Lecture Notes in Computer Science 1393

Edited by G. Goos, J. Hartmanis and J. van Leeuwen

T0223219

Springer
Berlin
Heidelberg
New York
Barcelona
Budapest
Hong Kong
London
Milan
Paris
Santa Clara
Singapore
Tokyo

Didier Bert (Ed.)

B'98: Recent Advances in the Development and Use of the B Method

Second International B Conference
Montpellier, France, April 22-24, 1998
Proceedings

 Springer

Series Editors

Gerhard Goos, Karlsruhe University, Germany
Juris Hartmanis, Cornell University, NY, USA
Jan van Leeuwen, Utrecht University, The Netherlands

Volume Editor

Didier Bert
CNRS, Laboratoire LSR, IMAG
681, rue de la Passerelle, BP 72
F-38402 Saint-Martin-d'Hères CEDEX, France
E-mail: Didier.Bert@imag.fr

Cataloging-in-Publication data applied for

Die Deutsche Bibliothek - CIP-Einheitsaufnahme

Recent advances in the development and use of the B method :
proceedings / B'98, Second International B Conference, Montpellier,
France, April 22 - 24, 1998. Didier Bert (ed.). - Berlin ; Heidelberg ;
New York ; Barcelona ; Budapest ; Hong Kong ; London ; Milan ;
Paris ; Santa Clara ; Singapore ; Tokyo : Springer, 1998
  (Lecture notes in computer science ; Vol. 1393)
  ISBN 3-540-64405-9

CR Subject Classification (1991): D.2,F.3.1

ISSN 0302-9743
ISBN 3-540-64405-9 Springer-Verlag Berlin Heidelberg New York

Typesetting: Camera-ready by author
SPIN 10636942   06/3142 – 5 4 3 2 1 0   Printed on acid-free paper

Preface

This volume contains the contributions of invited speakers and the refereed papers of the Second International B Conference (**B'98**) held in Montpellier, France, April 22-24, 1998. The first conference was held in Nantes (France) in November 1996. The **B** conferences aim to provide a forum for the rapidly growing community working in specification and software construction using the B method. The scope of the conferences covers all aspects of B technology, ranging from theoretical investigations to industrial applications, including methodological issues, B extension proposals, support tools, as well as comparisons or integration with other development methods.

At the current conference, an education session was organized on April 21st for the discussion of teaching experiences. Demonstrations were also presented during the three conference days.

B contains a notation for the abstract specification of *machines* and *systems* and a method for rigorously refining those modules to implementations and thence to code. The first contribution "On B" presents the essential goals of the method. They are simply providing assistance, including computer aided assistance, for the production of correct designs. This is intended to "trap the bugs" as early as possible in the development process.

Invited speakers are Dr. Carroll Morgan from Oxford University who proposes new advances in probabilistic programming, Patrick Behm, Pierre Desforges, and Jean-Marc Meynadier who speak about the project MÉTÉOR developed using the **B** method in RATP and Matra-Transport International, and François Pilarski who relates the use of formal methods at Aérospatiale.

The program committee received 29 contributions from seven countries. Only fifteen of them were chosen to be presented and published. Selected papers cover the main topics of the conference. Special attention is drawn to J.-R. Abrial's and L. Mussat's paper which presents advanced work to integrate specification of dynamic properties into **B** abstract systems, including the generation of proof obligations for these properties. Moreover such properties are made compatible with refinement. Conditions to ensure deadlock freeness and liveness properties during the refinement process can be stated and proved.

I sincerely thank all the program committee members, who actively collaborated electronically in the distribution and selection process. Thanks are due to Henri Habrias and Steve Dunne for their advice and for the organization of the education session. Many thanks to the organization committee: Claude Boksenbaum, Thérèse Libourel, Michel Sala, and Corine Zicler from the LIRMM.

February 1998   Didier Bert

Organization

B'98 was organized by the B Conference Steering Committee (APCB). It was supported by the Z User Group (ZUG) and the B User Group (BUG). Financial support was provided by the LIRM ("Laboratoire d'Informatique, de Robotique et de Micro-électronique de Montpellier", University of Montpellier II and CNRS) and the LSR-IMAG ("Laboratoire Logiciels, Systèmes, Réseaux", University Joseph Fourier, INPG and CNRS, Grenoble).

Program Committee

Didier Bert (Program Chair)	CNRS, LSR-IMAG, Grenoble, F
Pierre Bieber	ONERA-CERT, Toulouse, F
Claude Boksenbaum	Univ. of Montpellier, F
Egon Börger	Univ. of Pisa, I
Jonathan Bowen	ZUG, Univ. of Reading, UK
Pierre Desforges	RATP, Paris, F
Ranan Fraer	Intel, Israel
Robert B. France	Florida Atlantic Univ., FL, USA
Marc Frappier	Univ. of Sherbrooke, Canada
Philipp A. Heuberger	TUCS, Åbo Akademi Univ., Turku, Finland
David Lightfoot	Univ. of Oxford Brookes, UK
Fernando Mejia	GEC-Alsthom, Paris, F
Ken Robinson	Univ. of South Wales, Australia
Pierre-Yves Schobbens	Univ. of Namur, B

External Referees

All submitted papers, whether accepted or rejected, were refereed by three or four program committee members and a number of external referees. This symposium would not have been possible without their voluntary and dedicated work.

Jean-Raymond Abrial	Steve Dunne	Louis Mussat
Michel Allemand	Arnaud Durand	Christel Seguin
Christian Attiogbé	Andy Galloway	Bill Stoddart
Jean-Yves Chauvet	Henri Habrias	Virginie Wiels
Marielle Doche	Guy Laffitte	

Table of Contents

On B... 1
  Jean-Raymond Abrial

Invited Lectures

The Generalised Substitution Language Extended to Probabilistic Programs 9
  Carroll Morgan

MÉTÉOR: An Industrial Success in Formal Development 26
  Patrick Behm, Pierre Desforges, Jean-Marc Meynadier

Cost Effectiveness of Formal Methods in the Development of Avionics
Systems at AÉROSPATIALE...................................... 27
  François Pilarski

Theoretical Issues on B

Well Defined B 29
  Patrick Behm, Lilian Burdy, Jean-Marc Meynadier

Composition and Refinement in the B-Method........................ 46
  Marie-Laure Potet, Yann Rouzaud

Formalisation of B in Isabelle/HOL 66
  Pierre Chartier

B Extension Proposals

Introducing Dynamic Constraints in B.............................. 83
  Jean-Raymond Abrial, Louis Mussat

Retrenchment: An Engineering Variation on Refinement 129
  Richard H. Banach, Michael R. Poppleton

Methodological Issues

Synthesising Structure from Flat Specifications 148
  Brian Matthews, Brian Ritchie, Juan Bicarregui

An Object-Based Approach to the B Formal Method 162
  Alexander Malioukov

Graphical Design of Reactive Systems 182
  Emil Sekerinski

Process Control Engineering: Contribution to a Formal Structuring
Framework with the B Method 198
    Jean-François Pétin, Gérard Morel, Dominique Méry,
    Patrick Lamboley

Designing a *B Model* for Safety-Critical Software Systems 210
    Souâd Taouil-Traverson, Sylvie Vignes

Design of Distributed Systems

Abstract State Machines: Designing Distributed Systems with State
Machines and B 226
    Bill Stoddart, Steve Dunne, Andy Galloway, Richard Shore

Layering Distributed Algorithms within the B-Method 243
    Marina Waldén

Case Studies and Industrial Applications

Two Strategies to Data-Refine an Equivalence to a Forest 261
    Philipp Heuberger

Specification of an Integrated Circuit Card Protocol Application Using the
B Method and Linear Temporal Logic 273
    Jacques Julliand, Bruno Legeard, Thierry Machicoane,
    Benoit Parreaux, Bruno Tatibouët

Test Case Preparation Using a Prototype 293
    H. Treharne, J. Draper, S. Schneider

Author Index 313

On B

Jean-Raymond Abrial

Consultant,
26, rue des Plantes, 75014, Paris.
abrial@steria.fr

In the B-Book [Abr96], an introduction entitled "What is **B** ?" presents it in a few pages. There is no point in reproducing this introduction here. There is, however, clearly a need to have in this book a sort of informal presentation of **B** complementing that of the B-Book for those readers who are not familiar with this approach. This is the purpose of this short text, where the emphasis will be put on the question of the development process with **B**. At the end of the text, I will also cover some more general problems concerning **B** (tool, education, research, future).

B *is a "Debugger".*

The aim of **B** is very practical. Its ambition is to provide to industrial practitioners a series of techniques for helping them in the construction of software systems. As everyone knows, the complexity of such systems, as well as the context within which they are developed makes them very prone to errors. Within this framework, the goal of **B** is to accompany the system development process in such a way that the inevitable errors, produced either during the technical specification phase, or the design phase, or, of course, during the coding phase, that all these errors are trapped *as soon as they are produced*. In a sense, from that point of view, **B** is nothing else but a generalized debugging technology.

Classical Debugging Techniques are Based on Execution.

In classical software developments, errors are usually (but partially) discovered, and hopefully corrected, after the coding phase: this is done by checking the final product (or better, some parts of it) against a variety of *tests* supposed to cover the widest range of behaviors. Another technique, which becomes very popular these days, is that of *model checking* by which it is shown that the final system satisfies certain properties: this is done by an exhaustive search under all possible executions of the program.

As can be seen, both techniques, testing and model checking, work on the final product and are based on some "laboratory" *execution* of it. Since we believe in the great importance of trapping errors as soon as they are produced, it is clear that such techniques cannot be used during the technical specification and the design phases, where no execution can take place.

The B Debugging Technique is Based on Proofs. Conceptual Difficulties.

The debugging technology, which is proposed by **B**, is thus not based on execution, it is rather based on *mathematical proofs*. This apparently simple approach, which is widely used in other engineering disciplines, poses a number of specific problems.

When execution is the criterion, the developer obviously tends to write his formal text (his program) with *execution in mind*. He reasons in terms of data that are modified by some actions (assignments), and he constructs his program by means of a number of operations on such actions: conditionals, sequencing, loop, procedure calls, etc.

With **B**, the developer (at least, in the early phases) is *not supposed to reason in terms of execution*. Since the basic paradigm is that of proof, he has to think directly *in terms of properties* that have to be satisfied by the future system. This shift from execution to properties and proofs constitutes, in fact, a great step, which could sometimes represent an insurmountable difficulty to some persons. In our experience, it is not so much the manipulation of well defined mathematical concepts (sets, relations, functions, numbers, sequences, etc) that poses a serious problem to certain **B** practitioners, it is rather the necessary change of habit consisting in abandoning (for a while) the idea of execution.

Necessity of Re-writing the Requirement Documents.

As a matter of fact, some **B** novices use it as if it were a programming language with the classical concepts of discrete mathematics directly at their disposal. From our point of view, it is a mistake. We must say, however, that people are inclined to do so, since the informal requirements of the system they realize are often also written with execution in mind. Very often indeed, such requirements are already written in the form of a pseudo-implementation describing the future system in terms of data and algorithms acting on them.

This is the reason why, in our opinion, it is almost always indispensable, before engaging in any development with **B**, to spend a significant time (that is, for a large system, several months) to just *rewrite these requirements* in english, say, so as to re-orient them towards the precise statements of the properties of the future system. The natural language statements, the diagrams, or the tables describing these properties in one form or another must be identified, isolated and labeled in order to clearly separate them from the rest of the text (hypertext technology and "literate programming" helps here).

Such properties may concern either the *static* aspect of the system (that is, the permanent properties of its data), or its *dynamic* aspect (that is, the properties expressing how the data are allowed to evolve).

Obviously, such a rewriting should be performed hand in hand with the "client", who has to give his final agreement so that this second text becomes the new contractual basis of the future development.

Extracting Some Properties from the Requirement Documents.

Once this is done, the work of the **B** practitioner is to transcribe such informally stated properties into *mathematical models*. This has to be done *gradually*. It is out of the question to do this in a flat manner. One has first to extract from the informal text a few very fundamental properties that are the expression of the essence of the system.

The corresponding model takes the form of a, so-called, *abstract machine*, which encapsulates some *variables* whose types and static properties are formalized within a, so-called, *invariant* clause. These variables often denote some very abstract concepts related to the problem at hand. This is the reason why they are quite naturally "encoded" by equally abstract mathematical objects such as those mentioned above (sets, and the like).

The dynamics of the model is defined by a number of, so-called, *operations*, formalized as predicate transformers, called in **B** *generalized substitution*. Usually, at the top level, such operations are very straightforward: they take the form of a pre-condition followed by a simple, often highly non-deterministic, action defined on all (or part of) the variables at once (no sequencing, no loop). At this point, a first series of proofs must be performed in order to show that the static properties of the variables are indeed preserved by the operations. It constitutes a first form of debugging of the original informal text. Note that the requirement properties that have been chosen must be referenced. In this way, an easy navigation from the informal statements of these properties to their first formal setting counterparts is indeed possible.

Refinement as a Technique for Extracting more Details of the Problem.

Our first mathematical model is then *refined*, but still with properties and proofs in mind, not yet execution. It is done by extracting more properties from the informal specification in order to incorporate them in the model (without forgetting to reference them as above). Another set of proofs has then to be performed in order to certify that the extended model is itself coherent and, above all, that it is not contradictory with its abstraction (debugging continues). This extended model itself is then refined (that is, more properties are extracted) and more proofs are done, etc.

The Technique of Model Decomposition.

The process of refinement mentioned above can be complemented by that of *decomposition*. By this, we mean the splitting of a (possibly refined) model into several sub-models, which are then themselves refined and possibly decomposed independently, and so on. Such sub-models are said to be *imported* in their parent model.

Architecture Construction.

Note that in doing so (refinement and decomposition), the *architecture* of our future system is gradually emerging. It is interesting to note that it is realized solely in terms of the successive extractions of the properties of the system from within the informal requirements.

Refinement as a Technique for Transforming Models into Modules.

When all the original properties have been extracted in this way, we may claim that we have a complete mathematical model of our system. As we have seen above, such a model is already made of a number of abstract machines, together with their refinements and decompositions. This may already form a significantly large structure. At this point, the informal requirement document is of no use anymore. It is then time to start thinking in terms of execution. For this, we continue the refinement and decomposition processes as above, but, this time, we are not driven anymore by the incorporation of new properties, we are rather driven by the idea of gradually transforming our *mathematical models* into *software modules*.

Now refinement mainly acts on the variable spaces. It changes these spaces into others with components closer to programming variables (still represented, however, by well defined mathematical objects). Refinement also acts on the statements of the actions: pre-conditions are weakened (in fact, very shortly they disappear completely), non-determinacy is gradually reduced (in other words, postponed decisions are taken), conditionals, sequencing and loops gradually appear (the program takes shape). Proofs continue also to be performed, hence debugging is still active. At this point, we clearly think less as professionals of our system, more as pure informaticians concerned by efficiency.

Final Implementation on an Extraneous Environment.

It is now time to envisage the end of our **B** development process. We may have two opposite attitudes here, or a mixture of both.

Either, we continue down refining until each of our variables has a direct counterpart in a classical programming language (scalar of a limited size, arrays with well defined bounds, files, etc); in this case, the final formal text is indeed a program, which can be translated automatically into a classical programming language, or even directly into assembly code.

Or, we decide to stop earlier. In this case, we may use another collection of abstract machines, whose operations represent our "repertoire of instructions". These machines are used to implement the last refinements we have obtained; of course, such machines are never refined (at least by us), they only represent the formal **B** interface to the environment, on which we decide to implement our final refinements. This environment can be very low level (for instance: a simple library), or, on the contrary, a vast piece of data and code (for instance: an entire data base). This technique allows us to use **B** on the most vital parts of a system only. Notice that it can also be the beginning of yet another **B** development that has been made beforehand (bottom up construction and reusability).

The Proofs Accompany the Development Process.

As can be seen, the proof process has indeed *accompanied* the development process along each of its phases, namely the property extraction phases, the architecture building phases, and the implementation phases. Experience shows that the complexity of the proofs is a faithful indication of that of our development. If proofs are too complicated, a certain re-organization of the way the design is done might have, quite often, some spectacular effects. In fact, thinking in terms of proof constitutes, as experience shows, an extremely efficient heuristic for constructing large and complex software systems. Incorporating in one's mind the permanent idea of proving is, we think, a sign of maturity.

Why Use **B** *?*

As the text above has shown, doing a development with **B** is not a small enterprise. One might then wonder whether it is worth at all engaging in this direction. Sometimes people say that **B** should only be used for the development of safety critical systems, in other words that the decision to use **B** is dictated by the nature of the problem at hand. This view, in our opinion, is erroneous.

People, we think, should engage in a **B** development only if they are ready to do so. A measure of this readiness is indicated by their degree of disappointment with respect to their present development process. Should this process be well integrated in their organization and should it give entire satisfaction, then no **B** development is necessary, even worse it could be dangerous to destroy something that works well. On the other hand, when people have some doubts about the adequacy of their development process, then the utilization of **B** could be envisaged.

In other words, it is not so much the nature of the problem that counts for taking such a decision (of using **B**), than the understanding that something has gone wrong in the way systems are developed. And one of the first question to be solved is then, of course, that of the integration of **B** within the old development process. In particular, as we pointed out above, the question of the re-writing of the requirement documents (to be integrated at the beginning of the development process), and the question of the proofs (to be integrated as a permanent concern in each phase the development process) are of utmost importance.

How to Use **B**. *Questioning the Provers.*

It is clear that **B** cannot be used without some tools. On view of what has been said above, it is also clear that, among these tools, the provers (automatic and interactive) play a prominent rôle. On projects of a significant size and "average" difficulty, a classical figure is that the automatic prover should succeed in discharging 80% of the proofs. The remaining proofs have to be handled with the interactive prover. One should also remember the following rule of thumb: roughly speaking, a **B** development resulting in n lines of final code demands the proof of $n/2$ little lemmas, and an "average" trained person is able to conduct 15 interactive proofs per day. For instance, on a project whose part developed with **B** amounts to 50,000 lines, we have thus 25,000 proofs, among which 5,000 (that is 20%) are not discharged automatically. The manual (interactive) treatment of such proofs will then represent a work load that amounts to $5,000/15 = 333$ man-days, that is roughly 15 man-months [1]. This has to be compared with the testing effort (as well as with the "price" of the late discovery of bugs) that must be paid in the classical development of large software systems.

The inside of such provers must be visible and trustable. It is not conceivable that people take the "success/failure" answers of such programs for granted. In particular, all the inference rules of such provers should, not only be visible (this is obvious), but *they should themselves be proved*, with full visibility given on such second order proofs and on the corresponding second order prover. In fact, experience shows that, on the average, between 2 to 5% of such inference rules are wrong, if no care is taken. Moreover, for the purpose of extending the capabilities of the prover, people can add their own rules of inferences. Such added rules must also be proved "on line".

More generally, the industrial usage of such tools and the importance of the projects in which they are engaged, require that they obtain an industrial "recognition" of some sort on the part of an independent "body". Such an effort is very costly, but is, we think, an indispensable prerequisite for the industrial credibility of the **B** approach. To the best of our knowledge, **Atelier B** fulfills, to a large extent, these requirements: it has been formally approved by a consortium led by RATP, the Parisian Metro Authority.

---

[1] This figure can be lowered provided the interactive prover has the capability to largely re-use tactics and sub-proofs

People and Education

Technology is nothing without people. And people are able to develop and use a certain technology *provided they have received the adequate education.* In the case of **B**, what can be seen in some parts of the world is very encouraging. There is, however, an area where this education is, we think, too weak. This is precisely that part that is centered around the question of *formal proofs.* In our opinion, this subject is still taught in a way that is either too formal and theoretical, or, at the other end of the spectrum, entirely devoted to the study of some tools.

It seems to us that a new subject entitled "Proof and Prover Technology" has to be introduced in Computer Science curricula in the coming years. This has to be done in an independent fashion, in very much the same way as the "Language and Compiler Technology" subject has been introduced many decades ago independently of any particular language and compiler. By the way, a number of techniques of compiler technology could certainly be fruitfully incorporated in the prover technology (the static part of a compiler is, after all, a low level prover).

Formal methods in general, and **B** in particular, are still sometimes taught in an old-fashioned way, by concentrating the presentations around the linguistic aspects. Students then get the impression that these formalisms are just very high level programming languages. This is reinforced by the practical exercises they are asked to do, namely to put their knowledge into practice by just *writing* some formal specifications and designs. It is very important that they should also be asked to *prove* them, so as to figure out that it is not easy (in particular the first time), and that the idea of the proof must permanently influence the way they have to structure their formal texts.

Research and the Future of **B**

Research on **B** must continue, it is vital. The proceedings of this conference show, if at all necessary, that it is indeed very active and rich. People have already proposed a number of extensions to **B**, and they will do so in the future. This is normal and certainly shows the interest and the creativity of our community. It must therefore be warmly encouraged. There is a risk, however, that everyone knows: the proliferation of various incompatible dialects, all pretending to represent the "genuine" **B**. We have seen quite often this terrible tendency at work in other formalisms. It is dangerous. We have, however, the chance to still form a very small community.

In order to limit such risks, I thus propose that a (very small) committee be organized to think and propose some solutions to this problem. We have to remember that, on one hand, democracy is certainly indispensable, but that, on the other hand, no language or formalism project has ever been successfully achieved by a committee. Efficiency and reason should dictate our action here.

References

[Abr96] J.-R. Abrial, *The B-Book: Assigning programs to meanings*, Cambridge University Press, 1996.

The Generalised Substitution Language Extended to Probabilistic Programs

Carroll Morgan

Programming Research Group, Oxford University, UK.
carroll@comlab.ox.ac.uk,
http://www.comlab.ox.ac.uk/oucl/groups/probs.
The work is supported by the EPSRC.

Abstract. Let predicate P be converted from Boolean to numeric type by writing $\langle P \rangle$, with $\langle false \rangle$ being 0 and $\langle true \rangle$ being 1, so that in a degenerate sense $\langle P \rangle$ can be regarded as 'the probability that P holds in the current state'. Then add explicit numbers and arithmetic operators, to give a richer language of arithmetic formulae into which predicates are embedded by $\langle \cdot \rangle$.

Abrial's generalised substitution language GSL can be applied to arithmetic rather than Boolean formulae with little extra effort. If we add a new operator $_p\oplus$ for probabilistic choice, it then becomes '$pGSL$': a smooth extension of GSL that includes random algorithms within its scope.

Keywords: Probability, program correctness, generalised substitutions, weakest preconditions, B, GSL.

1   Introduction

Abrial's Generalised Substitution Language GSL [1] is a weakest-precondition based method of describing computations and their meaning; it is complemented by the structures of Abstract Machines, together with which it provides a framework for the development of correct systems. In this paper we extend it to probabilistic programs, those that implement random algorithms.

Most sequential programming languages contain a construct for 'deterministic' choice, where the program chooses from a number of alternatives in some predictable way: for example, in

$$\text{IF } test \text{ THEN } this \text{ ELSE } that \text{ END} \qquad (1)$$

the choice between *this* and *that* is determined by *test* and the current state.

In contrast, Dijkstra's language of guarded commands brings nondeterministic or 'demonic' choice to prominence, in which the program's behaviour is *not* predictable, not determined by the current state. At first [2], demonic choice was presented as a consequence of 'overlapping guards', almost an accident — but as its importance became more widely recognised it developed a life of its own. Nowadays it merits an explicit operator: the construct

$$this \parallel that$$

chooses between the alternatives unpredictably and, as a specification, indicates abstraction from the issue of which will be executed. The customer will be happy with either *this* or *that*; and the implementor may choose between them according to his own concerns.

With the invention of 'miracles' [12,16,18] the two forms of choice were unified, showing demonic choice to be the more fundamental: that innovation is exploited in *GSL* whenever one writes

$$test \rightarrow this \quad \parallel \quad \neg test \rightarrow that \qquad (2)$$

instead of the more conventional (1) above.

Early research on probabilistic semantics took a different route: demonic choice was not regarded as fundamental — rather it was abandoned altogether, being replaced by probabilistic choice [8,4,3,7,6]. Thus probabilistic semantics was divorced from the contemporaneous work on specification and refinement, because without demonic choice there is no means of abstraction.

More recently however it has been discovered [5,15] how to bring the two topics back together, taking the more natural approach of *adding* probabilistic choice, retaining demonic choice and seeing deterministic choice again as at (2). Probabilistic choice too is a special case of demonic choice: both deterministic and probabilistic choice refine demonic choice, but neither refines the other.

Because the probabilistic/demonic semantics is an extension of predicate transformers, it is possible to present its main ideas in the *GSL* idiom, which is what we do in this paper. The result could be called '*pGSL*'.

In Sec. 2 we give a brief and shallow overview of *pGSL*, somewhat informal and concentrating on simple examples. Sec. 3 sets out the definitions and properties of *pGSL* systematically, and Sec. 4 treats an example of reasoning about probabilistic loops.

An impression of *pGSL* can be gained by reading Sections 2 and 4, with finally a glance over Sections 3.1 and 3.2; more thoroughly one would read Sections 2, 3.1 and 3.2, then 2 (again) and finally 4. The more theoretical Sec. 3.3 can be skipped on first reading.

2   An impression of *pGSL*

Let angle brackets $\langle \cdot \rangle$ be used to embed Boolean-valued predicates within arithmetic formulae which, for reasons explained below, we call *expectations*; in this section we allow them to range over the unit interval $[0, 1]$. Stipulating that $\langle false \rangle$ is 0 and $\langle true \rangle$ is 1, we make the expectation $\langle P \rangle$ in a trivial sense the probability that a given predicate P holds: if false, P is said to hold with probability 0; if true, it holds with probability 1.

For our first example, we consider the simple program

$$x := -y \quad {}_{\frac{1}{3}}\oplus \quad x := +y \,, \tag{3}$$

over variables $x, y : \mathbb{Z}$, using a construct ${}_{\frac{1}{3}}\oplus$ which we interpret as 'choose the left branch $x := -y$ with probability $1/3$, and choose the right branch with probability $1 - 1/3$'.

Recall that for any predicate P over *final* states, and a standard[1] substitution S, the predicate $[S]P$ acts over *initial* states: it holds in those initial states from which S is guaranteed to reach P. Now suppose S is probabilistic, as Program (3) is; what can we say about the *probability* that $[S]P$ holds in some initial state?

It turns out that the answer is just $[S]\langle P \rangle$, once we generalise $[S]$ to expectations instead of predicates. We begin with the two definitions

$$[x := E]R \quad \widehat{=} \quad \text{`}R \text{ with } x \text{ replaced everywhere'}^2 \text{ by } E \tag{4}$$

$$[S \,{}_p\oplus T]R \quad \widehat{=} \quad p * [S]R + (1-p) * [T]R \,, \tag{5}$$

in which R is an expectation, and for our example program we ask

> what is the probability that the predicate 'the final state will satisfy $x \geq 0$' holds in some given initial state of the program?

To find out, we calculate $[S]\langle P \rangle$ in this case; that is

$$[x := -y \,{}_{\frac{1}{3}}\oplus x := +y]\langle x \geq 0 \rangle$$

$$\equiv^3 \qquad \begin{aligned} &(1/3) * [x := -y]\langle x \geq 0 \rangle \\ &+ (2/3) * [x := +y]\langle x \geq 0 \rangle \end{aligned} \qquad\qquad \text{using (5)}$$

$$\equiv \qquad (1/3)\langle -y \geq 0 \rangle + (2/3)\langle +y \geq 0 \rangle \qquad\qquad \text{using (4)}$$
$$\equiv \qquad \langle y < 0 \rangle /3 + \langle y = 0 \rangle + 2\langle y > 0 \rangle /3 \,. \qquad\qquad \text{arithmetic}$$

Our answer is the last arithmetic formula above, which we could call a 'pre-expectation' — the probability we seek is found by reading off the formula's value for various initial values of y, getting

when y is negative,	$1/3 + 0 + 2(0)/3 = 1/3$
when y is zero,	$0/3 + 1 + 2(0)/3 = 1$
when y is positive,	$0/3 + 0 + 2(1)/3 = 2/3$.

Those results indeed correspond with our operational intuition about the effect of ${}_{\frac{1}{3}}\oplus$.

---

[1] Throughout we use *standard* to mean 'non-probabilistic'.

[2] In the usual way, we take account of free and bound variables, and if necessary rename to avoid variable capture.

[3] Later we explain the use of '$\equiv$' rather than '$=$'.

The above remarkable generalisation of sequential program correctness is due to Kozen [8], but until recently was restricted to programs that did not contain demonic choice ⫿. When He *et al.* [5] and Morgan *et al.* [15] successfully added demonic choice, it became possible to begin the long-overdue integration of probabilistic programming and formal program development: in the latter, demonic choice — as *abstraction* — plays a crucial role in specifications.

To illustrate the use of abstraction, in our second example we abstract from probabilities: a demonic version of Program (3) is much more realistic in that we set its probabilistic parameters only within some tolerance. We say informally (but still with precision) that

- $x:=-y$ is to be executed with probability *at least* 1/3,
- $x:=+y$ is to be executed with probability *at least* 1/4 and   (6)
- it is certain that one or the other will be executed.

Equivalently we could say that alternative $x:=-y$ is executed with probability between 1/3 and 3/4, and that otherwise $x:=+y$ is executed (therefore with probability between 1/4 and 2/3).

With demonic choice we can write Specification (6) as

$$\left(x:=-y \;{}_{\frac{1}{3}}\!\oplus\; x:=+y\right) \quad \| \quad \left(x:=-y \;{}_{\frac{3}{4}}\!\oplus\; x:=+y\right),\qquad (7)$$

because we do not know or care whether the left or right alternative of ⫿ is taken — and it may even vary from run to run of the program, resulting in an 'effective' ${}_p\oplus$ with p somewhere between the two extremes.[4]

To examine Program (7), we define the generalised substitution

$$[S\,\|\,T]R \;\;\hat{=}\;\; [S]R \text{ min } [T]R,\qquad (8)$$

using min because we regard demonic behaviour as attempting to make the achieving of R as *im*probable as it can. Repeating our earlier calculation (but more briefly) gives this time

$$[\text{Program (7)}]\,\langle x \geq 0\rangle$$

$$\equiv \qquad \begin{array}{l} \langle y \leq 0\rangle\,/3 + 2\,\langle y \geq 0\rangle\,/3 \\ \text{min} \quad 3\,\langle y \leq 0\rangle\,/4 + \langle y \geq 0\rangle\,/4 \end{array} \qquad\qquad \text{using (4), (5), (8)}$$

$$\equiv \qquad \langle y < 0\rangle\,/3 + \langle y = 0\rangle + \langle y > 0\rangle\,/4. \qquad\qquad \text{arithmetic}$$

---

[4] A convenient notation for (7) would be based on the abbreviation

$$S \;{}_{[p,q]}\!\oplus\; T \;\;\hat{=}\;\; S\,{}_p\!\oplus T \;\|\; S\,{}_q\!\oplus T\,;$$

we would then write it $x:=-y \;{}_{[\frac{1}{3},\frac{3}{4}]}\!\oplus\; x:=+y.$

Our interpretation is now

- When y is initially negative, the demon chooses the left branch of $[\!]$ because that branch is more likely (2/3 *vs.* 1/4) to execute $x := +y$ — the best we can say then is that $x \geq 0$ will hold with probability at least 1/3.
- When y is initially zero, the demon cannot avoid $x \geq 0$ — either way the probability of $x \geq 0$ finally is 1.
- When y is initially positive, the demon chooses the right branch because that branch is more likely to execute $x := -y$ — the best we can say then is that $x \geq 0$ finally with probability at least 1/4.

The same interpretation holds if we regard $[\!]$ as abstraction. Suppose Program (7) represents some mass-produced physical device and, by examining the production method, we have determined the tolerance as above (6) on the devices produced. If we were to buy one arbitrarily, all we could conclude about its probability of establishing $x \geq 0$ is just as calculated above.

Refinement is the converse of abstraction: for two substitutions S, T we define

$$S \sqsubseteq T \;\;\hat{=}\;\; [S]R \Rrightarrow [T]R \;\; \text{for all } R, \tag{9}$$

where we write $\Rrightarrow$ for 'everywhere no more than' (which ensures $\langle \mathsf{false} \rangle \Rrightarrow \langle \mathsf{true} \rangle$ as expected). From (9) we see that in the special case when R is an embedded predicate $\langle P \rangle$, the meaning of $\Rrightarrow$ ensures that a refinement T of S is at least as likely to establish P as S is. That accords with the usual definition of refinement for standard programs — for then we know $[S]\langle P \rangle$ is either 0 or 1, and whenever S is certain to establish P (whenever $[S]\langle P \rangle \equiv 1$) we know that T also is certain to do so (because then $1 \Rrightarrow [T]\langle P \rangle$).

For our third example we prove a refinement: consider the program

$$x := -y \quad {}_{\frac{1}{2}}\oplus \quad x := +y \,, \tag{10}$$

which clearly satisfies Specification (6); thus it should refine Program (7). With Definition (9), we find for any R that

	$[\text{Program (10)}]R$	
$\equiv$	$([x := -y]R)/2 \quad + \quad ([x := +y]R)/2$	
$\equiv$	$R^-/2 + R^+/2$	introduce abbreviations
$\equiv$	$(3/5)(R^-/3 + 2R^+/3)$ $+ \quad (2/5)(3R^-/4 + R^+/4)$	arithmetic
$\Lleftarrow$	$\quad\quad R^-/3 + 2R^+/3$ min $\quad 3R^-/4 + R^+/4$	any linear combination exceeds min
$\equiv$	$[\text{Program (7)}]R \,.$	

The refinement relation (9) is indeed established for the two programs.

The introduction of 3/5 and 2/5 in the third step can be understood by noting that demonic choice $\|$ can be implement by any probabilistic choice whatever: in this case we used $_{\frac{3}{5}}\oplus$. Thus a proof of refinement at the program level might read

$$
\begin{array}{ll}
& \text{Program (10)} \\
= & x := -y \quad _{\frac{1}{2}}\oplus \quad x := +y \\[2ex]
= & \quad\ (x := -y \quad _{\frac{1}{3}}\oplus \quad x := +y) & \text{arithmetic} \\
& _{\frac{3}{5}}\oplus \quad (x := -y \quad _{\frac{3}{4}}\oplus \quad x := +y) \\[2ex]
\sqsupseteq & \quad\ x := -y \quad _{\frac{1}{3}}\oplus \quad x := +y & (\|) \sqsubseteq (_p\oplus) \text{ for any } p \\
& \|\quad x := -y \quad _{\frac{3}{4}}\oplus \quad x := +y \\[2ex]
\equiv & \text{Program (7) .}
\end{array}
$$

3 Presentation of probabilistic *GSL*

In this section we give a concise presentation of probabilistic *GSL* as a whole: its definitions, how they are to be interpreted and their (healthiness) properties.

3.1 Definitions of *pGSL* substitutions

In *pGSL*, substitutions act between 'expectations' rather than predicates, where an *expectation* is an expression over (program or state) variables that takes its value in the non-negative reals extended with ∞.[5] To retain the use of predicates, we allow expectations of the form $\langle P \rangle$ when P is Boolean-valued, defining $\langle \mathsf{false} \rangle$ to be 0 and $\langle \mathsf{true} \rangle$ to be 1.

Implication-like relations between expectations are

$$
\begin{array}{lll}
R \Rrightarrow R' & \mathrel{\widehat{=}} & R \text{ is everywhere no more than } R' \\
R \equiv R' & \mathrel{\widehat{=}} & R \text{ is everywhere equal to } R' \\
R \Lleftarrow R' & \mathrel{\widehat{=}} & R \text{ is everywhere no less than } R'.
\end{array}
$$

Note that $\models P \Rightarrow P'$ exactly when $\langle P \rangle \Rrightarrow \langle P' \rangle$, and so on; that is the motivation for the symbols chosen.

The definitions of the substitutions in *pGSL* are given in Fig. 1.

---

[5] This domain, more general than the $[0,1]$ of the previous section, makes the definitions easier... but perhaps makes intuition harder. In any case, the healthiness conditions of Sec. 3.3 show that we can restrict attention to $[0,1]$ if we wish, as indeed we do again in Sec. 4.

The probabilistic generalised substitution language *pGSL* acts over 'expectations' rather than predicates: *expectations* take values in $\mathbb{R}_{\geq 0} \cup \{\infty\}$.

$[x := E]R$ — The expectation obtained after replacing all free occurrences of x in R by E, renaming bound variables in R if necessary to avoid capture of free variables in E.

$[P \mid S]R$ — $\langle P \rangle * [S]R$, where $0 * \infty \mathrel{\hat=} 0$.

$[S \,[\!]\, T]R$ — $[S]R \min [T]R$

$[P \Longrightarrow S]R$ — $1/\langle P \rangle * [S]R$, where $\infty * 0 \mathrel{\hat=} \infty$.

$[\text{skip}]R$ — R

$[@z \cdot S]R$ — $\min z \cdot ([S]R)$, where z does not occur free in R.

$[S\,{}_p{\oplus}\,T]R$ — $p * [S]R + (1-p) * [T]R$

$S \sqsubseteq T$ — $[S]R \Rightarrow [T]R$ for all R

- R is an expectation (possibly but not necessarily $\langle P \rangle$ for some predicate P);
- P is a predicate (not an expectation);
- $*$ is multiplication;
- S, T are probabilistic generalised substitutions (inductively);
- p is an expression over the program variables (possibly but not necessarily a constant), taking a value in $[0, 1]$; and
- z is a variable (or a vector of variables).

Fig. 1. *pGSL* — the probabilistic Generalised Substitution Language

3.2 Interpretation of *pGSL* expectations

In its full generality, an expectation is a function describing how much each program state is 'worth'.

The special case of an embedded predicate $\langle P \rangle$ assigns to each state a worth of 0 or of 1: states satisfying P are worth 1, and states not satisfying P are worth 0. The more general expectations arise when one estimates, in the *initial* state of a probabilistic program, what the worth of its *final* state will be. That estimate , the 'expected worth' of the final state, is obtained by summing over all final states

the worth of the final state multiplied by the probability the program 'will go there' from the initial state.

Naturally the 'will go there' probabilities depend on 'from where', and so that expected worth is a function of the initial state.

When the worth of final states is given by $\langle P \rangle$, the expected worth of the initial state turns out — very nearly — to be just the probability that the program will reach P. That is because expected worth of initial state

$\equiv$ (probability S reaches P)
         $*$ (worth of states satisfying P)

    $+$ (probability S does not reach P)
         $*$ (worth of states not satisfying P)

$\equiv$ (probability S reaches P) $* 1$
    $+$ (probability S does not reach P) $* 0$

$\equiv$ probability S reaches P ,

where matters are greatly simplified by the fact that all states satisfying P have the same worth.

Typical analyses of programs S in practice lead to conclusions of the form

$$p \quad \equiv \quad [S]\langle P \rangle$$

for some p and P which, given the above, we can interpret in two equivalent ways:

1. the expected worth $\langle P \rangle$ of the final state is at least[6] the value of p in the initial state; or
2. the probability that S will establish P is at least p.

Each interpretation is useful, and in the following example we can see them acting together: we ask for the probability that two fair coins when flipped will show the same face, and calculate

$$\begin{bmatrix} x:= H \,_{\frac{1}{2}}\oplus\, x:= T \;; \\ y:= H \,_{\frac{1}{2}}\oplus\, y:= T \end{bmatrix} \langle x = y \rangle$$

$\equiv$ $_{\frac{1}{2}}\oplus, := $ and sequential composition
$[x:= H \,_{\frac{1}{2}}\oplus\, x:= T]((\langle x = H \rangle /2 + \langle x = T \rangle /2)$

$\equiv$ $(1/2)(\langle H = H \rangle /2 + \langle H = T \rangle /2)$ $_{\frac{1}{2}}\oplus$ and $:=$
   $+ (1/2)(\langle T = H \rangle /2 + \langle T = T \rangle /2)$

$\equiv$ $(1/2)(1/2 + 0/2) + (1/2)(0/2 + 1/2)$ definition $\langle \cdot \rangle$
$\equiv$ $1/2$.   arithmetic

---

[6] We must say 'at least' in general, because of possible demonic choice in S; and some analyses give only the weaker $p \Rrightarrow [S]\langle P \rangle$ in any case.

We can then use the second interpretation above to conclude that the faces are the same with probability (at least[7]) $1/2$.

But part of the above calculation involves the more general expression

$$[x := H \: {}_{\frac{1}{2}}\!\oplus\: x := T](\langle x = H \rangle /2 + \langle x = T \rangle /2) \;,$$

and what does that mean on its own? It must be given the first interpretation, since its post-expectation is not of the form $\langle P \rangle$, and it means

the expected value of $\langle x = H \rangle /2 + \langle x = T \rangle /2$ after executing $x := H \: {}_{\frac{1}{2}}\!\oplus\: x := T$,

which the calculation goes on to show is in fact $1/2$. But for our overall conclusions we do not need to think about the intermediate expressions — they are only the 'glue' that holds the overall reasoning together.

3.3   Properties of $pGSL$

Recall that all GSL constructs satisfy the property of conjunctivity[8] [1, Sec. 6.2] — that is, for any GSL substitution S and post-conditions P, P' we have

$$[S](P \wedge P') \quad = \quad [S]P \wedge [S]P' \;.$$

That 'healthiness property' [2] is used to prove general properties of programs.

In $pGSL$ the healthiness condition becomes 'sublinearity' [15], a generalisation of conjunctivity:

Let a, b, c be non-negative finite reals, and R, R' expectations; then all $pGSL$ constructs S satisfy

$$[S](aR + bR' \ominus c) \quad \Lleftarrow \quad a[S]R + b[S]R' \ominus c \;,$$

which property of S is called *sublinearity*.
We have written aR for $a * R$ etc., and truncated subtraction $\ominus$ is defined

$$x \ominus y \quad \hat{=} \quad (x - y) \max 0 \;,$$

with syntactic precedence lower than $+$.

Although it has a strange appearance, from sublinearity we can extract a number of very useful consequences, as we now show [15]. We begin with monotonicity, feasibility and scaling.[9]

---

[7] Knowing there is no demonic choice in the program, we can in fact say it is exact.

[8] They satisfy monotonicity too, which is implied by conjunctivity.

[9] Sublinearity characterises probabilistic *and demonic* substitutions. In Kozen's original probability-only formulation [8] the substitutions are not demonic, and there they satisfy the much stronger property of 'linearity' [9].

monotonicity: increasing a post-expectation can only increase the pre-expectation. Suppose $R \Rrightarrow R'$ for two expectations R, R'; then

$$
\begin{array}{ll}
& [S]R' \\
\equiv & [S](R + (R' - R)) \\
\Lleftarrow & [S]R + [S](R' - R) \qquad\qquad \text{sublinearity with } a,b,c \cong 1,1,0 \\
\Lleftarrow & [S]R \ . \qquad\qquad\qquad\qquad R' - R \text{ well defined, hence } 0 \Rrightarrow [S](R' - R)
\end{array}
$$

feasibility: pre-expectations cannot be 'too large'. First note that

$$
\begin{array}{ll}
& [S]0 \\
\equiv & [S](2 * 0) \\
\Lleftarrow & 2 * [S]0 \ , \qquad\qquad\qquad \text{sublinearity with } a,b,c \cong 2,0,0
\end{array}
$$

so that $[S]0$ must be either 0 or ∞. We say that S is *feasible* if $[S]0 \equiv 0$. Now write $\max R$ for the maximum of R over all its variables' values, and assume that S is feasible; then

$$
\begin{array}{ll}
& 0 \\
\equiv & [S]0 \qquad\qquad\qquad\qquad\qquad\quad \text{feasibility above} \\
\equiv & [S](R \ominus \max R) \qquad\qquad\qquad\quad R \ominus \max R \equiv 0 \\
\Lleftarrow & [S]R \ominus \max R \ , \qquad\qquad\qquad a,b,c \cong 1,0,\max R
\end{array}
$$

where we assume for the moment that $\max R$ is finite so that it can be used in sublinearity. Now from $0 \Lleftarrow [S]R \ominus \max R$ we have trivially that

$$
[S]R \quad \Rrightarrow \quad \max R \ , \tag{11}
$$

which we have proved under the assumption that S is feasible and $\max R$ is finite — but if $\max R$ is not finite, then (11) holds anyway.

Thus we have shown in any case that feasibility implies (11); but since (11) implies feasibility (take $R \cong 0$), it could itself be taken as the definition.[10]

scaling: multiplication by a non-negative constant distributes through feasible[11] substitution. Note first that $[S](aR) \Lleftarrow a[S]R$ directly from sublinearity. For $\Rrightarrow$ we have two cases: when a is 0, trivially from feasibility

$$
[S](0 * R) \equiv [S]0 \equiv 0 \equiv 0 * [S]R \ ;
$$

and for the other case $a \neq 0$ we reason

$$
\begin{array}{ll}
& [S](aR) \\
\equiv & a(1/a)[S](aR) \qquad\qquad\qquad\qquad\qquad a \neq 0 \\
\Rrightarrow & a[S]((1/a)aR) \qquad\qquad\qquad\quad \text{sublinearity using } 1/a \\
& a[S]R \ ,
\end{array}
$$

thus establishing $[S](aR) \equiv a[S]R$ generally.

---

[10] We can define fis (S) to be $\langle [S]0 = 0 \rangle$.

[11] The feasibility restriction is because when $[S](0 * R)$ is infinite it does not equal $0 * [S]R$.

That completes monotonicity, feasibility and scaling.

The remaining property we examine is probabilistic conjunction. Since standard conjunction $\land$ is not defined over numbers, we have many choices for a probabilistic analogue $\&$ of it, requiring only that

$$0 \,\&\, 0 = 0, \quad 0 \,\&\, 1 = 0, \quad 1 \,\&\, 0 = 0 \quad \text{and} \quad 1 \,\&\, 1 = 1 \qquad (12)$$

for consistency with embedded Booleans.

Obvious possibilities for $\&$ are multiplication $*$ and minimum min, and each of those has its uses; but neither satisfies anything like a generalisation of conjunctivity. Instead we define

$$R \,\&\, R' \quad \hat{=} \quad R + R' \ominus 1 \,, \qquad (13)$$

whose right-hand side is inspired by sublinearity when $a, b, c \,\hat{=}\, 1, 1, 1$. We now establish a (sub-) distribution property for it.

While discussing conjunction we restrict our expectations to the unit interval $[0, 1]$, as we did earlier, and assume all our substitutions are feasible.[12] In that case infinities do not intrude, and we have from feasibility that $R \Rrightarrow 1$ implies

$$[S]R \quad \Rrightarrow \quad \max R \quad \Rrightarrow \quad 1 \,,$$

showing that the restricted domain $[0, 1]$ is closed under (feasible) substitutions.

The distribution property is then a direct consequence of sublinearity.

sub-conjunctivity: the operator $\&$ subdistributes through substitutions. From sublinearity with $a, b, c \,\hat{=}\, 1, 1, 1$ we have

$$[S](R \,\&\, R') \quad \Lleftarrow \quad [S]R \,\&\, [S]R'$$

for all S.

Unfortunately there does not seem to be a full (rather than sub-) conjunctivity property.

Beyond sub-conjunctivity, we say that $\&$ generalises conjunction for several other reasons. The first is of course that it satisfies the standard properties (12).

The second reason is that sub-conjunctivity implies 'full' conjunctivity for standard programs. Standard programs, containing no probabilistic choices, take standard $\langle P \rangle$-style post-expectations to standard pre-expectations: they are the embedding of GSL in $pGSL$, and for standard S we now show that

$$[S](\langle P \rangle \,\&\, \langle P' \rangle) \quad \equiv \quad [S]\langle P \rangle \,\&\, [S]\langle P' \rangle \,. \qquad (14)$$

First note that '$\Lleftarrow$' comes directly from sub-conjunctivity above, taking R, R' to be $\langle P \rangle, \langle P' \rangle$.

Then '$\Rrightarrow$' comes from monotonicity, for $\langle P \rangle \,\&\, \langle P' \rangle \Rrightarrow \langle P \rangle$ whence $[S](\langle P \rangle \,\&\, \langle P' \rangle) \Rrightarrow [S]\langle P \rangle$, and similarly for P'. Putting those together gives

---

[12] We could avoid the feasibility assumption by using the domain $[0, 1] \cup \infty$, but in this presentation it is simpler not to introduce ∞.

$$[S](\langle P \rangle \& \langle P' \rangle) \quad \Rrightarrow \quad [S]\langle P \rangle \ \min \ [S]\langle P' \rangle \ ,$$

by elementary arithmetic properties of $\Rrightarrow$. But on standard expectations — which $[S]\langle P \rangle$ and $[S]\langle P' \rangle$ are, because S is standard — the operators min and & agree.

A last attribute linking & to $\wedge$ comes straight from elementary probability theory. Let A and B be two events, unrelated by $\subseteq$ and not necessarily independent:

> if the probability of A is at least p, and the probability of B is at least q,
>
> then the most that can be said about the joint event $A \cap B$ is that it has probability at least $p \& q$ [19].

The & operator also plays a crucial role in the proof (not given in this paper) of the probabilistic loop rule presented and used in the next section [13].

4 Probabilistic invariants for loops

To show *pGSL* in action, we state a proof rule for probabilistic loops and apply it to a simple example. Just as for standard loops, we can deal with invariants and termination separately.

We continue with the restriction to feasible programs, and expectations in $[0, 1]$.

4.1 Probabilistic invariants

In a standard loop, the invariant holds at every iteration of the loop: it describes a set of states from which the loop will establish the postcondition, if termination occurs.

For a probabilistic loop we have a post-expectation rather than a postcondition; but if that post-expectation is some $\langle P \rangle$ say, then — as an aid to the intuition — we can look for an invariant that gives a lower bound on the probability that we will establish P by (continuing to) execute the loop 'from here'. Often that invariant will have the form

$$p \quad * \quad \langle I \rangle \tag{15}$$

with p a probability and I a predicate, both expressions over the state. From the definition of $\langle \cdot \rangle$ we know that the interpretation of (15) is

probability p if I holds, and probability 0 otherwise.

We see an example of such invariants below.

4.2 Termination

The probability that a program will terminate generalises the usual definition: recalling that $\langle \text{true} \rangle \equiv 1$ we define

$$\text{trm}(S) \quad \hat{=} \quad [S]1 . \tag{16}$$

As a simple example of termination, suppose S is the recursive program

$$S \quad \hat{=} \quad S_p \oplus \text{skip} , \tag{17}$$

in which we assume that p is some constant strictly less than 1: elementary probability theory shows that S terminates with probability 1 (after an expected $p/(1-p)$ recursive calls). And by calculation based on (16) we confirm that

$$
\begin{array}{ll}
& \text{trm}(S) \\
\equiv & [S]1 \\
\equiv & p * ([S]1) + (1-p) * ([\text{skip}]1) \\
\equiv & p * \text{trm}(S) + (1-p) ,
\end{array}
$$

so that $(1-p) * \text{trm}(S) \equiv 1-p$. Since p is not 1, we can divide by $1-p$ to see that $\text{trm}(S) \equiv 1$. That agrees with the elementary theory above, that the recursion will terminate with probability 1 — for if p is not 1, the chance of recursing N times is p^N, which for $p < 1$ approaches 0 as N increases without bound.

4.3 Probabilistic correctness of loops

A loop is a least fixed point, as in the standard case [1, Sec. 9.2], which gives easily that if $\langle P \rangle * I \Rrightarrow [S]I$ then

$$I \Rrightarrow [\text{WHILE } P \text{ DO } S \text{ END}](\langle \neg P \rangle * I)$$

provided[13] the loop terminates; indeed, for the proof one simply carries out the standard reasoning almost without noticing that expectations rather than predicates are being manipulated. Thus the notion of invariant carries over smoothly from the standard to the probabilistic case.

When termination is taken into account we get the following rule [13].

> For convenience write T for the termination probability of the loop, so that
> $$T \quad \hat{=} \quad \text{trm}(\text{WHILE } P \text{ DO } S \text{ END}) .$$
>
> Then partial loop correctness — preservation of a loop invariant I — implies total loop correctness if that invariant I nowhere[14] exceeds T:
>
> $$
> \begin{array}{ll}
> \text{If} & \langle P \rangle * I \Rrightarrow [S]I \\
> \text{and} & I \Rrightarrow T \\
> \text{then} & I \Rrightarrow [\text{WHILE } P \text{ DO } S \text{ END}](\langle \neg P \rangle * I) .
> \end{array}
> $$

---

[13] The precise treatment of 'provided' uses weakest *liberal* pre-expectations [13, 10].

[14] Note that is not the same as 'implies total correctness in those states where I does not exceed T': in fact I must not exceed T in *any* state, and the weaker alternative is not sound.

We illustrate the loop rule with a simple example. Suppose we have a machine that is supposed to sum the elements of a sequence [1, Sec. 10.4.2], except that the mechanism for moving along the sequence occasionally sticks, and for that moment does not move. A program for the machine is given in Fig. 2, where the unreliable component

$$k := k + 1 \quad_c\oplus \quad \text{skip}$$

sticks (fails to move along) with probability $1-c$. With what probability does the machine accurately sum the sequence, establishing

$$r = \text{sum}(s) \tag{18}$$

on termination?

We first find the invariant: relying on our informal discussion above, we ask

during the loop's execution, with what probability are we in a state from which completion of the loop would establish (18)?

The answer is in the form (15) — take p to be $c^{\text{size}(s)+1-k}$, and let I be the standard invariant [1, p.459]

$$k \in 1..\text{size}(s)+1 \quad \wedge \quad r = \text{sum}(s \uparrow (k-1)) .$$

```
PRE
    s ∈ seq(u)
THEN
    VAR k IN
        r, k := 0, 1;
        WHILE k ≤ size(s) DO
            r := r + s(k);
            k := k + 1 c⊕ skip        ← failure possible here
        END
    END
END
```

Fig. 2. An unreliable sequence-accumulator

Then our probabilistic invariant — call it J — is just $p * \langle I \rangle$, which is to say it is

if the standard invariant holds then $c^{\text{size}(s)+1-k}$, the probability of going on to successful termination; if it does not hold, then 0.

Having chosen a possible invariant, to check it we calculate

$$\begin{bmatrix} r := r + s(k); \\ k := k + 1 \,_c\oplus \text{skip} \end{bmatrix} J$$

$$\equiv \quad [r := r + s(k)] \qquad\qquad\qquad\qquad ; \text{ and } _c\oplus$$
$$c * [k := k + 1]J + (1-c) * J$$

$\Leftarrow$ $\qquad\qquad\qquad\qquad\qquad\qquad\qquad\qquad\qquad\qquad$ drop $(1-c)*J$, and $:=$

$$[r:=r+s(k)]$$
$$c^{\text{size}(s)+1-k} \quad * \quad \left\langle \begin{matrix} k \in 0..\text{size}(s) \\ r = \text{sum}(s \uparrow k) \end{matrix} \right\rangle$$

$\equiv \qquad c^{\text{size}(s)+1-k} \quad * \quad \left\langle \begin{matrix} k \in 0..\text{size}(s) \\ r+s(k) = \text{sum}(s \uparrow k) \end{matrix} \right\rangle \qquad\qquad :=$

$\Leftarrow \qquad \langle k \leq \text{size}(s) \rangle * J$,

where in the last step the guard $k \leq \text{size}(s)$, and $k \geq 1$ from the invariant, allow the removal of $+s(k)$ from both sides of the lower equality.

Now we turn to termination: we note (informally) that the loop terminates with probability at least

$$c^{\text{size}(s)+1-k} \quad * \quad \langle k \in 1..\text{size}(s)+1 \rangle ,$$

which is just the probability of $\text{size}(s)+1-k$ correct executions of $k:=k+1$, given that k is in the proper range to start with; hence trivially $J \Rrightarrow \text{trm}\,(while)$, as required by the loop rule.

That concludes reasoning about the loop itself, leaving only initialisation and the post-expectation of the whole program. For the latter we see that on termination of the loop we have $\langle k > \text{size}(s) \rangle * J$, which indeed 'implies' (is in the relation $\Rrightarrow$ to) the post-expectation $\langle r = \text{sum}(s) \rangle$ as required.

Turning finally to the initialisation we finish off with

$$[r, k:= 0, 1]J$$
$\equiv \qquad c^{\text{size}(s)} \quad * \quad \left\langle \begin{matrix} 1 \in 1..\text{size}(s)+1 \\ 0 = \text{sum}(s \uparrow 0) \end{matrix} \right\rangle$
$\equiv \qquad c^{\text{size}(s)} \quad * \quad \langle \text{true} \rangle$
$\equiv \qquad c^{\text{size}(s)}$,

and our overall conclusion is therefore

$$c^{\text{size}(s)} \quad \Rrightarrow \quad [sequence\text{-}accumulator] \langle r = \text{sum}(s) \rangle ,$$

just as we had hoped: the probability that the sequence is correctly summed is at least $c^{\text{size}(s)}$.

Note the importance of the inequality $\Rrightarrow$ in our conclusion just above — it is not true that the probability of correct operation is *equal* to $c^{\text{size}(s)}$ in general. For it is certainly possible that r is correctly calculated in spite of the occasional malfunction of $k:=k+1$; but the exact probability, should we try to calculate it, would depend intricately on the contents of s. (It would be 1, for example, if s contained only zeroes, and could be very involved if s contained some mixture of positive and negative values.) If we were forced to calculate exact results (as in earlier work [20]), rather than just lower bounds as we did above, this method would not be at all practical.

Further examples of loops, and a discussion of probabilistic *variant* arguments, are given elsewhere [13].

5 Conclusion

It seems that a little generalisation can go a long way: Kozen's use of expectations and the definition of $_p\oplus$ as a weighted average [8] is all that is needed for a simple probabilistic semantics, albeit one lacking abstraction. Then He's *sets* of distributions [5] and our min for demonic choice together with the fundamental property of sublinearity [15] take us the rest of the way, allowing allowing abstraction and refinement to resume their central role — this time in a probabilistic context. And as Sec. 4 illustrates, many of the standard reasoning principles carry over almost unchanged.

Being able to reason formally about probabilistic programs does not of course remove *per se* the complexity of the mathematics on which they rely: we do not now expect to find astonishingly simple correctness proofs for all the large collection of randomised algorithms that have been developed over the decades [17]. Our contribution — at this stage — is to make it possible in principle to locate and determine reliably what are the probabilistic/mathematical facts the construction of a randomised algorithm needs to exploit... which is of course just what standard predicate transformers do for conventional algorithms.

Finally, there is the larger issue of probabilistic abstract machines, or modules, and the associated concern of probabilistic data refinement. That is a challenging problem, with lots of surprises: using our new tools we have already seen that probabilistic modules sometimes do not mean what they seem [11], and that equivalence or refinement between such modules depends subtly on the power of demonic choice and its interaction with probability.

Acknowledgements

This paper reports work carried out with Annabelle McIver, Jeff Sanders and Karen Seidel, and supported by the *EPSRC*.

References

1. J.-R. Abrial. *The B-Book*. Cambridge University Press, 1996.
2. E.W. Dijkstra. *A Discipline of Programming*. Prentice Hall International, Englewood Cliffs, N.J., 1976.
3. Yishai A. Feldman. A decidable propositional dynamic logic with explicit probabilities. *Information and Control*, 63:11–38, 1984.
4. Yishai A. Feldman and David Harel. A probabilistic dynamic logic. *J. Computing and System Sciences*, 28:193–215, 1984.

5. Jifeng He, K. Seidel, and A. K. McIver. Probabilistic models for the guarded command language. *Science of Computer Programming*, 28:171–192, 1997.
6. C. Jones. Probabilistic nondeterminism. Monograph ECS-LFCS-90-105, Edinburgh Univ. Edinburgh, U.K., 1990. (PhD Thesis).
7. C. Jones and G. Plotkin. A probabilistic powerdomain of evaluations. In *Proceedings of the IEEE 4th Annual Symposium on Logic in Computer Science*, pages 186–195, Los Alamitos, Calif., 1989. Computer Society Press.
8. D. Kozen. A probabilistic PDL. In *Proceedings of the 15th ACM Symposium on Theory of Computing*, New York, 1983. ACM.
9. Annabelle McIver and Carroll Morgan. Probabilistic predicate transformers: part 2. Technical Report PRG-TR-5-96, Programming Research Group, March 1996. Revised version to be submitted for publication under the title *Demonic, angelic and unbounded probabilistic choices in sequential programs*.
10. Annabelle McIver and Carroll Morgan. Partial correctness for probabilistic demonic programs. Technical Report PRG-TR-35-97, Programming Research Group, 1997.
11. Annabelle McIver, Carroll Morgan, and Elena Troubitsyna. The probabilistic steam boiler: a case study in probabilistic data refinement. In preparation, 1997.
12. C. C. Morgan. The specification statement. *ACM Transactions on Programming Languages and Systems*, 10(3), July 1988. Reprinted in [14].
13. C. C. Morgan. Proof rules for probabilistic loops. In He Jifeng, John Cooke, and Peter Wallis, editors, *Proceedings of the BCS-FACS 7th Refinement Workshop*, Workshops in Computing. Springer Verlag, July 1996.
14. C. C. Morgan and T. N. Vickers, editors. *On the Refinement Calculus*. FACIT Series in Computer Science. Springer-Verlag, Berlin, 1994.
15. Carroll Morgan, Annabelle McIver, and Karen Seidel. Probabilistic predicate transformers. *ACM Transactions on Programming Languages and Systems*, 18(3):325–353, May 1996.
16. J. M. Morris. A theoretical basis for stepwise refinement and the programming calculus. *Science of Computer Programming*, 9(3):287–306, December 1987.
17. Rajeev Motwani and Prabhakar Raghavan. *Randomized Algorithms*. Cambridge University Press, 1995.
18. G. Nelson. A generalization of Dijkstra's calculus. *ACM Transactions on Programming Languages and Systems*, 11(4):517–561, October 1989.
19. K. Seidel, C. C. Morgan, and A. K. McIver. An introduction to probabilistic predicate transformers. Technical Report PRG-TR-6-96, Programming Research Group, February 1996. Revised version to be submitted for publication under the title *Probabilistic Imperative Programming: a Rigorous Approach*.
20. M. Sharir, A. Pnueli, and S. Hart. Verification of probabilistic programs. *SIAM Journal on Computing*, 13(2):292–314, May 1984.

MÉTÉOR: An Industrial Success in Formal Development

Patrick Behm[1], Pierre Desforges[2], Jean-Marc Meynadier[1]

[1] Matra Transport International
48-56 rue Barbès 92120 Montrouge
tel : 01 49 65 71 41 fax : 01 49 65 70 55
e-mail : {behm,burdy,meynadier}@matra-transport.fr
[2] RATP
7, square Félix Nadar 94648 Vincennes Cedex
tel : 01 49 57 85 95 fax : 01 49 57 87 23
e-mail : soledad.valencia@ratp.fr

A new line of metro is Paris is going to open in August 1998. This line, operated by *RATP*, is equipped with the MÉTÉOR system, which enables fully automatic driverless trains as well as conventional trains. The safety critical software of the MÉTÉOR system was formally developed in 1996-1997 using the B method by *Matra Transport International*. The development includes :

- abstract models of the software components;
- refinement design to concrete models;
- automatic translation into Ada code.

The total size of the models is about 100.000 lines of B (excluding the comments and the empty lines); the total size of the software is about 87.000 lines of Ada code.

The validation includes :

- formal proof (up to 100%) of the proof obligations of the method (about 28.000 lemmas);
- proof of the mathematical rules added to discharge the proof of the lemmas (about 1.400 rules, 900 of which are automatically proved);
- a safety process to protect against errors in the translation to code.

The talk will emphasis on key points which led to the success, in particular:

- how the work had to be redefined for the development and validation teams at *Matra Transport International* and for the validation team at *RATP*;
- the method was enriched with a set of guidelines books (how to build the abstract models, how to refine to concrete models, how to prove, how to document models, etc.);
- the *Atelier B* was strenghthened to deal with very large models.

The talk will evaluate the use of a formal method for a large project in an industrial context.

Cost Effectiveness of Formal Methods in the Development of Avionics Systems at AÉROSPATIALE

François Pilarski

Aérospatiale Aéronautique, Etablissement de Toulouse
316 Route de Bayonne
BP M0141/6
F-31060 Toulouse Cedex 03, France
Tél : (+33|0) 5 61 93 98 86
Fax : (+33|0) 5 61 93 80 90
Francois.Pilarski@avions.aerospatiale.fr

AEROSPATIALE has been using formal methods since the early 80's to develop part of the embedded systems, and more specifically most of the avionics systems. During the last two decades, such an approach has demonstrated significant cost savings. This paper presents some aspect of this approach and focuses more precisely on the way it has helped in reducing embedded systems development and maintenance costs.

This first section of this paper is devoted to a general description of the overall context and it gives same elements of history. Basically this section is focused on the tool SCADE and its predecessors (SAO) which implements the main, though not only, formal method used at AEROSPATIALE.

In this section the reader will see that the first driver to introduce formal methods was to allow all the people involved in system development, to communicate. That was in the early 80's and was in itself the first cost reduction in reducing the number of mis understandings, re-design to more generally speaking design iterations. In fact this was a formalisation of a basic engineering language. This formalised language was finally named SAO which stands for the French translation of "Computer Aided Specification".

The next step in cost saving was achieved in the early 90's with the generalization of automatic coding and the simulation of the specifications themselves.

This improvement in the approach induced three main benefits :

- firstly, an appreciable shortening of the modification cycle which can be, in same cases, as short as one week and even less, between the identification of a need-to-modify and its flying-solution, compared to some weeks before.
- secondly, a significant reduction of the number of iterations to tune the specification by simulating it : the sometimes needed iterations are performed by the designer himself and so he produces a "good specification" the very first time, which is then coded and embedded. This is what can be found in the litterature as the "Y life cycle" instead of the "V life cycle".
- thirdly, a significant reduction of the unit testing (of the embedded code) thanks to the qualification of the code generators. This has induced a cost reduction by a factor of 2 and more.

The second section summarizes the benefits AEROSPATIALE have found in using SAO first and now SCADE and constitutes an attempt to synthesize the properties and characteristics which make a formal method efficient (at AEROSPATIALE).

In this second section the cost aspects are emphasized instead of safety aspects. Indeed when speaking about formal methods one generally thinks of proof techniques in order to ensure "a complete and exhaustive" validation. It is obvious that these techniques, when applicable are useful, but it is a fact that aircrafts (Airbus A320, A340, for example) have already been certified, and are now flying safely every day, thanks to classical techniques such as RAMS analysis, ground tests, flight tests, ... So, the benefits of formal methods are not related to safety. The point is that such methods allow :

- better communication between the people involved in the development process provided that these people do agree to use the language (almost) as naturally as their mother language. Indeed, as far as engineers are concerned, an engineering language is accepted, and as far as automatic subjects are addressed, block diagrams are certainly good candidates.
- automatic code generation and so simulation capability. Moreover, a "high fidelity" simulation of the specification can be achieved provided the semantics of the language are completely defined and broadcasted.
- qualified code generation provided the code generator is simple enough. Of course this last point is certainly not easy to achieve and generally needs pure mathematical research. Obviously the "synchronous" theory has been a definitely significant step towards the simplicity of the languages and the associated code generators.

The third section summarises some aspects of formal methods, which have not been extensively used yet but which are likely to induce extra cost reduction, namely proof techniques.

Indeed, proof techniques are alternate techniques for validating specifications. Of course the current state of the art will not allow the use of such techniques on the overall system specification because of its size, and even if this could be done it may not be of major interest because of some reasons detailed in this 3rd section. Nevertheless proof techniques are definitely of great interest because :

- they can be applied statically on the specification itself which means very early in the design process.
- when they are applicable, and within their intrinsic limits, they provide exhaustive results.
- finally, these techniques generally produce counter examples in the case of nogo results and they may produce test cases to be executed on benches which allow a better confidence in the result of the proof in itself.

As a conclusion it is recalled that formal methods have been demonstrated to be cost effective at AEROSPATIALE, especially SAO and now SCADE. In addition same extra cost saving is expected, thanks to the industrial maturity of proof techniques.

Well Defined B

Patrick Behm[1], Lilian Burdy[1,2], Jean-Marc Meynadier[1]

[1] Matra Transport International
48-56 rue Barbès 92120 Montrouge
tel : 01 49 65 71 41 fax : 01 49 65 70 55
e-mail : {behm,burdy,meynadier}@matra-transport.fr
[2] Laboratoire CEDRIC
Conservatoire National des Arts et Métiers
292 rue St Martin 75141 Paris Cedex 3
e-mail : burdy@cnam.fr

Abstract. B is a language with a three-valued semantics: terms like $\min(\emptyset)$ or $1/0$ are ill-defined, consequently formulas containing ill-defined terms may also be ill-defined. Therefore the deduction system we use to discharge the proof obligations should be constructed from a three-valued logic. In this paper, we introduce a deduction system that allows to reason in a two-valued logic if new proof obligations called well-definedness lemmas are also proved. We define this deduction s ystem and the new proof obligations that ensure the well-definedness of B components. The practical benefits on the proof mechanisms are then outlined.

1 Introduction

Most of the time, in mathematics, we are not interested in reasoning about meaningless expressions[1]. If a division by 0 occurs in a demonstration, we usually consider it to be faulty and skip the demonstration. In computer science, the situation is more intricate for, at least, two reasons:

- in the domain of the semantics of programming languages, since meaningless expressions (such as $1/0$) cannot be forbidden by the syntax of programs, a specific denotation has to be introduced to modelize these expressions;
- if one uses a software tool to reason about pieces of program or specification which may include meaningless expressions, the tool has to handle such expressions.

But how to deal with meaningless expressions? In particular, what is the truth-value of a predicate including meaningless expressions? Is $1/0 = 1/0$ really true? What about $1/0 < 2/0$?) One way to tackle this problem is to introduce a third value, besides *true* and *false*, to denote a predicate for which you don't know whether it is true or false, and to extend the logic to reason about specifications

---

[1] Such expressions appear as soon as a partial operator or function is used out of its domain, e.g. $1/0$.

and programs with meaningless expressions. The *Logic for Partial Functions* of VDM is an example of a three-valued logic.

For the developer, the drawback of this type of approach is to complicate the proofs with a logic that may appear unnatural (in particular the deduction rule and the law of the excluded middle do not hold in *LPF*; in other three-valued logics, conjunction and disjunction are not commutative). We are all the more concerned with this problem as, in our industrial context, we cannot ask developers to be expert in sophisticated mathematics.

The alternative approach we have experimented and formalized at *Matra Transport International* for several years is quite different. The idea is: before proving any other property on a formal model, first make sure that the model is well-defined (free from meaningless expressions). This is achieved, in the context of the B method, by producing well-definedness lemmas from the models; these lemmas are proved in the usual two-valued set theory logic with a restriction: you may only introduce well-defined expressions during proofs (when a hypothesis is added and when a quantifier is instantiated).

In other words, in the chain of validation of formal models, we add a step before the classic proof obligations: the *well-definedness of models*.

validation step	technique used
syntax	automatic checking
type	automatic checking
Well definedness	proof
proof obligation of the method	proof

The aim of this paper is to formalize this approach and to outline its advantages: how it fully addresses the problem of meaningless expressions keeping as close as possible to the usual two-valued logic framework, and, as a by-product, how it simplifies and strengthens the proof mechanisms.

In section 2, a three-valued semantics is provided for B: an extension of the first order logic with partial functions is introduced; the semantics is then defined, with the support of the Δ_e operator which returns whether a term is well-defined or not.

In section 3, a well-definedness operator on predicates (Δ_p) is used to define a deduction system; we then give the main result of the paper: the deduction system is consistent and complete if, before proving a predicate, you first prove that it is well-defined.

In section 4, we restrict Δ_p (from Kleene to Mc Carthy) to ease the definition and the implementation of the well-definedness of B components (machines, refinements and implementations) and the well-definedness operator on B substitutions Δ_s is introduced. We finally define the Δ operator on a B component that gives lemmas sufficient to establish the well-definedness of the component.

In section 5, we focus on practical benefits on the proof mechanisms, in particular at the B0 level.

2 The B Language: A Three-Valued Semantics

2.1 Syntax

The language signature Σ is defined by a set V of variable symbols, a set F of function symbols and a set P of total predicate symbols.

Definition 1. T_Σ, *the set of Σ-terms is inductively defined by:*
each variable of V is a term;
if $f \in F$, $\mathrm{arity}(f) = n$ and $e_1, ..., e_n$ are terms, then $f(e_1, ..., e_n)$ is a term.

Example 1. Let F be $\{succ, pred, zero, one\}$ then,
$pred(zero)$ is a term of T_Σ but it is ill-defined: intuitively, a term is ill-defined if it contains a function that is called out of its domain;
$succ(pred(zero))$ is also ill-defined because it contains an ill-defined subterm.

Definition 2. *We inductively define F_Σ, the set of Σ-formulas:*

$p(e_1, ..., e_n)$	*is a formula if $p \in P$, $\mathrm{arity}(p) = n$ and $e_1, ..., e_n$ are terms;*
$True$	*is a formula;*
$False$	*is a formula;*
$\varphi \wedge \psi$	*is a formula if φ and ψ are formulas;*
$\varphi \vee \psi$	*is a formula if φ and ψ are formulas;*
$\varphi \Rightarrow \psi$	*is a formula if φ and ψ are formulas;*
$\neg\varphi$	*is a formula if φ is a formula;*
$\forall x.\varphi$	*is a formula if $x \in V$ and φ is a formula;*
$\exists x.\varphi$	*is a formula if $x \in V$ and φ is a formula.*

Since all predicates are total, ill-definedness only comes from terms.

Example 2. Let P be $\{equal\}$ then,
$\forall x.equal(succ(pred(x)), x)$ is ill-defined;
$\forall x.\neg equal(x, zero) \Rightarrow equal(succ(pred(x)), x)$ is well-defined because the ill-defined subformula is guarded by a formula that ensures the well-definedness of the global formula;
$equal(pred(zero), zero) \Rightarrow equal(succ(zero), one)$ is well-defined or ill-defined depending of the definition of well-definedness.

These notions of well-definedness are defined in the next paragraph.

2.2 Semantics

We define a model and then an interpretation of terms and formulas. We introduce an interpretation defined by Kleene: the model and interpretation definitions are unusual because we are in a three-valued logic so we do not have a usual interpretation as we do in first order logic. To deal with ill-definedness, we introduce an operator Δ_e that allows to construct the interpretations.

Models. Let A be a set with $\perp_A$ not belonging to A. We define $A_\perp$ as $A \cup \{\perp_A\}$. Let F_A be a set of total functions from $A_\perp^n$ to $A_\perp$, and P_A a set of total predicates from $A_\perp^n$ to $\{t, f, \perp\}$. We say that $< A, F_A, P_A >$ is a model for our language that associates to each function of zero arity c an element c_A from A, to each partial function of non zero arity f of F a total function f_A of F_A and to each total predicate p of P a total predicate p_A of P_A.

We have an interpretation $\mathcal{J}$ for terms $\mathcal{J} : T_\Sigma \to A_\perp$ such that:

$\mathcal{J}(x) = x$

$\mathcal{J}(c) = c_A$

$\mathcal{J}(f(e_1, ..., e_2)) = \begin{cases} f_A(\mathcal{J}(e_1), .., \mathcal{J}(e_n)) & \text{if } f \text{ is defined in } e_1, ..., e_n \\ \perp_A & \text{otherwise} \end{cases}$

We get a three-valued interpretation $\mathcal{J} : F_\Sigma \to \{t, f, \perp\}$ for formulas. $\perp$ represents ill-definedness and t, f respectively the two well-known values: true and false.

Example 3. Let $A_\perp$ be $\{0, 1, 2, \perp\}$ then

$\mathcal{J}(succ(zero)) = 1,$

$\mathcal{J}(pred(zero)) = \perp$

The Δ_e Operator. We define the Δ_e operator on terms, $\Delta_e : T_\Sigma \to F_\Sigma$ assigns a well-definedness predicate to each term. A term is either well-defined or not: the well-definedness predicate should not be ill-defined. To do this, a predicate d_f is associated to each function f. d_f represents the domain of the function. We can say that if this predicate instantiated with $e_1, ..., e_n$ is true and the e_i are recursively all well-defined then the term $f(e_1, ..., e_n)$ is well-defined too.

We inductively define Δ_e on T_Σ:

$\Delta_e v = True$ for each variable v from V

$\Delta_e c = True$ for each function c from F with zero arity

$\Delta_e f(e_1, ..., e_n) = \begin{cases} d_f(e_1, ..., e_n) \land & \text{for each function } f \text{ from } F \text{ with arity } n \\ \bigwedge_{i=1}^{n} \Delta_e e_i & \text{and each terms } e_1, ..., e_n \end{cases}$

d_f corresponds to the side-conditions defined in [Abr96] for each operator. To ensure well-definedness of the well-definedness predicate, this predicate should only contain total predicates and functions.

Example 4. Let d_{pred} be $\neg(equal(x, zero))$ and d_{succ} be $True$ then

$\Delta_e(succ(zero)) = True,$

$\Delta_e(pred(zero)) = \neg(equal(zero, zero)).$

Interpretation. We now present a formula interpretation called Kleene's interpretation, denoted $\mathcal{J}$. This interpretation is as close as possible to the classic interpretation.

$$\mathcal{J}(False) \quad = f$$
$$\mathcal{J}(True) \quad = t$$

$$\mathcal{J}(p(e_1, ..., e_n)) = \begin{cases} t \text{ if } p_A(\mathcal{J}(e_1), ..., \mathcal{J}(e_n)) = t \text{ and } \bigwedge_{i=1}^{n} \mathcal{J}(\Delta_e e_i) = t \\ f \text{ if } p_A(\mathcal{J}(e_1), ..., \mathcal{J}(e_n)) = f \text{ and } \bigwedge_{i=1}^{n} \mathcal{J}(\Delta_e e_i) = t \\ \bot \text{ otherwise} \end{cases}$$

$$\mathcal{J}(\varphi \wedge \psi) \quad = \begin{cases} t \text{ if } \mathcal{J}(\varphi) = t \text{ and } \mathcal{J}(\psi) = t \\ f \text{ if } \mathcal{J}(\varphi) = f \text{ or } \mathcal{J}(\psi) = f \\ \bot \text{ otherwise} \end{cases}$$

$$\mathcal{J}(\varphi \vee \psi) \quad = \begin{cases} t \text{ if } \mathcal{J}(\varphi) = t \text{ or } \mathcal{J}(\psi) = t \\ f \text{ if } \mathcal{J}(\varphi) = f \text{ and } \mathcal{J}(\psi) = f \\ \bot \text{ otherwise} \end{cases}$$

$$\mathcal{J}(\varphi \Rightarrow \psi) \quad = \begin{cases} t \text{ if } \mathcal{J}(\varphi) = f \text{ or } \mathcal{J}(\psi) = t \\ f \text{ if } \mathcal{J}(\varphi) = t \text{ and } \mathcal{J}(\psi) = f \\ \bot \text{ otherwise} \end{cases}$$

$$\mathcal{J}(\neg\varphi) \quad = \begin{cases} t \text{ if } \mathcal{J}(\varphi) = f \\ f \text{ if } \mathcal{J}(\varphi) = t \\ \bot \text{ otherwise} \end{cases}$$

$$\mathcal{J}(\forall x.\varphi) \quad = \begin{cases} t \text{ if for all } a \text{ in } A, \mathcal{J}(\varphi)[x \leftarrow a] = t \\ f \text{ if there exists an } a \text{ in } A \text{ such that } \mathcal{J}(\varphi)[x \leftarrow a] = f \\ \bot \text{ otherwise} \end{cases}$$

$$\mathcal{J}(\exists x.\varphi) \quad = \begin{cases} t \text{ if there exists an } a \text{ in } A \text{ such that } \mathcal{J}(\varphi)[x \leftarrow a] = t \\ f \text{ if for all } a \text{ in } A, \mathcal{J}(\varphi)[x \leftarrow a] = f \\ \bot \text{ otherwise} \end{cases}$$

Remark 1. This interpretation is close to the usual interpretation because if we erase the lines $\bot$ otherwise, we get the usual interpretation of operators.

Example 5. To ease the reading, we shall use the notation $a = b$ instead of $equal(a, b)$:
$$\mathcal{J}(\forall x.(\neg(pred(x) = zero))) = f$$
$$\mathcal{J}(pred(zero) = pred(zero)) = \bot$$
$$\mathcal{J}(x = one \Rightarrow pred(x) = zero) = t$$
$$\mathcal{J}(pred(zero) = zero \Rightarrow succ(zero) = zero) = \bot$$
$$\mathcal{J}(pred(zero) = zero \Rightarrow succ(zero) = one) = t$$
$$\mathcal{J}(succ(zero) = zero \Rightarrow pred(zero) = zero) = t$$

The interpretation permits to have an ill-defined subformula in a well-defined formula if the context contains the subformula well-definedness. In the third formula of the previous example, $pred(x) = zero$ is an ill-defined subformula but the negative occurrence of the implication ($x = one$) ensures the global formula well-definedness. Also, the fifth formula of the previous example is well-defined even though the subformula $pred(zero) = zero$ is ill-defined, because the positive occurrence is obviously true.

3 Deduction Systems and Well Definedness Operator

3.1 Weak Strong Validity Notion

In a three-valued logic, unlike in a two-valued logic, different validity notions may be defined. The validity notion depends on the way ill-definedness is treated. The different consequence relations (and consequently validity notions) are described in [GL90]. So we have to choose a validity notion for the B language.

Definition 3. $\Gamma \models \varphi$ if and only if for every interpretation $\mathcal{J}$,
$\mathcal{J}(\Gamma) = f$ or $\mathcal{J}(\varphi) = t$

The validity notion that we choose, is like the interpretation, as close as possible to the usual validity notion. It is completely described in [Owe93]. If we look at the previous definition, we could believe that it is the same as the usual validity notion but we should note that, here, the negation of t is not f but f or $\bot$. In fact we can give an equivalent definition which would be:

Proposition 1. $\Gamma \models \varphi$ if and only if for every interpretation $\mathcal{J}$,
if $\mathcal{J}(\Gamma) = t$ or $\mathcal{J}(\Gamma) = \bot$ then $\mathcal{J}(\varphi) = t$

Example 6. Let us look at the validity of the formulas in the previous example :
$\not\models \forall x.(\neg(pred(x) = zero))$
$\not\models pred(zero) = pred(zero)$
$x = one \models pred(x) = zero$
$pred(zero) = zero \not\models succ(zero) = zero$
$pred(zero) = zero \models succ(zero) = one$
$succ(zero) = zero \models pred(zero) = zero$

3.2 The Δ_p^K Operator

To construct a sound and complete deduction system, we have to define the operator Δ_p^K.
Δ_p^K assigns a well-definedness predicate to each predicate, like term well-definedness predicates the formula well-definedness predicates are well-defined.

Definition 4. $\Delta_p^K : F_\Sigma \to F_\Sigma$ is defined as
$$\Delta_p^K \varphi = \begin{cases} t \text{ if for all } \mathcal{J}, \mathcal{J}(\varphi) = t \text{ or } f \\ f \text{ if for all } \mathcal{J}, \mathcal{J}(\varphi) = \bot \end{cases}$$

Proposition 2. *We can give an inductive definition too, this definition is equivalent to the precedent :*

$$\Delta_p^K(p(e_1, ..., e_n)) = \bigwedge_{i=1}^n \Delta_e(e_i)$$
$$\Delta_p^K True = True$$
$$\Delta_p^K False = True$$

$$\Delta_p^K(\varphi \wedge \psi) \quad = (\Delta_p^K\varphi \wedge \Delta_p^K\psi) \vee (\Delta_p^K\varphi \wedge \neg\varphi) \vee (\Delta_p^K\psi \wedge \neg\psi)$$
$$\Delta_p^K(\varphi \vee \psi) \quad = (\Delta_p^K\varphi \wedge \Delta_p^K\psi) \vee (\Delta_p^K\varphi \wedge \varphi) \vee (\Delta_p^K\psi \wedge \psi)$$
$$\Delta_p^K(\varphi \Rightarrow \psi) \quad = (\Delta_p^K\varphi \wedge \Delta_p^K\psi) \vee (\Delta_p^K\varphi \wedge \neg\varphi) \vee (\Delta_p^K\psi \wedge \psi)$$
$$\Delta_p^K(\neg\varphi) \quad = \Delta_p^K\varphi$$
$$\Delta_p^K(\forall x.\varphi) \quad = \forall x.\Delta_p^K\varphi \vee \exists x.(\Delta_p^K\varphi \wedge \neg\varphi)$$
$$\Delta_p^K(\exists x.\varphi) \quad = \forall x.\Delta_p^K\varphi \vee \exists x.(\Delta_p^K\varphi \wedge \varphi)$$

Example 7. $\Delta_p^K(pred(zero) = pred(zero)) = False$
$\Delta_p^K(x = one \Rightarrow pred(x) = zero) = True$
$\Delta_p^K(pred(zero) = zero \Rightarrow succ(zero) = zero) = False$
$\Delta_p^K(pred(zero) = zero \Rightarrow succ(zero) = one) = True$
$\Delta_p^K(succ(zero) = zero \Rightarrow pred(zero) = zero) = True$

3.3 Two Proofs For One

$$\frac{}{\Gamma, P \vdash P}\ axiom \qquad\qquad \frac{\Gamma \vdash P}{\Gamma, Q \vdash P}\ weakening$$

$$\frac{\Gamma, P, P \vdash Q}{\Gamma, P \vdash Q}\ contraction \qquad \frac{\Gamma_1, P, Q, \Gamma_2 \vdash R}{\Gamma_1, Q, P, \Gamma_2 \vdash R}\ permutation$$

$$\frac{\Gamma, P \vdash Q}{\Gamma \vdash P \Rightarrow Q}\ \Rightarrow\text{-}right \qquad \frac{\Gamma \vdash P \quad \Gamma, Q \vdash R}{\Gamma, P \Rightarrow Q \vdash R}\ \Rightarrow\text{-}left \qquad \frac{\Gamma \vdash P \quad \Gamma \vdash Q}{\Gamma \vdash P \wedge Q}\ \wedge\text{-}right$$

$$\frac{\Gamma, P, Q \vdash R}{\Gamma, P \wedge Q \vdash R}\ \wedge\text{-}left \qquad \frac{\Gamma \vdash P}{\Gamma \vdash P \vee Q}\ \vee\text{-}right \qquad \frac{\Gamma \vdash Q}{\Gamma \vdash P \vee Q}\ \vee\text{-}right$$

$$\frac{\Gamma, P \vdash R \quad \Gamma, Q \vdash R}{\Gamma, P \vee Q \vdash R}\ \vee\text{-}left \qquad \frac{\Gamma, P \vdash False}{\Gamma \vdash \neg P}\ \neg\text{-}right$$

$$\frac{\Gamma \vdash P}{\Gamma, \neg P \vdash Q}\ \neg\text{-}left \qquad \frac{}{\Gamma, False \vdash P}\ False\text{-}left$$

$$\frac{\Gamma \vdash P}{\Gamma \vdash \forall x\ P}\ \forall\text{-}right\ if\ x \setminus \Gamma \qquad \frac{\Gamma, P \vdash Q}{\Gamma, \exists x.P \vdash Q}\ \exists\text{-}left\ if\ x \setminus \Gamma$$

$$\frac{\Gamma \vdash \Delta_p^K P \quad \Gamma \vdash P \quad \Gamma, P \vdash Q}{\Gamma \vdash Q}\ cut$$

$$\frac{\Gamma, P[x \leftarrow t] \vdash Q \quad \Gamma \vdash \Delta_e t}{\Gamma, \forall x.P \vdash Q}\ \forall\text{-}left \qquad \frac{\Gamma \vdash P[x \leftarrow t] \quad \Gamma \vdash \Delta_e t}{\Gamma \vdash \exists x\ P}\ \exists\text{-}right$$

Fig. 1. B-Logic

We define (fig. 1) the B-Logic. The logic is close to the classic sequent calculus, only the *cut* ,∀ − *left* and ∃ − *right* rules have been changed because they can introduce ill-defined formulas.

These three rules are the only rules that introduce formulas or terms. The *cut* rule gets a new antecedent that represents the new formula's well-definedness proof. The ∀ − *left* and ∃ − *right* rules get a new antecedent too which represents the introduced term's well-definedness proof. These rules are difficult to use in an automatic prover, because it has to find a new term, however they are useful in an interactive prover. It means that when new terms are introduced in a manual proof, their well-definedness has to be proved.

The following theorem means that this logic is sound and complete with the validity notion that we defined if we make two proofs for one formula.

Theorem 1. *Given a set of formula Γ and a formula φ,*
$\Gamma \vdash \varphi$ and $\vdash \Delta_p^K (\Gamma \Rightarrow \varphi)$ if and only if $\Gamma \models \varphi$

We call the first lemma validation lemma and the second well-definedness lemma.

We could have constructed a deduction system in which one proof would have been sufficient but it would have been much less efficient while the axiom rule would not have been sound. So we prefer to prove two lemmas in an efficient deduction system rather than one lemma in a less efficient one.

When one proves a lemma, rather than proving the well-definedness at the leaves of the proof tree (at the axiom rules), the well-definedness of the lemma is proved at the beginning of the proof and the well-definedness of introduced terms is also checked.

We will see in the next section that the well-definedness lemmas associated to each B proof obligations will not be really proved. Instead they will be factorised in new lemmas defined directly from machines: we will call them delta lemmas.

4 Well Defined Proof Obligations and Proof Obligations of Well Definedness

Our aim is to apply the previous result to the proof obligations of B. The first idea is to really discharge proof obligations and their associated well-definedness lemmas in our deduction system. But we consider that the well-definedness lemmas of the proof obligations of a given machine could be factorised in what we call delta lemmas.

We first define the proof obligations of machines, refinements and implementations and then we define the lemmas that are sufficient to be proved to ensure the well-definedness of these proof obligations. To do this we have to define what is a well-defined substitution. Moreover we define a weaker Δ_p^K operator.

4.1 A Weaker Δ

First, we define a new Δ_p^{MC} operator for all formulas of the B language, we use a delta defined by Mc Carthy that is a weaker version of the Δ_p^K operator. We use Δ_p^{MC} because it produces predicates that are simpler and easier to prove automatically than Δ_p^K.

Definition 5. *We define well-definedness of formulas:*

$$\Delta^{MC}{}_p(P \Rightarrow Q) \equiv \Delta^{MC}{}_p P \wedge (P \Rightarrow \Delta^{MC}{}_p Q)$$
$$\Delta_p^{MC}(P \wedge Q) \equiv \Delta_p^{MC} P \wedge (P \Rightarrow \Delta_p^{MC} Q)$$
$$\Delta_p^{MC}(\neg P) \equiv \Delta_p^{MC} P$$
$$\Delta_p^{MC}(\forall x.P) \equiv \forall x.\Delta_p^{MC} P$$
$$\Delta_p^{MC}(a = b) \equiv \Delta_e a \wedge \Delta_e b$$
$$\Delta_p^{MC}(a \in s) \equiv \Delta_e a \wedge \Delta_e s$$
$$\Delta_p^{MC}(P \vee Q) \equiv \Delta_p^{MC} P \wedge (\neg P \Rightarrow \Delta_p^{MC} Q)$$
$$\Delta_p^{MC}(P \Leftrightarrow Q) \equiv \Delta_p^{MC} P \wedge \Delta_p^{MC} Q$$
$$\Delta_p^{MC}(\exists x.P) \equiv \forall x.\Delta_p^{MC} P$$
$$\Delta_p^{MC}(True) \equiv True$$
$$\Delta_p^{MC}(False) \equiv True$$
$$\Delta_p^{MC}(s \subset t) \equiv \Delta_e s \wedge \Delta_e t$$
$$\Delta_p^{MC}(s \subseteq t) \equiv \Delta_e s \wedge \Delta_e t$$
$$\Delta_p^{MC}(n < m) \equiv \Delta_e n \wedge \Delta_e m$$
$$\Delta_p^{MC}(n \leq m) \equiv \Delta_e n \wedge \Delta_e m$$
$$\Delta_p^{MC}(n > m) \equiv \Delta_e n \wedge \Delta_e m$$
$$\Delta_p^{MC}(n \geq m) \equiv \Delta_e n \wedge \Delta_e m$$

Proposition 3. *Given a formula P, if $\Delta_p^{MC} P$ is true then $\Delta_p^K P$ is also true.*

Checking Mc Carthy's delta is sufficient to ensure Kleene's delta, so the next proposition may be deduced from theorem 1.

Proposition 4. *Given a set of formula Γ and a formula φ, if $\Gamma \vdash \varphi$ and $\vdash \Delta_p^{MC}(\Gamma \Rightarrow \varphi)$ then $\Gamma \models \varphi$*

This proposition is weaker than the theorem 1; with Mc Carthy's delta, we lose the completeness but the soundness is preserved.

Remark 2. Notice that $\Delta_p^{MC}(P \wedge Q)$ may be true whereas $\Delta_p^{MC}(Q \wedge P)$ may not. It does not mean that the conjunction is not commutative any more, but only that one has to use the right order when writing models. No order is required during proofs. Exactly the same constraint exists for the type checking in B: $x \in \mathbb{N} \wedge x \leq 1$ is well-typed whereas $x \leq 1 \wedge x \in \mathbb{N}$ is not.

Example 8. $x = zero \vee pred(x) = pred(x)$ is still well-defined but $pred(x) = pred(x) \vee x = zero$ is no more well-defined.

In the remainder of the text, we shall write Δ_p instead of Δ_p^{MC}.

4.2 Well Defined Proof Obligations

We give in this section the different proof obligations and their well-definedness lemmas. We distinguish machines, refinements and implementations because they do not have the same validation lemmas but we will show that, because a formula and its negation have the same well-definedness, the delta lemmas are quite similar for the three abstract machine types. We call $VL(M)$, the validation lemmas of the abstract machine M.

Definition 6. *An abstract machine M is well-defined if and only if its proof obligations are well-defined i.e. if and only if there exists a proof $\vdash \Delta_p(VL(M))$.*

This definition of machine well-definedness does not care about ill-defined terms that do not occur in any of proof obligations.
In order to clarify the definitions, we only present abstract machines without parameters and constraints.

Machine Proof Obligations.

Definition 7. *We remind the validation lemmas of a machine as defined in [Abr96]:*

$$
VL \left(
\begin{array}{l}
\text{MACHINE } M \\
\text{CONSTANTS } c \\
\text{PROPERTIES } P \\
\text{VARIABLES } v \\
\text{INVARIANT } I \\
\text{ASSERTIONS } J \\
\text{INITIALISATION } U \\
\text{OPERATIONS} \\
\quad u \leftarrow O(w) = \\
\quad \text{PRE } Q \\
\quad \text{THEN } V \\
\quad \text{END} \\
\text{END}
\end{array}
\right)
\equiv
\left\{
\begin{array}{l}
P \Rightarrow [U]I \\[2mm]
P \wedge I \Rightarrow J \\[2mm]
P \wedge I \wedge J \wedge Q \Rightarrow [V]I
\end{array}
\right.
$$

Applying the definition of a well-defined machine, we obtain the next proposition.

Proposition 5. *The machine M is well-defined if an only if*
$\vdash \Delta_p((P \Rightarrow [U]I) \wedge (P \wedge I \Rightarrow J) \wedge (P \wedge I \wedge J \wedge Q \Rightarrow [V]I))$

Applying the definition of Mc Carthy's Delta, we obtain this sufficient definition of a well-defined machine.

A machine is well-defined if its properties, invariant, assertions, preconditions are well-defined, if the initialisation applied to the invariant gives a well-defined formula and for each operation, if the precondition is well defined and the formula resulting from the application of the substitution to the invariant is well-defined.

Proposition 6. *The machine M is well-defined if*
$\vdash \Delta_p P$ *and*
$\vdash P \Rightarrow \Delta_p([U]I)$ *and*
$\vdash P \Rightarrow \Delta_p I$ *and*
$\vdash P \wedge I \Rightarrow \Delta_p J$ *and*
$\vdash P \wedge I \wedge J \Rightarrow \Delta_p Q$ *and*
$\vdash P \wedge I \wedge J \wedge Q \Rightarrow \Delta_p([V]I)$

Refinement Proof Obligations.

Definition 8. *We remind the validation lemmas of a refinement as defined in [Abr96]:*

$$
VL \left(
\begin{array}{l}
\text{REFINEMENT } M_r \\
\text{REFINES } M \\
\text{CONSTANTS } c_r \\
\text{PROPERTIES } P_r \\
\text{VARIABLES } v_r \\
\text{INVARIANT } I_r \\
\text{INITIALISATION } U_r \\
\text{OPERATIONS} \\
\quad u \leftarrow O(w) = \\
\quad \text{PRE } Q_r \\
\quad \text{THEN } V_r \\
\quad \text{END} \\
\text{END}
\end{array}
\right)
\equiv
\left\{
\begin{array}{l}
P \wedge P_r \Rightarrow [U_r]\neg[U]\neg I_r \\[2mm]
P \wedge P_r \wedge I \wedge I_r \wedge J \wedge Q \Rightarrow Q_r \\[2mm]
P \wedge P_r \wedge I \wedge I_r \wedge J \wedge Q \wedge Q_r \\
\quad \Rightarrow [V_r]\neg[V]\neg I_r
\end{array}
\right.
$$

Proposition 7. *The refinement M_r is well-defined if
the machine M that it refines is well-defined and if*
$\vdash P \Rightarrow \Delta_p P_r$ *and*
$\vdash P \wedge P_r \Rightarrow \Delta_p([U_r]\neg[U]\neg I_r)$ *and*
$\vdash P \wedge P_r \Rightarrow \Delta_p I_r$ *and*
$\vdash P \wedge P_r \wedge I \wedge I_r \wedge J \wedge Q \Rightarrow \Delta_p Q_r$ *and*
$\vdash P \wedge P_r \wedge I \wedge I_r \wedge J \wedge Q \wedge Q_r \Rightarrow \Delta_p([V_r]\neg[V]\neg I_r)$ *and*

Implementation Proof Obligations.

Definition 9. *We remind the validation lemmas of an implementation as defined in [Abr96]:*

$$
VL \left| \begin{array}{l} \text{IMPLEMENTATION } M_i \\ \text{REFINES } M_r \\ \text{CONSTANTS } c_i \\ \text{PROPERTIES } P_i \\ \text{VALUES } c_i = d_i \\ \text{VARIABLES } v_i \\ \text{INVARIANT } I_i \\ \text{INITIALISATION } U_i \\ \text{OPERATIONS} \\ \quad u \leftarrow O(w) = \\ \quad \text{PRE } Q_i \\ \quad \text{THEN } V_i \\ \quad \text{END} \\ \text{END} \end{array} \right\rangle \equiv \left\{ \begin{array}{l} P \wedge P_r \wedge P_i \Rightarrow [U_i]\neg[U_r]\neg I_i \\[2mm] P \wedge P_r \wedge P_i \wedge I \wedge I_r \wedge I_i \wedge \\ J \wedge Q \wedge Q_r \Rightarrow Q_i \\[2mm] P \wedge P_r \wedge P_i \wedge I \wedge I_r \wedge I_i \wedge \\ J \wedge Q \wedge Q_r \wedge Q_i \\ \Rightarrow [V_i]\neg[V_r]\neg I_i \\[2mm] \exists(c,c_r).([c_i := d_i](P \wedge P_r \wedge P_i)) \end{array} \right.
$$

Proposition 8. *The implementation M_i is well-defined if the abstract machines that it refines are well-defined and if*

$\vdash P \wedge P_r \Rightarrow \Delta_p P_i$ *and*

$\vdash P \wedge P_r \wedge P_i \Rightarrow \Delta_p([U_i]\neg[U_r]\neg I_i)$ *and*

$\vdash P \wedge P_r \wedge P_i \wedge I \wedge J \wedge I_r \Rightarrow \Delta_p I_i$ *and*

$\vdash P \wedge P_r \wedge P_i \wedge I \wedge J \wedge I_r \wedge I_i \wedge Q \wedge Q_r \Rightarrow \Delta_p Q_i$ *and*

$\vdash P \wedge P_r \wedge P_i \wedge I \wedge J \wedge I_r \wedge I_i \wedge Q \wedge Q_r \wedge Q_i \Rightarrow \Delta_p([V_i]\neg[V_r]\neg I_i)$ *and*

$\vdash \forall(c,c_r).\Delta_p([c_i := d_i](P \wedge P_r \wedge P_i))$

Remark 3. The lemmas from propositions 7,8 are close to the machine proof obligations of well-definedness (proposition 6); except for the hypothesis, we have almost the same lemmas.

4.3 Well-Definedness of Generalised Substitutions

In propositions 6,7,8 we have to prove predicates like $\Delta_p([S]P)$. For this, we define the Δ_s operator that assigns a well-definedness predicate to each substitution such that the following theorem holds.

Theorem 2. $\Delta_p I \wedge \Delta_s S \Rightarrow \Delta_p([S]I)$

This theorem means that if a substitution is well-defined then it transforms a well-defined predicate into a well-defined predicate.

Definition 10. *We define the well-definedness of substitutions:*

$\Delta_s(x := E) \equiv \Delta_e E$

$\Delta_s(skip) \equiv True$

$\Delta_s(P \mid S) \equiv \left\{ \begin{array}{l} \Delta_p P \wedge \\ P \Rightarrow \Delta_s S \end{array} \right.$

$\Delta_s(S_1 \| S_2) \equiv \left\{ \begin{array}{l} \Delta_s S_1 \wedge \\ \Delta_s S_2 \end{array} \right.$

$$\Delta_s(P \Longrightarrow S) \equiv \begin{cases} \Delta_p P \wedge \\ P \Rightarrow \Delta_s S \end{cases}$$

$$\Delta_s(@x.S) \equiv \forall x. \Delta_s S$$

$$\Delta_s(S_1 \| S_2) \equiv \begin{cases} \Delta_s S_1 \wedge \\ \Delta_s S_2 \end{cases}$$

$$\Delta_s \begin{pmatrix} \text{WHILE } P \\ \text{DO } S \\ \text{INVARIANT } I \\ \text{VARIANT } V \\ \text{END} \end{pmatrix} \equiv \begin{cases} \forall x. \Delta_p I \wedge \\ \forall x. (I \Rightarrow \Delta_p P) \wedge \\ \forall x. (I \Rightarrow \Delta_e V) \wedge \\ \forall x. (I \wedge P \Rightarrow \Delta_s S) \end{cases}$$ where x is the list of the variables modified in the body of the loop

$$\Delta_s((x := E); T) \equiv \begin{cases} \Delta_e E \wedge \\ [x := E]\Delta_s T \end{cases}$$

$$\Delta_s((S_1 \| S_2); T) \equiv \begin{cases} \Delta_s(S_1; T) \wedge \\ \Delta_s(S_2; T) \end{cases}$$

$$\Delta_s \begin{pmatrix} \text{WHILE } P \\ \text{DO } S \\ \text{INVARIANT } I \\ \text{VARIANT } V \\ \text{END}; \\ T \end{pmatrix} \equiv \begin{cases} \forall x. \Delta_p I \wedge \\ \forall x. (I \Rightarrow \Delta_p P) \wedge \\ \forall x. (I \Rightarrow \Delta_e V) \wedge \\ \forall x. (I \wedge P \Rightarrow \Delta_s S) \wedge \\ \forall x. (I \wedge \neg P \Rightarrow \Delta_s T) \end{cases}$$ where x is the list of the variables modified in the body of loop

This definition is sufficient to ensure the previous theorem. We can remark that the well-definedness of substitution mainly depends on the well-definedness of affected terms and conditions.

The well-definedness of a sequence of two substitutions cannot be defined using only the well-definedness of the two substitutions. We choose to define it by induction on the first substitution, finally we get only three definitions (for assignment, parallel and loop), since sequencing operator distributes on the other operators.

The well-definedness of proof obligations does not ensure the well-definedness of the source. For example, the proof obligation generated by the substitution $x := 1/0; x := 1$ does not contain the term $1/0$. So we could have defined $\Delta_s(x := E; x := F)$ to be $\Delta_e F$ and the theorem 2 would still have been valid.

In fact, our definition of Δ_s ensures that all the terms of a substitution are well defined. So the Δ - lemmas that we define in the next section ensure not only that the proof obligations are well defined, but also that the source does not contain any ill-defined term.

4.4 Proof Obligations of Well Definedness: Δ - lemmas

Finally, we define the Δ - lemmas associated to machines, refinements and implementations. These lemmas are sufficient to ensure the well-definedness of proof obligations. Formally, we define the Δ_m operator that assigns lemmas to abstract machines, so that the next proposition holds.

Proposition 9. Δ_m *correctness* :

1. $\Delta_m(M) \Rightarrow \Delta_p(VL(M))$
2. $\Delta_m(M) \wedge \Delta_m(M_r) \Rightarrow \Delta_p(VL(M_r))$
3. $\Delta_m(M) \wedge \Delta_m(M_r) \wedge \Delta_m(M_i) \Rightarrow \Delta_p(VL(M_i))$

Definition 11. *We define well-definedness of machine, refinement and implementation:*

$$
\Delta_m \left(
\begin{array}{l}
\text{MACHINE } M \\
\text{CONSTANTS } c \\
\text{PROPERTIES } P \\
\text{VARIABLES } v \\
\text{INVARIANT } I \\
\text{INITIALISATION } U \\
\text{OPERATIONS} \\
\quad u \leftarrow O(w) = \\
\quad \text{PRE } Q \\
\quad \text{THEN } V \\
\quad \text{END} \\
\text{END}
\end{array}
\right)
\equiv
\left\{
\begin{array}{l}
\Delta_p P \\
\\
P \Rightarrow \Delta_p I \\
\\
P \Rightarrow \Delta_s U \\
\\
P \wedge I \Rightarrow \Delta_p Q \\
\\
P \wedge I \wedge Q \Rightarrow \Delta_s V
\end{array}
\right.
$$

$$
\Delta_m \left(
\begin{array}{l}
\text{REFINEMENT } M_r \\
\text{REFINES } M \\
\text{CONSTANTS } c_r \\
\text{PROPERTIES } P_r \\
\text{VARIABLES } v_r \\
\text{INVARIANT } I_r \\
\text{INITIALISATION } U_r \\
\text{OPERATIONS} \\
\quad u \leftarrow O(w) = \\
\quad \text{PRE } Q_r \\
\quad \text{THEN } V_r \\
\quad \text{END} \\
\text{END}
\end{array}
\right)
\equiv
\left\{
\begin{array}{l}
P \Rightarrow \Delta_p P_r \\
\\
P \wedge P_r \Rightarrow \Delta_p I_r \\
\\
P \wedge P_r \Rightarrow \Delta_s U_r \\
\\
P \wedge P_r \wedge I \wedge I_r \wedge Q \Rightarrow \Delta_p Q_r \\
\\
P \wedge P_r \wedge I \wedge I_r \wedge Q \wedge Q_r \Rightarrow \Delta_s V_r
\end{array}
\right.
$$

Remark 4. As $\Delta_p \neg P$ is equivalent to $\Delta_p P$, the double negation of proof obligations does not influence the well-definedness lemma; if we know that the substitutions of machine operations preserve well-definedness, we just have to check that the substitutions of refinement operations have the same property, i.e. this property holds : $\Delta_p P \wedge \Delta_s S \wedge \Delta_s T \Rightarrow \Delta_p([T]\neg[S]\neg I)$

$$\Delta_m \left(\begin{array}{l} \text{IMPLEMENTATION} \\ \quad M_i \\ \text{REFINES } M_r \\ \text{CONSTANTS } c_i \\ \text{PROPERTIES } P_i \\ \text{VALUES } c_i = d_i \\ \text{VARIABLES } v_i \\ \text{INVARIANT } I_i \\ \text{INITIALISATION} \\ \quad U_i \\ \text{OPERATIONS} \\ \quad u \leftarrow O(w) = \\ \quad \text{PRE } Q_i \\ \quad \text{THEN } V_i \\ \quad \text{END} \\ \text{END} \end{array} \right) \equiv \left\{ \begin{array}{l} P \wedge P_r \Rightarrow \Delta_p P_i \\ \\ P \wedge P_r \wedge P_i \wedge I \wedge I_r \Rightarrow \Delta_p I_i \\ \\ P \wedge P_r \wedge P_i \wedge I \wedge I_r \Rightarrow \Delta_s U_i \\ \\ P \wedge P_r \wedge P_i \wedge I \wedge I_r \wedge I_i \wedge Q \wedge Q_r \Rightarrow \Delta_p Q_i \\ \\ P \wedge P_r \wedge P_i \wedge I \wedge I_r \wedge I_i \wedge \\ Q \wedge Q_r \wedge Q_i \Rightarrow \Delta_s V_i \\ \\ \Delta_e d_i \end{array} \right.$$

We see that we do not check the Δ-lemmas due to the values lemmas because the well-definedness of the properties is checked in the machines and refinements.

5 Repercusions

5.1 Consequences on the rules

As we have seen in section 3, the proof of each lemma is divided into two parts. The first one is the proof of the well-definedness of the lemma, and the second one is the proof of the lemma itself, assuming its well-definedness. This hypothesis allows to simplify the demonstration and especially the rules used for this demonstration. Indeed, assuming that the lemma is well defined, the rules need no more be protected against ill-defined expressions.

For example the following backward and rewriting rules can be simplified as shown in the table:

	Initial rule	Simplified rule
R1	$c \neq 0 \wedge a = b \Rightarrow a/c = b/c$	$a = b \Rightarrow a/c = b/c.$
R2	$c = a \Rightarrow \{a \mapsto b\}(c) == b$	$\{a \mapsto b\}(c) == b$
R3	$s \neq \emptyset \wedge s \in FIN(\mathbb{Z})$ $\Rightarrow min(s) \leq max(s)$	$min(s) \leq max(s)$
R4	$x \in dom(f) \wedge$ $f \in dom(f) \mapsto\mapsto ran(f) \wedge f^{-1} \in ran(f) \mapsto\mapsto dom(f)$ $\Rightarrow f^{-1}(f(x)) == x$	$f^{-1}(f(x)) == x$

This simplification of the rule base has two advantages. First of all, the rules are easier to write, to understand and to validate. Secondly, it improves significantly the speed of the tool and the number of the lemmas proved, as we had noticed in 1992 on our automatic prover based on such a simplified rule base.

5.2 Consequences on the method

In B, the arithmetic symbols have a dual interpretation: in machines (or refinements) they denote the mathematical operator, whereas in implementations, they also denote the corresponding function of the programming language into which the implementations are to be translated.

Consequently, in the machines the domain of each operator is the one given by the mathematical theory (Cf. [Abr96]) whereas in the implementations it is the more restrictive (the intersection) between the one given by the theory and the one given by the programming language [2]. In order to take into account the inherent partialness of the arithmetic operator in programming languages, the B-method limits drastically the use of these operators in the implementations (Cf. [Abr96] *12.1.11. Allowed Constructs in an Implementation*). For example, the operators /, + and − are syntaxically forbidden in IF and WHILE conditions (the source : IF (a+1 < 2) THEN ... is not allowed in implementations), because their evaluation could overflow at run time. In this restrictive way, the B-method guarantees that all the expressions in implementations can be correctly evaluated.

These limitations on the expressivity of B in implementations could be removed by using the notion of well-defined model introduced previously. Indeed, the definition of Δ that we have chosen (Cf. 4) guarantees that if the well definedness lemmas are proved, then there is no ill-defined term in the source. In other words it means that programming operators are used in their domain and then that the computer can evaluate them.

We just have to notice that the definition of Δ_e for the arithmetic operators is not the same in machines and in implementations because we have to take into account the duality of the arithmetic symbols in implementations. In machines the definition of Δ_e is based on the mathematical domain whereas in implementations it is based on the domain of the corresponding function in the programming language. For example, in machine, $\Delta_{e\_mch}(x+y) \equiv \Delta_{e\_mch}x \wedge \Delta_{e\_mch}y$ but in implementation, $\Delta_{e\_imp}(x+y) \equiv \Delta_{e\_imp}x \wedge \Delta_{e\_imp}y \wedge (x+y \in minint..maxint)$ which means that the result must be in the range of the language (supposed to be *minint..maxint*).

6 Conclusion

How to deal with the meaningless expressions that may occur in formal models without disturbing engineers which unnecessary mathematical complexities? This paper answers, in the context of the B method, by an original approach in which new proofs obligations, the Δ-lemmas, have to be discharged before the proof obligations of the method. All the proofs can be done in the usual two-valued framework if you check the well-definedness of the terms you introduce during the proofs.

---

[2] to be more precise we should also take into account the compiler and the hardware.

45

This technique was first prototyped at *Matra Transport* in 1992: an extension of the proof obligation generator of the B-Toolkit was developed internally to produce the Δ-lemmas. A major benefit was to simplify and to improve significantly the performances of the automatic prover we were developing at that time.

It is now currently being implemented in the Atelier B. This article provides the specification of the tool and formally establishes the results upon which the specification is built.

Acknowledgements

This work is partly supported by the ASCOT project.

References

[Abr96] Abrial J.R., The B Book (1996)
[BCJ84] Barringer H., Cheng J.H., Jones C.B., A Logic Covering Undefinedness in Program Proofs; Acta Informatica 21:251-269 (1984)
[BKT88] Blikle A., Konikowska B., Tarlecki A., A Three Valued Logic for Software Specification and Validation; LNCS 328 (1988)
[CJ90] Cheng J.H., Jones C.B., On the Usability of Logics Which Handle Partial Functions; Proceedings of the Third Refinement Workshop 51-69 (1990)
[EO93] Elvang-Gøransson M., Owe O., A Simple Sequent Calculus for Partial Functions; TCS 114:317-330 (1993)
[GL90] Gavilanes-Franco A., Lucio-Carrasco F. A First Order Logic for Partial Functions; TCS 74 37-69 (1990)
[Hol91] Holden M., Weak Logic Theory; TCS 79:295-321 (1991)
[Owe93] Owe O., Partial Logics Reconsidered: a Conservative Approach, Research Report 155, Department of Informatics, University of Oslo, 1991; Formal Aspects of Comput. 5:208-223 (1993)

Composition and Refinement in the B-Method

Marie-Laure Potet and Yann Rouzaud
LSR-IMAG, Grenoble, France

Laboratoire Logiciels Systèmes Réseaux - Institut IMAG (UJF - INPG - CNRS)
BP 72, F-38402 Saint Martin d'Hères Cedex - Fax +33 4 76827287
Marie-Laure.Potet@imag.fr, Yann.Rouzaud@imag.fr

Abstract. In this paper, we propose a framework to study refinement of abstract machines in the B-method. It allows us to properly deal with shared variables, possibly introduced by composition primitives SEES and IMPORTS. We exhibit local conditions on components which are sufficient to ensure global correctness of a software system. Finally, we show how restrictions on the architecture of software systems may guarantee these conditions.

1 Introduction

Modularity is pointed out as a principle allowing to master the complexity of software development or maintenance. A modular method must help designers to produce software systems from autonomous components. Modularity must be offered at each level of software development: programming as well as specification and design.

In the framework of formal methods, *modules* or *components* correspond to syntactic entities which can be combined by *composition primitives*. If a method offers stepwise refinement, adding modularity requires to precisely define composition primitives and how they interact with the process of refinement. Modularity and refinement has been widely studied in the framework of algebraic specifications [ST88]. In the framework of model oriented specifications, some methods offer a concept of modularity (for instance B [Abr96], VDM [Gro94]) but problems appear when combining refinement and composition.

The work presented in this paper was initially motivated by an example communicated by P. Behm, from Matra Transport International. This example exhibits an incorrect B-development in which each component refinement is locally correct. We aimed to extend the architectural conditions given in the B-book (transitivity and circularity, p. 583), in order to detect such pathological examples. So we developed a framework to define refinement of structured components, in order to prove their correctness. This paper presents a simplified version of this framework.

Section 2 presents the B-clauses which allows designers to build structured development (in particular SEES and IMPORTS clauses), and we give a paradigmatic example, illustrating the problem due to refinement composition (section 2.4). In section 3, we propose a semantics for structured components, in terms of *flat components*. From this definition, we show that the proofs obligations relative to each refinement step of structured components, as defined by the B-method, are correct. Then, we introduce a notion of *code component* and we exhibit sufficient conditions to prove its correctness. This amounts to study how monotonicity and transitivity of the refinement relation interact. By a top-down approach we propose several sufficient conditions. The last one is presented in section 4. It is based on the dependency graph between components and it corrects the conditions proposed in the B-Book.

1.1 Composition Primitives

Designing appropriate composition primitives for a specification language or method is a non-trivial task. During the various phases of the software life cycle, expected characteristics can differ. For instance, at the stage of system specification, composition primitives must allow to easily combine pieces of specifications and, if possible, their properties. At the architectural design stage, major system components and their inter-relationships must be identified. So composition primitives must favour the independence of coding activity. This duality is illustrated by the *open-closed* principle [Mey88]. The open view means building larger components by extension. The closed view means making a component available for blind use by others components.

So a method should offer several styles of composition primitives, suitable for the stages of specification, design or programming.

1.2 Composition and Refinement

In a method which offers stepwise refinement, the relationship between different levels of specification is defined by a *refinement relation*. When specifications use composition primitives, a way to refine such structured specifications must be included. At the specification level, some structured specifications can be interpreted as new "flattened" specifications. In this case, the new resulting specification can be refined in any way. Otherwise, if the structure is inherent in the specification, the refinement must preserve the global structure. For instance, in the Z notation [Spi88], a reference to a schema is interpreted as a local copy of the schema text and the new schema may be refined in an independent way. On the contrary, in the programming language Ada, links between packages which are introduced at the specification level, are implicitly preserved in the body.

At the level of architectural design, the final structure of the system is elaborated and components will be implemented separately. This structure must be kept by the latter steps of refinement. This is the property of *compositional refinement* (also referenced as the property of horizontal refinement), which permits to compose refinements to form a large composite refinement architecture.

Refinement composition abilities naturally depend on the relations between components (see for instance discussions about inheritance in the object-oriented approach [LW94]). Several cases can be considered:

1. Refinement composition is always valid. This is the case for instance if the refinement relation is proved to be monotonic [BW90], for such compositions.
2. Global correctness depends on the semantics of the involved components. In this case, a case-by-case proof is mandatory. For instance, if a specification is built as an extension of another specification, the compositionality of refinement depends on the form of this extension.
3. Global correctness depends on the global structure of the system. This is generally the case when sharing is allowed.

Sharing occurs when the same object is used into several modules. In that case, two main problems arise. First, semantics of sharing must be preserved by the refinement process. For instance, if an abstract data type is duplicated, conversion between the different representations must be insured. Secondly, correctness of each independent development does not necessarily guarantee correctness of the composition. Some possible interferences relative to the shared part can break down refinement. This is the classical problem about aliasing and side effects. This point is crucial in the method/language dealing with with states, as we will see.

2 Component, Composition and Refinement in B

2.1 B-Components

In the B-method, there are three kinds of component: *abstract machines, refinements* and *implementations. Abstract machines* are the visible part of specifications. In particular, all composition primitives connect components with abstract machines. *Refinements* are intermediary steps between interface (abstract machines) and executable code (implementations). These components can be seen as traces of a development. *Implementations* are the last level of a development. Implementations are particular refinements in which substitutions are executable, so they can be translated into code. Moreover, either variables are concrete ones, or they come from other abstract machines, so they must be used via operation calls.

The introduction of several kinds of component, linked to the different steps of the development process, is a particularity of the B-method. In other languages or methods, there is generally only one kind of component, and some syntactic restrictions characterize implementations. This distinction in the B-method is based on the following arguments:

1. Refinements and implementations are not only specifications, but they also contain information about the refinement (the *gluing invariant*, describing the change of variables).
2. Each kind of components has specific syntactic restrictions. For instance, sequencing cannot occur in an abstract machine, in order to favour the abstraction at the first level of a development.
3. The target of composition primitives is always an abstract machine. This restriction favours the decomposition/composition criterion which permits to develop pieces of specification in an independent way.

2.2 B Composition Primitives

The B-method offers, at present, four composition primitives. Two of them (IN-CLUDES and IMPORTS) exclude possibility of sharing and two of them (USES and SEES) allow a controlled form of sharing.

Includes/Imports. The INCLUDES primitive links abstract machines or refinements to abstract machines. This primitive can be seen as a schema inclusion in Z, without possibility of sharing: this primitive is interpreted as a local copy of the included machines. Due to some syntactic restrictions, the INCLUDES primitive permits to extend an abstract machine (enforcing and adding variables state, adding and hiding operations).

The IMPORTS primitive links implementations to abstract machines. This primitive corresponds to classical component primitives of programming languages. It allows to build a layered software. This primitive can be seen as the closed version of the INCLUDES primitive: use of IMPORTS encapsulates the state of the imported abstract machines.

Implementions are not refinable in the B-method, so the IMPORTS primitive is a final composition primitive. A composition using INCLUDES primitive, with its copy semantics, is not necessarily preserved during the refinement process. If an abstract machine M is included in a component C, being either an abstract machine or a refinement, there are two possibilities:

1. C is refined by its proper structure. In this case, the abstract machine M will be implemented only if it is imported in another implementation.
2. C is implemented using a IMPORTS primitive on M. This possibility is not directly supported by the method, because refinement does not exploit the preservation of this kind of structure.

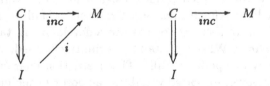

Fig. 1. If a component C includes a machine M, an implementation I of C may or may not import M.

Uses/Sees. The USES primitive introduces a form of sharing between abstract machines. In the B-method, sharing is introduced by a link on a component entity. The use of this primitive permits to extend an abstract machine in multiple ways. A final abstract machine must include all shared machines and their extensions. For more explanations about this construction, see [BPR96].

The SEES primitive can appear in abstract machines, refinements or implementations. The use of this primitive allows to share sets, definitions and variables in a very limited way: variables must not be modified by the seing components, in any way. From the refinement point of view, there are some restrictions:

1. abstract machines containing a USES primitive are not considered as refinable specifications.
2. if a SEES primitive is introduced at a given level of a development, this primitive must be preserved in the lowest levels of the development, to guarantee the unicity of the implementation of the shared part.

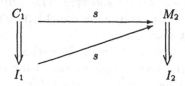

Fig. 2. A SEES primitive must be preserved in a refinement.

The USES and INCLUDES primitives are only syntactic facilities. So in the study of refinement composition, only the SEES and IMPORTS primitives have to be considered.

Comparison between Sees and Imports. The SEES and IMPORTS primitives differ in their use, due to their proper restrictions, whose aim is to limit interference between local refinements. Some restrictions fall on local use of these primitives and some of them are relative to a development, taken as a whole.

Local Restrictions. When an IMPORTS primitive is used, values of variables are accessible only by operation calls. This restriction guarantees the invariant preservation. Moreover, imported variables can occur in the invariant part. This possibility allows designers to constrain imported variables and use them to represent abstract variables. In this way, a layered software is produced. When a SEES primitive is used, variables can be consulted (directly or via operation calls), but cannot be modified. Variables of the seen machine are not visible in the invariant part of the seeing component. As a result, seen variables cannot be used in a refinement to represent abstract variables.

Global Restrictions. Abstract machines which are seen by other ones must be imported once, and only once, in the development. Abstract machines can be imported at most once in a development, so variables cannot be shared by this way (if necessary, renaming, which produces a new copy of a machine, can be used). Another important property is the absence of cycle: an abstract machine cannot see or import itself, directly or indirectly.

2.3 Refinement of a Single B-Component

Refinement relates an "abstract" model of a B-component to a more "concrete" one. In the B-method, it is based on observational substitutivity: any behaviour of the refined specification is one of the possible behaviours of the initial specification. More specifically, B-refinement allows designers to reduce non-determinism of operations, to weaken their preconditions, and to change the variable space.

In the following, we recall some results on B-refinement (chapter 11 of the B-book).

Refinement Component. A refinement component is defined as a differential to be added to a component. A refinement component can have proper variables which are linked to variables of the refined component by a *gluing invariant*. Moreover, refined operations must be stated on the new variables.

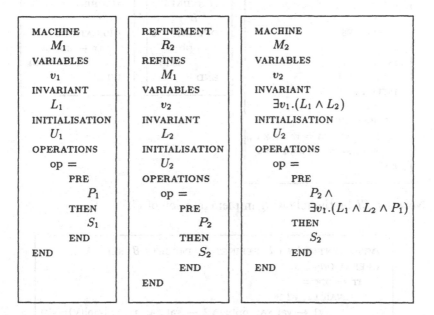

Fig. 3. Refinement R_2 of M_1, seen as an independant machine M_2.

Proof Obligations. The proof obligations for refinement R_2 of Fig. 3 are, provided that there are no common variables (B-book, p. 530):

1. Initialisation: $[U_2]\neg[U_1]\neg L_2$
2. Operation op: $L_1 \wedge L_2 \wedge P_1 \Rightarrow P_2 \wedge [S_2]\neg[S_1]\neg L_2$

In the most general case, there is a chain of refinements $M_1, R_2, \ldots, R_n$ to be considered. The proof obligation for an operation of R_n is, provided that M_1 and its refinements have no common variables:

$$L_1 \wedge L_2 \wedge \ldots \wedge L_n \wedge P_1 \wedge \ldots \wedge P_{n-1} \Rightarrow P_n \wedge [S_n]\neg[S_{n-1}]\neg L_n \ .$$

2.4 Compositional Refinement

In languages based on states, a major difficulty is relative to the sharing of states. In presence of sharing, we must prove that some local reasoning about values of variables are always valid in a global system. Such a problem appears in the B refinement process.

Example 1. Let A, B, C be the following abstract machines:

```
MACHINE
   A
VARIABLES
   xa
INVARIANT
   xa : 0..1
INITIALISATION
   xa := 0
OPERATIONS
   rr ← val_xa = rr := xa ;
   mod_xa = xa := 1 - xa
END
```

```
MACHINE
   B
OPERATIONS
   opb =
      skip
END
```

```
MACHINE
   C
OPERATIONS
   rr ← opc =
      rr := TRUE
END
```

Now, let CI be the following implementation of C:

```
IMPLEMENTATION CI REFINES C IMPORTS B SEES A
OPERATIONS
   rr ← opc =
      VAR v1, v2 IN
            v1 ← val_xa; opb; v2 ← val_xa; rr := bool(v1=v2)
      END
END
```

This refinement is valid. Using B-definitions on substitutions, we have to prove that TRUE=bool(xa=xa), which is true. Now machine B is implemented, with the help of D and DI, by BI:

```
IMPLEMENTATION          MACHINE          IMPLEMENTATION
     BI                    D                   DI
REFINES                 OPERATIONS          REFINES
     B                    opd = skip            D
SEES                    END                 IMPORTS
     D                                          A
OPERATIONS                                  OPERATIONS
  opb = opd                                   opd = mod_xa
END                                         END
```

These two refinements are also valid. But, despite the fact that proof obligations proposed by the B-method can be discharged, the code of the operation *opc* is not correct (see below).

```
rr ← opc =
    VAR v1, v2 IN
        v1 := xa ;  xa := 1 - xa ;  v2 := xa ;  rr := bool(v1=v2)
    END
```

The resulting substitution is bool(xa=(1-xa)), which is FALSE. Where is the flaw? When implementing the abstract machine C, we implicitly suppose that the operation *opd* of the machine D does not affect the variable xa. But this hypothesis is broken by the implementation DI (see Fig. 4).

The B-method imposes conditions on architecture to eliminate some incorrect cases (B-book, p. 583): it is not possible for a machine, a refinement or an implementation to see a machine that is one of its ancestors or descendants through a chain of IMPORTS primitives. But the architecture of our example does not fit this condition, because A is imported through a SEES primitive.

Fig. 4. Architecture of Example 1.

The problem comes from two different views on abstract machines. When abstract machines are combined, only modifications described in the abstract definition of operations are observable. So, we implicitly suppose that abstract machines, and *a fortiori* their code, do not modify anything else. When abstract machines are refined, new variables can be introduced. So we implicitly suppose that operations can alter other variables, in a way compatible with the refinement invariant.

If variables introduced by a refinement are local to this refinement, the composition is valid. But if these variables can be referenced in other abstract machines by composition, these two views can become inconsistent and some unpleasant side effects can appear. New conditions are necessary to simultaneously adopt these two points of view.

2.5 Notation, Operations and Properties on Refinements

In this paper, in order to highlight the essential part of a proof obligation, the notation $\sqsubseteq_L$ will be used, and gluing invariants of intermediate refinements, as well as preconditions of their operations, will be omitted and considered as hidden hypotheses. We will also assume that the precondition of the refining operation is already proved. So, *in such an implicit context*, the proof obligation of an operation op, refined in a chain of refinements $R_1, \ldots, R_n$, will be written $L_n \Rightarrow op_{R_{n-1}} \sqsubseteq_{L_n} op_{R_n}$, where L_n is the gluing invariant of R_n.

Definition 1. *Refinement Relation $\sqsubseteq_L$.*

Let L be a predicate, $op_1 \equiv P_1|S_1$ and $op_2 \equiv P_2|S_2$ be two operations with the same signature. Then:

$$op_1 \sqsubseteq_L op_2 \equiv [S_2]\neg[S_1]\neg L .$$

Definition 2. *Notation var and free.*

1. $var(C)$ is the set of variables of the component C, in the VARIABLES clause.
2. $free(L)$ is the set of free variables of the predicate L.

Renaming Common Variables. When a B-component C and its immediate refinement R, with gluing invariant L, share some variables v, a renaming must be introduced, in order to properly deal with proof obligations. Let v' be a set of fresh variables, related to v. Then v will be renamed by v' in R (and in the chain of refinements beginning with R), so the proof obligation for an operation op becomes:

$$L \wedge v = v' \Rightarrow op_C \sqsubseteq_{L \wedge v = v'} [v := v']op_R .$$

Translating a B-Refinement into an Independant Machine. This operation takes a refinement R_n in a chain $M_1, R_2, \ldots, R_n$, and delivers the corresponding independant abstract machine M_n, which looks like abstract machine M_2 of Fig. 3. Main characteristic of this translation is that intermediate variables are hidden by existential quantification. Notice that renaming of common variables is prerequisite. Invariant of the resulting machine is:

$$\exists x_1, \ldots, x_{n-1} \cdot (L_1 \wedge L_2 \wedge \ldots \wedge L_n)$$

and the precondition of an operation is:

$$P_n \wedge \exists x_1, \ldots, x_{n-1} \cdot (L_1 \wedge L_2 \wedge \ldots \wedge L_n \wedge P_1 \wedge \ldots \wedge P_{n-1}) .$$

Reducing a Chain of Refinements. Reducing a chain of refinements M_1, $R_2, \ldots, R_n$ consists in defining a direct refinement R'_n of abstract machine M_1. Let M_n be the independant abstract machine, corresponding with R_n. Then R'_n is the differential to be added to M_1, in order to build M_n. Notice that renaming of common variables is prerequisite. Gluing invariant between M_1 and R'_n is:

$$\exists x_2, \ldots, x_{n-1} \cdot (L_2 \wedge \ldots \wedge L_n)$$

and the precondition of an operation of R'_n is:

$$P_n \wedge \exists x_1, \ldots, x_{n-1} \cdot (L_1 \wedge \ldots \wedge L_n \wedge P_1 \wedge \ldots \wedge P_{n-1}) \ .$$

Invariant Splitting. In the following, the invariant splitting property will be used to establish sufficient conditions for a proof obligation of a refinement, when its gluing invariant L takes the form $L_1 \wedge L_2$.

Lemma 1. Let S be a substitution and P, Q be two predicates, such that S does not modify the free variables of Q. We have:

$$Q \wedge \neg[S]\neg P \Rightarrow \neg[S]\neg(P \wedge Q).$$

Proof: by structural induction on substitutions.

Lemma 2. Let S_1 and S_2 be two substitutions, and A, B two predicates, such that S_1 does not modify the free variables of B. We have:

$$[S_1]B \wedge [S_2]\neg[S_1]\neg A \Rightarrow [S_2]\neg[S_1]\neg(A \wedge B)$$

Notice that in general, we cannot deduce $[S_2]\neg[S_1]\neg(A \wedge B)$ from the hypotheses $[S_2]\neg[S_1]\neg A$ and $[S_2]\neg[S_1]\neg B$.

Proof: by lemma 1, we have $B \wedge \neg[S_1]\neg A \Rightarrow \neg[S_1]\neg(A \wedge B)$. By monotonicity of substitutions through implication (B-Book, p. 287), we obtain $[S_2](B \wedge \neg[S_1]\neg A) \Rightarrow [S_2]\neg[S_1]\neg(A \wedge B)$. The property is then established by distributivity of substitutions through conjunction (B-Book, p. 287).

Property 1. *Invariant splitting.*
    Let C be a B-component, R a refinement of C, $L \equiv L_1 \wedge L_2$ the gluing invariant of R, and op_C an operation of C, whose refinement is op_R. Property $op_C \sqsubseteq_L op_R$ holds if:

1. op_C does not modify the free variables of L_2,
2. $[op_R]L_2$,
3. $op_C \sqsubseteq_{L_1} op_R$.

Proof: direct application of lemma 2.

3 A Framework for Compositional Refinement

We call *B-component* a B-entity: an abstract machine, a refinement or an implementation. A B-component is *flat* if it includes neither SEES nor IMPORTS primitive. Otherwise it is *structured*.

First, we propose a semantics for structured components. Following the work presented in [BPR96], the chosen semantics consists in interpreting such components as new "flattened" components. Thus refinement of structured components can be reduced to refinement of flat components. Finally, we use this framework to define the last step of a development: how the code of an abstract machine is elaborated. Studying the correctness of this code comes down to study the monotonicity of the refinement relation with respect to the structural SEES and IMPORTS primitives. This form of monotonicity is not always valid (recall example 1), and some sufficient conditions will be pointed out.

3.1 Flattening Structured B-Components

We define a *flattening* operation, denoted by $\mathcal{F}$, which produces a new flat component, in which all SEES and IMPORTS primitives are expanded. In such a flat component, the keywords MACHINE, REFINEMENT, IMPLEMENTATION are replaced with COMPONENT. If no REFINES clause appears in a component, it comes from an abstract machine. Otherwise, it comes from a refinement or an implementation. This change of keyword is done to underline that there is no syntactic restriction on the allowed substitutions in our components.

In the flattening operation, we only consider variables and clauses related to variables (initialisation, invariant and operations), because problems of refinement composition come from variables. The SEES and IMPORTS primitives will be treated in the same way, because they have the same semantics (call of operations on an encapsulated state). The difference lays on the possibility of sharing for the SEES primitive: in this case some components $\mathcal{F}(M_i)$ can have some variables in common, coming from seen machines.

Definition 3. *The Flattening Operation.*
Let C be a B-component. If C is stand-alone, then $\mathcal{F}(C)$ is C, with the header "COMPONENT $\mathcal{F}(C)$". Otherwise, C has some SEES or IMPORTS primitives on machines M_1, ..., M_n. The flat component $\mathcal{F}(C)$ is defined as follows:

1. Header of $\mathcal{F}(C)$ is "COMPONENT $\mathcal{F}(C)$".
2. If C refines a B-component C', then a clause "REFINES $\mathcal{F}(C')$" is introduced.
3. Variables of $\mathcal{F}(C)$ are variables of C, $\mathcal{F}(M_1)$, ..., $\mathcal{F}(M_n)$. Because variables of C, M_1, ..., M_n are distinct (a restriction imposed by the B-method), common variables may only come from the machines which are seen (several times) and imported (almost once).
4. Invariant of $\mathcal{F}(C)$ is the conjunction of invariant of C and invariants of $\mathcal{F}(M_1)$, ..., $\mathcal{F}(M_n)$. For the same reason as above, invariants on shared variables are necessarily identical.

5. Initialisation of $\mathcal{F}(C)$ is the substitution $((U_1 \otimes \ldots \otimes U_n) \, ; U)$, where each U_i is the initialisation of the component $\mathcal{F}(M_i)$ and U is the initialisation of M. The operator $\otimes$ is the extension of the operator $\parallel$ when variables are shared (see [BPR96] for more explanations).

6. Operations of $\mathcal{F}(C)$ are expanded operations of C. Expansion consists in replacing the calls to operations with their bodies, where formal parameters are replace with effective parameters (B-book, page 314). We suppose here that operations are not recursive.

Property 2. *Invariant Preservation by an Operation Call.*

Let M be a component corresponding abstract machine and I be its invariant. It can be proved that I is preserved by a substitution S, calling operations of M, if these operations are called into their precondition. Such a condition is imposed by the B-method. In consequence, for a component C, seeing or importing a component M, each operation of $\mathcal{F}(C)$ preserves the invariant of M.

Example 2. The flat component associated with implementation DI of Example 1 is:

```
COMPONENT F(DI)  REFINES F(D)
VARIABLES xa
INVARIANT xa : 0..1
INITIALISATION xa := 0
OPERATIONS opd =  xa := 1 - xa
END
```

3.2 Structured Refinement

Let C be a B-component, seeing abstract machines $M_1, \ldots, M_k$, and let R be a B-refinement of C, seeing the same machines, and possibly seeing or importing other machines $M_{k+1}, \ldots, M_n$. We suppose here that common variables between $\mathcal{F}(C)$ and $\mathcal{F}(R)$ only come from seen machines, i.e. $M_1, \ldots, M_k$ (other common variables can be renamed, if necessary).

To prove the correctness of this refinement, we have to prove that $\mathcal{F}(C)$ is refined by $\mathcal{F}(R)$:

1. By the flattening operation, invariant of $\mathcal{F}(R)$ is $L \wedge L_1 \ldots \wedge L_n$, where L is the gluing invariant between C and R and each L_i is the invariant of $\mathcal{F}(M_i)$.

2. Because $\mathcal{F}(C)$ and $\mathcal{F}(R)$ have some common variables (variables of $M_1, \ldots, M_k$), renaming must be done and the gluing invariant must be strengthened. Let v_s be this set of variables and v'_s be a set of corresponding fresh variables. We rename v_s by v'_s in the component $\mathcal{F}(R)$ and the new invariant becomes $L \wedge L_1 \ldots \wedge L_n \wedge v_s = v'_s$. Thus we must establish, for each operation of C:

$$L \wedge L_1 \ldots \wedge L_n \wedge v_s = v'_s \Rightarrow op_{\mathcal{F}(C)} \sqsubseteq_{L \wedge L_1 \ldots \wedge L_n \wedge v_s = v'_s} [v_s := v'_s] op_{\mathcal{F}(R)}$$

3. Two applications of the splitting invariant property will simplify this formula:

   (a) Splitting into $L_1 \wedge \ldots \wedge L_k \wedge v_s = v_s'$ and $L \wedge L_{k+1} \wedge \ldots \wedge L_n$.

   i. $op_{\mathcal{F}(C)}$ does not modify variables of $L_1 \wedge \ldots \wedge L_k \wedge v_s = v_s'$: variables v_s' are fresh variables, and, for variables v_s, only consulting operations can be called in $op_{\mathcal{F}(C)}$.

   ii. With similar arguments about $op_{\mathcal{F}(R)}$, $[[v_s := v_s']op_{\mathcal{F}(R)}](L_1 \wedge \ldots \wedge L_k \wedge v_s = v_s')$ can be reduced to $L_1 \wedge \ldots \wedge L_k \wedge v_s = v_s'$, which belongs to hypotheses.

   iii. So it remains to prove $L \wedge L_1 \wedge \ldots \wedge L_n \wedge v_s = v_s' \Rightarrow op_{\mathcal{F}(C)} \sqsubseteq_{L \wedge L_{k+1} \wedge \ldots \wedge L_n} [v_s := v_s']op_{\mathcal{F}(R)}$, which is equivalent to $L \wedge L_1 \wedge \ldots \wedge L_n \Rightarrow op_{\mathcal{F}(C)} \sqsubseteq_{L \wedge L_{k+1} \wedge \ldots \wedge L_n} op_{\mathcal{F}(R)}$ (proof by structural induction on substitutions).

   (b) Splitting into L and $L_{k+1} \wedge \ldots \wedge L_n$.

   i. The operations $op_{\mathcal{F}(C)}$ do not modify variables of $L_{k+1}, \ldots, L_n$ because variables of these machines are not accessible from C.

   ii. By property 2, $L \wedge L_1 \wedge \ldots \wedge L_n \Rightarrow [op_{\mathcal{F}(R)}]L_i$ holds for each i.

   iii. So it remains to prove $L \wedge L_1 \wedge \ldots \wedge L_n \Rightarrow op_{\mathcal{F}(C)} \sqsubseteq_L op_{\mathcal{F}(R)}$.

In conclusion, the final condition is $L \wedge L_1 \wedge \ldots \wedge L_n \Rightarrow op_{\mathcal{F}(C)} \sqsubseteq_L op_{\mathcal{F}(R)}$, which is the one proposed by Atelier-B [AtB] in presence of SEES or IMPORTS primitives.

3.3 Code Components

In this section, we introduce the notion of code component, in order to build the code attached to abstract machines. Code components are flat components in which references to abstract machines, introduced by SEES or IMPORTS clauses, are replaced by the code associated with these abstract machines. In the following, we define two kinds of code component:

1. $\mathcal{C}(I)$ is the code component refining $\mathcal{F}(I)$, if I is an implementation.
2. $\mathcal{C}(M)$ is the code component refining $\mathcal{F}(M)$, if M is an abstract machine. It is obtained from $\mathcal{C}(I)$ by reducing the refinement chain $\mathcal{F}(M)$, $\mathcal{F}(I)$, $\mathcal{C}(I)$.

For simplicity reasons, we suppose that variables of an implementation can only come from seen and imported machines (dealing with local concrete variables should not be a problem).

Definition 4. *Code Component Operation* $\mathcal{C}$.

1. Let I be a B-implementation and let I' be I, without its gluing invariant and with the clause "REFINES $\mathcal{F}(I)$".

   (a) If I has neither SEES nor IMPORTS primitive, I has no variables (see above), and $\mathcal{C}(I)$ is I'.

(b) If I is a structured B-implementation with SEES or IMPORTS primitives on components $M_1, \ldots, M_n$, $\mathcal{C}(I)$ is obtained by flattening together I' and the code components $\mathcal{C}(M_1), \ldots \mathcal{C}(M_n)$. The resulting invariant of $\mathcal{C}(I)$ is $L_1 \wedge \ldots \wedge L_n$, where each L_i is the invariant of $\mathcal{C}(M_i)$.

2. Let M be a B-abstract machine.

   (a) If M is a basic machine, $\mathcal{C}(M)$ is obtained from $\mathcal{F}(M)$ by adding the clause "REFINES $\mathcal{F}(M)$", by renaming its variables v with fresh variables v', then by adding to its invariant the gluing invariant $v = v'$. Recall that a basic machine has no B-implementation.

   (b) If M has the implementation I, $\mathcal{C}(M)$ is obtained by reducing the refinement chain $\mathcal{F}(M)$, $\mathcal{F}(I)$, $\mathcal{C}(I)$, as defined in section 2.5.

Property 3. *Code Component Variables.*

1. Let C be a B-component, then variables of its code $\mathcal{C}(C)$ only come from the code of basic machines: $var(\mathcal{C}(C)) \subseteq \bigcup \{var(\mathcal{C}(M)) : M \text{ is a basic machine}\}$.
2. Let I a B-implementation. Since variables of the code of basic machines are fresh variables, $var(\mathcal{F}(I)) \cap var(\mathcal{C}(I)) = \emptyset$.

Property 4. *Variables of Gluing Invariants of Code Components.* Let L be the gluing invariant of a code component $\mathcal{C}(M)$, where M is an abstract machine; we have: $free(L) = var(\mathcal{F}(M)) \cup var(\mathcal{C}(M))$.

Example 3. We suppose here that the abstract machine A of example 1 is a basic machine. So the code components $\mathcal{C}(D)$ and $\mathcal{C}(DI)$, respectively associated with components $\mathcal{F}(D)$ and $\mathcal{F}(DI)$ are:

COMPONENT
$\mathcal{C}(D)$
REFINES
$\mathcal{F}(D)$
VARIABLES
xa'
INVARIANT
$\exists$ xa . (xa : 0..1 $\wedge$ xa' : 0..1 $\wedge$ xa = xa')
INITIALISATION
xa' := 0
OPERATIONS
opd =
xa' := 1 - xa'
END

COMPONENT
$\mathcal{C}(DI)$
REFINES
$\mathcal{F}(DI)$
VARIABLES
xa'
INVARIANT
xa' : 0..1 $\wedge$ xa = xa'
INITIALISATION
xa' := 0
OPERATIONS
opd =
xa' := 1 - xa'
END

3.4   Code Correctness

Now we have to prove that $\mathcal{F}(I)$ is refined by $\mathcal{C}(I)$. If I has neither SEES nor IMPORTS primitive, the proof is obvious. Otherwise, the condition is:

Condition 1. *A Compositional Proof Obligation.*

If $\mathcal{F}(I)$ has been obtained from a structured B-implementation with some SEES or IMPORTS primitives on components $M_1, \ldots, M_n$, it suffices to prove :

$$\boxed{L_1 \wedge \ldots \wedge L_n \Rightarrow op_{\mathcal{F}(I)} \sqsubseteq_{L_1 \wedge \ldots \wedge L_n} op_{\mathcal{C}(I)}}$$

where each L_i denotes the invariant of $\mathcal{C}(M_i)$, i.e. the gluing invariant between $\mathcal{C}(M_i)$ and $\mathcal{F}(M_i)$.

3.5 A Sufficient Condition

Condition 1 cannot be directly reduced using the splitting invariant property, so we now inspect the structure of operations.

This analysis only works when SEES primitives only occur at the level of implementations. In this case, we have $var(\mathcal{F}(M)) = var(M)$, for any machine M. A complete analysis, giving the same results, will be published later.

1. Because operations in $\mathcal{F}(I)$ and $\mathcal{C}(I)$ only differ in the expansion of the operations which are called in I, the property of monotonicity of refinement can be used (B-Book, p. 504). Thus, operations of $\mathcal{C}(I)$ refine operations of $\mathcal{F}(I)$ if we can prove that, for each i, $L_1 \wedge \ldots \wedge L_n \Rightarrow op_{\mathcal{F}(M_i)} \sqsubseteq_{L_1 \wedge \ldots \wedge L_n} op_{\mathcal{C}(M_i)}$. This use of monotonicity amounts to prove that gluing invariants L_j are also verified by operations op_{M_i} and their refinements.

2. Now the invariant splitting property can be used:

   (a) Operations $op_{\mathcal{F}(M_i)}$ cannot modify variables in $free(L_j)$ for $i \neq j$, because, by property 4, $free(L_j) = var(\mathcal{F}(M_j)) \cup var(\mathcal{C}(M_j))$: variables of abstract machines are supposed to be disjoint (after renaming if necessary), variables of a code are fresh variables, and op_{M_i} can only call consulting operations.

   (b) $L_1 \wedge \ldots \wedge L_n \Rightarrow op_{\mathcal{F}(M_i)} \sqsubseteq_{L_i} op_{\mathcal{C}(M_i)}$ is a consequence of the refinement proof obligation on M_i, which is $L_i \Rightarrow op_{\mathcal{F}(M_i)} \sqsubseteq_{L_i} op_{\mathcal{C}(M_i)}$.

   (c) Then it suffices to prove $L_1 \wedge \ldots \wedge L_n \Rightarrow [op_{\mathcal{C}(M_i)}](\bigwedge_{j \neq i} L_j)$.

3. Using distributivity of substitution through conjunction, we obtain the following sufficient condition:

Condition 2. *A sufficient condition.*

If $\mathcal{F}(I)$ has been obtained from a structured B-implementation with some SEES or IMPORTS primitives on components $M_1, \ldots, M_n$, a sufficient condition is, for each i and j with $i \neq j$:

$$\boxed{L_1 \wedge \ldots \wedge L_n \Rightarrow [op_{\mathcal{C}(M_i)}]L_j}$$

where each L_i denotes the invariant of $\mathcal{C}(M_i)$, i.e. the gluing invariant between $\mathcal{C}(M_i)$ and $\mathcal{F}(M_i)$.

4 An Architectural Condition

The sufficient condition stated above preserves, in some sense, the composition of refinement because proof obligations of each local refinement are reused. But new proofs are necessary. Less fine sufficient conditions can be stated on the architecture of developments, in order to guarantee that no potentially incorrect configuration appears. For that purpose, first we define some dependency relations between abstract machines. Secondly a finer analysis of gluing invariants of code components is proposed, using a restriction on the SEES primitive. Finally, we examine the sufficient condition in terms of easily checkable conditions on dependencies.

Definition 5. *Dependency relations.*

1. M_1 *sees* M_2 iff the implementation of M_1 sees the machine M_2.
2. M_1 *imports* M_2 iff the implementation of M_1 imports the machine M_2.
3. M_1 *depends_on* M_2 iff the code of M_1 is built by using M_2: *depends_on* $= (sees \cup imports)^+$.
4. M_1 *can_consult* M_2 iff the code of M_1 can consult the variables of the code of M_2: *can_consult* $= (depends\_on^*; sees)$.
5. M_1 *can_alter* M_2 iff the code of M_1 can modify the variables of the code of M_2: *can_alter* $= (depends\_on^*; imports)$.

   Relational notation is the one of the B-method: transitive closure ($^+$), reflexive and transitive closure (*) and composition (;).

4.1 Variables and Dependency Relations

To ensure the sufficient condition $[op_{\mathcal{C}(M_i)}]L_j$ in terms of dependency relations, a condition is the following: variables which both appear in $op_{\mathcal{C}(M_i)}$ and in L_j cannot be modified by $op_{\mathcal{C}(M_i)}$. To state this condition, $var(C)$, the set of variables of a component C must be analyzed, in the case of a code component.

Property 5. *Variables of Code Components.*

1. For a basic machine M, $var(\mathcal{C}(M))$ is the set of variables obtained from $var(M)$ by renaming variables v by v'.
2. For a non-basic machine M, $var(\mathcal{C}(M))$ is the set of the variables of the code of an abstract machine which is in the dependency graph of $\mathcal{C}(M)$, i.e.: $var(\mathcal{C}(M)) = \bigcup\{var(\mathcal{C}(N)) : N \in depends\_on[\{M\}]\}$.

   Now we come back to the sufficient condition. Variables of $op_{\mathcal{C}(M_i)}$ which can be modified come from code of machines in the set $can\_alter[\{M_i\}]$. On the other hand, by properties 4 and 5, free variables of L_j come from machines or their code in the set $\{M_j\} \cup depends\_on[\{M_j\}]$. Because $\{M_j\} \subseteq depends\_on * [\{M_j\}]$, condition 2 is ensured if for each i and j, with $j \neq i$:

$$can\_alter[\{M_i\}] \cap depends\_on^*[\{M_j\}] = \emptyset .$$

This structural condition is too restrictive, because it rejects too many architectures. For instance, architecture of Fig. 5 does not fit this condition but can be proved correct if refinements are locally correct:

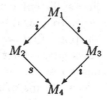

Fig. 5. A correct architecture.

4.2 Using Restrictions on Clauses

In this section, a finer analysis of the gluing invariant of code components is made, using a restriction specific to the SEES primitive: variables coming from a seen machine cannot be referenced into gluing invariants of seing components. In consequence, a continuous chain of IMPORTS primitives is needed to alter variables of an abstract machine: it explains why architecture of Fig. 5 is correct.

Property 6. *Form of the Gluing Invariant of Code Components.*

Let L be the gluing invariant of $\mathcal{C}(M)$, where M is an abstract machine with no SEES primitive, then L takes the form $A \wedge B$, with:

1. $free(A) = \bigcup \{var(\mathcal{C}(N_i)) : N_i \in can\_consult[\{M\}]\}$. In this case, $A \equiv \bigwedge A_i$, where each A_i is the invariant of the independant abstract machine corresponding to $\mathcal{C}(N_i)$ (section 2.5).
2. If M is a basic machine $free(B) = var(M) \cup var(\mathcal{C}(M))$.
3. Otherwise $free(B) = var(\mathcal{F}(M)) \cup \bigcup \{var(\mathcal{C}(N)) : N \in imports^+[\{M\}]\}$.

Proof by induction. In the case of a basic machine M, A is true and B is the gluing invariant of $\mathcal{C}(M)$.

Now we analyse the inductive step on a simplified case (with no loss of generality). Let M be an abstract machine and I be its implementation, seeing a machine M_s and importing a machine M_i. Then we have:

1. Invariant of $\mathcal{C}(M_s)$ takes the form $A_s \wedge B_s$.
2. Invariant of $\mathcal{C}(M_i)$ takes the form $A_i \wedge B_i$.
3. A_s and A_i are conjuctions of invariants of independant machines.
4. $imports^+[\{M\}] = \{M_i\} \cup imports^+[\{M_i\}]$.
5. $can\_consult^+[\{M\}] = \{M_s\} \cup can\_consult^+[\{M_i\}] \cup can\_consult^+[\{M_s\}]$.

6. Invariant of $\mathcal{C}(M)$, as defined in section 3.3, is:

$$\exists v_s, v_i \cdot (L \wedge A_s \wedge B_s \wedge A_i \wedge B_i \wedge L_s \wedge L_i)$$

where L is the gluing invariant between $\mathcal{F}(I)$ and $\mathcal{F}(M)$, L_s is the invariant of M_s, and L_i is the invariant of M_i.

7. (a) $v_s \notin free(L)$ because a seen variable cannot occur into gluing invariants.
   (b) $v_s \notin free(A_i \wedge B_i)$ and $v_i \notin free(A_s \wedge B_s)$, thanks to property 5.
   (c) $v_s \notin free(L_i)$ and $v_i \notin free(L_s)$ because machines have disjoint variables (after renaming if necessary).
   (d) $v_s \notin free(A_s)$ and $v_i \notin free(A_i)$, by inductive hypothesis.
   (e) So invariant of $\mathcal{C}(M)$ becomes, after putting some subformulae out of the scope of the quantifiers:

$$\exists v_s \cdot (A_s \wedge B_s \wedge L_s) \wedge A_i \wedge \exists v_i \cdot (L \wedge B_i \wedge L_i) \ .$$

8. $A \equiv \exists v_s \cdot (A_s \wedge B_s \wedge L_s) \wedge A_i$ and $\exists v_s \cdot (A_s \wedge B_s \wedge L_s)$ is the invariant of the independant machine corresponding to $\mathcal{C}(M_s)$.

9. $B \equiv \exists v_i \cdot (L \wedge B_i \wedge L_i)$.

4.3 An Architectural Sufficient Condition

Recall that we want to ensure condition $[op_{\mathcal{C}(M_i)}]L_j$ for each i and j, with $i \neq j$, where $M_1, \ldots, M_n$ are seen or imported in the implementation I of machine M, and $L_1, \ldots, L_n$ are respectively the gluing invariants of $[op_{\mathcal{C}(M_1)}], \ldots, [op_{\mathcal{C}(M_n)}]$. We suppose that M has no SEES primitive.

1. Using property 6 and distributivity of substitution through conjonction, L_j takes the form $A_j \wedge B_j$ and condition 2 becomes:
   (a) $L_1 \ldots \wedge L_n \Rightarrow [op_{\mathcal{C}(M_i)}]A_j$
   (b) $L_1 \ldots \wedge L_n \Rightarrow [op_{\mathcal{C}(M_i)}]B_j$
   First formula holds, due to property 2 and to the fact that A_j is a conjonction of invariants of independant machines. So a sufficient condition is second formula.

2. By property 6, free variables of B_j come from machines or their code in the set $\{M_j\} \cup imports^+[\{M_j\}]$. So it suffices to prove that $op_{\mathcal{C}(M_i)}$ cannot modify variables of B_j:

$$can\_alter[\{M_i\}] \cap (\{M_j\} \cup imports^+[\{M_j\}]) = \emptyset \ .$$

3. Using the fact that an abstract machine is imported once only, we obtain:

$$can\_alter[\{M_i\}] \cap \{M_j\} = \emptyset \ .$$

4. Next step consists in stating this condition in terms of machine M.
   (a) If M_j is imported by I then M_i cannot import M_j, so condition holds.

(b) The remaining case is when M_i is seen by I. So condition becomes:

$$can\_alter[\{M\}] \cap sees[\{M\}] = \emptyset .$$

5. Now, considering the global architecture of developments, we obtain:

Condition 3. *An Architectural Condition.*

An architecture of developpements, where SEES primitives only occur at the level of implementations, is correct if all components are proved and if:

$$\boxed{can\_alter \cap sees = \emptyset}$$

The B-Book (p. 583) and the Atelier-B (up to version 3.2) propose architectural conditions which can be translated, in terms of our relations, into:

$$(imports^+ \cup (sees; imports^+)) \cap sees = \emptyset .$$

This condition is not sufficient, because it does not consider can_alter. So the incorrect architecture of example 1, which does not respect condition 3, is accepted by the B-method.

5   Conclusion

A practical issue of our work results in a set of conditions to guarantee the correctness of refinements in the presence of SEES and IMPORTS primitives, when SEES primitives only occur at the level of implementations

1. Translation of SEES and IMPORTS primitives in terms of flat components has given condition 1 which consists in proving that refinements can be combined.
2. Use of monotonicity has given stronger condition 2, which exploits the fact that a SEES primitive only allows calls of consulting operations. This condition is simpler to verify than condition 1.
3. Proper restrictions on the clauses SEES and IMPORTS, which can be seen as the impossibility to represent two independent abstract states on the same implementation, have given the final condition 3 on the dependency graph.

A complete analysis, with no restriction on SEES primitive, is under development and it will be published later. Under reasonable assumptions about chains of SEES primitives, it gives the same sufficient conditions.

Under this analysis, it is possible to consider several levels of checkings. For instance, if condition 3 is not valid, we can try to verify condition 2 or 1, before reconsidering the global development, in order to eliminate the undesirable sharing.

The second issue is, following [BPR96], a framework for dealing with structured components in the B-method, in order to study how proofs of invariant properties and proofs of refinement can be combined. Within this framework, extensions of B-method primitives can be proposed. Structural clauses offered by the B-method have some restricting conditions which could be removed. If semantics of new structural clauses can be defined in terms of flat components, then a proper analysis of their properties of compositional refinement can be done in a rigourous way. For instance, the compositionality of some forms of INCLUDES or USES can be studied, resulting in a more flexible form of sharing. Following [MQR95], it seems to us that sharing must be introduced at the specification level and must be strictly controlled in the refinement process. In that case, fine reasoning about sharing is possible. The problem met in the B-method comes from the fact that reasoning is done at the level of abstract machines, in which sharing is not always specified.

References

[Abr96] J-R. Abrial, *The B-Book*, Cambridge University Press, 1996.

[AtB]   Steria Méditerranée, *Le Langage B. Manuel de référence version 1.5* , S.A.V. Steria, BP 16000, 13791 Aix-en-Provence cedex 3, France.

[BPR96] D. Bert, M-L. Potet, Y. Rouzaud, *A Study on Components and Assembly Primitives in B*, In First Conference on the B Method, 47–62, H. Habrias, editor, 1996.

[BW90]   R. J. R. Back, J. von Wright, *Refinement calculus I: Sequential Nondeterministic Programs*, In Stepwise Refinement of Distributed Systems, J. W. deBakker, W. P. deRoever, and G. Rozenberg, editors, LNCS 430, 42–66, Springer-Verlag, 1990.

[Gro94] The VDM-SL Tool Group, *User's Manual for the IFAD VDM-SL Toolbox*, IFAD, Forskerparken 10, 5230 Odense M, Denmark, 1994.

[LW94]   B. Liskov, J. Wing, *A Behavioural Notion of Subtyping*, ACM Transactions on Programming Languages and Systems, 16(6), 1811–1841, 1994.

[Mey88] B. Meyer, *Object-Oriented Construction*, Prentice-Hall, 1988.

[MQR95] M. Moriconi, X. Qian, R. A. Riemenschneider, *Correct Architecture Refinement*, IEEE Transactions on Software engineering, 21(4), 356–372, 1995.

[Spi88] M. Spivey, *Understanding Z: a Specification Language and its Formal Semantics*, Cambridge University Press, 1988.

[ST88]   D. Sannella, A. Tarlecki, *Towards Formal Development of Programs from Algebraic Specifications: Implementations Revisited*, Acta Informatica, 25, 233–281, 1988.

[Wir86] M. Wirsing, *Structured Algebraic Specifications: A Kernel Language*, Theoretical Computer Science, 42, 123–249, 1986.

Formalisation of B in Isabelle/HOL

Pierre Chartier

University of Cambridge Computer Laboratory
New Museums Site, Pembroke Street, Cambridge CB2 3QG, UK
tel 44(0)1223334422 — fax 44(0)1223334678
Pierre.Chartier@cl.cam.ac.uk

Abstract. We describe a semantic embedding of the basic concepts of the B language in the higher-order logic instance of the generic theorem prover Isabelle (Isabelle/HOL). This work aims at a foundation to formalise the full abstract machine notation, in order to produce a formally checked proof obligation generator. The formalisation is based on the B-Book. First we present an encoding of the mathematical basis. Then we formalise generalised substitutions by the before-after model and we prove the equivalence with the weakest precondition axiomatic model. Finally we define operations and abstract machines.

1 Introduction

Formal methods are mostly used in safety-critical domains to produce high quality software or hardware. For industrial use (for large programs), the use of formal methods by hand is long, complex and error-prone. Tools have been developed to put formal methods into practice. Are these tools safety-critical systems? Of course it depends on the degree of safety we require. But the question is not irrelevant: if it is difficult to apply formal methods by hand, we do not see why it would be easier to construct "by hand" tools to this task. Thus ultimately, the application of formal methods should be checked by *formally verified* tools to reach the highest degree of safety.

It would certainly be very ambitious to develop such tools by, say, the formal method they intend to implement. However formal methods rely on logical foundations which can be embedded in a logical system. So an implementation of tools within a theorem prover seems promising for establishing their soundness as well as providing a unified framework to develop and prove programs. Indeed following Gordon [4], embeddings of simple imperative programming languages have been done in HOL [7] and in Isabelle/HOL [9]. These works enable us to generate and prove verification conditions about programs in a unified framework, and more important, in a sound way relative to the logical system they use. The specification language Z [11] has been encoded in several theorem provers too (see [3] or [8] for a summary of such works). Refinement technology for modular programs has been developed in HOL [12, 13] and has been used among other things to verify a proof-checker formally.

These successful works give us motivation to follow a similar approach with the **B** language [1]. **B** aims at developing a whole system architecture, from formal specification to implementation. The *B-Book* serves us as a guide. We found some inspiration too for the long term goal, in the paper of Bert et al. [2].

Our aim in this paper is to develop foundations to make a full formalisation of **B** possible. We mean a formalisation of abstract machine theory which would enable us to formally check the consistency of proof obligations of the abstract machine notation, and thus obtain the equivalent of a formally verified proof obligation generator.

We suppose the reader familiar with **B** but we give a short presentation of Isabelle/HOL in the next section. In Sect. 3 we describe the encoding of the mathematical basis necessary to construct generalised substitutions in the following section. We end with the formalisation of operations and abstract machines.

2 Isabelle/HOL

Isabelle [10] is a generic interactive theorem prover whose soundness is ensured by an LCF approach [6]. Isabelle/HOL implements the higher-order logic of Church which is very close to Gordon's HOL system [5]. In the rest of the paper HOL stands for Isabelle/HOL.

We describe here some features of Isabelle and the syntax we have used from HOL. Readers can skip this section and come back when they encounter notations they want to make precise.

Meta-level logic Isabelle's meta-logic is higher-order, based on the simply typed λ-calculus. It is used to express axioms, rules and definitions. $\Longrightarrow$ and $\bigwedge$ denote meta implication and meta universal quantification respectively, the nested implication $P_1 \Longrightarrow (\ldots (P_n \Longrightarrow Q) \ldots)$ is abbreviated as $[\![P_1; \ldots; P_n]\!] \Longrightarrow Q$. $\equiv$ is the meta equality to express definition.

Theories Declarations are organised in theories, inside which we can define constants (**consts**), non-recursive definitions (**defs**), primitive recursive definitions (**primrec**) and inductive definitions (**inductive**). The latter specifies the least set closed under given rules.

Types The type of formulae is bool. $\Rightarrow$ is the function constructor. Greek letters denote type variables. Type constraints are written $x :: t$ (the type of x is t). We can introduce type synonyms (**types**) and type definitions (**typedef**). The latter introduces a new type T in a safe way from some subset S. It adds the function Abs_T from S to T and the converse function Rep_T with the axioms $\mathsf{Abs\_T}(\mathsf{Rep\_T}(x)) = x$ and $x : S \Longrightarrow \mathsf{Rep\_T}(\mathsf{Abs\_T}(x)) = x$.

Logical connectives Classical notations $\neg$, $\wedge$, $\vee$, $\longrightarrow$, $\forall$, $\exists$. The equivalence is simply $=$ since we are in a higher-order logic. We use $\longrightarrow$ and $=$ instead of **B** notation ($\Rightarrow$ and $\Leftrightarrow$). ϵ is Hilbert's description operator (equivalent of a choice operator): ($\epsilon x.\ P$) denotes some x satisfying P if P is satisfiable, an arbitrary value otherwise. It is used to define a polymorphic arbitrary value: arbitrary $\equiv \epsilon x.$ False.

Sets Classical notations ∪ (union), ∩ (intersection) ... UNIV denotes the universal set of a certain type (all the elements of this type).

Lists We use HOL notations instead of **B** ones, except for the concatenation of two lists written as $x ⌢ y$. $\{\!| x |\!\}$ denotes the set of elements of the list x. $\mathsf{map}(f)(l)$ is the list of images of elements of the list l through f.

All the definitions below have been implemented in HOL, and whenever we speak of a theorem, a property or a result, that means a theorem formally proved in HOL.

3 Mathematical Basis

In this paper we focus on generalised substitution and abstract machines. We do not want to formalise all the mathematical background presented in Part I of the B-Book. Of course we need to manipulate predicates, expressions and substitution over them, but we shall not define the syntax of predicates and expressions. Instead we encapsulate them in a HOL abstract type which captures the essential properties we need. We then define substitutions on predicates and expressions.

3.1 Predicates and Expressions

First, we define an abstract type **name** to denote variable names. We let expressions be undefined, so their type is just **value**, another abstract type. For example in practical use, **name** could be instantiated by **string**. If we want to be very close to **B**, it is a little more complicated for **value**, since we need to define a recursive datatype containing the integers, the powerset and the cartesian product constructors, and a corresponding type-checker. All this is possible but outside the scope of this paper.

From these basic types we define a state as a mapping from variable names to values, and represent a predicate (resp. expression) depending on free variables by a function from state to bool (resp. value). That corresponds to the following declarations in HOL:

types   name
        value
        state = name ⇒ value
        pred = state ⇒ bool
        expr = state ⇒ value

This semantic representation of predicates and expressions is classical, but it gives us some undesirable functions. Indeed the definitions of **pred** and **expr** admit functions depending on an infinite set of free variables, which obviously we do not need in practice, and which would cause problems for the generation of fresh variables for alpha-conversion (renaming of bound variables).

Normally we should deduce the finiteness of the set of free variables of a predicate or an expression from its structural definition. Because we do not have such a definition, we need to constrain the state functions from the "outside". We want to consider functions which only depend on a finite subset of images of a state. That is, there exists a finite **name** set D such that the image of a state s through a function f does not depend on the values of s outside D (but f can depend on the values of s on a strict subset of D):[1]

$$\exists D. \text{finite } D \wedge (\forall s\, t.\ s =\!\!\mid_D t \longrightarrow f(s) = f(t)) \tag{1}$$

To abbreviate this property and because we shall reuse this concept later, we introduce the constant **depend**[2] and define the type constructor Sfun:

defs $\text{depend}(f)(D) \equiv \forall s\, t.\ s =\!\!\mid_D t \longrightarrow f(s) = f(t)$

typedef $\alpha\, \text{Sfun} = \{(f :: \text{state} \Rightarrow \alpha).\ \exists D.\text{finite } D \wedge \text{depend}(f)(D)\}$

Obviously all constant functions are members of Sfun set, which guarantees that the new type is not empty. The construct **typedef** ensures that for all F of type $\alpha\, \text{Sfun}$, its concrete representation satisfies (1). Predicates and expressions are instances of Sfun:

types   Pred = bool Sfun
        Expr = value Sfun

Application and abstraction are denoted by $F's$ and $(\lambda s.\ f)$. For convenience, we lift the logical connectives from **bool** (in normal font) to **Pred** (in bold font) such that:

$$(\neg P)'s \equiv \neg P's$$
$$(P \oplus Q)'s \equiv P's \oplus Q's \qquad \oplus \text{ stands for } \wedge, \vee, \longrightarrow, =$$
$$(\otimes x.\ P)'s \equiv \otimes v.\ P's[v/x] \qquad \otimes \text{ stands for } \forall \text{ and } \exists$$

The definition of $=$ is polymorphic as in HOL: that is $P's$ and $Q's$ must simply have the same type, **bool** or **value**. $s[v/x]$ denotes the assignment of v to x in the state s, that is:

defs $s[v/x] \equiv \lambda y.\ \text{if } y = x \text{ then } v \text{ else } s(y)$

Finally we use $\$x$ to denote the expression that returns the value of the variable whose name is x: $\$x's \equiv s(x)$. We establish the injectivity of $\$$,

$$(\$x = \$y) = (x = y), \tag{2}$$

with the help of a supplementary axiom about the abstract type **value** which states that there are at least two distinct elements of type **value** (obvious for an interesting use): $\exists(a :: \text{value})\, b.\ a \neq b$

---

[1] $=\!\!\mid$ is an equality on restricted functions, defined by $s =\!\!\mid_D t \equiv \forall x \in D.\ s(x) = t(x)$

[2] In fact depend is overloaded to be used later with substitution or several elements at the same time. At this point it is extended to cartesian product by $\text{depend}(f, g)(D) \equiv \text{depend}(f)(D) \wedge \text{depend}(g)(D)$, list by $\text{depend}([])(D) = \text{True} \wedge \text{depend}(f \# G)(D) = (\text{depend}(f)(D) \wedge \text{depend}(G)(D))$, name set by $\text{depend}(N)(D) \equiv N \subseteq D$ and Sfun (after its definition below) by $\text{depend}(F) \equiv \text{depend}(\lambda s.\ F's)$, .

An important result for α Sfun elements is the extensionnality property

$$(\bigwedge s.\ F's = G's) \Longrightarrow F = G \tag{3}$$

which comes directly from the extensionnality axiom for functions.

3.2 Substitution

We now define substitution on predicates and expressions. By substitution we mean here only substitution of variables by expressions (or other variables) in predicates or expressions. To avoid the use of explicit type constraints with an overloaded operator, we use $[x := E]F$ for substitution, and we reserve $[S]$ to denote the weakest precondition operator defined by the *generalised* substitution S. Abrial defines the substitution syntactically, but this requires a syntactic definition of predicates and expressions. Since we consider these from the semantic view, we give a semantic definition using the assignment function. Later we shall define substitution on generalised substitutions (to be able to define operation calls), so that the operator subst is defined for a polymorphic type β. The definition for $\beta = \alpha$ Sfun follows:

    consts   subst :: [name, Expr, β] $\Rightarrow \beta$ ("$[\_ := \_]\_$")

    defs $[x := E]F \equiv \lambda s.\ F's[E's/x]$

Variable renaming is a particular case of subst where the expression is $\$y$ for some y. We can easily establish some results like

$$[x := E]\$x = E$$
$$[x := E](P \oplus Q) = ([x := E]P \oplus [x := E]Q)$$

But to go further (to deal with bound variables and multiple substitution), we need to make precise what is a fresh variable: a variable which has no free occurrence in a predicate or an expression. In fact the non-freeness side-condition is the dual of the constant depend introduced earlier: "the variables of v are not free in F" ($v\backslash F$) is equivalent to "F depends only on the variables in $\overline{v}$"[3]. Then "$.\backslash.$" is just an abbreviation and in the rest of the paper we use alternatively "$.\backslash.$" or depend, depending on which is more "intuitive".

    syntax $v\backslash F \equiv \mathsf{depend}(F)(\overline{v})$

Since we use set-theoretic notation, it is a little different to B notation. For example to express that variable x is not free in F, we write $\{x\}\backslash F$. The advantage is that we can speak of any set of variables, even an infinite one. We are able to prove the following theorems:

$$v\backslash\$x = x \notin v$$
$$(v - \{x\})\backslash P \Longrightarrow v\backslash(\otimes x.\ P)$$

---

[3] $\overline{v}$ is the complement of v.

$$\{x\}\backslash P \Longrightarrow \otimes x.\, P = P$$

$$\{x\}\backslash P \Longrightarrow [x := E]P = P$$

$$\{x\}\backslash(\$y, F) \Longrightarrow [x := [y := F]E]/[y := F]P = [y := F]/[x := E]P \tag{4}$$

$$\{y\}\backslash P \Longrightarrow \otimes y.\, [x := \$y]P = \otimes x.\, P \tag{5}$$

$$\{y\}\backslash(\$x, E) \Longrightarrow [x := E]/(\otimes y.\, P) = \otimes y.\, [x := E]P \tag{6}$$

We can always apply (6) with the renaming of the bound variable (5) when necessary to satisfy the side-condition by exhibiting a y such that $\{y\}\backslash(P, \$x, E)$. The existence of such a y is a consequence of the property which defines Sfun (1) and of an axiom that states the infiniteness of variable names: $\neg$finite (UNIV :: name set). Notice that the formal proof of (4) points to an omission in Abrial's corresponding axiom [1, p. 35, axiom SUB 11]: the side-condition $\{x\}\backslash\$y$ (or $x\backslash y$ in **B** parlance).

With ".\." we can define the multiple substitution in the same way that Abrial does. We use the HOL list type to represent lists of variables and lists of expressions[4]. Then we have to provide two rules: an obvious one for the "empty" multiple substitution, and one for the "real" multiple substitution (we keep HOL syntax for lists, thus $x\#Y$ corresponds to x, Y in the *B-Book*):

rules
$$[[] := []]F = F \tag{7}$$

$$[\,\{x\}\backslash\$Y;\ \{z\}\backslash(F, \$Y, D)\,] \tag{8}$$
$$\Longrightarrow [x\#Y := c\#D]F = [z := c]/[Y := D][x := \$z]F$$

We have removed the side-condition $z\backslash(\$x, c)$, which is pointless. We do not say what happens if the lengths of the list of variables and the list of expressions are different. That means we always need an hypothesis of equality on these lengths to prove general properties about multiple substitutions. Here too, the property which defines Sfun (1) is essential to prove general properties about multiple substitution like distributivity over logical connectives, since we can always exhibit a fresh variable z verifying the non-freeness property of (8).

To simplify proofs about multiple substitution (to avoid too much interactivity during proof due to non-freeness side-conditions and inductions on lists) we introduce a multiple assignment on states and prove that multiple substitution is equivalent to, first evaluating all the expressions involved and then, assigning (in any order) each obtained value to the corresponding variable, provided the variables are distinct[5] and the lengths of the lists are the same[6]. This is the theorem:

$$[\,\text{distinct}X;\ X \stackrel{\text{len}}{=} E\,] \Longrightarrow [X := E]F = (\lambda s.\, F`s[\text{map}(\lambda e.e`s)(E)/X])$$

The multiple assignment is defined by primitive recursion on the list of variable names (we keep the same notation as simple assignment to avoid too much different syntax):

---

[4] For this purpose $ is extended to lists of names: $X \equiv \text{map(op } \$)(X)$.

[5] The operator distinct is defined by primitive recursion on list.

[6] $x \stackrel{\text{len}}{=} y$ is short for length$(x) = $ length(y).

primrec   assign list
$$s[V/[]] \quad = (\text{case } V \text{ of } [] \Rightarrow s \mid v\#W \Rightarrow \text{arbitrary})$$
$$s[V/x\#Y] = (\text{case } V \text{ of } [] \Rightarrow \text{arbitrary} \mid v\#W \Rightarrow s[v/x][W/Y])$$

At this point, all axioms about non-freeness and substitution (series NF and SUB of [1, Appendix E]) that we can express in our framework, can be established.

4   Generalised Substitution

Abrial defines the language of generalised substitutions (for short GSL) from a weakest precondition axiomatic system. Then he shows the equivalence of this system with the before-after model. Finally he links them to two set-theoretic models: the set transformer model and the relational model which corresponds directly to the before-after model with sets instead predicates.

Of these constructions, we eliminate the set-theoretic models because of their typing rigidity which, perhaps, simplifies reasoning at the level of substitutions in a *single* machine, but which is not suitable for reasoning about machine architectures. Finally, we choose the before-after model because we find it easier to formalise in our framework. However, to be close to the *B-Book*, we show the equivalence with the axiomatic model.

4.1   Before-After Model

As stated by the normalised form theorem [1, Theorem 6.1.1], for all generalised substitutions S working on the variable x there exists two predicates P and Q such that[7]:

$$S = P \mid @x'. \, Q \Longrightarrow x := x'$$

Such a P is unique, but not Q. More precisely any Q', such that $P \longrightarrow \forall x'.Q = Q'$ defines the same generalised substitution as Q. However there is only one Q such that $(\forall x. \, \neg P \longrightarrow \forall x'. \, Q)$. Of course, as we will prove later, P and Q are exactly the termination predicate $\text{trm}(S)$ and the before-after predicate $\text{prd}_x(S)$.

Obviously, the variable x on which the substitution works is also characteristic. In fact, Q also depends on another variable denoted by priming the former one: x', which denotes the after-value of x. The priming is only a convention; what is important is that x' is *fresh*, that is, is distinct of x.

Then formally, a substitution is a 4-tuple (P, Q, x, x') where P and Q are predicates, and x and x' are lists of variable names all distinct and of the same length. To derive the injectivity property of the weakest-precondition operator[8] (16), any generalised substitution needs to have a unique representation. For P

---

[7] Readers familiar with HOL should notice that we use @ for the unbounded choice operator of **B**, instead of Hilbert's choice operator denoted ϵ in this paper.

[8] Two generalised substitutions are equal if they establish the same post-conditions.

and Q it suffices they verify $(\forall x.\ \neg P \longrightarrow \forall x'.\ Q)$. Lists of variables are not suitable since the repetition and the order of variables are irrelevant: $(x, x := e, f)$ is not well-formed, and $(x, y := e, f)$ and $(y, x := f, e)$ are equal. Furthermore the explicitness of x' is artificial since a substitution does not depend at all on the particular names chosen for x'.

So we use of a finite set instead of a list to denote variables involved in a substitution. We bypass the last point by making Q dependent on two parameters instead of one: the before-state and the after-state. Since we want the only relevant values of the after-state to be those of the variables x, we have a non-freeness condition on the second parameter of the before-after predicate (expressed with depend). With these properties we define the type of generalised substitutions:

> **typedef** $\text{Sub} = \{(P :: \text{Pred}, Q :: \text{Pred Sfun}, D :: \text{name set}).\ \text{finite}\,(D)\ \wedge$
> $(\forall s.\ \text{depend}(Q\text{`}s)(D)) \wedge (\forall s.\ \neg P\text{`}s \longrightarrow (\forall s'.\ Q\text{`}s\text{`}s'))\}$

We add some syntax for convenience. $(P|D : Q)$ is used as concrete syntax for the substitution abstracted from the 3-tuple $(P, \lambda s\,s'.\ P\text{`}s \longrightarrow Q\text{`}s\text{`}s', D)$. Conversely trm, prd, dom map a substitution to its three components[9]. $\text{dom}(S)$ is the set of variables which S may modify, intuitively those are the variables which appear on the left-hand side of substitutions. Initially trm and prd are just considered as syntactic features to retrieve the characteristic predicates of an element of Sub, but they indeed correspond to what we expect, as proved after the next definition.

The formalisation of generalised substitutions is completed with the semantics of the weakest precondition of a postcondition R w.r.t. a substitution S (classically denoted by $\text{wp}(S, R)$, but we follow Abrial's notation $[S]R$):

$$[S]R \equiv \lambda s.\ \text{trm}(S)\text{`}s \wedge (\forall s'.\ \text{prd}(S)\text{`}s\text{`}s' \wedge s =\!\!\!\mid_{\overline{\text{dom}(S)}} s' \longrightarrow R\text{`}s')$$

The condition $s =\!\!\!\mid_{\overline{\text{dom}(S)}} s'$ tells us that the variables not involved in the substitution are not modified.

We are now able to justify the choice of trm and prd by the proof of the following theorems:

$$\text{trm}(S) = [S](\lambda s.\ \text{True})$$
$$\text{prd}(S) = \lambda s\,s'.\ \neg[S](\lambda s.\ \neg\ s' =\!\!\!\mid_{\text{dom}(S)} s)\text{`}s)$$

They are exactly Abrial's definitions in our formalism. $(\lambda s.\ \text{True})$ stands for the predicate $x = x$, and $(\lambda s.\ \neg\ s' =\!\!\!\mid_{\text{dom}(S)} s)\text{`}s)$ for $\neg\ x' = x$.

---

[9] The use of $(\lambda s\,s'.\ P\text{`}s \longrightarrow Q\text{`}s\text{`}s')$ instead of simply $Q$ guarantees the condition $(\forall s.\ \neg P\text{`}s \longrightarrow (\forall s'.\ Q\text{`}s\text{`}s'))$ and does not change the semantics of the substitution. P, Q and D must verify the properties of Sub to obtain the equalities $\text{trm}(P|D:Q) = P$, $\text{prd}(P|D:Q) = Q$, and $\text{dom}(P|D:Q) = D$. The notation $(P|D:Q)$ is reminiscent of the standard **B** notation.

This foundation lets us define the operators of the GSL easily:

$$\mathsf{skip} \equiv (\lambda s.\ \mathsf{True}\,|\,\emptyset : \lambda s\, s'.\ \mathsf{True}) \tag{9}$$

$$x := E \equiv (\lambda s.\ \mathsf{True}\,|\,\{x\} : \lambda s\, s'.\ s'(x) = E\text{'}s) \tag{10}$$

$$P\,|\,S \equiv (P \wedge \mathsf{trm}(S)\,|\,\mathsf{dom}(S) : \mathsf{prd}(S)) \tag{11}$$

$$P \Longrightarrow S \equiv (P \longrightarrow \mathsf{trm}(S)\,|\,\mathsf{dom}(S) : \lambda s\, s'.\ P\text{'}s \wedge \mathsf{prd}(S)\text{'}s\text{'}s')$$

$$S\,[\,]\,T \equiv (\mathsf{trm}(S) \wedge \mathsf{trm}(T)\,|\,\mathsf{dom}(S) \cup \mathsf{dom}(T) : \tag{12}$$

$$\lambda s\, s'.\ (\mathsf{prd}(S)\text{'}s\text{'}s' \wedge s =\!\!|_{\mathsf{dom}(T)-\mathsf{dom}(S)}\, s') \vee$$
$$(\mathsf{prd}(T)\text{'}s\text{'}s' \wedge s =\!\!|_{\mathsf{dom}(S)-\mathsf{dom}(T)}\, s')\ )$$

$$@x.\ S \equiv (\forall x.\ \mathsf{trm}(S)\,|\,\mathsf{dom}(S) - \{x\} : \lambda s\, s'.\ \exists v\, v'.\ \mathsf{prd}(S)\text{'}s[v/x]\text{'}s'[v'/x])$$

$$S\,|\,|\,T \equiv (\mathsf{trm}(S) \wedge \mathsf{trm}(T)\,|\,\mathsf{dom}(S) \cup \mathsf{dom}(T) : \tag{13}$$

$$\lambda s\, s'.\ \mathsf{prd}(S)\text{'}s\text{'}s' \wedge \mathsf{prd}(T)\text{'}s\text{'}s')$$

Apart from the unusual look of the before-after predicate due to its functional representation, certain definitions merit some comments. According to us, this definition of skip (9) is more intuitive than $x := x$ since it does not involve any variable at all. With (10) we can establish the expected relation between the simple substitution of GSL and the semantic substitution developed in the previous section: $[x := E]R = [x := E]R$. We just use $\mathsf{prd}(S)$ instead of $P \longrightarrow \mathsf{prd}(S)$ in (11) according to the note 9. The only definition which is perhaps a little surprising is the choice operator (12). Indeed following the substitution which is *chosen* in $S\,[\,]\,T$, say S, we have to specify that the variables involved in T are not modified except if they are involved in S, that is $s =\!\!|_{\mathsf{dom}(T)-\mathsf{dom}(S)}\, s'$, conversely for T. Our definition of the parallel operator[10] (13) is more general than Abrial's, since it allows S and T to work on common variables. When domains of S and T are disjoint it is exactly Abrial's definition. We could have defined it as (if $\mathsf{dom}(S) \cap \mathsf{dom}(T) = \emptyset$ then ... else arbitrary) but that is needlessly complex. In fact, because of the normalisation form theorem, we can write this generalised substitution anyway with or without the domain condition. So we think this condition would be better placed as a limitation on the GSL we can use for abstract machines, as the use of composition and loop substitutions is forbidden at the abstract level, and the use of the specification statement ($x : P$) is forbidden at the implementation level.

4.2 Axiomatic Model

In this section we establish the equivalence between the before-after model we developed above and the axiomatic model from which Abrial starts.

First, from the definitions above we derive the axioms of GSL (the results about skip and [] could be derived from the three others with a definition based on the normalised form of substitutions, but we follow Abrial's presentation):

$$[\mathsf{skip}]R = R$$

---

[10] Bert et al. introduce this definition in [2] but for another specific need.

$$[P \mid S]R = P \wedge [S]R$$
$$[P \Longrightarrow S]R = P \longrightarrow [S]R$$
$$[S \, [] \, T]R = [S]R \wedge [T]R$$
$$\{x\} \backslash R \Longrightarrow [@x. \, S]R = \forall x. \, [S]R \tag{14}$$

Conversely, we show that every substitution as we defined them (element of Sub type) can be expressed in a normal form using only the precondition, the guarded substitution, the unbounded choice and the (multiple) simple substitution, that is

$$\forall S. \, \exists P \, D \, D' \, Q. \, S = P \mid (@D'. \, Q \Longrightarrow D := D') \tag{15}$$

The proof is relatively easy if S involves only a single variable (i.e. the domain of S is a singleton). To do the general proof we need to deal with lists of variables. So we extend by primitive recursion the binding operators $\forall$, $\exists$, and @:

primrec   "op $\otimes$" list

$$\otimes[]. \, R \quad \ = R$$
$$\otimes(x \# Y). \, R = \otimes x. \, \otimes Y. \, R$$

We extend the simple substitution to the multiple substitution when it makes sense (that is when the variables involved are distinct and when there is the same number of expressions as variables):

defs $X := E \equiv$ if $\text{distinct}(X) \wedge E \stackrel{\text{len}}{=} X$

then $(\lambda s. \, \text{True} \mid \{\!\mid X \mid\!\} : \lambda s \, s'. \, \text{map}(s')(X) = \text{map}(\lambda e. \, e's)(E))$

else arbitrary

The general proof of (15) is not really complicated but needs several specific properties of operators on lists. The correct P is found automatically by Isabelle, it is of course $\text{trm}(S)$. The others are instantiated by hand. For D we take any list such that its elements are distinct and are those of $\text{dom}(S)$[11]. For D' we need distinct fresh variables in the same number as D. At last Q is $\text{prd}(S)$ where the relevant after-values are mapped to the fresh variables D'.

$$P = \text{trm}(S)$$
$$D = (\epsilon D. \, \{\!\mid D \mid\!\} = \text{dom}(S) \wedge \text{distinct}(D))$$
$$D' = (\epsilon D'. \, \{\!\mid D' \mid\!\} \backslash S \wedge \text{distinct}(D') \wedge D' \stackrel{\text{len}}{=} D)$$
$$Q = (\lambda s. \, \text{prd}(S)'s's[\text{map}(s)(D')/D])$$

The obtained result is just formal, and is not used in practice. More useful is the injectivity property of the weakest precondition operator "[.]" which states that two substitutions are equal if they have the same domain and if they

---

[11] It is possible since $\text{dom}(S)$ is finite.

establish exactly the same postconditions. Its proof uses the injectivity of the encoding of Sub and the extensionnality property of α Sfun (3):

$$[\![\, \mathsf{dom}(S) = \mathsf{dom}(T); \, \forall R. \, [S]R = [T]R \,]\!] \Longrightarrow S = T \tag{16}$$

Equipped with this theorem and the axioms of GSL, we can forget the heavy definitions in terms of trm, prd and dom of the operators of GSL, and prove almost automatically[12] all the various properties which mix different substitution operators. For properties involving the parallel operator we need to prove

$$[\![\, \mathsf{dom}(S) \cap \mathsf{dom}(T) = \emptyset; \, \mathsf{dom}(S) \backslash Q; \, \mathsf{dom}(T) \backslash P;$$
$$[S]P; \, [T]Q \,]\!] \Longrightarrow [S \, || \, T](P \wedge Q)$$

4.3 Substituted Substitution

We close the section on GSL by extending the non-freeness and the substitution to generalised substitutions, which we need to define operation calls in the next section.

The variables manipulated by a generalised substitution S are the variables of $\mathsf{trm}(S)$, and the before- and after-variables of $\mathsf{prd}(S)$. By the definition of the Sub type, the after-variables are included in $\mathsf{dom}(S)$. The extension of the non-freeness condition is defined through the extension of depend (see note 2):

defs $\mathsf{depend}(S) \equiv \mathsf{depend}(\mathsf{trm}(S), \mathsf{prd}(S), \mathsf{dom}(S))$

At this point we can derive the theorem $\{x\} \backslash S \Longrightarrow @x. \, S = S$.

The substituted substitution is less easy to define because it is only partial: $[x := E](x := F)$ is only defined when E is itself a variable. More generally, to define a substituted substitution $[x := E]S$, we have to consider two cases:

- The substituted variable x is in the domain of S. Then the substituted substitution makes sense only when there exists y such that $E = \$y$. The injectivity of $\$$ (2) guarantees that, *if it exists*, such a y is unique. The domain of the substituted substitution is obtained by replacing x by y, that is $\{y\} \cup (\mathsf{dom}(S) - \{x\})$, x is replaced by y in $\mathsf{trm}(S)$ and in $\mathsf{prd}(S)$ where we *also* replace x' by y' ($\lambda s. \, [x := \$y]([x := \$y](\mathsf{prd}(S))'s)$).
- The substituted variable x is not in the domain of S. In this case the substituted substitution is defined for all E, and its domain is $\mathsf{dom}(S)$.

We split the definition of a substituted substitution in two rules:

rules $x \in \mathsf{dom}(S) \Longrightarrow [x := \$y]S = ([x := \$y](\mathsf{trm}(S)) \, |$
$\{y\} \cup (\mathsf{dom}(S) - \{x\}) : \lambda s. \, [x := \$y]([x := \$y](\mathsf{prd}(S))'s))$
$x \notin \mathsf{dom}(S) \Longrightarrow [x := E]S =$
$([x := E](\mathsf{trm}(S)) \, | \, \mathsf{dom}(S) : [x := E](\mathsf{prd}(S)))$

---

[12] In general, with a single call to Isabelle's classical reasoner [10].

Note that we do not need to redefine the multiple substituted substitution, since (7) and (8) were defined in terms of simple substitution.

We prove various distributivity properties on (multiple) substituted substitution. Two useful results are

$$\{y\}\backslash S \Longrightarrow (@y.\ [x := \$y]S) = (@x.\ S)$$

and $\quad [\ y \overset{\text{len}}{=} x;\ \text{distinct}(x);\ \{\!|\,x\,|\!\} \subseteq \text{dom}(S);$

$$e \overset{\text{len}}{=} z;\ \text{distinct}(z);\ \{\!|\,z\,|\!\} \cap \text{dom}(S) = \emptyset\ ]$$

$$\Longrightarrow [x^\frown z := \$y^\frown e](P \mid S) = ([x^\frown z := \$y^\frown e]P \mid [x^\frown z := \$y^\frown e]S)$$

The former enables us to rename a variable under the unbounded choice, in practice to apply the axiom of @ (14) when the non-freeness condition about x is not realised. The latter is connected with operation calls. It distributes the replacement of formal parameters (output x, input z) by actual parameters (output y, input e) over the basic shape of an operation (a precondition P and a generalised substitution S).

5 Abstract Machine

In this section we formalise the abstract machine theory. We characterise basic machines, i.e. the elements of abstract machine notation which start by MACHINE and do not contain any assembly clause (INCLUDES, EXTENDS, USES or SEES). First we define operations and then abstract machines; we end with the combination of operations (in a generalised substitution) in order to give an idea of our future work.

5.1 Operation

An operation is characterised by a 5-tuple (N, i, o, P, S): N is the name, i and o are respectively the list of input and output parameters, P is the explicit precondition of the operation, and S is the substitution performed when the operation is called. There are constraints to obtain a well-formed operation: the names of lists i and o must be all distinct, o must not be free in P, i must not be modified by S, and conversely o must be in $\text{dom}(S)$. We define the type Op

typedef $\text{Op} = \{(N :: \text{name}, i :: \text{name list}, o :: \text{name list}, P :: \text{Pred}, S :: \text{Sub}).$

$$\text{distinct}(i) \wedge \text{distinct}(o) \wedge \{\!|\,o\,|\!\}\backslash P \wedge$$

$$\{\!|\,i\,|\!\} \cap \text{dom}(S) = \emptyset \wedge \{\!|\,o\,|\!\} \subseteq \text{dom}(S)\}$$

We explicitly separate the precondition from the substitution of the operation since it plays a particular rôle in the axioms of abstract machines.

The operators name, in, out, pre and body map an operation to its internal components. We define an operator to denote the local variables of an operation and a predicate to control the set of readable variables:

defs $\text{local}(O) \quad \equiv \text{dom}(\text{body}(O)) - \text{out}(O)$

$\quad\quad\quad \text{read}(O)(V) \equiv \text{depend}(\text{pre}(O), \text{trm}(\text{body}(O)), \text{prd}(\text{body}(O)))(V)$

An operation call $o \leftarrow O(i)$ is simply the generalised substitution (pre | body) where the formal parameters in and out have been replaced by the actual parameters (o :: name list) and (i :: Expr list). Of course we need a side-condition to say that such a call is well-formed: the actual output variables o are distinct, o and i have the same length than their corresponding formal parameters, and o is different from the local variables of O. Finally we define preserve which states that an operation preserves a predicate.

$$
\begin{aligned}
\textbf{defs} \quad o \leftarrow O(i) \quad &\equiv\ /\mathsf{out}(O)^\frown \mathsf{in}(O) := \$o^\frown i/(\mathsf{pre}(O) \mid \mathsf{body}(O)) \\
\mathsf{wfcall}(O)(i)(o) \quad &\equiv\ \mathsf{distinct}(o) \wedge o \overset{\mathsf{len}}{=} \mathsf{out}(O) \wedge i \overset{\mathsf{len}}{=} \mathsf{in}(O) \wedge \\
&\qquad \{\!|o|\!\} \cap \mathsf{local}(O) = \emptyset \\
\mathsf{preserve}(O)(I) \quad &\equiv\ \lambda s.\ \forall i\, o.\ \mathsf{wfcall}(O)(i)(o) \\
&\qquad \longrightarrow (I \wedge /\mathsf{in}(O) := i/\mathsf{pre}(O) \\
&\qquad\qquad \longrightarrow [o \leftarrow O(i)]I)\text{`}s)
\end{aligned}
$$

5.2 Abstract Machine

We have now all the necessary concepts to define abstract machines. However in this paper we simplify some features: we do not include the clauses SETS, (ABSTRACT_)CONSTANTS and PROPERTIES, and we do not distinguish between CONCRETE_VARIABLES and VARIABLES, since for the moment our formalisation does not go far enough to exploit these concepts.

An abstract machine is a 7-tuple (N, X, C, V, I, U, O) where N is the name, X the list of formal parameters, C the constraints on these parameters, V the set of variables, I the invariant, U the initialisation and O the set of operations. The machine is well-formed when X and V are distinct, C depends on X only, if there is no parameter[13] ($X = [\,]$) then $C = (\lambda s.\ \mathsf{True})$, V is finite, I depends on X and V only, U works on V and depends on X only, O is finite and for each element of O their local variables are equal to V[14] and they can only read their input parameters, V and X. The type Mch is then

$$
\begin{aligned}
\textbf{typedef} \quad \mathsf{Mch} = \{ &(N :: \mathsf{name}, X :: \mathsf{name\ list}, C :: \mathsf{Pred}, V :: \mathsf{name\ set}, \\
&I :: \mathsf{Pred}, U :: \mathsf{Sub}, O :: \mathsf{Op\ set}). \\
&\mathsf{distinct}(X) \wedge \{\!|X|\!\} \cap V = \emptyset \wedge \mathsf{depend}(C)(\{\!|X|\!\}) \wedge \\
&(X = [\,] \longrightarrow C = (\lambda s.\ \mathsf{True})) \wedge \\
&\mathsf{finite}(V) \wedge \mathsf{depend}(I)(\{\!|X|\!\} \cup V) \wedge \\
&\mathsf{dom}(U) = V \wedge \mathsf{depend}(U)(\{\!|X|\!\}) \wedge \mathsf{finite}(O) \wedge \\
&(\forall B \in O.\ \mathsf{local}(B) = V \wedge \mathsf{read}(B)(\mathsf{in}(B) \cup V \cup \{\!|X|\!\}) \wedge \\
&\qquad (\forall A \in O.\ \mathsf{name}(A) = \mathsf{name}(B) \longrightarrow A = B))\}
\end{aligned}
$$

---

[13] In this case there is no CONSTRAINTS clause in **B**. However, to have a unified type for abstract machine, we take this view, consistent with abstract machine axioms.

[14] In general the local variables of an operation just have to be included in the variables of a machine, but we can always extend the domain of a substitution S (then of an operation) with x by $S||x := x$ to obtain that equality.

As previously, we provide selector functions name, prm, ctr, var, inv, ini and ops, to access to components of Mch. The axioms of abstract machines are expressed in the definition of the consistency predicate: initialisation establishes the invariant under the constraints, and all the operations preserve the invariant under the constraints.

defs consistent(M) $\equiv$ ($\forall s$. (ctr(M) $\longrightarrow$ [ini(M)](inv(M)))'s) $\wedge$
$\qquad$ ($\forall B \in$ ops(M). $\forall s$. (ctr(M) $\longrightarrow$
$\qquad\qquad\qquad\qquad\qquad\qquad\qquad$ preserve(B)(inv(M)))'s)

At this point we can develop and prove single machines. The encapsulation of operations and machines in abstract types guarantees that all the conditions about non-freeness, dependence, distinctness etc. are formally verified.

5.3 Combining Operations

In this section we look at the use of operations in generalised substitutions (as in bodies of operations of including machines). Such generalised substitutions (we call them commands) are defined with operation calls combined with generalised substitutions on variables other than the local one of the operations (following the *hiding principle*). First we give a precise definition of which combinations are accepted, and then we prove a theorem which ensures the soundness of the proof obligations for the INCLUDES clause.

We need to define hidden, which collects all the local variables of a set of operations (hidden(O) $\equiv$ {n. $\exists U \in O$. $n \in$ local(U)}).

cmd(O), the set of commands constructed on the set of operations O, is defined inductively. The first two cases introduce operation calls and generalised substitutions on variables other than hidden(O). The next four rules authorise the GSL basic operators. Finally, the parallel operator is permitted for disjoint substitutions.

inductive cmd(O)

$[\, U \in O$; wfcall(U)(i)(o); hidden(O)\$o\,]$ $\Longrightarrow$ $o \leftarrow U(i) \in$ cmd(O)

hidden(O)\dom(S) $\qquad\qquad\qquad\Longrightarrow$ $S \in$ cmd(O)

$S \in$ cmd(O) $\qquad\qquad\qquad\qquad\Longrightarrow$ ($P \mid S$) $\in$ cmd(O)

$S \in$ cmd(O) $\qquad\qquad\qquad\qquad\Longrightarrow$ ($P \Longrightarrow S$) $\in$ cmd(O)

$[\, S \in$ cmd(O); $T \in$ cmd(O) $]$ $\qquad\Longrightarrow$ ($S \,[\,]\, T$) $\in$ cmd(O)

$[\, x \notin$ hidden(O); $S \in$ cmd(O) $]$ $\qquad\Longrightarrow$ (@x. S) $\in$ cmd(O)

$[\, S \in$ cmd(O); $T \in$ cmd(O); dom(S) $\cap$ dom(T) $= \emptyset\,]$
$\qquad\qquad\qquad\qquad\qquad\qquad\qquad\Longrightarrow$ ($S \,||\, T$) $\in$ cmd(O)

For example, the well-formed operations for a machine M which includes the machines M_1 and M_2 are exactly cmd(ops(M_1) $\cup$ ops(M_2)), provided that var(M_1) and var(M_2) are disjoint.

The INCLUDES mechanism enables us to prove separately the proof obligations of the included and the including machines. The theorem below ensures that the operations of the *including* machine indeed preserve the invariant of the *included* machines. That is, with the example above, for all operations C of M, C preserves $\mathsf{inv}(M_1)$ and $\mathsf{inv}(M_2)$.

$$\begin{aligned}
\llbracket\ & C \in \mathsf{cmd}(O); \\
& \forall U \in O.\ \forall V \in O.\ \mathsf{local}(U) = \mathsf{local}(V) \lor \mathsf{local}(U) \cap \mathsf{local}(V) = \emptyset; && (17) \\
& \exists U \in O.\ \mathsf{depend}(I)(\mathsf{local}(U)); && (18) \\
& \forall U \in O.\ \forall s.\ \mathsf{preserve}(U)(I)'s\ \rrbracket && (19) \\
\implies\ & \forall s.\ (I \land \mathsf{trm}(C) \longrightarrow [C]I)'s
\end{aligned}$$

This general theorem does not refer to abstract machines. However the link with the INCLUDES mechanism is straightforward: O is a set of operations (the union of the operations of the included machines), I is a predicate (the invariant of an included machine), C is a command constructed from O (the body of an operation of the including machine).

Note the side-conditions (realised in the case of an INCLUDES clause) which state, (17) that the local variables of the operations form a partition of all the hidden variables (as it must be the case for operations coming from different machines included in the same machine), (18) that the invariant depends only on local variables of some operation (we suppose that all the operations of a same machine have the same local variables, see note 14), and (19) that the invariant is preserved by all the operations (which is trivial for the operations from other included machines than the one of the invariant, because of the partition of hidden variables).

This theorem is the key to prove the consistency of the proof obligations of an including machine. That is informally:

$\textit{proof\_obligation}(\textsc{Machine}\ M\ \textsc{includes}\ N \ldots \textsc{end})$

$\implies \mathsf{consistent}(\textit{abstract\_machine}(\textsc{Machine}\ M\ \textsc{includes}\ N \ldots \textsc{end}))$

where *proof_obligation* and *abstract_machine* map a **B** component to respectively its proof obligations and the corresponding element of type Mch.

6 Conclusion

In this paper we have started a formalisation of **B** in Isabelle/HOL. We have bypassed the encoding of the syntax of predicates and expressions by taking a semantic view, to focus on generalised substitutions and abstract machines. Then we have formalised generalised substitutions by the before-after model, and proved the equivalence with the weakest precondition axiomatic model. Finally we have formalised abstract machines.

The construction enables us to define single abstract machines and to prove their consistency inside HOL. This encoding of **B** basic concepts in HOL is also promising for the formalisation of the whole abstract machine notation, as our current exploration with the INCLUDES clause and the refinement of generalised substitutions shows us.

This outlines our future work. First we have to define machines assembly clauses in term of abstract machines as described in this paper. Then we could formally establish rules (*proof obligations*) for proving the consistency of these constructs. We follow the same process for the refinement of abstract machines.

Apart from interesting theoretical concepts (generalised substitutions, abstract machines, refinement...), we also tried to define and use formally the non-freeness conditions. These hypotheses seem generally obvious and tedious for people, but they are necessary to construct practical tools. Our experiments with assembly clauses emphasise their importance and show they do not really complicate proofs. Indeed proof scripts are rather short (a few lines of Isabelle's tactics), except for theorems involving lists which require more interactivity.

The main advantage of using HOL is its static type-checking system. It avoids to "pollute" formulae with side-conditions to ensure the well-formedness of expressions[15]. This would not be the case in a flattened universe like Isabelle/ZF (the ZF set theory instance of Isabelle). We are peculiarly satisfied with the **typedef** construct which encapsulates the properties characterising a new type. By hiding these properties it enables us to write very readable and concise theorems. This is specially valuable in case of rewriting rules because the less side-conditions there are, the more efficient is Isabelle's simplifier. In addition the proof guidance provided by types certainly improves the work of Isabelle's automatic tools.

Obviously this work provides a sort of validation of some **B** concepts. It also leads to a formally developed proof obligation generator for abstract machine notation. This tool is valuable in itself. More interesting perhaps, could be its use to check existing proof obligation generators (Atelier B, B-toolkit). From the theoretical point of view, it is a framework which enables us to check formally the soundness of extensions and/or modifications of the **B** language.

Finally the work would be complete with an encoding of the syntax of predicates and expressions. With an appropriate type-checker, the whole construction would provide a unified framework to write and prove **B** programs.

Acknowledgements. I wish to thank Larry Paulson and Mark Staples for comments on a draft of this paper, Larry Paulson for providing interest and advice for this work, the RATP (France) for funding me, and the EPSRC (grant GR/K57381, Mechanising Temporal Reasoning).

References

1. J.-R. Abrial. *The B-Book — Assigning Programs to Meanings*. Cambridge University Press, 1996.
2. D. Bert, M.-L. Potet, and Y. Rouzaud. A study on components and assembly primitives in b. In H. Habrias, editor, *Proc. of First B Conference*, pages 47–62, IRIN, Nantes, 1996.

---

[15] Side-conditions like "S is a generalised substitution", "P is a predicate" ...

3. J. P. Bowen and M. J. C. Gordon. Z and HOL. In J. P. Bowen and J. A. Hall, editors, *Z Users Workshop*, pages 141–167. Springer-Verlag, 1994.

4. M. J. C. Gordon. Mechanizing programming logics in higher order logic. In G. Birtwistle and P. A. Subrahmanyam, editors, *Current Trends in Hardware Verification and Automated Theorem Proving*. Springer-Verlag, 1989.

5. M. J. C. Gordon and T. Melham. *Introduction to HOL — A Theorem Proving Environment for Higher-Order Logic*. Cambridge University Press, 1993.

6. M. J. C. Gordon, R. Milner, and C. P. Wadsworth. *Edinburgh LCF: A Mechanised Logic of Computation*, volume 78 of *Lecture Notes in Computer Science*. Springer-Verlag, 1979.

7. P. V. Homeier and D. F. Martin. A mechanically verified verification condition generator. *The Computer Journal*, 38(2):131–141, 1995.

8. Kolyang, T. Santen, and B. Wolff. A structure preserving encoding of Z in Isabelle/HOL. In J. von Wright, J. Grundy, and J. Harrison, editors, *Theorem Proving in Higher-Order Logics*, volume 1125 of *Lecture Notes in Computer Science*, pages 283–298. Springer-Verlag, 1996.

9. T. Nipkow. Winskel is (almost) right: Towards a mechanized semantics textbook. In V. Chandru and V. Vinay, editors, *Foundations of Software Technology and Theoretical Computer Science*, volume 1180 of *Lecture Notes in Computer Science*, pages 180–192. Springer-Verlag, 1996.

10. L. C. Paulson. *Isabelle — A Generic Theorem Prover*, volume 828 of *Lecture Notes in Computer Science*. Springer-Verlag, 1994.

11. J. M. Spivey. *The Z Notation — A Reference Manual*. Prentice Hall, 1992.

12. J. von Wright. Program refinement by theorem prover. In *Proc. of the 6th Refinement Workshop*, London, 1994. Springer-Verlag.

13. J. von Wright. Verifying modular programs in HOL. Technical Report 324, University of Cambridge Computer Laboratory, 1994.

Introducing Dynamic Constraints in B

Jean-Raymond Abrial[1] and Louis Mussat[2]

[1] Consultant*
26, rue des Plantes   75 014 Paris
abrial@steria.fr

[2] Service Central de la Sécurité des Systèmes d'Information
18, rue du Dr. Zamenhof   92 131 Issy-les-Moulineaux
ssi19@calva.net

Abstract. In **B**, the expression of dynamic constraints is notoriously missing. In this paper, we make various proposals for introducing them. They all express, in different complementary ways, how a system is allowed to evolve. Such descriptions are independent of the proposed evolutions of the system, which are defined, as usual, by means of a number of operations. Some proof obligations are thus proposed in order to reconcile the two points of view. We have been very careful to ensure that these proposals are compatible with refinement. They are illustrated by several little examples, and a larger one. In a series of small appendices, we also give some theoretical foundations to our approach. In writing this paper, we have been heavily influenced by the pioneering works of Z. Manna and A. Pnueli [11], L. Lamport [10], R. Back [5] and M. Butler [6].

1   Introduction

Background

This paper is the continuation of a study [2] that appeared in the First B Conference, where we showed how **B** could be used for specifying and designing distributed systems. Since then, we have explained, by means of a rather detailed case study [3], how the concepts introduced in [2] could be handled in practice and proved correct with **Atelier B** [13]. These two studies also showed that **B** could be used "as it is", at least to a certain extent.

Previous Work

The main idea conveyed in the mentioned papers is that **B** abstract machines, normally used to specify and develop software modules, might also be used to model the evolution of certain "global" situations. For instance, the state of such a "machine" might be a complete network. And its "operations" might be simple, so called, events, which may occur "spontaneously" rather than being invoked, as is the case with a normal abstract machine operation. For instance,

---

* Supported by STERIA, SNCF, RATP and INRETS

such an event might be a specific action involved in a communication protocol executed by an agent that is situated somewhere in the mentioned network. Rather than being pre-conditioned, each event is guarded by a certain predicate, which states precisely the condition under which the event can be enabled. Finally, new events, which were not explicitly present in an abstraction, might be introduced in a refinement. Such events are all supposed to refine the non-event (that modifies nothing) of the abstraction. The gradual introduction of new events in successive refinement steps makes it possible to slowly develop a system by starting from a non-distributed abstraction (describing, say, in one shot, the main goal of a certain protocol) and ending eventually in a completely distributed concrete realization.

Purpose of Paper

As we became more and more familiar with the problems raised by the specification and design of such distributed systems, it clearly appeared that some of their requirements were sometimes elegantly presented informally in terms of certain "dynamic constraints" that are rather difficult to express, prove and refine with **B** "as it is". The purpose of this paper is thus the following: (1) to present some simple extensions to **B** able to handle such constraints, (2) to show them at work on some examples, (3) to present their theoretical foundations. In doing so, we shall always keep in mind that such extensions must be easily implementable on **Atelier B**.

Dynamic Constraints

Dynamic constraints have been popular among researchers for quite a long time. They have been studied intensively for many years (an excellent survey can be found in [12]). They appear in the literature under different names such as: temporal logic constraints, liveness constraints, eventuality properties, fairness, deadlock, livelock etc. Unlike a static constraint (an invariant), which expresses that a certain property involving the state variables of a system must hold when the system is in a steady state, a dynamic constraint is a law expressing *how the system is allowed to evolve*.

Handling Dynamic Constraints in B

Our idea is to practically handle dynamic constraints in **B** in exactly the same way as we have handled so far static constraints. Let us thus recall in what follows the way we handle static constraints in **B**. As we know, it is possible to express a number of static properties of a system (in the INVARIANT clause of an abstract machine), and also to define a number of named operations (in the OPERATIONS clause) whose rôle is to describe the evolution of the system (possibly in a very abstract way, which is to be refined later). Once this is done, we are required to prove that the proposed evolution of the system is compatible with the (independently proposed) static properties: these are the so called "proof obligations". As can be seen, our main philosophy is one of *separation of concern.* Notice that in a specification language such as **Z** [8], the invariant has *not* to be proved to be maintained, it is *automatically* incorporated in the before-after expressions defining the dynamics of the specified system.

It seems then that everything has been said, that there is no room for further properties to be defined. The purpose of this paper is to say, no, everything has not been said: in the same way as we have defined some static properties of the system independently of the operations describing its evolution, we might also define a number of dynamic properties *independently* of the proposed operations. And, as seen above in the case of the static constraints, it will then be required to prove that the proposed operations of the system are compatible with such dynamic constraints. In other words, we want to be sure that the system indeed evolves as it has been allowed to. Notice that in a specification language such as **TLA** [10] (like in **Z** for the invariant, as we have noticed above), the dynamic constraints have *not* to be proved to be satisfied, they are *automatically* incorporated in the before-after expressions defining the dynamics of the specified system.

Short Examples

A classical generic example of a dynamic constraint, which can be defined for a system, expresses that, under some conditions, which hold *now*, a certain state of affair will certainly be reached *in the future*. In a system involving the control of some requests together with the handling of the corresponding services (such a system is thus modeled with at least two events, one introducing some new request and another honoring some pending request), we might require, as a dynamic constraint, that any pending request will not be pending for ever, that it will be honored eventually. And, again, we are then required to prove that the proposed events gently handle such a dynamic constraint. For instance, we might require of a lift system that any request for a lift at a certain floor will be satisfied in the future. Likewise, we might require that an automatic maintenance system eventually succeeds in repairing what it is supposed to repair at a given moment or explain why it cannot do so. We want to exclude the possibility for the system to do nothing and never report anything.

Another classical situation is one where, in a system, we require that once a certain property holds it then holds "for ever": that any further evolution of the system will not destroy the property in question. For instance, in a system recording historical information, we might require that a piece of data stays in it for ever once it has been entered.

2 The Proposal

None of the proposals we present in what follows is new. They are just new in **B** and, perhaps, in the way each of them is packaged and integrated in a single language. We have been inspired by the ideas of various researchers on different systems. Certainly the work by Z. Manna and A. Pnueli [11], and that of L. Lamport [10]. But clearly, the work of M. Butler as it is presented in [6] has been fundamental to us.

Our proposal is made of five parts. (1) We first introduce a general notion of abstract system (complementary to that of abstract machine). (2) Then we present the idea of a variant in an abstract system refinement, whose rôle is to limit the possibilities for new events, introduced in that refinement, to take control for ever. (3) We then define the concept of a dynamic invariant expressing how data are allowed to evolve in an abstract system. (4) The important notion of modality is then developed, which states how the repeated occurrences of certain events can lead to certain wishful situations. (5) Finally, we give some rules concerning the problem of deadlock.

Each of these concepts will more or less be introduced in the same systematic fashion. First, we shall present the concept (sometimes with a short background) together with its linguistic representation in **B**. Then we shall give (if any) the corresponding proof rules. At this point, we might present a little example illustrating the concept and its proof rules (the proof rules will be recognizable immediately as they will be boxed in a special way). Finally, we shall explain how the concept is influenced by refinement.

The latter point is *fundamental*. We have always to keep in mind that any technique for expressing some (dynamic) properties in the development of a system has to be compatible with some further refinements. Once you have stated a certain property at some point in the construction of a system, you demand that that property is maintained in further refinements. This is certainly part of the very definition of what refining means (the abstract promises should be honored), but dually, this is also part of the semantical definition of any *wishful* property you want to express. In fact, this gives a primary criterion for considering a property: again, it should be maintained by refinement.

2.1 Abstract Systems

Description

In order to make a clear distinction between an "ordinary" abstract machine and one that is used to model a global situation driven by some events, we do not call the latter an abstract MACHINE any more, but rather an abstract SYSTEM. Likewise, the OPERATIONS clause of such a system is now called the EVENTS clause. The other clauses are left unchanged.

A Short Example

As a toy example, next is a little system with two events:

```
SYSTEM
   toy
VARIABLES
   x, y
INVARIANT
   x, y ∈ ℕ × ℕ
INITIALIZATION
   x, y := 0, 0
EVENTS
   evt_x ≙ x := x + 1 ;
   evt_y ≙ y := y + 1
END
```

No Hidden Fairness Assumptions

In such a description, there is *no hidden assumptions* concerning the firing of the events: what you get, is only what you read. And what we can read is the following: when the system moves (notice that the "willingness" of the system to move is *not* our concern), any occurrences of the two events evt_x and evt_y may take place. However, there is no implicit "fairness" assumptions saying that both events must occur infinitely often (as is the case in **UNITY** [7]). On the contrary, here it is quite possible that the event evt_x never occur, or occur just once, or many times, and similarly with the event evt_y. In fact, besides the ability of observing any of the two events, we have no extra knowledge concerning the possible sequences of observation we will be able to make.

Abstract Scheduler

If a more specific behavior is needed, *it has to be specified explicitly*. For instance, if we want to be sure that no event can occur indefinitely without letting the other occur from time to time, and vice versa, we have to "implement" this explicitly (and we shall also see in section 2.4 how to state this, so that we will be able to prove our "implementation"). Such an implementation is called an *abstract scheduler* (a variety of such abstract schedulers is discussed in [4]).

As will be seen, such an abstract scheduler can be so abstract that it *does not commit ourselves to a specific policy*. As a consequence, any kind of more specific policy can be realized in a refinement. There are various possibilities for defining such abstract schedulers, including one consisting in introducing an explicit scheduler event.

An Abstract Scheduler Example

In what follows, we propose to distribute an abstract (fair) scheduler among the two events evt_x and evt_y incrementing the state variables x and y respectively:

```
SYSTEM
    toy_with_scheduler
VARIABLES
    x, y, c, d
INVARIANT
    x, y, c, d ∈ ℕ × ℕ × ℕ × ℕ    ∧    ( c > 0 ∨ d > 0 )
INITIALIZATION
    x, y := 0, 0 ∥ c, d :∈ ℕ₁ × ℕ₁
EVENTS
    evt_x  ≙  SELECT c > 0 THEN x, c := x + 1, c − 1 ∥ d :∈ ℕ₁ END ;
    evt_y  ≙  SELECT d > 0 THEN y, d := y + 1, d − 1 ∥ c :∈ ℕ₁ END
END
```

As can be seen, the firing of the event evt_x depends on the *positive* value of a certain variable c. The value of this variable represents, in a given state, the maximum number of time evt_x can be enabled without evt_y being itself executed. Such a variable is decreased by evt_x and, at the same time, evt_x chooses non-deterministically a *positive* value for a certain variable d handled similarly by the event evt_y. The invariant $c > 0 \lor d > 0$ ensures that the system never deadlocks. In section 2.4, it will be shown how to express (and indeed prove) formally that each of these two events is "fair" to the other.

Abstract System and Refinement

We shall postpone the discussion on the effect of refinement on an abstract system until the next section and section 2.5 (where this question will be studied in details). Let us just say for the moment that what is "promised" by an abstract system should not be destroyed by refinement. And what is promised is a number of events which can happen freely within certain (guarded) conditions. We do not want refinement to offer less concerning the occurrence of the events in question. To take the terminology of **CSP** [9] and also that of **Action Systems** as presented by Butler in [6], we do not want to restrict in any way the *external* non-determinism that is offered by an abstract system at the top level.

2.2 Refining an Abstract System: the VARIANT Clause

Description

For refining a SYSTEM, we use a REFINEMENT component whose OPERATIONS clause is also, of course, replaced by an EVENTS clause. This is also the case for a refinement refining a refinement refining itself an abstract system, and so on.

Besides the events of its abstraction, such a refinement may introduce some *new* events that are not present in the abstraction. Such new events are all supposed to refine a "virtual" event of the abstraction that does nothing (skip). This is amply described and justified in [2] and [3] (this has already been introduced for a long time in **TLA** [10] as the "stuttering steps" and also in **Action**

Systems [5] as the "internal actions"). However, as such a "virtual" skip might, in principle, take control for ever, which is certainly not desirable, we have to assume that the corresponding new event only refines a *bounded* skip. In order to ensure this limitation, we introduce a new clause: the VARIANT clause. Such a clause contains a natural number expression. A corresponding proof obligation states that each *new* event decreases that quantity, so that the *old* events cannot be postponed for ever. Notice that the variant could also be an expression denoting a natural number sequence, in which case each new event is supposed to decrease that quantity lexicographically.

Proof Obligations

Let $\mathcal{H}$ be a new event introduced in a refinement. Suppose that the variant expression stated in the VARIANT clause is V. We have then to prove the following (where v denotes a *fresh* variable):

$$\boxed{\begin{array}{l} V \in \mathbb{N} \\ [v := V]\,[\mathcal{H}]\,(V < v) \end{array}} \qquad\qquad \text{(PO\_1)}$$

Such a proof has to be done, as usual, under the assumptions of the various invariants we depend on in this refinement.

A Short Example

Next is another little system, in which the unique event evt_1 non-deterministically chooses a number x and assign it to both variables a and b:

```
SYSTEM
    another_toy_0
VARIABLES
    a, b
INVARIANT
    a ∈ ℕ ∧ b ∈ ℕ ∧ b = a
INITIALIZATION
    a, b := 0, 0
EVENTS
    evt_1 ≙ ANY x WHERE x ∈ ℕ THEN a, b := x, x END
END
```

The idea is to now refine this system as follows: the concrete event evt_1 only assigns x to a. The variable b', the refined version of b, is set to 0. This new version of evt_1 is only enabled when b' is equal to a. A new event, named evt_2, gradually transports the content of a to b' by incrementing b' while it is strictly smaller than a. The gluing invariant $(b' = a) \Rightarrow (b' = b)$ precisely states at which moment the abstract b and the concrete b' do agree: this is indeed when the value of b' has reached that of a.

REFINEMENT
  another_toy_1
REFINES
  another_toy_0
VARIABLES
  a, b'
INVARIANT
  $b' \in (0 \, . \, . \, a) \,\wedge\, (b' = a \,\Rightarrow\, b' = b)$
VARIANT
  $a - b'$
INITIALIZATION
  $a, b' := 0, 0$
EVENTS
  evt_1 $\widehat{=}$ ANY x WHERE $x \in \mathbb{N} \,\wedge\, b' = a$ THEN $a, b' := x, 0$ END ;
  evt_2 $\widehat{=}$ SELECT $b' < a$ THEN $b' := b' + 1$ END

It is not difficult to prove that the new version of **evt_1** refines its abstract counterpart, and that **evt_2** refines skip. The proof obligations concerning the VARIANT clause reduce to the following, which holds trivially:

$$a \in \mathbb{N} \,\wedge\, b' \in (0 \, . \, . \, a) \,\Rightarrow\, a - b' \in \mathbb{N}$$
$$a \in \mathbb{N} \,\wedge\, b' \in (0 \, . \, . \, a) \,\wedge\, b' < a \,\Rightarrow\, a - (b' + 1) < a - b'$$

The VARIANT Clause and Refinement

Another way to look at the above proof obligation is to consider that the new event $\mathcal{H}$ *refines* a generalized substitution defined by the before-after predicate $V' < V$, where V' denotes the expression V with each state variable x replaced by its after-value x'. In other words, $\mathcal{H}$ refines a certain non-deterministic substitution that strictly decreases the quantity V. Since refinement is transitive, we can then conclude that any refinement of $\mathcal{H}$ still refines the before-after predicate $V' < V$. In conclusion, the VARIANT clause is *compatible with refinement*.

2.3 Dynamic Invariant: the DYNAMICS Clause

Description

A dynamic invariant is a rule stating how certain variables are allowed to evolve. For instance, it might be the case that we are sure that a certain numerical variable cannot be decreased: this is part of what we mean by this variable. It might then be useful to state this explicitly in our specification (subjected, of course, to a proof obligation expressing that each event indeed satisfies this property). We know that, in a sense, this is redundant with the events (hence the proof obligation) but we feel it important to express such redundancies in a specification.

Such dynamic invariants are defined in a special clause called DYNAMICS. It can be introduced in an abstract system or in any of its refinements. Such a clause contains a number of conjuncted before-after predicates involving certain (before) variables and also some "primed" (after) variables. Each of these before-after predicates expresses how variables are allowed to evolve when modified by the events. For instance, given a natural number variable x, the dynamic invariant $x \leq x'$ states that the variable x is not allowed to decrease, only to increase or stay unchanged.

Proof Obligation

Of course, a proof obligation has to be generated in order to ensure that each event is indeed consistent with the contents of the dynamic invariant. For instance, an event with the substitution $x := x + 1$ satisfies the dynamic invariant $x \leq x'$ while the substitution $x := x - 1$ does not.

In general, given an event $\mathcal{E}$ and a dynamic invariant of the form $P(x, x')$ (where x denotes the variables of the considered abstract system), the shape of the proof obligation is the following, where $\mathsf{prd}_x(\mathcal{E})$ is the before-after predicate associated with the event $\mathcal{E}$ (this is described in the B-Book [1] in section 6.3.1):

$$\boxed{\mathsf{prd}_x(\mathcal{E}) \;\Rightarrow\; P(x, x')} \qquad \text{(PO\_2)}$$

This has to be proved under the invariant of the abstract system. It exactly says what is meant by the dynamic invariant. Namely, if x and x' are related by the before-after predicate corresponding to the event $\mathcal{E}$ then the dynamic invariant should also hold between these variables.

A Short Example

In what follows it is shown how the system *toy* of section 2.1 can be equipped with a dynamic invariant.

```
SYSTEM
    toy_with_dynamics
VARIABLES
    x, y
INVARIANT
    x, y ∈ ℕ × ℕ
DYNAMICS
    x ≤ x′ ∧ y ≤ y′
INITIALIZATION
    x, y := 0, 0
EVENTS
    evt_x ≙ x := x + 1 ;
    evt_y ≙ y := y + 1
END
```

As, clearly, the before-after predicate of evt_x is $x' = x + 1 \land y' = y$, and that of evt_y is $y' = y + 1 \land x' = x$, we are led to prove the following which holds trivially:

$$x, y \in \mathbb{N} \times \mathbb{N} \land x' = x + 1 \land y' = y \Rightarrow x \leq x' \land y \leq y'$$
$$x, y \in \mathbb{N} \times \mathbb{N} \land y' = y + 1 \land x' = x \Rightarrow x \leq x' \land y \leq y'$$

Dynamic Invariant and Refinement

As for the case of the VARIANT clause in the preceding section, we can consider that, in the proof obligation (PO_2), the event $\mathcal{E}$ *refines* a generalized substitution defined by the before-after predicate $P(x, x')$. And, again, since refinement is transitive, we can then conclude that any refinement of $\mathcal{E}$ will still refine the before-after predicate $P(x, x')$. In conclusion the DYNAMICS clause is *compatible with refinement*.

2.4 Modality Properties: the MODALITIES Clause

Background

A variety of temporal operators have been introduced in the literature [11] for reasoning about the way systems can behave dynamically. The most classical are □ (always), ◇ (eventually), ⤳ (leadsto) and until. In what follows, we shall give a brief informal description of each of them.

Given a certain predicate P defined on the state variables of an evolving system, then $\Box P$ means that P always holds whatever the evolution of the system. In other words, this clearly means that P is invariant in our terminology.

Given a certain predicate P, the statement $\Diamond P$ means that P holds at system start up or that it will certainly hold after system start up whatever the evolution of the system. Notice that, once it holds, there is no guarantee that P holds for ever. This operator is rarely used on its own, but rather together with the operator $\Box$, as in the statement $\Box \Diamond P$. This statement means that it is always the case that P holds eventually: in other words, if P does not hold in a certain state then it will certainly hold in some other state that is reachable from the former whatever the evolution of the system.

Given two predicates P and Q, the statement $P \leadsto Q$ (pronounced P leads to Q) means that it is always the case that once P holds then Q holds eventually. Notice that, once the very process, by which some progress is made towards Q, has started, then P is not required to hold any more (P is only required to hold at the initialization of this process). The statement $P \leadsto Q$ can be defined by the following combination of the two previous operators:

$$P \leadsto Q \quad \hat{=} \quad \Box(P \Rightarrow \Diamond Q)$$

As can be seen, the statement $\Box \Diamond Q$ is clearly a special case of $P \leadsto Q$.

Given two predicates P and Q, the statement P until Q means two different things: (1) that P leads to Q, and (2) that P holds as long as Q does not. Notice that it is not required that P still holds when Q just holds. Up to the last evolution, we can say that P is a "local invariant", which holds during the active part of the process by which P "leads to" Q.

Introducing modalities in B

It seems that a combination of the two operators $\leadsto$ and until covers most of the "modalities" that one may encounter in practice. In both cases, as we have already mentioned, there is an implicit usage of a certain process that is effectively at work in order to *progress* from a certain situation characterized by the predicate P to another one characterized by the predicate Q.

Following what is done in **TLA** [10], we would like to make this process *explicit*. In other words, we would like to express that P leads to Q only when certain events $\mathcal{F}_1, \cdots, \mathcal{F}_n$ do occur.

For instance, suppose that we would like to express that a certain event evt in a system cannot prevent indefinitely the other events in the system to occur. This is clearly expressed by stating that the guard G of evt leads to $\neg G$ and this when the only means of progress is precisely evt. If this is the case then any attempt for evt to take control for ever will fail.

The "eventuality" aspect of these operators means that the process in question *must come to an end*. Clearly this can be expressed as the termination of a certain loop whose body is made by the bounded choice of the concerned events and whose guard is the negation of the predicate we want to reach.

This view of our modality as a loop termination is supported by the small theoretical development that the interested reader can consult in the appendices.

Description: First Form

The first form of our modality involves five distinct components (all possibly defined in terms of the state variables x of our abstract system): (1) a predicate P which is our "point of departure", (2) a predicate Q which is our eventual "destination", (3) a non-empty list of event names $\mathcal{F}_1, \dots, \mathcal{F}_n$ (possibly separated by the keyword OR) that are involved by the loop in progress to go from P to Q (this list is optional, when it is missing then all the events of the system are implicitly involved), (4) an invariant predicate J that must hold during the loop (this predicate is optional) and (5) a natural number expression V denoting the decreasing variant of our loop (alternatively, an expression denoting a sequence of natural numbers):

```
SELECT
    P
LEADSTO
    Q
WHILE
    F₁ OR ··· OR Fₙ
INVARIANT
    J
VARIANT
    V
END
```

This construct is, in fact, a proof obligation stipulating that a loop of the form below indeed terminates (where I stands for the invariant of our component):

```
SELECT
    P
THEN
    WHILE ¬Q DO
        CHOICE F₁ OR ··· OR Fₙ END
    INVARIANT
        I ∧ J
    VARIANT
        V
    END
END
```

The termination of this loop, however, may not necessarily lead to a state where Q holds. This is because the loop may terminate *before* we reach that state. This is due to the fact that the events $\mathcal{F}_1$ to $\mathcal{F}_n$ *have their own guards*. In other words, the effective guard of the loop is not $\neg Q$ but rather the following (in the B-Book, the construct grd is called fis in section 6.3.2):

$$\neg Q \ \wedge \ \big(\, \mathrm{grd}(\mathcal{F}_1) \vee \cdots \vee \mathrm{grd}(\mathcal{F}_1) \,\big)$$

Consequently, when the loop terminates we have

$$Q \lor (\neg \, \text{grd}(\mathcal{F}_1) \land \cdots \land \neg \, \text{grd}(\mathcal{F}_n))$$

As we certainly do not want to terminate in a state where $(\neg \, \text{grd}(\mathcal{F}_1) \land \cdots \land \neg \, \text{grd}(\mathcal{F}_n))$ holds whereas Q does not, we require the following condition to hold:

$$\neg Q \Rightarrow \text{grd}(\mathcal{F}_1) \lor \cdots \lor \text{grd}(\mathcal{F}_n)$$

When $\neg Q$ is stronger that the disjunction of the guards then the effective guard of the loop is exactly $\neg Q$. When the loop terminates then we certainly are in a state where Q holds (this is justified in Appendix **A7**).

How to Achieve the until *Effect*

The until effect can easily be achieved by means of the following modality:

```
SELECT
    P
LEADSTO
    Q
WHILE
    F₁ OR ··· OR Fₙ
INVARIANT
    J ∧ (P ∨ Q)
VARIANT
    V
END
```

Since the involved loop is, as we know, guarded by $\neg Q$, the invariance of $P \lor Q$ means that *inside* the loop (where $\neg Q$ holds) then P holds, whereas *at the end* of the loop (where Q holds) P may not hold any more: it is then indeed the case "(1) that P leads to Q and (2) that P holds as long as Q does not".

As a syntactic sugar, we can thus introduce the following construct to replace the special case above:

```
SELECT
    P
UNTIL
    Q
WHILE
    F₁ OR ··· OR Fₙ
INVARIANT
    J
VARIANT
    V
END
```

Proof Obligation for First Form

The following proof obligations (except the last one) constitute a direct derivation of the loop proof rules that one may find in the B-Book in section 9.2.9. Notice that the third and fourth proof obligations have to be repeated for each concerned event. Also notice that we do not have to prove that each of the event maintains the invariant I of the abstract system, since this has clearly been covered by the "standard" proof obligations. Note that the corresponding proofs have to be performed under the assumption of the invariant I. Finally note that the quantification is done on the variable z, which denotes the collection of state variables *that are modified in the loop*.

$$
\begin{array}{l}
P \Rightarrow J \\[4pt]
P \Rightarrow \forall z \cdot (I \wedge J \Rightarrow V \in \mathbb{N}) \\[4pt]
P \Rightarrow \forall z \cdot (I \wedge J \wedge \neg Q \Rightarrow [\mathcal{F}_i] \, J) \\[4pt]
P \Rightarrow \forall z \cdot (I \wedge J \wedge \neg Q \Rightarrow [v := V] \, [\mathcal{F}_i] \, (V < v)) \\[4pt]
P \Rightarrow \forall z \cdot (I \wedge J \wedge \neg Q \Rightarrow \mathrm{grd}(\mathcal{F}_1) \vee \cdots \vee \mathrm{grd}(\mathcal{F}_n))
\end{array}
\qquad \text{(PO\_3)}
$$

The first of these proof obligations expresses that the extra invariant is established by the guarding condition P. The second proof obligation expresses that under the invariant and the guard of the loop the variant is indeed a natural number (alternatively, an expression denoting a natural number sequence). The third proof obligation states that the predicate J is indeed an extra "local" invariant of the corresponding event. The fourth proof obligation states that the variant decreases under the corresponding event. The final proof obligation states that $\neg Q$ is the effective guard of our loop.

Notice the importance of the universal quantification over z (the state variables modified in the loop). This has the effect of separating the context of what is to be proved "dynamically" from the initial condition which does not always hold.

Description: Second Form

There exists a second form for our "leads to" property. It involves an initial non-deterministic choice. Clearly this second form generalizes the former.

```
ANY y WHERE
    P
LEADSTO
    Q
WHILE
    F₁ OR ··· OR Fₙ
INVARIANT
    J
VARIANT
    V
END
```

And this second construct is, as the former, a proof obligation stipulating that a loop of the form below indeed terminates:

```
ANY y WHERE
    P
THEN
    WHILE ¬Q DO
        CHOICE F₁ OR ··· OR Fₙ END
    INVARIANT
        I ∧ J
    VARIANT
        V
    END
END
```

Proof Obligation for Second Form

By analogy with those obtained for the first form, next are the proof obligations for the second form of modality. As previously the third and fourth are to be repeated for each of the n concerned events. Notice again that these proofs have to be performed under the assumption of the current invariant I.

$$\forall y \cdot (P \Rightarrow J)$$
$$\forall y \cdot (P \Rightarrow \forall z \cdot (I \wedge J \Rightarrow V \in \mathbb{N}))$$
$$\forall y \cdot (P \Rightarrow \forall z \cdot (I \wedge J \wedge \neg Q \Rightarrow [\mathcal{F}_i] J)) \qquad \text{(PO\_4)}$$
$$\forall y \cdot (P \Rightarrow \forall z \cdot (I \wedge J \wedge \neg Q \Rightarrow [v := V][\mathcal{F}_i](V < v)))$$
$$\forall y \cdot (P \Rightarrow \forall z \cdot (I \wedge J \wedge \neg Q \Rightarrow \mathrm{grd}(\mathcal{F}_1) \vee \cdots \vee \mathrm{grd}(\mathcal{F}_n)))$$

As for the previous case, the variable z is supposed to denote those variables that are modified in the loop.

A Short Example

As an example, we can now state that in the system *toy_with_scheduler* of section 2.1, the event evt_x (resp. evt_y) does not keep the control for ever. We have just to say that, provided its guard holds, then the recurrent occurrence of this event leads to a certain state where the guard does not hold any more, formally:

```
SYSTEM
    toy_with_scheduler_dynamics_and_modality
VARIABLES
    x, y, c, d
INVARIANT
    x, y, c, d ∈ ℕ × ℕ × ℕ × ℕ    ∧    (c > 0 ∨ d > 0)
DYNAMICS
    x ≤ x' ∧ y ≤ y'
INITIALIZATION
    x, y := 0, 0 ‖ c, d :∈ ℕ₁ × ℕ₁
EVENTS
    evt_x ≙ SELECT c > 0 THEN x, c := x + 1, c − 1 ‖ d :∈ ℕ₁ END ;
    evt_y ≙ SELECT d > 0 THEN y, d := y + 1, d − 1 ‖ c :∈ ℕ₁ END
MODALITIES
    SELECT c > 0 LEADSTO c = 0 WHILE evt_x VARIANT c END ;
    SELECT d > 0 LEADSTO d = 0 WHILE evt_y VARIANT d END
END
```

Notice that since the guard of evt_x is exactly $c > 0$, we trivially have $c > 0 \Rightarrow$ grd(evt_x) (and the like for evt_y). We can conclude, provided the corresponding proofs are done, that these two events are "fair" to each other.

Modalities and Refinement

For each of the two forms of modality we have introduced in this section, the four first proof obligations are clearly maintained by the refinements of the events: this is obvious for the first and second ones that are not concerned by the events; in the third and fourth proof obligations the events, say $\mathcal{F}$, are only present in subformulae of the form $[\mathcal{F}]\,R$ for some conditions R. Such statements are maintained by refinement according to the very definition of refinement, which says that if an abstraction $\mathcal{F}$ is such that $[\mathcal{F}]\,R$ holds, and if $\mathcal{G}$ refines $\mathcal{F}$ then $[\mathcal{G}]\,R$ holds.

However, the main purpose of the proof obligations was to ensure that the considered loop terminated. The problem is that the implicit concrete loop now contains not only the refined versions of our events but also the new events introduced in the refinement and supposed to refine skip. So that the "body" of our refined implicit loop is now the following:

CHOICE $\mathcal{G}_1$ OR $\cdots$ OR $\mathcal{G}_n$ OR $\mathcal{H}_1$ OR $\cdots$ OR $\mathcal{H}_m$ END where the $\mathcal{G}_i$ are supposed to be the refinements of the more abstract $\mathcal{F}_i$, and where the $\mathcal{H}_j$ are supposed to be the new events. Fortunately, we know that, thanks to the VARIANT clause introduced in section 2.2, the new events $\mathcal{H}_j$ cannot take control for ever. It just then remains for us to be sure again that the loop does not terminate *before* its normal abstract end (as we know, refinement may have the effect of strengthening the guard of an event). In fact the following condition, which has been proved (this was a proof obligation)

$$\boxed{\neg Q \Rightarrow \mathsf{grd}(\mathcal{F}_1) \vee \cdots \vee \mathsf{grd}(\mathcal{F}_n)}$$

is now refined by the condition (to be proved under the assumption of the "gluing" invariant of the refinement):

$$\boxed{\neg Q \Rightarrow \mathsf{grd}(\mathcal{G}_1) \vee \cdots \vee \mathsf{grd}(\mathcal{G}_n) \vee \mathsf{grd}(\mathcal{H}_1) \vee \cdots \vee \mathsf{grd}(\mathcal{H}_m)}$$

which has no reason to be true. We thus impose the following refinement condition (again, to be proved under the assumption of the "gluing" invariant of the refinement), which clearly is sufficient to ensure a correct refinement of each of the fifth proof obligations:

$$\boxed{\begin{array}{l} \mathsf{grd}(\mathcal{F}_1) \vee \cdots \vee \mathsf{grd}(\mathcal{F}_n) \\ \Rightarrow \\ \mathsf{grd}(\mathcal{G}_1) \vee \cdots \vee \mathsf{grd}(\mathcal{G}_n) \vee \mathsf{grd}(\mathcal{H}_1) \vee \cdots \vee \mathsf{grd}(\mathcal{H}_m) \end{array}} \qquad \text{(PO\_5)}$$

This condition says that the concrete events $\mathcal{G}_i$ (refining the abstract events $\mathcal{F}_i$) together with the new events $\mathcal{H}_j$ do not deadlock more often than the abstract events $\mathcal{F}_i$. As we shall see in the next section, this condition must be maintained along the complete development. This is essentially the "progress condition" introduced in [6].

2.5 Deadlockfreeness

The Problem

At the top level, an abstract system "offers" a number of events able to occur "spontaneously" (guard permitting of course). Following the terminology used in **CSP** [9] and in **Action Systems** [5, 6], such possibilities correspond to a certain *external non-determinism* that has to be guaranteed. But, as we know, refinement (besides other effects) can strengthen guards, so that it could very well happen that an abstract event, say $\mathcal{E}$, offered at the top level, disappears completely in the refinement because of the following correct refinement

SELECT false THEN $\mathcal{E}$ END

In order to prevent this to happen, it seems sufficient to impose that the abstract guard implies the concrete guard. But as the converse certainly holds (because of refinement), this implies that the abstract and concrete guards are identical (under the gluing invariant, of course). This is certainly too drastic a rule in the case where the refinement introduces some new events.

Proof Obligations

In fact, as we know, an abstract system can be refined by another one introducing *new* events. And we also know that such events cannot take control for ever because of the VARIANT clause (section 2.2). The idea is to impose a certain "progress condition" [6] allowing us to relax the above constraint on the refinement of the guard of an event. More precisely, in the case of the *first* refinement of an abstract system, the law is the following for each abstract event $\mathcal{F}$ refined by $\mathcal{G}$ and with the new events $\mathcal{H}_1, \cdots, \mathcal{H}_n$ (this has to be proved under the assumption of the abstract and concrete gluing invariants):

$$\boxed{\boxed{\ \mathsf{grd}(\mathcal{F}) \ \Rightarrow\ \mathsf{grd}(\mathcal{G}) \lor \mathsf{grd}(\mathcal{H}_1) \lor \cdots \lor \mathsf{grd}(\mathcal{H}_n)\ }} \qquad \text{(PO\_6)}$$

Such a rule does not disallow the guard of $\mathcal{F}$ to be strengthen in $\mathcal{G}$, it only gives a certain limitation to this strengthening: it should at least be "absorbed" by the new events. If we perform yet another refinement, we have to prove the following rule which gradually transports the progress condition along the development (again, this has to be proved under the relevant invariant assumptions):

$$\boxed{\boxed{\begin{array}{l} \mathsf{grd}(\mathcal{G}) \lor \mathsf{grd}(\mathcal{H}_1) \lor \cdots \lor \mathsf{grd}(\mathcal{H}_n) \\[4pt] \Rightarrow \\[4pt] \mathsf{grd}(\mathcal{M}) \lor \mathsf{grd}(\mathcal{K}_1) \lor \cdots \lor \mathsf{grd}(\mathcal{K}_n) \lor \mathsf{grd}(\mathcal{L}_1) \lor \cdots \lor \mathsf{grd}(\mathcal{L}_m) \end{array}}} \qquad \text{(PO\_7)}$$

where $\mathcal{M}$ is a refinement of $\mathcal{G}$, each $\mathcal{K}_i$ is a refinement of the corresponding more abstract event $\mathcal{H}_i$, and the $\mathcal{L}_j$ are the new events of the refinement. A similar proof obligation has to be generated for each further refinement, and so on.

Example

It is easy to check that the above progress condition is satisfied in the case of the refinement *another_toy_1* of *another_toy_0* (section 2.2). We have in the more abstract system

$$\mathsf{grd}(\mathsf{evt\_1}) \ \Leftrightarrow\ \exists x \cdot x \in \mathbb{N} \ \Leftrightarrow\ \mathsf{true}$$

And in the concrete system

$$\mathsf{grd}(\mathsf{evt\_1}) \ \Leftrightarrow\ \exists x \cdot (x \in \mathbb{N} \land b' = a) \ \Leftrightarrow\ b' = a$$

$$\mathsf{grd}(\mathsf{evt\_2}) \ \Leftrightarrow\ b' < a$$

The progress condition reduces to the following (which holds trivially):

$$b' \in (0 \mathinner{\ldotp\ldotp} a) \Rightarrow (b' = a) \lor (b' < a)$$

Modalities Revisited

As we have just done for the guard of an abstract event, the proof obligation presented for the disjunction of the guards of events involved in a modality (section 2.4), has to be extended for any further refinement.

3 A Larger Example

In this section, we present a complete example able to illustrate the proposal made above.

3.1 Informal Presentation

The problem consists in specifying and refining an event system concerned with requests and services. An agency is supposed to offer n different services (n is thus a positive natural number). Clients of this agency are supposed to issue requests for these services. Once a request for a service is pending, that service cannot be requested again. On the other hand, a pending request cannot be pending for ever. At this stage, we do not require any specific scheduling strategy for honoring the pending requests. In other words, the choice of any future correct strategy must be left open. Again, our only requirement concerning any future implemented strategy is that there cannot be any pending request starvation. Although we do not specify a precise strategy, we nevertheless require a proof guaranteeing that a pending request will be served "some time".

The system is then refined in two different ways, which both concerns the scheduling strategy: (1) a FIFO strategy, (2) a LIFT strategy. With the FIFO strategy a request is supposed to be honored according to its arrival: the oldest the first. With the LIFT strategy the n services are supposed to correspond to the n floors of a building. The clients are the passengers of the lift. The requests are issued by clients when they push the floor buttons within the lift, thus asking for the lift to stop at certain floors. The lift strategy is then the following: the lift does not change direction unless it has no more passenger to serve within that direction, and, of course, within a given direction, the lift serves its passengers in the natural order of the requested floors.

3.2 Developing the Specification

In what follows, we shall develop our formal treatment of the above problem by means of a gradual approach. Clearly, our final abstract system will have at least two events: one for issuing new requests, another for honoring pending requests. In a first phase however, we shall consider one event only, namely that corresponding to honoring requests. In a subsequent refinement, we shall then introduce the requesting event. And only at this stage shall we be able to state the dynamic constraint stipulating that no pending request can be pending for ever.

Phase 0

The (very abstract) state of our abstract system at this level, essentially formalizes the "history" of what has happened so far concerning the services that have been honored. This state consists in a "log", named l_0, recording which services have been honored and when. It is not our intention to formalize a notion of time in our future system: our point of view is just to consider that our model of the system *at this stage* consists in saying that certain services have been honored (one at a time) and that, clearly, such services have been honored "at some time".

Invariant

Our variable l_0 is then just typed as follows

$$l_0 \in \mathbb{N} \nrightarrow (1 \mathinner{.\,.} n)$$

This typing invariant must be made a little more precise by expressing that our history being the history "so far" is clearly finite. We write thus the following extra condition:

$$\mathsf{dom}(l_0) \in \mathbb{F}(\mathbb{N})$$

If t is in the domain of l_0, this means that the service $l_0(t)$ has been honored at "time" t. As can be seen, we have used the set of natural number to denote the results of time measurements. Clearly, we do not know what such a time measurement represents in terms of any precise output as given by a real clock (in particular, we are not interested in any time unit). Our only reason for formalizing time measurements with $\mathbb{N}$ is a pragmatic one. By doing so, we shall be able to compare various time measurements, and thus easily express such concepts as before, after, next, and so on.

Of course, we could have removed completely any reference to the time by just recording the services in the order in which they have been honored (that is, in the form of a finite sequence). However, as we shall see below, such a "trace" technique is not accurate enough in our case.

It is also convenient to have a second variable recording the time, named c_0, of the "youngest" recorded service in the log (when it exists). This variable is typed as follows:

$$\boxed{c_0 \in \mathbb{N}}$$

together with the following invariant (notice that, in this invariant, $\max(\mathrm{dom}(l_0))$ is well defined in the place where it appears because $\mathrm{dom}(l_0)$ is then a finite and non-empty set):

$$\boxed{l_0 \neq \emptyset \;\Rightarrow\; c_0 = \max(\mathrm{dom}(l_0))}$$

Dynamic Invariant

At this point, it is possible to write down a number of dynamic properties of our state variables, properties expressing that such variables can only be modified according to certain constraints. Such properties will secure the very "raison d'être" of these variables, namely to record the history of some "past" events. For instance, no service can ever be removed from the log l_0, and no time nor any service can be modified either. Likewise, the variable c_0 can only be incremented: this formalizes that events are recorded in the log l_0 as soon as they effectively take place. This results in the following simple dynamic invariant:

$$\boxed{\begin{array}{l} l_0 \subseteq l_0' \\ c_0 < c_0' \end{array}}$$

Events

We are now ready to formalize our unique event, named **serve**. This event "spontaneously" records in the log l_0 that, at an *arbitrary* time t, necessarily strictly greater than c_0 however, some *arbitrary* service x has been honored.

$$
\begin{array}{l}
\textbf{serve} \quad \widehat{=} \\
\quad \text{ANY } t, x \text{ WHERE} \\
\qquad t \in \mathbb{N} \quad \wedge \\
\qquad x \in (1\,..\,n) \quad \wedge \\
\qquad c_0 < t \\
\quad \text{THEN} \\
\qquad c_0 := t \quad \| \\
\qquad l_0 := l_0 \cup \{t \mapsto x\} \\
\quad \text{END}
\end{array}
$$

What is important to mention here is that we do not know (and we are not interested in) the "cause" of this event. The only thing we say is that *it is possible to observe* that, subjected to certain conditions, such an arbitrary event does occur. Of course, the question is now: are we able to always observe that event ? The answer to this question lies in the guard (the enabling condition) of our event, namely

$$
\exists\,(t, x) \cdot (t \in \mathbb{N} \wedge x \in (1\,..\,n) \wedge c_0 < t)
$$

As can be seen, this condition is always valid (under the invariant). This means that our event, as we expect, can always be observed. In other words, our system is always ready to honor any service. Notice that, at this point, we have not yet introduced any notion of request. This is precisely the subject of the next phase of our development where it will be clear that honoring a service is not done in a way that is as arbitrary as it appears in the present abstraction. It is not difficult to prove that this event maintains the static as well as the dynamic invariant.

Modality

It is interesting to note that, at this point, we can introduce the following modality expressing that time passes: any "future time" t (strictly greater than c_0) will eventually be a "past time" (some service will have occurred after it).

$$
\begin{array}{l}
\text{ANY } t \text{ WHERE} \\
\quad c_0 < t \\
\text{LEADSTO} \\
\quad t \leq c_0 \\
\text{VARIANT} \\
\quad \max(\{0, t - c_0\}) \\
\text{END}
\end{array}
$$

Final System

Next is our complete SYSTEM (in subsequent phases we shall not show our components with all there clauses put together like this):

```
SYSTEM
    phase_0
CONSTANTS
    n
PROPERTIES
    n ∈ ℕ₁
VARIABLES
    l₀, c₀
INVARIANT
    l₀ ∈ ℕ ⇸ (1 .. n)    ∧
    dom(l₀) ∈ 𝔽(ℕ)    ∧
    c₀ ∈ ℕ    ∧
    l₀ ≠ ∅  ⇒  c₀ = max(dom(l₀))
DYNAMICS
    l₀ ⊆ l'₀    ∧
    c₀ < c'₀
INITIALIZATION
    l₀, c₀ := ∅, 0
EVENTS
    serve    ≙
        ANY t, x WHERE
            t ∈ ℕ    ∧
            x ∈ (1 .. n)    ∧
            c₀ < t
        THEN
            c₀ := t    ‖
            l₀ := l₀ ∪ {t ↦ x}
        END
MODALITIES
    ANY t WHERE
        c₀ < t
    LEADSTO
        t ≤ c₀
    VARIANT
        max({0, t − c₀})
    END
END
```

Phase 1

The purpose of this phase is to introduce a requesting event together with some new interesting dynamic constraints.

Gluing Invariant

We first introduce two variables l_1 and c_1 that are just copies of their corresponding abstractions. For the sake of readability we introduce them explicitly, together with the following trivial gluing invariant:

$$\boxed{\begin{aligned} l_1 &= l_0 \\ c_1 &= c_0 \end{aligned}}$$

Invariant

We now introduce a variable r_1 which records the various requests that have been made so far. This variable is typed as follows:

$$\boxed{r_1 \in \mathbb{N} \twoheadrightarrow (1 \mathinner{\ldotp\ldotp} n)}$$

As for the log l_0 above, we have the extra constraints that r_1 is finite, namely:

$$\boxed{\mathsf{dom}(r_1) \in \mathbb{F}(\mathbb{N})}$$

Dynamic Invariant

We also have to express, as for l_1 above, that r_1 records the history of the requests. Such an history cannot be modified, it can only be augmented. We have thus the following dynamic invariant:

$$\boxed{r_1 \subseteq r_1'}$$

Invariant Again

As can be seen, the type of r_1 is the same as that of l_1. Contrary to what one might expect however, the expression $r_1(t)$ does *not* denote a certain service that has been *requested* at time t. It rather denotes the "knowledge" we suppose to have in this abstraction of the (possibly future) time where the corresponding service has been (or will be) honored. In other words r_1 is a log as is l_1. But this log possibly already records a little of the future of l_1: it anticipates l_1. Of course, it seems rather strange that we can guess the future time where a pending request will be honored. We give ourselves the right to do so only because we are still in an abstraction. But, as we shall see below, this right is precisely the least committed way by which we can express that no pending request will be pending for ever. The fact that r_1 anticipates l_1 is clearly described in the following invariant:

$$l_1 \subseteq r_1$$

As a consequence the pending requests are exactly those requests that are in $r_1 - l_1$. It is time now to express that a service that is pending cannot be requested until it is honored. This is formalized very easily by requiring that the function $r_1 - l_1$ is injective:

$$r_1 - l_1 \in \mathbb{N} \rightarrowtail (1 \mathinner{\ldotp\ldotp} n)$$

It remains now for us to express that the guessed times of service of the pending requests (if any) "belong to the future". Taking into account that c_1 denotes the time of the youngest honored service (if any), we have thus the following extra invariant:

$$r_1 - l_1 \neq \emptyset \Rightarrow c_1 < \min(\mathrm{dom}(r_1 - l_1))$$

Variant

As we shall see, we have a new event, called **request**. This new event must not have the possibility to be enabled for ever. It has thus to decrease a certain variant, which is, in fact, the following:

$$n - \mathsf{card}(r_1 - l_1)$$

Events

We are now ready to define our **request** event as follows

```
request    ≘
    ANY t, y WHERE
        t ∈ ℕ − dom(r₁ − l₁)    ∧
        y ∈ (1 .. n) − ran(r₁ − l₁)    ∧
        c₁ < t
    THEN
        r₁ := r₁ ∪ {t ↦ y}
    END
```

It is easy to prove that this event maintains the static as well as the dynamic invariant, that it refines **skip**, and that it decreases the above variant.

Next is the refinement of the event **serve**. As expected, the idea is to now deterministically honor the pending request (if any) whose guessed service time is the smallest.

$$
\begin{array}{l}
\textbf{serve} \quad \hat{=} \\
\quad \textbf{SELECT} \\
\quad\quad r_1 - l_1 \neq \emptyset \\
\quad \textbf{THEN} \\
\quad\quad \textbf{LET } t \textbf{ BE} \\
\quad\quad\quad t = \min(\mathrm{dom}(r_1 - l_1)) \\
\quad\quad \textbf{IN} \\
\quad\quad\quad c_1 := t \quad \| \\
\quad\quad\quad l_1 := l_1 \cup \{t \mapsto r_1(t)\} \\
\quad\quad \textbf{END} \\
\quad \textbf{END}
\end{array}
$$

It is interesting to compare this event with its abstraction:

$$
\begin{array}{l}
\textbf{serve} \quad \hat{=} \\
\quad \textbf{ANY } t, x \textbf{ WHERE} \\
\quad\quad t \in \mathbb{N} \quad \wedge \\
\quad\quad x \in (1 \mathinner{\ldotp\ldotp} n) \quad \wedge \\
\quad\quad c_0 < t \\
\quad \textbf{THEN} \\
\quad\quad c_0 := t \quad \| \\
\quad\quad l_0 := l_0 \cup \{t \mapsto x\} \\
\quad \textbf{END}
\end{array}
$$

As can be seen the refined version is now completely deterministic. Of course, the guard of the refined event must be stronger than that of the abstraction. This is certainly the case since, as we have already seen, the guard of the abstraction is always valid. The refinement proof also requires that we give some witness values for the arbitrary variables t and x in the abstraction: these are clearly $\min(\mathrm{dom}(r_1 - l_1))$ and $r_1(\min(\mathrm{dom}(r_1 - l_1)))$.

Modality

It finally remains for us to express that no pending request will be pending for ever. We have just to say that if any request for the service x is in the range of $r_1 - l_1$ (is waiting to be honored) then, it will not stay there for ever under the recurrent occurrences of the two events **request** and **serve**. At some point in the future it should disappear (may be shortly, of course). This is done as follows:

```
ANY x WHERE
    x ∈ ran(r₁ − l₁)
LEADSTO
    x ∉ ran(r₁ − l₁)
VARIANT
    [((1 .. n) × {c₁} ⋖ (r₁ − l₁)⁻¹)(x) − c₁, n − card(r₁ − l₁)]
END
```

Notice that, in this modality, we have not mentioned any event since both events
serve and **request** are concerned. Also note that our variant is lexicographic. The
apparent complexity of the first part of this variant is due to the fact that when
x is not a member of $\mathsf{ran}(r_1 - l_1)$ (at the end of the process), the expression
$(r_1 - l_1)^{-1}(x)$ is not defined. On the other hand, the second part of this variant
is a mere copy of our VARIANT clause.

It is easy to prove that both events are compatible with this modality.

Deadlockfreeness

According to the outcome of section 2.5, it remains for us to ensure deadlockfreeness. In other words, we have to prove that the abstract guard of event **serve**
implies the disjunction of the concrete guards. This reduces to proving:

$$r_1 - l_1 = \emptyset \Rightarrow$$
$$\exists (t, y) \cdot (t \in \mathbb{N} - \mathsf{dom}(r_1 - l_1) \wedge y \in (1 .. n) - \mathsf{ran}(r_1 - l_1) \wedge c_1 < t)$$

Notice that this also proves that our abstract modality is correctly transported
within the present refinement.

Conclusion

What we have done in this refinement was *not* to define a particular scheduler
that has been, by any chance, able to satisfy our modality. By using the artifact
of the "guessed" service time of a coming request, we have just been able to
implement again a very *abstract scheduler*. As we shall see below, any policy
that will not be contradictory with this abstraction will be a correct policy. In
other words, we will not have to verify any more in the coming refinements that
our modality is satisfied, we will just have to implement a concrete scheduler
that refines this very general abstract one.

Phase 2

The second refinement is just a technical phase consisting in throwing away
the log l_1 that has no purpose any more. The variable c_1 will thus also disappear.
In fact, we are just going to keep the pending requests (corresponding to $r_1 - l_1$)
but not with their guessed *service* time, only their guessed *waiting* time. This
results in some drastic simplifications of the model.

Invariant

The new variable, named w_2, is typed as follows:

$$w_2 \in (1 \mathrel{..} n) \rightarrowtail \mathbb{N}_1$$

Notice that w_2 is injective as expected and that the waiting times are strictly positive as one would also expect.

Gluing Invariant

This variable is glued as follows to the abstraction:

$$w_2 = (r_1 - l_1)^{-1} \mathbin{;} \mathsf{minus}(c_1)$$

The function $\mathsf{minus}(c_1)$ is the function that subtracts c_1.

Events

We can now propose the following refinement of the event **request**:

> **request** $\;\widehat{=}$
>   **ANY** y, w **WHERE**
> $y \in (1 \mathrel{..} n) - \mathsf{dom}(w_2)$ $\wedge$
> $w \in \mathbb{N}_1 - \mathsf{ran}(w_2)$
>   **THEN**
> $w_2 := w_2 \cup \{y \mapsto w\}$
>   **END**

It is not difficult to prove that it refines its abstraction (the witness for t being clearly $c_1 + w$):

> **request** $\;\widehat{=}$
>   **ANY** t, y **WHERE**
> $t \in \mathbb{N} - \mathsf{dom}(r_1 - l_1)$ $\wedge$
> $y \in (1 \mathrel{..} n) - \mathsf{ran}(r_1 - l_1)$ $\wedge$
> $c_1 < t$
>   **THEN**
> $r_1 := r_1 \cup \{t \mapsto y\}$
>   **END**

Next is the proposed refinement of the event serve:

```
serve  ≙
   SELECT
      w₂ ≠ ∅
   THEN
      LET t BE
         t = min(ran(w₂))
      IN
         w₂ := (w₂ ▷ {t}) ; minus(t)
      END
   END
```

This event clearly refines its abstraction:

```
serve  ≙
   SELECT
      r₁ − l₁ ≠ ∅
   THEN
      LET t BE
         t = min(dom(r₁ − l₁))
      IN
         c₁ := t   ∥
         l₁ := l₁ ∪ {t ↦ r₁(t)}
      END
   END
```

Deadlockfreeness

The trivial equivalence of the abstract and concrete guards of each event clearly implies the deadlockfreeness condition and the correct transportation of our modalities.

3.3 Towards some implementations

In this section, our intention is to propose two different refinements of the above abstract scheduler corresponding to the FIFO and the LIFT policies respectively.

The FIFO Policy

Invariant

In this policy we are going to reduce the inverse of the previous variable w_2 to a mere injective sequence q_3. This yields the following typing:

$$q_3 \in \mathsf{iseq}(1 \, .. \, n)$$

Gluing Invariant

We have the following gluing invariant:

$$q_3 = w_2^{-1}$$

Notice that we can deduce the following assertion:

$$w_2 \neq \emptyset \Rightarrow \min(\mathrm{ran}(w_2)) = 1$$

As can be seen, the waiting times are now all "dense" (starting at 1): they together form the domain of the sequence q_3.

Events

The event **request** is now very simple (just the appending of the new request in the queue):

$$
\begin{array}{l}
\textbf{request} \quad \widehat{=} \\
\quad \text{ANY } y \text{ WHERE} \\
\qquad y \in (1 \mathbin{..} n) - \mathrm{ran}(q_3) \\
\quad \text{THEN} \\
\qquad q_3 := q_3 \leftarrow y \\
\quad \text{END}
\end{array}
$$

We can fruitfully compare it to its abstraction:

$$
\begin{array}{l}
\textbf{request} \quad \widehat{=} \\
\quad \text{ANY } y, w \text{ WHERE} \\
\qquad y \in (1 \mathbin{..} n) - \mathrm{dom}(w_2) \quad \wedge \\
\qquad w \in \mathbb{N}_1 - \mathrm{ran}(w_2) \\
\quad \text{THEN} \\
\qquad w_2 := w_2 \cup \{y \mapsto w\} \\
\quad \text{END}
\end{array}
$$

As can be seen, the guessed waiting "time" of the abstraction is now completely determined as $\mathsf{size}(q_3) + 1$. It is precisely this determination that implements the FIFO policy together with the event **serve**. This event just consists in removing the first element of the queue:

$$
\begin{array}{l}
\textbf{serve} \quad \widehat{=} \\
\quad \text{SELECT} \\
\qquad q_3 \neq [\,] \\
\quad \text{THEN} \\
\qquad q_3 := \mathrm{tail}(q_3) \\
\quad \text{END}
\end{array}
$$

Again, it can fruitfully be compared to its abstraction:

$$
\begin{array}{|l|}
\hline
\textsf{serve} \quad \widehat{=} \\
\quad \text{SELECT} \\
\qquad w_2 \neq \emptyset \\
\quad \text{THEN} \\
\qquad \text{LET } t \text{ BE} \\
\qquad\quad t = \min(\text{ran}(w_2)) \\
\qquad \text{IN} \\
\qquad\qquad w_2 := (w_2 \rhd \{t\}) \,;\, \text{minus}(t) \\
\qquad \text{END} \\
\quad \text{END} \\
\hline
\end{array}
$$

We can see how the new version simulates its abstraction: the pair with the smallest index, 1, is removed, and 1 is indeed subtracted from the other indices (this is, in fact, exactly what tail does).

The LIFT Policy

Invariant

As for the FIFO policy, the LIFT policy will be a refinement of our phase 2 above. In the present case, the n services are supposed to denote the n floors of a building. We shall therefore suppose that there are at least two floors (otherwise there is no point in having a lift at all !).

$$
\boxed{n \geq 2}
$$

This phase will consist in making the waiting time function w_2 (now renamed w_4) more precise. We already know from phase 2 that it should be injective from $1 .. n$ to $\mathbb{N}_1$. We have the following trivial gluing invariant.

$$
\boxed{w_4 = w_2}
$$

We introduce to more variables. First, the lift position l_4 (this is a floor) and second the lift direction d_4 (*up* or *down*). We have thus the following typing invariant:

$$
\boxed{
\begin{aligned}
&l_4 \in 1 .. n \\
&d_4 \in \{\, up,\ down \,\}
\end{aligned}
}
$$

We now have an extra invariant stipulating that, when it is at the bottom floor, the lift goes up, whereas it goes down, when it is at the top floor (here it helps to have at least two floors).

$$l_4 = 1 \implies d_4 = up$$
$$l_4 = n \implies d_4 = down$$

Given the position and direction of the lift, our idea is to have a pre-defined function yielding the waiting time for a coming request for floor x. It corresponds to the number of floors the lift has to pass (including the last one x) in order to reach floor x. For instance, next are the two functions corresponding to the lift being at floor 4 (in a building with 7 floors) and going either down or up as indicated:

$$f_4 = \{\, 7 \mapsto 9, \qquad\qquad g_4 = \{\, 7 \mapsto 3,$$
$$6 \mapsto 8, \qquad\qquad\qquad\quad 6 \mapsto 2,$$
$$5 \mapsto 7, \qquad\qquad\qquad\quad 5 \mapsto 1, \qquad \uparrow$$
$$4 \mapsto 6, \quad \boxed{lift} \qquad\qquad 4 \mapsto 6, \quad \boxed{lift}$$
$$3 \mapsto 1, \qquad \downarrow \qquad\qquad\quad 3 \mapsto 7,$$
$$2 \mapsto 2, \qquad\qquad\qquad\quad 2 \mapsto 8,$$
$$1 \mapsto 3 \,\} \qquad\qquad\qquad 1 \mapsto 9 \,\}$$

Next are the formal definitions of these two functions (notice that they are both injective from $1 \mathinner{.\,.} n$ to $\mathbb{N}_1$ as required):

$$f_4 \mathrel{\widehat{=}} \lambda x \cdot (x \in 1 \mathinner{.\,.} l_4 - 1 \mid l_4 - x) \,\cup\, \lambda x \cdot (x \in l_4 \mathinner{.\,.} n \mid l_4 + x - 2)$$
$$g_4 \mathrel{\widehat{=}} \lambda x \cdot (x \in l_4 + 1 \mathinner{.\,.} n \mid x - l_4) \,\cup\, \lambda x \cdot (x \in 1 \mathinner{.\,.} l_4 \mid 2n - (l_4 + x))$$

We put them together in a function h_4 parametrized by the direction of the lift:

$$h_4 \mathrel{\widehat{=}} \{\, down \mapsto f_4,\ up \mapsto g_4 \,\}$$

It remains for us to write our main invariant stating that w_4 is always included (because not all requests are present in general) in $h_4(d_4)$:

$$w_4 \subseteq h_4(d_4)$$

It is now very simple to propose the following refinement for **request**

request $\mathrel{\widehat{=}}$
  ANY y WHERE
    $y \in (1 \mathinner{.\,.} n) - \mathrm{dom}(w_4)$
  THEN
    $w_4 := w_4 \cup \{\, y \mapsto h_4(d_4)(y) \,\}$
  END

This can be fruitfully compared with its abstraction (clearly the witness for w is $h_4(d_4)(y)$):

```
request    ≙
    ANY y, w WHERE
        y ∈ (1 .. n) − dom(w₂)    ∧
        w ∈ ℕ₁ − ran(w₂)
    THEN
        w₂ := w₂ ∪ {y ↦ w}
    END
```

Next is the new version of the event **serve**

```
serve    ≙
    SELECT
        w₄ ≠ ∅
    THEN
    LET t BE
        t = min (ran (w₄))
    IN
        LET z BE
            z = w₄⁻¹(t)
        IN
            w₄ := (w₄ ▷ {t}) ; minus (t)    ‖
            l₄ := z    ‖
            IF z = n ∨ (z ≠ 1 ∧ l₄ > z) THEN
                d₄ := down
            ELSE
                d₄ := up
            END
        END
    END
END
```

It can be compared with its abstraction

```
serve    ≙
    SELECT
        w₂ ≠ ∅
    THEN
    LET t BE
        t = min(ran(w₂))
    IN
        w₂ := (w₂ ▷ {t}) ; minus(t)
    END
END
```

APPENDICES

In the following Appendices, we present a formal model of certain aspects of abstract systems. The rôle of this model is essentially to formalize the concept of "reachability" as described in the linguistic construct LEADSTO introduced in section 2.4 of the main text. In doing so, we shall be able to justify the proof obligations presented in the paper.

In Appendix **A1**, we recall the definition and main properties of conjunctive set transformers. In Appendix **A2**, we quickly present and define the main classical operators applicable to conjunctive set transformers. We recall that these operators maintain conjunctivity. In Appendix **A3**, we remind the definitions and main properties of the fixpoints of conjunctive set transformers. This allows us to introduce (in Appendix **A4**) more operators dealing with the concept of iteration. We show that these operators also maintain conjunctivity. We indicate how the least fixpoint of a conjunctive set transformer is connected with the "termination" of the iteration. In Appendices **A5** and **A6** we give more properties of the least fixpoint, properties supporting this notion of termination. In Appendix **A7** we define the notion of reachability of a certain set. This is based on the termination (fixpoint) of a certain conjunctive set transformer. In Appendix **A8**, we study how the "classical" refinement influences reachability. In Appendix **A9**, we study the main assumptions concerning the new events that may be introduced in the refinement of an abstract system. Finally, in Appendix **A10**, our study culminates with the refinement of reachability *in the presence of new events*.

A1. Conjunctive Set Transformers

The events of an abstract system are formally described by means of conjunctive set transformers (see B-Book in section 6.4.2). Let F be such a set transformer built on a set s (this is the "state" of our abstract system). We have thus:

$$F \in \mathbb{P}(s) \to \mathbb{P}(s) \tag{1}$$

In what follows, we shall make the frequent abuse of language consisting in identifying an event with its set transformer. Given a subset p of s, the set $F(p)$ denotes, as we know, the largest subset of s in which we have to be, in order for the "event" formalized by F to "terminate" in a state belonging to p.

The conjunctivity property of our set transformer F is defined as follows for each non-empty set σ of subsets of s:

$$F\left(\bigcap_{t \in \sigma} t\right) = \bigcap_{t \in \sigma} F(t) \tag{2}$$

When specialized to a set σ with two elements, the above condition reduces to the following where p and q are two subsets of s:

$$F(p \cap q) = F(p) \cap F(q) \tag{3}$$

This means that if we want to terminate within both sets p and q, we better start from within both sets $F(p)$ and $F(q)$. A simple consequence of this property is that our set transformer is *monotone*. That is, for any two subsets p and q of s, we have

$$p \subseteq q \Rightarrow F(p) \subseteq F(q) \tag{4}$$

We now define the, so-called, termination set, $\mathsf{pre}(F)$, of F as follows (see B-Book, property 6.4.9):

$$\mathsf{pre}(F) \;\widehat{=}\; F(s) \tag{5}$$

According to this definition, the set $\mathsf{pre}(F)$ thus denotes the largest set in which we have to be in order for the event F to "terminate" in a state belonging to s. As "belonging to s" is not adding any constraints on the outcome, the set $\mathsf{pre}(F)$ then just denotes the set where we have to be for the event F to simply "terminate". In what follows, we shall suppose (unless otherwise stated) that our termination set is always equal to s itself, that is

$$F(s) = s \tag{6}$$

We now present the, so called, before-after relation, $\mathsf{rel}(F)$, associated with F (see B-Book, property 6.4.9). When a pair (x, x') belongs to this relation, this means that the event F is able to transform the state x into the state x'. It is defined indirectly by means of the image of a subset p of s under $\mathsf{rel}(F)^{-1}$:

$$\mathsf{rel}(F)^{-1}[p] \;\widehat{=}\; \overline{F(\overline{p})} \tag{7}$$

In what follows we shall use the letter f to denote the relation $\mathsf{rel}(F)$. The domain, $\mathsf{dom}(f)$, of the relation f is called the *guard*, $\mathsf{grd}(F)$, of the set transformer F. We have thus:

$$\mathsf{grd}(F) = \mathsf{dom}(f) = f^{-1}[s] = \overline{F(\emptyset)} \tag{8}$$

A2. Operations on Conjunctive Set Transformers

We now present the classical operations applicable to conjunctive set transformers. This is done in the following table, where F, F_1, F_2 and F_z are conjunctive set transformers built on a certain set s, where p is a subset of s, and t is a set:

Identity	skip_s
Pre-conditioning	$p \mid F$
Guarding	$p \Longrightarrow F$
Bounded choice	$F_1 \, [] \, F_2$
Unbounded choice	$[]_{z \in t} \, F_z$
Sequencing	$F_1 \, ; \, F_2$

Notice that in the B-Book the operators ($\mid$, $\Longrightarrow$, etc) were supposed to work with predicates and predicate transformers (generalized substitutions). Here they are rather applied to sets and set transformers. This slight shift in the notation leads, we think, to a certain simplification of the formal presentation.

We have the following definitions yielding the values of the above set transformer constructions for a given subset q of s:

$\text{skip}_s(q)$	q
$(p \mid F)(q)$	$p \cap F(q)$
$(p \Longrightarrow F)(q)$	$\bar{p} \cup F(q)$
$(F_1 \, [] \, F_2)(q)$	$F_1(q) \cap F_2(q)$
$([]_{z \in t} \, F_z)(q)$	$\bigcap_{z \in t} F_z(q)$
$(F_1 \, ; \, F_2)(q)$	$F_1(F_2(q))$

It is easy to prove that each of the above operation transforms conjunctive set transformers into other conjunctive set transformers.

A3. Fixpoints of Conjunctive Set Transformers

As we shall use them in the sequel, we remind in this Appendix the definition and main properties of the fixpoints of conjunctive set transformers. Let $\text{fix}(F)$ and $\text{FIX}(F)$ be defined as follows:

$$\text{fix}(F) = \bigcap \{ p \mid p \subseteq s \land F(p) \subseteq p \} \tag{9}$$

$$\text{FIX}(F) = \bigcup \{ p \mid p \subseteq s \land p \subseteq F(p) \} \tag{10}$$

Since F is monotone according to (4), then these definitions indeed lead (Tarski) to fixpoints, that is:

$$F(\text{fix}(F)) = \text{fix}(F) \tag{11}$$

$$F(\text{FIX}(F)) = \text{FIX}(F) \tag{12}$$

From (9) and (10) , we can easily deduce the following, which is valid for any subset p of s:

$$F(p) \subseteq p \;\Rightarrow\; \text{fix}(F) \subseteq p \tag{13}$$

$$p \subseteq F(p) \;\Rightarrow\; p \subseteq \text{FIX}(F) \tag{14}$$

These laws will be useful to prove certain properties involving the fixpoints. For instance, from them it is easy to prove that $\text{fix}(F)$ and $\text{FIX}(F)$ are indeed respectively the least and greatest fixpoints of F. So that we have

$$\text{fix}(F) \subseteq \text{FIX}(F) \tag{15}$$

A4. More Operations on Conjunctive Set Transformers: Iterates

We are now ready to present more operations on conjunctive set transformers. They are all dealing with some form of iteration. This concept is important in our framework since the formal behavior of an abstract system (with events) is intuitively formalized by all the possible iterations one is able to perform with these events. Such operations are introduced in the following table, where F is a conjunctive set transformer, and n is natural number:

nth iterate	F^n
Closure	F°
Opening	$F^{\,\hat{}}$

The nth iterate is defined recursively as follows:

F^0	skip_s
F^{n+1}	$F \; ; \; F^n$

The values of the other two at the subset q of s are defined as follows:

$F^\circ(q)$	$\text{FIX}(q \mid F)$
$F^\wedge(q)$	$\text{fix}(q \mid F)$

The intuitive rationale behind these definitions will appear in the sequel. For the moment, let us just see what kind of property we can derive from these *fixpoint* definitions. Concerning F°, we deduce the following, supposed to be valid for any subset q of s:

$$F^\circ(q)$$
$$=$$
$$(q \mid F)(F^\circ(q))$$
$$=$$
$$q \cap F(F^\circ(q))$$
$$=$$
$$\text{skip}_s(q) \cap (F \; ; \; F^\circ)(q)$$
$$=$$
$$(\text{skip}_s \, [] \, (F \; ; \; F^\circ))(q)$$

As this development could have been performed on $F^\wedge$ as well, we have thus:

$$F^\circ = \text{skip}_s \; [] \; (F \; ; \; F^\circ) \tag{16}$$

$$F^\wedge = \text{skip}_s \; [] \; (F \; ; \; F^\wedge) \tag{17}$$

We have obtained the classical unfolding properties. Clearly, such properties show the iteration at work. More precisely, by developing these equations, we obtain something like this:

$$F^\circ = \text{skip}_s \; [] \; F \; [] \; F^2 \; [] \; \cdots \tag{18}$$

$$F^\wedge = \text{skip}_s \; [] \; F \; [] \; F^2 \; [] \; \cdots \tag{19}$$

It seems then that the two are indeed the same. This would be a wrong conclusion in general: in fact the "$\cdots$" are, as usual, misleading. F°, being defined by a greatest fixpoint, denotes a kind of infinite object, whereas $F^{\hat{}}$ contains some finiteness requirement in its definition. In fact, the conjunctivity of F allows one to prove the following:

$$F^{\circ} = \bigcap_{n \in \mathcal{N}} F^{n} \qquad (20)$$

$$F^{\hat{}} = \text{fix}(F) \mid F^{\circ} \qquad (21)$$

Equality (20) is easily shown by first proving $F^{\circ}(q) \subseteq F^{n}(q)$ for any natural number n. This is done by mathematical induction. From this, $F^{\circ}(q) \subseteq (\bigcap_{n \in \mathcal{N}} F^{n})(q)$ follows immediately. Then the second part of (20), namely $(\bigcap_{n \in \mathcal{N}} F^{n})(q) \subseteq F^{\circ}(q)$, is proved using (14) and (2). Equality (21) is essentially Theorem 9.2.1 of the B-Book.

As can be seen on (20), F° just denotes all the possible iterations without any direct concerns about termination. On the other hand, as can be seen on (21), $F^{\hat{}}$ is exactly F° together with the fundamental *termination requirement* that one has to start the iterations from within $\text{fix}(F)$. Consequently, as we shall see in the next Appendix, no iteration started in $\text{fix}(F)$ *can be pursued indefinitely*: we shall necessarily *reach* some points where we cannot move further.

From the definition of the termination set of a set transformer, we deduce easily (B-Book sections 9.1.3 and 9.2.4) the following (since $F(s) = s$):

$$\text{pre}(F^{n}) = s \qquad (22)$$

$$\text{pre}(F^{\circ}) = s \qquad (23)$$

$$\text{pre}(F^{\hat{}}) = \text{fix}(F) \qquad (24)$$

The set $\text{fix}(F)$ thus represents the set from which one has to start in order for the iterate $F^{\hat{}}$ to *terminate*.

The before-after relation of this iterators can be calculated easily (B-Book sections 9.1.3 and 9.2.4). We obtain (since $F(s) = s$) the following:

$$\text{rel}(F^{n}) = f^{n} \qquad (25)$$

$$\text{rel}(F^{\circ}) = f^{*} \qquad (26)$$

$$\text{rel}(F^{\hat{}}) = \overline{\text{fix}(F)} \times s \cup f^{*} \qquad (27)$$

where f^{*} denotes the transitive and reflexive closure of f. Notice that in case $\text{fix}(F)$ is equal to s then $\text{rel}(F^{\hat{}})$ is exactly f^{*}.

Finally, we can prove by mathematical induction that, for each natural number n, F^{n} is conjunctive. From this and from (20) and (21) it follows that F° and $F^{\hat{}}$ are also conjunctive.

A5. A Property of the Least Fixpoint of a Conjunctive Set Transformer

We now prove that $\text{fix}(F)$ only contains *finite chains* of points related by the before-after relation f. This finiteness of the chains built within $\text{fix}(F)$ nicely supports the idea that we cannot "run" for ever by iterating F from a point of $\text{fix}(F)$. The proof is by contradiction. We suppose that there exists a non-empty subset c of $\text{fix}(F)$, that is

$$c \neq \emptyset \ \wedge \ c \subseteq \text{fix}(F) \tag{28}$$

such that each element of c participates in an infinite chain (included in c) relative to the before-after relation f. Under these assumptions, we are going to prove now that c is necessarily *empty*. This contradiction indicates that there is no such set c, thus $\text{fix}(F)$ only contains finite chains.

By definition, for any element x of c, we are sure that there is an element y of c such that x and y are related through f. Thus starting from x we can continue for ever following f while remaining in c. We have thus, by definition

$$\forall x \cdot (x \in c \ \Rightarrow \ \exists y \cdot (y \in c \ \wedge \ (x, y) \in f)) \tag{29}$$

That is, equivalently (by set contraposition and according to (29))

$$c \subseteq f^{-1}[c] \quad \Leftrightarrow \quad \overline{f^{-1}[c]} \subseteq \overline{c} \quad \Leftrightarrow \quad F(\overline{c}) \subseteq \overline{c} \tag{30}$$

Consequently, we have (according to (13))

$$\text{fix}(F) \subseteq \overline{c} \tag{31}$$

According to (28), (31) and the transitivity of set inclusion, it turns out that we have $c \subseteq \overline{c}$, thus $c = \emptyset$.

A6. Property of the Finite Chains of the Fixpoint

In this Appendix, we prove that all the finite chains of $\text{fix}(F)$ end up in $\text{dom}(f)$. This property will be exploited in the next Appendix.

Since $\text{fix}(F)$ is a fixpoint, we have $F(\text{fix}(F)) = \text{fix}(F)$. Consequently, we also have $\text{fix}(F) \subseteq F(\text{fix}(F))$. Thus $\text{fix}(F)$ is *invariant* under F. In other words, when, from any point x of $\text{fix}(F)$, we follow the before-after relation f, we stay within $\text{fix}(F)$.

As we have seen in Appendix A5, we have no infinite chain within $\text{fix}(F)$. That is, if we start from a point x_1 of $\text{fix}(F)$, choosing *any* point x_2 of $f[\{x_1\}]$ (x_2 is thus in $\text{fix}(F)$), then *any* point x_3 in $f[\{x_2\}]$ (x_3 is thus in $\text{fix}(F)$), and so on, we necessarily reach a certain point x_n of $\text{fix}(F)$ where we cannot move further because $f[\{x_n\}]$ is empty. In other words, we *eventually* reach a point lying outside the domain of f, a point of $\overline{\text{dom}(f)}$. In conclusion, all the chains of $\text{fix}(F)$ are finite and end up in $\overline{\text{dom}(f)}$.

In order to be sure that an iteration $F^\frown$ *always* terminate (whatever its point of departure) and reaches eventually $\overline{\text{dom}(f)}$, it is thus necessary and sufficient to prove that $\text{fix}(F)$ is equal to s. It is well known (see B-Book at section 9.2.8) that for proving this, it is sufficient to show that F "decreases" a certain natural number expression. More generally, it is sufficient to prove that F "decreases" a certain quantity whose value belongs to a set that is well-founded by a certain relation.

Notice that $F^\frown$ not only reaches $\overline{\mathrm{dom}(f)}$ when it terminates but also the various elements obtained after executing skip_s, F, F^2, and so on. In order to reach exactly the elements of $\overline{\mathrm{grd}(F)}$, it is necessary to only keep those points lying within $\mathrm{grd}(F)$. This can be done by means of the following set transformer:

$$F^\frown \; ; \; (\overline{\mathrm{grd}(F)} \Longrightarrow \mathrm{skip}_s) \qquad\qquad (32)$$

This is just Dijkstra's "do F od" command and also a special form of the WHILE construct introduced in the B-Book in section 9.2.1. However, as far as termination is concerned, both $F^\frown$ and $F^\frown \; ; \; (\overline{\mathrm{grd}(F)} \Longrightarrow \mathrm{skip}_s)$ have the same termination set, namely $\mathrm{fix}(F)$.

A7. Reachability of any Set

Notice that, most of the time, an abstract system, whose events are collectively formalized by a conjunctive set transformer F, *does not terminate*. In general, such systems are constructed to run for ever. Resisting to failures that would force them to stop, is even one of their main requirements. One might then ask why we insisted so much in the preceding Appendices on this question of the *termination* of the iteration $F^\frown$ since, clearly, the corresponding termination set, namely $\mathrm{fix}(F)$, is in general empty. In what follows, we shall clarify this point.

Since an abstract system is supposed to run for ever, it cannot be characterized by a, so-called, *final* state that it is supposed to reach eventually. This contrasts with the classical view of a computer program supposed to deliver a certain *final result*. The validation of such a program is ensured by means of a proof establishing that the specified outcome is indeed reached. If such a program is formalized by means of a conjunctive set transformer S together with a termination set p (also called the *pre-condition* set), and if the outcome is characterized by a certain subset q, then proving $p \subseteq S(q)$ means that, provided we start the program within p, then we are sure to obtain the outcome characterized by q. In a sense, a terminating program S is entirely characterized by all the possible *permanent outcomes* (such as q) we can think of.

By analogy with a program, an ever running system might be entirely characterized by all the possible *temporary outcomes* we can think of (this is a thesis). In other words, reaching one of these outcomes is not synonymous with system stop as for a program. Such an outcome might be abandoned when the system proceeds further. But what must be proved is that such an outcome can be reached as often as possible, so that it is not the case that one is *always* outside it. Given a subset p of s (the temporary outcome in question), we study thus in this Appendix the notion of *reachability* of that set. And this is where the concept of termination will reappear.

We are interested in characterizing the subset of s, from which we have to start, in order to be certain to temporarily (but eventually) reach p by following the before-after relation f of the set transformer F defined as above. The idea is to put (just for the reasoning) a supplementary constraint on the events F in the form of the extra guard $\overline{p}$. We are then led to prove that the set transformer

$(\overline{p} \Longrightarrow F)\hat{\ }$ indeed terminates. In other words, allowing the system to proceed only when it is outside p, forces it to stop (hopefully thus in a state that is within p). If we want this to be always the case then we have to prove that the set $\mathsf{fix}(\overline{p} \Longrightarrow F)$ is equal to s. More precisely, we have to prove that the following set transformer does terminate:

$$(\overline{p} \Longrightarrow F)\hat{\ } \ ; \ (p \Longrightarrow \mathsf{skip}_s) \tag{33}$$

This set transformer is exactly (see B-Book in section 9.2.1):

$$\text{WHILE } \overline{p} \text{ DO } F \text{ END} \tag{34}$$

This leads to the proof obligations (PO_3) and (PO_4) presented in section 2.4. Nothing proves however that we have reached p (we only know that we have stopped at points that are outside the guard of $\overline{p} \Longrightarrow F$). In fact, we shall prove that in order to reach p we need the extra condition: $\overline{p} \subseteq \mathsf{dom}(f)$. We thus consider the set transformer $\overline{p} \Longrightarrow F$ whose definition is (for any subset q of s):

$$(\overline{p} \Longrightarrow F)(q) = p \cup F(q) \tag{35}$$

The guard of this set transformer can be calculated as follows:

$$\mathsf{grd}(\overline{p} \Longrightarrow F) = \overline{(\overline{p} \Longrightarrow F)(\emptyset)} = \overline{p \cup F(\emptyset)} = \overline{p} \cap \overline{F(\emptyset)} = \overline{p} \cap \mathsf{dom}(f)$$

As a consequence and according to what has been done above in Appendices **A5** and **A6**, the set $\mathsf{fix}(\overline{p} \Longrightarrow F)$ denotes exactly the set of points from which one can eventually reach the set $p \cup \overline{\mathsf{dom}(f)}$ by following the before-after relation of $\overline{p} \Longrightarrow F$ (this is $\overline{p} \lhd f$). If we want to be certain to reach p, it is thus sufficient to require that $\overline{\mathsf{dom}(f)}$ is included in p, that is, alternatively:

$$\overline{p} \subseteq \mathsf{dom}(f) \tag{36}$$

This corresponds to the last proof obligations of (PO_3) and (PO_4) obtained in section 2.4.

A8. Refining the Reachability Condition

In this Appendix, we shall study the problem of the refinement of the reachability studied in the preceding Appendix. We shall thus consider that the set transformer F, defined as above, is now *refined* to a certain set transformer G built on a set t, that is:

$$G \in \mathbb{P}(t) \to \mathbb{P}(t) \tag{37}$$

We also suppose that the termination set of G is trivial, that is:

$$G(t) = t \tag{38}$$

This refinement is performed by means of a certain total refinement relation r from t to s:

$$r \in t \leftrightarrow s \ \wedge \ \mathsf{dom}(r) = t \tag{39}$$

The set transformer F is said to be refined by G by means of the refinement relation r when the following condition holds between their respective before-after relations f and g, and between their termination sets (see B-Book in section 11.2.4)

$$r^{-1} \; ; g \subseteq f \; ; r^{-1} \tag{40}$$

$$r^{-1}[\mathsf{pre}(F)] \subseteq \mathsf{pre}(G) \tag{41}$$

Notice that condition (41) holds trivially. This is because we supposed that $\mathsf{pre}(F)$ is equal to s (this is condition (6)), thus $r^{-1}[\mathsf{pre}(F)]$ is equal to $\mathsf{dom}(r)$, that is t (since r is total according to (39)), which is certainly included in $\mathsf{pre}(G)$ since $\mathsf{pre}(G)$ is equal, by definition, to $G(t)$, which was supposed to be equal to t (this is (38)).

The set p whose reachability was studied in the previous Appendix is now transformed into the set $r^{-1}[p]$ (the image of p through r^{-1}). So that the reachability of $r^{-1}[p]$ will now be ensured within the termination set of the set transformer $(r^{-1}[p] \Longrightarrow G)\hat{\ }$. What remains to be proved is that the reachability of p in the abstraction indeed ensures that of $r^{-1}[p]$ in the concrete world. For this, we first have to prove that $r^{-1}[p] \Longrightarrow G$ is a refinement of $\overline{p} \Longrightarrow F$. Formally, we have to prove (under the conditions (38) and (39)):

$$r^{-1} \; ; (\overline{r^{-1}[p]} \lhd g) \subseteq (\overline{p} \lhd f) \; ; r^{-1} \tag{42}$$

This proof is left to the (favorite theorem prover of the) reader. A consequence of this refinement is that the iterate $(\overline{p} \Longrightarrow F)\hat{\ }$ is refined to the iterate $(\overline{r^{-1}[p]} \Longrightarrow G)\hat{\ }$ (according to the monotonicity of refinement with respect to opening, see B-Book section 11.2.4). From this, we can deduce (again B-Book section 11.2.4) that the image of the termination set of $(\overline{p} \Longrightarrow F)\hat{\ }$ is included into the termination set of $(\overline{r^{-1}[p]} \Longrightarrow G)\hat{\ }$, that is

$$r^{-1}[\mathsf{fix}(\overline{p} \Longrightarrow F)] \subseteq \mathsf{fix}(\overline{r^{-1}[p]} \Longrightarrow G) \tag{43}$$

As we know (according to Appendix A6), the finite chains of $\mathsf{fix}(\overline{r^{-1}[p]} \Longrightarrow G)$ all end up in the set $r^{-1}[p] \cup \mathsf{dom}(g)$. In order for the concrete set $r^{-1}[p]$ to be reached, we have to prove that $\mathsf{dom}(g)$ is included in $r^{-1}[p]$, alternatively $\overline{r^{-1}[p]} \subseteq \mathsf{dom}(g)$. In order to ensure that this is the case, we claim that it is sufficient to have the following extra condition:

$$r[\overline{\mathsf{dom}(g)}] \subseteq \overline{\mathsf{dom}(f)} \tag{44}$$

It then remains for us to prove the following (notice that we have supposed condition (36) stating that the set p is indeed reached by the repeated execution of $\overline{p} \Longrightarrow F$):

$$\overline{p} \subseteq \mathsf{dom}(f) \ \wedge \ r[\overline{\mathsf{dom}(g)}] \subseteq \overline{\mathsf{dom}(f)} \ \Rightarrow \ \overline{r^{-1}[p]} \subseteq \mathsf{dom}(g) \tag{45}$$

The proof of (45) is left to the (favorite theorem prover of the) reader (you will notice that the hypothesis concerning the totality of the refinement relation r is fundamental).

Condition (44) can be transformed equivalently as follows, by set contraposition:

$$\text{dom}(f) \subseteq \overline{r[\overline{\text{dom}(g)}]} \tag{46}$$

A9. Formal Hypotheses and Results concerning the New Events

In the next Appendix, we are going to study the problem of reachability of a certain set p when the set transformer F is refined to a concrete set transformer G by means of a certain refinement relation r, as it was studied in Appendix **A8**, except that this time we shall suppose that we have some extra events formalized by a set transformer H refining skip$_s$ and "terminating".

In this Appendix, we are going to formalize the relevant hypotheses concerning such new events and establish a simple result about them. More precisely, all our extra events are together formalized by means of a set transformer H defined on the set t as is G in (37):

$$H \in \mathbb{P}(t) \to \mathbb{P}(t) \tag{47}$$

We also suppose, as usual that $H(t)$ is equal to t. The before-after relation rel(H) associated with H is h. Since H is supposed to refine skip$_s$ by means of the refinement relation r, we have thus the following, as a special case of the condition (40):

$$r^{-1} \,;\, h \subseteq r^{-1} \tag{48}$$

Moreover, we suppose that $H\hat{}$ always "terminates", this is formalized by stating that the fixpoint of H is exactly the set t:

$$\text{fix}(H) = t \tag{49}$$

This is ensured in the main text by the proof obligation (PO_1). From this, we shall now prove that $H\hat{}$ indeed refines skip$_s$. The refinement condition to be proved (see B-Book page 520) reduces to:

$$r^{-1} \,;\, h^* \subseteq r^{-1} \tag{50}$$

For proving this it suffices to prove the following for any natural number n (since h^* is equal to $\bigcup_{n \in \mathcal{N}} h^n$)):

$$r^{-1} \,;\, h^n \subseteq r^{-1} \tag{51}$$

This can easily be proved by mathematical induction, using (48). By extension, it is easy to prove that the set transformer $(r^{-1}[p] \implies H)\hat{}$ also refines skip$_s$.

A10. Refining the Reachability Condition in the Presence of New Events

In this Appendix, we shall prove the central result of our study. It essentially says that, *as far as reachability is concerned*, a set transformer F can be "simulated" by the set transformer $G \, [] \, H$ where G refines F, and where the set transformer H (as described in Appendix **A9**) formalizes the new events refining skip$_s$.

We have written "simulated" rather than "refined". In fact, the simple set transformer $\overline{r^{-1}[p]} \implies (G \,[]\, H)$ does *not* refine $\overline{p} \implies F$. What we shall prove is that $(\overline{r^{-1}[p]} \implies (G \,[]\, H))\hat{\ }$ refines $(\overline{p} \implies F)\hat{\ }$. In other words, the *repeated* "execution" of $\overline{p} \implies F$ is refined by the repeated "execution" of $\overline{r^{-1}[p]} \implies (G \,[]\, H)$. The new events, formalized by H, do not induce any spoiling side effects on the *global* behavior of our system.

Let us define F', G' and H' as follows:

$$F' \mathrel{\hat{=}} \overline{p} \implies F \tag{52}$$

$$G' \mathrel{\hat{=}} \overline{r^{-1}[p]} \implies G \tag{53}$$

$$H' \mathrel{\hat{=}} \overline{r^{-1}[p]} \implies H \tag{54}$$

We have thus to prove that $F'\hat{\ }$ is refined by $(G'[]H')\hat{\ }$ by means of the refinement relation r. For this, we shall first observe that clearly $F'\hat{\ }$ is refined by $(H'\hat{\ } \; ; \; G')\hat{\ } \; ; \; H'\hat{\ }$ by means of the refinement relation r. This is because G' refines F' (Appendix **A3**) and $H'\hat{\ }$ refines skip$_s$ (Appendix **A4**) both by means of the refinement relation r, and also because of the monotonicity of refinement under the operators ";" and "$\hat{\ }$" (see B-Book section 11.2.4). It then just remains for us to prove that $(H'\hat{\ } \; ; \; G')\hat{\ } \; ; \; H'\hat{\ }$ is (algorithmically) refined by $(G' \,[]\, H')\hat{\ }$, since the transitivity of refinement thus ensures that $F'\hat{\ }$ is refined by $(G' \,[]\, H')\hat{\ }$. For proving this, we have to show (B-Book section 11.1.2) that for any subset a of t, we have:

$$((H'\hat{\ } \; ; \; G')\hat{\ } \; ; \; H'\hat{\ })(a) \subseteq (G' \,[]\, H')\hat{\ }(a) \tag{55}$$

that is

$$(H'\hat{\ } \; ; \; G')\hat{\ }(H'\hat{\ }(a)) \subseteq (G' \,[]\, H')\hat{\ }(a) \tag{56}$$

that is equivalently

$$\mathsf{fix}(H'\hat{\ }(a) \mid (H'\hat{\ } \; ; \; G')) \subseteq \mathsf{fix}(a \mid (G' \,[]\, H')) \tag{57}$$

Let q be defined as follows

$$q \mathrel{\hat{=}} \mathsf{fix}(a \mid (G' \,[]\, H')) \tag{58}$$

In order to prove (57), it is sufficient to prove the following (B-Book section 3.2.2):

$$H'\hat{\ }(a) \cap (H'\hat{\ } \; ; \; G')(q) \subseteq q \tag{59}$$

that is

$$H'\hat{\ }(a) \cap H'\hat{\ }(G'(q)) \subseteq q \tag{60}$$

that is (since $H'\hat{\ }$ is conjunctive))

$$H'\hat{\ }(a \cap G'(q)) \subseteq q \tag{61}$$

For this it is sufficient to prove (again B-Book section 3.2.2)

$$a \cap G'(q) \cap H'(q) \subseteq q \tag{62}$$

which is obvious since $q = a \cap G'(q) \cap H'(q)$ according to (58).

We have eventually proved that $(\overline{p} \Longrightarrow F)\hat{}$ is refined by $(r^{-1}[p] \Longrightarrow G[\,]H)\hat{}$. As above in Appendix **A8**, we now have to find the condition under which the set $r^{-1}[p]$ is reached. By an argument that is very similar to the one developed in Appendix **A8**, this condition is an extension of condition (46)

$$\mathrm{dom}(f) \subseteq \overline{r[\overline{\mathrm{dom}(g) \cup \mathrm{dom}(h)}]} \tag{63}$$

yielding

$$\forall (x,y) \cdot ((y,x) \in r \;\Rightarrow\; (x \in \mathrm{dom}(f) \;\Rightarrow\; y \in \mathrm{dom}(g) \vee y \in \mathrm{dom}(h))) \tag{64}$$

This is essentially a formal setting of the proof obligation **PO_5** presented in the main text.

Acknowledgments: We thank D. Méry, L. Lamport, M. Butler, and B. Legeard and his colleagues for a number of discussions and comments.

References

1. J.-R. Abrial. *The B-Book: Assigning Programs to Meanings.* Cambridge University Press (1996)
2. J.-R. Abrial. *Extending B Without Changing it (for Developing Distributed Systems).* First B Conference (H. Habrias editor). Nantes (1996)
3. J.-R. Abrial and L. Mussat. *Specification and Design of a Transmission Protocol by Successive Refinements Using B.* in *Mathematical Methods in Program Development* Edited by M.Broy and B. Schieder. Springer-Verlag (1997)
4. K.R. Apt and E.-R. Olderog. *Proof Rules and Transformations Dealing with Fairness.* Science of Computer Programming (1983)
5. R.J.R. Back and R. Kurki-Suonio. *Decentralization of Process Nets with Centralized Control.* 2nd ACM SIGACT-SIGOPS Symp. on Principles of Distributed Computing (1983)
6. M.J. Butler. *Stepwise Refinement of Communicating Systems.* Science of Computer Programming (1996)
7. K.M. Chandy and J. Misra. *Parallel Program Design: A Foundation.* Addison-Wesley (1988)
8. I.J. Hayes (editor). *Specification Case Study.* Prentice-Hall (1987)
9. C.A.R. Hoare. *Communicating Sequential Processes.* Prentice-Hall (1985)
10. L. Lamport. *The Temporal Logic of Actions.* SRC Report 57 (1991)
11. Z. Manna and A. Pnueli. *Adequate Proof Principles for Invariance and Liveness Properties of Concurrent Systems.* Science of Computer Programming (1984)
12. A. Udaya Shankar *An Introduction to Assertional Reasoning for Concurrent Systems.* ACM Computing Survey (1993)
13. Steria. *Atelier B Version 3.3.* (1997)

Retrenchment: An Engineering Variation on Refinement

R. Banach[a], M. Poppleton[a,b]

[a]Computer Science Dept., Manchester University, Manchester, M13 9PL, U.K.
[b]School of Mathl. and Inf. Sciences, Coventry University, Coventry, CV1 5FB, U.K.

banach@cs.man.ac.uk , m.r.poppleton@coventry.ac.uk

Abstract: It is argued that refinement, in which I/O signatures stay the same, preconditions are weakened and postconditions strengthened, is too restrictive to describe all but a fraction of many realistic developments. An alternative notion is proposed called retrenchment, which allows information to migrate between I/O and state aspects of operations at different levels of abstraction, and which allows only a fraction of the high level behaviour to be captured at the low level. This permits more of the informal aspects of design to be formally captured and checked. The details are worked out for the B-Method.

1 Idealised and Realistic Modelling: The Inadequacy of Pure Refinement

Like all good examples of terminology, the word "refinement" is far too evocative for its use ever to have been confined to exactly one concept. Even within the formal methods community, the word is used in at least two distinct senses. The first is a strict sense. An operation O_C is a refinement of an operation O_A iff the precondition of O_C is weaker than the precondition of O_A and the relation of O_C is less nondeterministic than the relation of O_A. The well known refinement calculus [Back (1981), Back (1988), Back and von Wright (1989), von Wright (1994), Morris (1987), Morgan (1990)] captures this in a formal system within which one can calculate precisely.

However there is a second, much less strict use of the word. In formalisms such as Z or VDM [Spivey (1993), Hayes (1993), Jones (1990), Jones and Shaw (1990)], requirements are frequently captured at a high level of abstraction, often involving for instance *divine* natural numbers or *divine* real numbers[1], and neglecting whole rafts of detail not appropriate to a high level view, in order that the reader of the high level description "can see the wood for the trees". Such descriptions are then "refined" to lower levels of abstraction where the missing details are filled in, typically yielding longer, more tortuous and much less transparent but much more realistic definitions of the system in question. Indeed the complexity of such descriptions can often be comparable to or greater than that of their implementations, a fact cited by detractors of formal methods as undermining the value of formal methods themselves, though this seems to us to be like denigrating stereoscopic vision because the image seen by the left eye is of comparable complexity to that seen by the right.

In truth the world is a complex place and developing descriptions of some part of it in two distinct but reconcilable formalisms (the specification and implementation), rather

---

1. By *divine* naturals, integers or reals, we mean the natural numbers, integers or real numbers that God made, abstract and infinite, in contrast to the finite discrete approximations that we are able to implement on any real world system. The latter we call *mundane* natural numbers, integers or real numbers.

than just one, is always likely to help rather than hinder, even if the "more abstract" description is not significantly simpler than the other. (For an entertaining example of the undue weight attatched to the brevity of descriptions see Fig. 16.2 of [Wand and Milner (1996)].)

In this paper we address the main problem posed by the second use of the "refinement" word, namely that there is not a refinement relationship in the strict sense between the idealised high level specification, and the "real" but lower level specification. We will use the B framework throughout the paper, but will frequently pretend that B contains many more liberal types, à la Z or VDM , than it actually does. For instance we will assume available to us divine types such as D-NAT , D-INT , D-REAL as well as their mundane counterparts M-NAT , M-INT , M-FLOAT ; we can identify M-NAT with the normal B type of NAT .

Let us illustrate with a small example, namely addition. In negotiating the requirement for a proprietary operation with a customer we might write:

$$
\begin{array}{ll}
\text{MACHINE} & \textit{My\_Divine\_Machine} \\
\text{VARIABLES} & \textit{aa , bb , cc} \\
\text{INVARIANT} & \textit{aa} \in \text{D-NAT} \wedge \textit{bb} \in \text{D-NAT} \wedge \textit{cc} \in \text{D-NAT} \\
& \ldots\ldots \\
\text{OPERATIONS} & \\
& \textit{MyPlus} \;\hat{=}\; \textit{cc} := \textit{aa} + \textit{bb} \text{ ;} \\
& \ldots\ldots
\end{array}
$$

In D-NAT , the + operation is the familiar one given by (say) the Peano axioms for addition, and is an ideal and infinite operation, making *MyPlus* equally ideal, but allowing us to see the essence of what is required. Having assured ourselves and the customer that we were on the right lines, we would want to describe more precisely what we could achieve, writing say:

$$
\begin{array}{ll}
\text{MACHINE} & \textit{My\_Mundane\_Machine} \\
& \ldots\ldots \\
\text{VARIABLES} & \textit{aaa , bbb , ccc} \\
\text{INVARIANT} & \textit{aaa} \in \text{M-NAT} \wedge \textit{bbb} \in \text{M-NAT} \wedge \textit{ccc} \in \text{M-NAT} \\
& \ldots\ldots \\
\text{OPERATIONS} & \\
& \textit{resp} \longleftarrow \textit{MyPlus} \;\hat{=} \\
& \quad \text{IF} \\
& \qquad \textit{aaa} + \textit{bbb} \leq \textit{MaxNum} \\
& \quad \text{THEN} \\
& \qquad \textit{ccc} := \textit{aaa} + \textit{bbb} \parallel \\
& \qquad \textit{resp} := \textit{TRUE} \\
& \quad \text{ELSE} \\
& \qquad \textit{resp} := \textit{FALSE} \\
& \quad \text{END ;} \\
& \ldots\ldots
\end{array}
$$

My_Mundane_Machine could never be a refinement of *My_Divine_Machine* . Partly this is for trivial syntactic reasons, eg. we would have to write REFINEMENT *My_Mundane_Machine* REFINES *My_Divine_Machine* .... Apart from that, there are three further important issues. Firstly the INVARIANT of the more concrete machine does not contain any refinement relation that would relate the abstract and concrete variables. This could easily be fixed if we were to write in the concrete INVARIANT say:

INVARIANT $aaa \in$ M-NAT $\wedge$ $bbb \in$ M-NAT $\wedge$ $ccc \in$ M-NAT $\wedge$
                  $aa = aaa \wedge bb = bbb \wedge cc = ccc$

assuming the obvious theory that allowed the identification of the mundane naturals as a subset of the divine ones. Secondly the signatures of *MyPlus* in the two machines are different; this is not allowed in normal notions of refinement. Thirdly, since not all divine naturals are refined to mundane ones, the standard proof obligation of refinement:

$$PA_{A,C} \wedge INV_A \wedge INV_C \wedge \text{trm}(MyPlus_A)$$
$$\Rightarrow \text{trm}(MyPlus_C) \wedge [MyPlus_C] \neg [MyPlus_A] \neg INV_C$$

cannot possibly be satisfied, as the *aaa + bbb > MaxNum* situation yields incompatible answers in the divine and mundane cases. (In the preceding the A and C subscripts refer to abstract and concrete respectively, $\text{trm}(S)$ is the predicate under which operation S is guaranteed to terminate, and $PA_{A,C}$ is the usual collection of clauses about the parameters and constants of the two machines).

The latter two reasons in particular show that the primary motivation for classical refinement, i.e. that the user should not be able to tell the difference between using the abstract or concrete version of an operation, does not hold sway here. What we are doing is adding real world detail to a description in a disciplined manner in order to aid understandability, not performing an implementation sleight of hand that we do not intend the user to notice.

Sometimes the process of adding detail can nevertheless be captured, albeit perhaps inelegantly, within the classical notion of refinement. For example the following would be a valid refinement if D-NAT were a valid type in B:

MACHINE   *Your_Divine_Machine*
VARIABLES   *aa , bb , cc*
INVARIANT $aa \in$ D-NAT $\wedge bb \in$ D-NAT $\wedge cc \in$ D-NAT

... ...
OPERATIONS
  YourPlus $\hat{=}$ $cc := aa + bb$ [] *skip* ;

... ...
END

REFINEMENT   *Your_Mundane_Machine*
REFINES   *Your_Divine_Machine*

... ...
VARIABLES   *aaa , bbb , ccc*
INVARIANT $aaa \in$ M-NAT $\wedge bbb \in$ M-NAT $\wedge ccc \in$ M-NAT $\wedge$
              $aa = aaa \wedge bb = bbb \wedge cc = ccc$

... ...
OPERATIONS
  YourPlus $\hat{=}$
      IF
          $aaa + bbb \leq MaxNum$
      THEN
          $ccc := aaa + bbb$

END ;

    ... ...

END

Thus as long as the extra detail is hidden at the lower level, one can conceal a certain amount of low level enrichment by specifying *skip* as the whole or an optional part of the higher level definition. This is frequently done in B when what one really wants to do is to give a detailed description at (say) the implementation level, but one nevertheless needs a specification of one sort or another because the B method always demands a machine at the top level of a development. Under such circumstances one writes *skip* at the top level (usually omitting to define any abstract variables too), relying on the fact that any operation (whose effect on the concrete variables does not entail any visible consequences on the abstract variables via the refinement invariant) refines it. In effect one simply avoids the issue.

However we argue that such uses of *skip* , though technically neat where they can accomplish what is desired, are somewhat misleading. They mix concerns in the following sense. The job of the abstract specification is to set out the idealised model as clearly as possible. Matters are therefore not helped by occurences here and there of *skip* , whose purpose is to mediate between the abstract model and concrete model in order that the relationship between them should be a refinement in the strict sense. In fact the *skip* is signalling that the relationship between the abstract and concrete models is *not* one of pure refinement, but something more intricate. And thus a cleaner design strategy would place the data that described this relationship in an appropriate position, rather than clog up the abstract model with *skip*s.

Situations much more involved than either of the above can arise routinely in the development of certain types of critical system; in particular if the system in question must model phenomena described in the real world by continuous mathematics. In such cases, system construction may well be founded upon a vast aggregate of conventional mathematics, perhaps supported by semiempirical considerations, and having an accuracy requirement for calculations measured in percent rather than in terms of the exact embedding of M-FLOAT in D-REAL . In such cases, the derivation of the discrete model actually cast in software from the original high level model, is a complex process of reasoning steps, some more precise than others, and all in principle belonging in the safety case for the implemented system, as justification for the purported validity and range of applicability of the low level discrete model. In these cases, current refinement technology cannot speak about any but the last step or two, as the premise on which it is founded, namely that the user should not be able to tell if it is the abstract or concrete version of a system that he is using, is neither applicable nor relevant to most of the justification.

The use of *skip* to circumvent the gap between levels of abstraction is even less convincing than previously when starting from a continuous model. Suppose one is modelling Newton's Second Law, which equates acceleration with force divided by mass. Newton did not state "$a := f \, / \, m$ [] *skip*" or anything similar, and the interpolation of *skip*s in the statement of such continuous laws for the purposes stated is particularly unattractive and intrusive.

And yet it is very unsatisfying to say that the corroboration that formal methods can offer in critical developments should be abandoned in such cases because the nature of the reasoning involved is "out of scope" of the conventional notion of refinement. Rather we should look to enrich what we might accomplish by "refinement-like" concepts in the hope of bringing more useful engineering within the remit of formal methods. As the pressure to include software in more and more critical systems increases, and the pressure to verify such systems mechanically against state of the art methodology increases too, the market for such enrichments can only grow. Our conclusion then is that there is an identifiable need to search for more flexible ways of "refining" abstract requirements into implementable specifications. In Section 2 we introduce a liberalisation of refinement, retrenchment, as a step in this direction. Section 3 makes the proposal more precise by discussing the incorporation of retrenchment in the B-Method, while Section 4 looks at scenarios involving the passage from continuous to discrete mathematics, scenarios that are gaining importance in the serious application of formal methods to real world safety critical systems; places indeed where the notion of retrenchment is particularly likely to prove useful. Section 5 concludes.

2 Retrenchment

A refinement as everyone knows, weakens the precondition and strengthens the postcondition of an operation. Since an operation is specified by a precondition/postcondition pair, to go beyond refinement to relate an abstract operation O_A and a concrete operation O_C, either the precondition of O_C must be stronger than or unrelated to the precondition of O_A, or the postcondition of O_C must be weaker than or unrelated to the postcondition of O_A, or both. There are no other possibilities.

Retrenchment is, very loosely speaking, the strengthening of the precondition and the weakening of the postcondition though technically it's more subtle than that. This is like the opposite of refinement, except that we avail ourselves of the opportunity to liberalise the connection between abstract and concrete operations even more widely. For instance not only will we allow changes of data type in the state component of an operation, we will also allow flexibility in the input and output components. Thus we allow inputs and outputs to change representation between abstract and concrete operations, and moreover we allow information to drift between I/O and state aspects during a retrenchment. Thus some data that was most conveniently viewed as part of the input at the abstract level say, might be best recast as partly input data and partly state at a more concrete level, or vice versa. Similar things might occur on the output side. This greater flexibility in involving properties of the inputs and outputs in the relation between versions of an operation, gives more leeway for building realistic but complex specifications of real systems out of oversimplified but more comprehensible subsystems.

These things go way beyond what is conceivable in refinement. Correspondingly, the usual way of controlling refinement, via a joint invariant, will be inadequate as a means of expressing the properties of this more liberal situation. We will need to split up the "local invariant" and "retrieve relation" in the joint invariant, and a couple of extra predicates per operation, one for the before-aspect and one for the after-aspect, and if it is necessary to relate the two in a general manner, a means of declaring logical variables with both of these predicates as scope. We see this in detail in the next section.

Of course this means that the litmus test of conventional refinement, that the correspondence between states at different levels of abstraction, and the identity of the inputs and outputs of corresponding operation instances, can be extended to a similar correspondence for sequences of operation applications, no longer applies if information can be moved between the I/O and state aspects of an operation in a retrenchment. When such a state of affairs holds, then there will usually be additional properties of histories of the two systems in question that are of interest in the overall understanding of the problem being solved. These sequence-oriented properties might typically include liveness and other fairness properties [see eg. Abadi and Lamport (1991)]. We do not pursue these aspects in the present paper, any more than fairness properties are covered by conventional formal methods of the model oriented kind, though further work may reveal the desirability of doing so.

It must be borne in mind that despite the similarities in the terminology in which it is phrased, the retrenchment technique proposed here is intended to be regarded in an entirely different light than conventional refinement. Refinement has as its objective a sort of black box role. The user does not need to enquire into the contents of the refinement black box, and the mathematical soundness of the notion of refinement guarantees that he is never wrong-footed by not doing so, since the observable behaviour of a refinement is always a possible behaviour of the abstraction. Retrenchment on the other hand, has as its objective very much a white box role. Retrenchment is a conscious decision to solve a different problem, and this must always be a deliberate engineering decision, deemed acceptable under prevailing circumstances. We envisage that the extent to which any particular retrenchment step can be justified on entirely self-contained mathematical grounds will very much vary from application to application; we imagine most will not be able to be so justified without input from non-mathematically-derivable real world considerations. (For example, mathematics can *express* the fact that the mundane naturals are finite, but it cannot *derive* this fact from some convincingly self-evident abstract criteria.)

3 Incorporating Retrenchment in the B-Method

The B-Method [Abrial (1996), Lano and Haughton (1996), Wordsworth (1996)] is a semantically well founded and structurally rich methodology for full-lifecycle formal software development. As such it provides an ideal framework into which to embed the retrenchment concept, since it already provides syntactic structure for expressing the refinement relation between specifications and implementations. Retrenchment will need a mild generalisation of this.

3.1 Syntax for Retrenchment

We propose the following outline syntax for retrenchment constructs where the square brackets indicate that LVAR A is optional:

MACHINE	*Concrete_Machine_Name (params)*
RETRENCHES	*Abstract_Machine-or-Refinement_Name*
... ...	
INVARIANT	J
RETRIEVES	G
... ...	
OPERATIONS	

$out \longleftarrow OpName\ (\ in\ ) \triangleq$
    BEGIN T [LVAR A] WITHIN P CONCEDES C END ;
    ... ...
END

In the above, we propose that the retrenchment construct be a MACHINE, as a retrenchment, being a decision to solve a new problem, should have a MACHINE as its top level statement. The RETRENCHES clause relates the retrenching machine to the retrenched construct that it remodels. We propose that the latter be either a MACHINE or a REFINEMENT for maximum flexibility. The RETRENCHES clause is similar to the REFINES clause in standard B, in that it opens the retrenched construct and makes its contents visible in the retrenching machine for the purpose of building predicates involving the contents of both. We assume that the name spaces of retrenching and retrenched constructs are disjoint aside from the operation names, which must admit an injection from operation names of the retrenched construct to operation names of the retrenching machine. (The reason we do not demand a bijection is that, given that we wish to allow the retrenched construct to be a proper oversimplification of the retrenching machine, there may well be operations of the retrenching machine that do not make sense at the more abstract level of the retrenched construct. Such operations could be modelled at the abstract level by by *skip*s of course, but we would just as soon not do so. Having an injection instead of a bijection on operation names can lead to interesting repercussions at the level of simulation, as indicated below.)

The retrenching machine can be parameterised (in contrast to refinements), so the CONSTRAINTS clause of the retrenching machine becomes in principle a joint predicate involving parameters of both retrenching and retrenched constructs if there is a need to express a relationship between them.

Being a machine, we propose that all the familiar machine structuring facilities: INCLUDES, USES, SEES, PROMOTES, EXTENDS, are available to the retrenching machine in the normal way. These aspects of machine construction are orthogonal to the retrenching idea.

Like machines but unlike refinements, the INVARIANT clause of a retrenching machine is a predicate in the local state variables only. Joint properties of state variables of both retrenching and retrenched constructs are held in the RETRIEVES clause, as they need to be treated a little differently compared to refinements.

The main difference between ordinary machines and retrenching machines appears in the operations. We propose to call the body of an operation of a retrenching machine a *ramified generalised substitution*. A ramified generalised substitution BEGIN T LVAR A WITHIN P CONCEDES C END , consists of a generalised substitution T as for any normal operation, together with its ramification, which consists of the following: the LVAR A clause which can declare logical variables A whose scope is both the WITHIN P and CONCEDES C clauses; the WITHIN P clause which is a predicate that defines the logical variables A and can strengthen the precondition of T by involving the abstract state and input; and the CONCEDES C clause which is a predicate that can weaken the postcondition of T by involving the abstract state and output and the logical variables A .

As mentioned in the previous section, global properties of system histories might well be expected to play a more significant role in a retrenchment than is usually the case in a refinement. There may thus be good reason to include a "SIMULATION Θ" clause in a retrenchment construct, where Θ describes a relationship between sets of sequences of operations at the two levels of abstraction, and including where appropriate relationships between values of input and output for corresponding operation instances. However in the general case, one might well have to incorporate properties of the system's environment, and so we do not pursue such a possibility in this paper.

3.2 Proof Obligations for Retrenchment

In order to discuss the proof obligations for retrenchment in detail, consider the following two machines. For simplicity we will assume that these machines contain no ASSERTIONS or DEFINITIONS which could be dealt with in the standard way.

MACHINE	$M(a)$	MACHINE	$N(b)$
		RETRENCHES	M
VARIABLES	u	VARIABLES	v
INVARIANT	$I(u)$	INVARIANT	$J(v)$
		RETRIEVES	$G(u,v)$
INITIALISATION	$X(u)$	INITIALISATION	$Y(v)$
OPERATIONS		OPERATIONS	

$$o \longleftarrow OpName(i) \triangleq$$
$$S(u,i,o)$$
END

$$p \longleftarrow OpName(j) \triangleq$$
BEGIN
$$T(v,j,p)$$
LVAR
$$A$$
WITHIN
$$P(i,j,u,v,A)$$
CONCEDES
$$C(u,v,o,p,A)$$
END
END

For these machines there will be the usual machine existence proof obligations (unless one postpones them till machine instantiation time as in standard B). Moreover, we point out that if the CONSTRAINTS clause of the retrenching machine is a joint predicate, then if there are a number of retrenchments and refinements in a development, the CONSTRAINTS proof obligations will grow to encompass all of them simultaneously, as $\exists x.P \wedge \exists x.Q \not\Rightarrow \exists x.(P \wedge Q)$; i.e. the values that witness joint machine existence in two adjacent retrenchment steps need not be the same ones for the middle machine. We do not foresee this as a major difficulty as a realistic development is unlikely to contain very many retrenchment steps.

There will be standard operation proof obligations viewing both M and N as machines in isolation. These include showing that the initialisation Y establishes J , i.e. that $PA_N \Rightarrow [Y(v)] J(v)$; and that $OpName$ in machine N preserves J , disregarding the retrieve and ramifications in N , i.e. that $PA_N \wedge J(v) \wedge \text{trm}(T(v,j,p)) \Rightarrow [T(v,j,p)] J(v)$. There is also a standard "refinement style" obligation to prove that both initialisations establish the retrieve relation G , i.e. that $PA_{M,N} \Rightarrow [Y(v)] \neg [X(u)] \neg G(u,v)$.

The most interesting proof obligations are the retrenchment ones. For a typical abstract operation $OpName$ given abstractly by S and retrenched to a ramified operation given by BEGIN $T \ldots$, this reads as follows.

$$PA_{M,N} \wedge (I(u) \wedge G(u,v) \wedge J(v)) \wedge (\text{trm}(T(v,j,p)) \wedge P(i,j,u,v,A))$$
$$\Rightarrow \text{trm}(S(u,i,o)) \wedge [T(v,j,p)] \neg [S(u,i,o)] \neg$$
$$(G(u,v) \vee C(u,v,o,p,A))$$

We regard this statement as a definition of the semantics of retrenchment, as opposed to refinement where the corresponding statement in Section 1 supports a more abstract formulation, based upon set transformer or relational inclusion etc., (see eg. Abrial (1996) Chapter 11). We base our definition on the following.

Let us reexamine refinement for a moment. In refinement, the objective is to ensure that the concrete system is able to emulate the abstract system, and in general there will be a many-many relationship between the steps that the abstract and concrete systems are able to make such that this is true. In particular, whenever an abstract operation is ready to make a terminating step, the corresponding concrete operation must be prepared to make a terminating step, which is the first conjunct of the refinement proof obligation. Furthermore, whenever a concrete operation actually makes a step, the result must be not incompatible with some step that the corresponding abstract operation could have made at that point. For this it is sufficient to exhibit for every concrete step, an appropriate abstract step: the second conjunct. Thus the $\forall Conc\text{-}Op\exists Abs\text{-}Op...$ structure of the second conjunct comes from ensuring that no concrete step "does anything wrong".

Retrenchment is different since the abstract and concrete systems are definitely incompatible. The white box nature of retrenchment implies that the relationship between abstract and concrete systems should be viewed first and foremost as an enhancement to the description of the concrete system, for that is the purpose of retrenchment. A retrenchment proof obligation ought to reflect this.

As before, there will in general be a many-many relationship between those steps that the abstract and concrete systems are able to make, that we might want to regard as related. Since in a retrenchment, it is the more concrete system that is considered more important, in the hypotheses of the proof obligation, it is the concrete trm condition for an operation that is present. We strengthen this by the WITHIN clause P to take into account aspects arising from the abstract state, abstract and concrete inputs, and to allow further fine tuning of the related before-configurations above and beyond that given by the RETRIEVES clause G, if required.

What then ought the conclusions of such a proof obligation to assert? The trm condition for the corresponding abstract operation is the obvious first thing. And the obvious second thing would speak about results in related steps. For these we would require the truth of the RETRIEVES clause G, but weakened by the CONCEDES clause C to take into account aspects arising from the abstract state, abstract and concrete output, and to allow deviations from strictly "refinement-like" behaviour to be expressed. We must say which pairs of abstract and concrete after-configurations should be ($G \vee C$)-related in the proof obligation. The essentially arbitrary nature of the many-many relation between steps makes expressing it verbatim within the proof obligation impractical and certainly not mechanisable. We are left with the possibility of stating some stylised subrelation of this relation, obvious candidates being subrelations of the form $\forall-\exists-...$ of which there are two possibilities to consider, namely $\forall Abs\text{-}Op\exists Conc\text{-}Op(G \vee C)$ and $\forall Conc\text{-}Op\exists Abs\text{-}Op(G \vee C)$. We discuss these in turn.

If we take the $\forall Abs\text{-}Op\exists Conc\text{-}Op(G \vee C)$ form, we must consider four things. Firstly, this form makes the resulting proof obligation resemble a refinement from concrete to abstract systems (aside from P and C of course), taking us in a direction we do not intend to go. Secondly, the $\forall Abs\text{-}Op$ part forces us to say something about all possible abstract steps. There may be many of these that are quite irrelevant to the more definitive concrete system, since the abstract system is intended to be merely a simplifying guide to the concrete one; the necessity of mentioning them, or excluding them via the P clause, would be an unwelcome complication. Thirdly, this form does *not* make us say something about all possible concrete steps, limiting its usefulness as an enhancement to the description of the concrete system. And fourthly, we have not identified any negative criterion that we must ensure the abstract system fulfils, as was the case for concrete systems in refinement. All of these considerations mitigate against adopting the $\forall Abs\text{-}Op \exists Conc\text{-}Op(G \vee C)$ form.

So we turn to the $\forall Conc\text{-}Op \exists Abs\text{-}Op(G \vee C)$ form. Here we consider three points. Firstly, we are not required to say something about all abstract steps, which in view of the remarks above we regard as beneficial. Secondly, we must say something about all concrete steps, which helps to enhance the description of the concrete system, and which we thus regard as good. In particular we must consider for any concrete step, whether it is: (a), excluded from consideration because P is not validated; (b) included but requires essential use of C to satisfy the obligation; (c), included but does not require C. The third point follows on from (c): there may well be sensible portions of the state and I/O spaces in which P and C are trivial. In such places, when both trm clauses hold, it will be possible to derive from the truth of the retrenchment obligation, the truth of the refinement obligation; this would tie in neatly with the joint initialisation proof obligation $PA_{M,N} \Rightarrow [Y(v)] \neg [X(u)] \neg G(u, v)$ mentioned above. Such a state of affairs supports our intention that retrenchment is regarded as a liberalisation of refinement, i.e. it is like refinement "except round the edges".

The heuristic reasoning above aimed to justify a proof obligation that is simple and convenient to mechanise and to use in real designs; and in the light of the preceding remarks we see that saying that retrenchment is merely a "the strengthening of the precondition and the weakening of the postcondition" is deceptively simplistic. The current lack of a more abstract underlying model for retrenchment is not regarded as a fundamental obstacle to its usefulness, though such a model would clearly be of great interest. Indeed, as the third point above indicated, we can expect at minimum, various special cases of retrenchment to lend themselves to deeper mathematical treatment. It might be that there is no "best" such theory and that increasing ingenuity will reveal increasingly complex special cases. The inevitable consequence of this would be, that treated in a standalone fashion, the special cases would generate standalone proof obligations of an increasingly complex and thus less practically convenient nature. Such an outcome would strongly support our strategy of defining retrenchment directly via a simple proof obligation. These fascinating matters will be explored more fully elsewhere.

3.3 Composability of Retrenchments

We have deliberately designed retrenchment to be a very flexible relation between machines, to afford designers the maximum convenience and expressivity in constructing complex solutions to complex problems by reshaping oversimplified but more comprehensible pieces. We indicated above that the mathematics of retrenchment will be more complex that that of refinement and we do not embark on a full discussion here. Nevertheless we show here that retrenchments compose to give retrenchments. To see this suppose machine $N (b)$ is retrenched to machine $O (c)$ whose structure is defined by "schematically alphabetically incrementing" $N (b)$, i.e. by replacing in the schematic text of $N (b)$ above, occurrences of $N, b, M, v, J, G, Y, p, j, T, P, C$, by occurrences of $O, c, N, w, K, H, Z, q, k, U, Q, D$, respectively. The retrenchment proof obligation for N and O then becomes:

$$PA_{N,O} \wedge (J(v) \wedge H(v, w) \wedge K(w)) \wedge (\text{trm}(U(w, k, q)) \wedge Q(j, k, v, w, B))$$
$$\Rightarrow \text{trm}(T(v, j, p)) \wedge [\, U(w, k, q)\,] \neg [\, T(v, j, p)\,] \neg$$
$$(H(v, w) \vee D(v, w, p, q, B))$$

From this and the preceding proof obligation we can show in a relational model that:

$$PA_{M,N,O} \wedge (I(u) \wedge (\exists v \bullet G(u, v) \wedge J(v) \wedge H(v, w)) \wedge K(w)) \wedge$$
$$\big(\text{trm}(U(w, k, q)) \wedge (\exists v, j, A \bullet G(u, v) \wedge J(v) \wedge H(v, w) \wedge$$
$$P(i, j, u, v, A) \wedge Q(j, k, v, w, B))\big)$$
$$\Rightarrow \text{trm}(S(u, i, o)) \wedge [\, U(w, k, q)\,] \neg [\, S(u, i, o)\,] \neg$$
$$\big((\exists v \bullet G(u, v) \wedge J(v) \wedge H(v, w)) \vee$$
$$(\exists v, p \bullet G(u, v) \wedge D(v, w, p, q, B)) \vee$$
$$(\exists v, p, A \bullet C(u, v, o, p, A) \wedge H(v, w)) \vee$$
$$(\exists v, p, A \bullet C(u, v, o, p, A) \wedge D(v, w, p, q, B))\big)$$

This corresponds to the retrenchment:

MACHINE	$O(c)$
RETRENCHES	M
VARIABLES	w
INVARIANT	$K(w)$
RETRIEVES	$\exists v \bullet G(u, v) \wedge J(v) \wedge H(v, w)$
INITIALISATION	$Z(w)$
OPERATIONS	

$\qquad q \longleftarrow OpName(k) \triangleq$
$\qquad$ BEGIN
$\qquad\qquad U(w, k, q)$
$\qquad$ LVAR
$\qquad\qquad B$
$\qquad$ WITHIN
$\qquad\qquad (\exists v, j, A \bullet G(u, v) \wedge J(v) \wedge H(v, w) \wedge$
$\qquad\qquad\qquad P(i, j, u, v, A) \wedge Q(j, k, v, w, B))$
$\qquad$ CONCEDES
$\qquad\qquad (\exists v, p \bullet G(u, v) \wedge D(v, w, p, q, B)) \vee$
$\qquad\qquad (\exists v, p, A \bullet C(u, v, o, p, A) \wedge H(v, w)) \vee$
$\qquad\qquad (\exists v, p, A \bullet C(u, v, o, p, A) \wedge D(v, w, p, q, B))$
$\qquad$ END
END

We take this as the natural definition of composition of retrenchments, and we note that it is built out of the syntactic pieces of the component retrenchments in such a manner that composition of retrenchments will be associative.

We point out straight away that the above is not the only possible definition: an easy variation on what is given includes $J(v)$ in the three existentially quantified clauses of the CONCEDES clause of the composition. This works because the stronger clauses arise naturally when the two original proof obligations are combined, so the given form is entailed by the stronger form. We dropped the $J(v)$ in all of them because designers are likely to be most interested in the interaction of the WITHIN and CONCEDES clauses in practical situations and the additional presence of $J(v)$ is likely to be seen only as a complicating nuisance.

We observe that the composed retrenchment is a different retrenchment than that obtained by alphabetically incrementing $N(b)$, even though the same machine $O(c)$ is involved. This is best understood from a categorical perspective. We could define a category $\mathcal{M}ch^{Ret}$ say, of machines and retrenchments, in which machines (given by the normal syntactic data for machines, and assuming (for convenience) that the machine name uniquely identifies the machine) constitute the objects, and abstract retrenchments (given by the syntactic data of the names of the retrenched and retrenching machines, the retrieve clause, and the ramification data) constitute the arrows. Roughly speaking, the law of composition of retrenchments, is the associative law of composition of arrows in this category[1]. The fact that there may be many different retrenchments to a given machine reflects the fact that there may be many different arrows to an object in a category, even many from the same source object. The concrete syntax proposed for retrenchments mixes object and arrow aspects in a single construct, and a good case could be made for their separation, especially since the connection between retrenched and retrenching machines is looser than in refinement. It is this categorical perspective that caused us to separate the local INVARIANT J from the RETRIEVE relation G in the definition of a retrenchment. And one could say much the same things about the usual refinement notion of course.

3.4 Simple Examples

With the preceding machinery in place, we can redo the earlier *My_Divine_Machine / My_Mundane_Machine* example properly as a retrenchment. We give first a minimal but self contained version of *My_Divine_Machine*:

```
MACHINE          My_Divine_Machine_0
VARIABLES        aa , bb , cc
INVARIANT        aa ∈ D-NAT ∧ bb ∈ D-NAT ∧ cc ∈ D-NAT
INITIALISATION   aa := 3 ‖ bb := 4 ‖ cc := 5
OPERATIONS
     MyPlus ≙ cc := aa + bb
END
```

And now we give a retrenchment of it along the lines of the original *My_Mundane_Machine*.

```
MACHINE          My_Mundane_Machine_1
RETRENCHES       My_Divine_Machine_0
VARIABLES        aaa , bbb , ccc
INVARIANT        aaa ∈ M-NAT ∧ bbb ∈ M-NAT ∧ ccc ∈ M-NAT
RETRIEVES        aa = aaa ∧ bb = bbb ∧ cc = ccc
INITIALISATION   aaa := 3 ‖ bbb := 4 ‖ ccc := 5
OPERATIONS
     resp ⟵ MyPlus ≙
         BEGIN
```

---

1. We say "roughly speaking", because there are minor irritations concerning the identities in such a syntactic category since eg. *TRUE* ∧ *TRUE* is semantically but not syntactically the same as *TRUE*. One can circumvent these by: having merely formal identities, or by allowing empty formulae in the syntax, or by defining the arrows as equivalence classes of syntactic data which identify eg. ϕ ∧ *TRUE* with ϕ. We will not go into details.

```
                IF
                    aaa + bbb ≤ MaxNum
                THEN
                    ccc := aaa + bbb ||
                    resp := TRUE
                ELSE
                    resp := FALSE
                END
            LVAR
                CC
            WITHIN
                CC = ccc
            CONCEDES
                aa = aaa & bb = bbb & CC = ccc
            END
    END
```

We are able to describe the case in which the variable ccc is not changed, with the help of the logical variable CC, noting that the CONCEDES clause refers to the after condition of the variables involved and that CC is not substituted. This situation is evidently outside the scope of normal refinement. To illustrate the flexibility of the retrenchment concept we give another, different retrenchment of $My\_Divine\_Machine$:

```
        MACHINE             My_Mundane_Machine_2
        RETRENCHES          My_Divine_Machine_0
        VARIABLES           aaa
        INVARIANT           aaa ∈ M-NAT
        RETRIEVES           aa = aaa
        INITIALISATION      aaa := 3
        OPERATIONS
            resp , ccc ⟵ MyPlus ( bbb ) ≙
                BEGIN
                    IF
                        aaa + bbb ≤ MaxNum
                    THEN
                        ccc := aaa + bbb ||
                        resp := TRUE
                    ELSE
                        ccc := 0 ||
                        resp := FALSE
                    END
                WITHIN
                    bb = bbb
                CONCEDES
                    (resp = TRUE ⟹ cc = ccc) & (resp = FALSE ⟹ ccc = 0)
                END
        END
```

Note that in this version, the status of bb has been changed to that of an input and the status of cc has been changed to that of an output, thus obviating the need to take their properties into account in the RETRIEVES clause. The WITHIN and CONCEDES clauses instead take on the jobs of relating *bb* and *bbb* , and *cc* and *ccc* respectively; and in this simple example the RETRIEVES clause always holds anyway.

These two examples are rather trivial. Nevertheless they are small enough to show some of the technical details of retrenchment clearly. In the next section we will discuss a more convincing scenario, albeit only superficially for lack of space.

4 Continuous and Discrete Systems

In this section we discuss the prospects for applying retrenchment in the development of systems that need to model physical aspects of the real world, both in general terms and with regard to specific examples.

4.1 Modelling the Real World

As the application of formal methods for system development in the real world continues to grow, the interest in applying them to systems which capture the properties of physical situations requiring continuous mathematics for their description grows likewise. See for example [Maler (1997), Alur, Henzinger and Sontag (1996)]. In the bulk of such work the continuous component is time, and the problem is to describe and control a one dimensional dynamics typically governed by laws of the form

$$\dot{f} = \Phi(f, e)$$

where f is a (tuple of) quantities of interest, $\dot{f}$ is the tuple of their first order time derivatives, and $\Phi(f, e)$ is a tuple of formulae in the f and the external input e . In addition the typically smooth evolution of the system according to the above law is punctuated from time to time with certain discrete events which interrupt the overall continuity of the system's behaviour. Over the years, a large amount of work has been directed at taming the difficulties that arise.

However there are also increasingly problems that involve applied mathematics of a different kind. Dose calculation in cancer radiotherapy is a typical case in point [Johns and Cunningham (1976), Khan (1994), Cunningham (1989), Hounsell and Wilkinson (1994)]. Here the problem to be solved centres on the Boltzmann transport equation [Huang (1963)], a three dimensional nonlinear integro-differential equation that describes the electron (or X-ray) density. Not only is this not a typical one dimensional problem, but there are no known exact solutions or calculation techniques for this equation applicable to the kind of spatial configurations of interest in practice; solutions to practical examples rely on heuristic techniques whose efficacy is gauged by comparison with experiment. No formal technique is ever going to be able to "justify" the procedures undertaken, on the basis of primitive axioms, in the same way that simple calculations with natural numbers are justified on the basis of the Peano axioms in a modern theorem prover. But that is not to say that automated support is out of the question.

The fact that continuous mathematics has been done with rigour for a century or more is good evidence that what has been done there is formalisable. The paucity of published material in this area is more a question of logicians' and computer scientists' ignorance of and/or distaste for the subject than any issue of principle. In fact continuous mathematics has received some attention from the mechanical theorem proving community lately [Harrison (1996)]. The cited work shows that a formal approach to analysis is entirely feasible, but is a big job. The sheer breadth of applied mathematics that may be needed in applications makes it clear that simply formalising a large general purpose body of continuous mathematics that would serve as a foundation for "all" formal developments where such mathematics is required is an unrealistic proposition.

The alternative, to reinvent the core continuous mathematics wheel formally as a precursor to the more specialised reasoning required in a specific application is equally unrealistic. Not only would the cost of rederiving any significant piece of applied mathematics from first principles be prohibitive, but many different developments would overlap significantly in the mathematics needed despite the remarks above, and this would lead to wasteful duplication.

Moreover applied mathematics does not work by deriving everything from first principles. Rather, it reaches a certain stage of maturity, turns the results obtained into algebra, and uses the equations of that algebra as axioms for further work. Thus it seems reasonable for computerised developments that depend on such mathematics to select a suitable suite of already known results as axioms (whether these be formally derived or merely results that have achieved equivalent status through years of successful use), to capture these as axioms in the theory underlying the development, and to use these to support the specifics of the development. Where one starts from in the vast sea of extant mathematics to select an axiom basis which will be both useful in providing good support for the development at hand, and also tractable for automated reasoning technology, would become a matter for engineering judgement.

Even the heuristic semi-empirical reasoning alluded to above can be incorporated in such an approach. Suppose for example that it is believed that within certain bounds of applicability, such and such a parametrised expression can, by suitable choice of parameters, yield a function that is within such and such an error margin of a solution to a particular nonlinear integro-differential equation (say). Then that belief can be expressed as a rule in the system and its use controlled by the same theorem proving environment that supports the rest of the development.

At the moment, to the extent that developments incorporating the passage from continuous to discrete mathematics are attempted at all using a formal approach, what one sees is a little disconcerting. Typically some continuous mathematics appears, describing the problem as it is usually presented theoretically. When this is done, there comes a violent jolt. Suddenly one is in the world of discrete mathematics, and a whole new set of criteria come into play. There is almost never any examination of the conditions under which the discrete system provides an acceptable representation of the continuous one, and what "acceptability" means in the situation in question. But surely these questions are of vital importance if the discrete model is truly to be relied on. Results from mathematics which have investigated the reliability of discrete approximations to continuous situations have shown that there are useful general situations in which the discrete approximation can be depended on. Such results ought to make their way into the justification of the appropriate development steps in real world applications wherever possible. Evidently incorporating them into strict refinement steps is too much to ask in general, and the greater flexibility of the retrenchment formalism we propose seems to us to be much better suited to the task in hand.

4.2 A Furnace Example

We describe in outline a hypothetical situation in which the flexibility of retrenchment comes into its own. Suppose we have undertaken to control an ultraefficient furnace, into which pulverised solid fuel is injected along with preheated air. Magnetic fields help to keep the resulting burning ionised gas evenly suspended throughout the volume of the combustion chamber in order to maximise efficiency, and away from the walls in order to prevent them from disintegrating at the high temperatures used. The objective is to keep the temperature as high and as evenly distributed as possible for efficiency's sake, to keep the hot gas away from the walls, and to ensure that fluctuations do not cause explosive hot spots to arise that could give rise to shock waves which could damage the combustion chamber. A number of sensors in the combustion chamber report periodically on the temperature and electromagnetic flux in their vicinity. The physics of the situation is described by the partial differential equations of magnetohydrodynamics. Needless to say it is not possible to solve these equations in closed form. We want to model this situation in order to develop software that will control the magnetic fields and inflow of air and fuel, so as to maximise efficiency while keeping the system safe.

The top layer of the model simply reflects the classical mathematics of the problem. Thus suppose that the vessel occupies a volume Ω, with boundary $\partial\Omega$. The problem is then to control the flow of ionised gas, given by its temperature θ, mass density ρ, pressure p, adiabaticity γ, velocity v, and current density J, by adjusting the applied magnetic field M, air input a, and fuel input s. The current values and rates of change of the physical quantities act as inputs, and the outputs are to be the future values of the physical variables and M, a, s, such that over a finite ensuing period, the behaviour of the system is safe; i.e. no instabilities arise, and the ionised gas stays away from the solid parts of $\partial\Omega$. In B terms, one could have a single operation

$$\theta \ldots M, a, s \longleftarrow furnace\_control\,(\,\theta, \rho, p, \gamma, v, J, \dot\theta, \dot\rho, \dot p, \dot\gamma, \dot v, \dot J\,)$$

whose body was a relation which specified the future behaviour and the control outputs, against the input data. The substitution could be a typical ANY $\theta \ldots M$, a, s WHERE *MHD_EQNs* END construct, where the body *MHD_EQNs* could simply quote the conjunction of the standard magnetohydrodynamic equations for the system with the desired bounds on future behaviour. This is specification at its most eloquent as the system is not capable of being solved in closed form, and the operation *furnace_control* would alter no state since we are at the textbook level of reasoning. Indeed the required relation could be captured in B constants, were it not for the desire to have an operation to retrench ultimately into an IMPLEMENTATION.

The intermediate layer of the model is a discretisation step in which continuous functions over space and time are replaced by finite sets of values at a grid of points in the combustion chamber Ω. So the operation would become something like

$$\theta_i \ldots M_i, a_i, s_i \longleftarrow furnace\_control\,(\,\theta_i, \rho_i, p_i, \gamma_i, v_i, J_i, \dot\theta_i, \dot\rho_i, \dot p_i, \dot\gamma_i, \dot v_i, \dot J_i\,)$$

where the subscripts range over a suitable grid. Furthermore, while the top layer simply states the desired properties of the outputs, the intermediate layer now gives them as a more concrete function of the inputs, reflecting the structure of the finite element calculations needed to generate actual numerical answers, though not necessarily in full detail. The retrenchment between these layers would, if done thoroughly enough, cover the detailed justification for the discretisation. This would include bounds on the permitted fluctuations of the continuous system in order that it can still be adequately represented by the discrete system, as evidently not all violently fluctuating behaviours can be faithfully mirrored within a fixed grid. The mathematics required for the WITHIN and CONCEDES clauses, and to properly discharge the relevant proof obligations from first principles, would be demanding to say the least. It is likely that if this were a genuine development, some heuristic rules would be invoked to discharge the proof obligations, expressing accumulated engineering wisdom in such situations. The retrenchment would then be doing little more than documenting the arguments, but in a manner consistent with the rest of the development, and capable of some mechanical checking. There is still no state, so we still have pure I/O.

The lowest layer of the model takes the idealised finite element scenario above, and relates it to the actual configuration of input and output devices in the real system. Thus the only inputs at this level will be temperature and electromagnetic flux sensor readings, and the only outputs will be the control parameters to the air and fuel injectors and magnetic field controls. The signature will thus look like

$$M_j \, , a_j \, , s_j \longleftarrow furnace\_control\,(\; \theta_j \, , J_j \,)$$

where j ranges over the actual input and output devices, and the remaining data of the intermediate model is committed to state variables of the machine. This arrangement is justified on the basis that the system changes sufficiently slowly that an iterative calculation of the required future behaviour can be done much faster and more accurately starting from the previous configuration, than ab initio from just the inputs. Furthermore, the model at this layer could stipulate numerical bounds on the values of the mathematical variables which occur, in order to ease the transition to computationally efficient arithmetic types later. The retrenchment from the layer above to this one will be rather easier than was the preceding retrenchment step, as the relationship between the I/O and state variables of the present model, and the I/O of the model above will consist of straightforward algebraic formulae, leading to relatively simple proof obligations. In particular the $\forall Conc\text{-}Op \exists Abs\text{-}Op(G \vee C)$ form of the retrenchment proof obligation enables the drawing up of a suitable C cognisant of these bounds rather more easily than the opposite form.

At this point we have reached the level that a conventional formal development might have started at. The operation of interest has reached a stage where its I/O signature and the information in its state has stabilised, so what remains is in the province of normal refinement. Such refinements could address the efficiency of the algorithms used, exploiting architectural features of the underlying hardware if appropriate, and could also address the precise representation of the state. We are assuming that the bounded mathematical types used in the model are such that casting them down to actual hardware arithmetic types can be done within a refinement; if not then another retrenchment would be required.

Surveying the above, we see how much of the reasoning that would otherwise fall outside of the remit of formal development has been brought into the fold by the use of retrenchment. Admittedly this was a hypothetical example, and not worked out in full detail, but the outline above shows us how the engineer's model building activity may be organised within a formal process, and the ultimate very detailed and obscure model that is cast into implementation, may be made more approachable thereby. The whole development process also reveals the mathematically most challenging parts for what they are, and documents to what extent they have been resolved through utilising either deep results on discretisability from real analysis, or the adoption of pragmatic engineering rules of thumb.

5 Conclusions

In the preceding sections we have argued that refinement is too restrictive to describe many developments fully, and have proposed retrenchment as a liberalisation of it. The objective was to allow more of the informal aspects of design to be formally captured and checked. We described the technical details of what retrenchment is within B, we considered some basic formal properties such as the proof obligations and composability, and discussed some examples.

Much of what we said regarding the applicability of retrenchment to realistic situations assumed the incorporation of ideal and richer types into B; this merits further discussion. Take the reals. Because the reals are based on non-constructive features, any finitistic approach to them will display weaknesses regarding what can be deduced, and different approaches will make different tradeoffs. (M-FLOAT is one possibility, and we could also mention different theories of constructible reals, as well as approaches that exploit laziness (in the functional programming sense) to yield so called computable exact reals.) The B attitude, to design a conservative framework for development, has the merit that a laudable degree of completeness of coverage can be achieved in the method. However to address many types of real world problem, this conservatism would need to be relaxed. It seems to us that the best way forward is to consider adding certified libraries to B, offering a variety of theories for richer types (eg. various types of reals), to give users the foundations for the applications they need. These idealisations could be retrenched away in the passage to an IMPLEMENTATION.

The lack of richer types in B is also felt at the I/O level, as B I/O only permits simple types to occur which thus can force premature concretisation. In this regard our work bears comparison with [Hayes and Sanders (1995)] who focus exclusively on I/O aspects, and who show how describing the I/O of an operation in excessively concrete terms, can lead to obscure specifications. Their decomposition of operations into an input abstraction phase, an abstract operation phase, and an output concretisation phase, corresponds to a special case of retrenchment in which there is no mixing of I/O and state aspects, but where the WITHIN and CONCEDES clauses permit translation from one I/O format to another. One can see this as further affirmation of the inadequacy of pure refinement as the only mechanism for turning abstract descriptions into concrete ones, as was indicated in Section 1.

The present work, the first on retrenchment, raises more questions than it solves. The true value of any development technique can only be judged by its usefulness in practice. For that, a significant body of case studies must be developed, and then those whose livelihood depends on doing developments right, must come to a verdict, either explicitly or implicitly, on whether the technique offers a worthwhile improvement on current practice or not. Retrenchment should be subjected to such critical appraisal in order to prove its worth. The authors envisage retrenchment as being useful both in continuous problems as discussed in the preceding section, and in entirely discrete situations too, where the complexity of the real system is built up in digestible steps from simpler models. We have given enough of the basic theory of retrenchment in this paper, to enable such application work and its evaluation to proceed. The other facet of retrenchment needing to be pursued, the underlying theory, aspects of which were discussed at the end of Section 3.2, is under active investigation and the results will be reported in future papers.

References

Abadi M., Lamport L. (1991); The Existence of Refinement Mappings. Theor. Comp. Sci. **82**, 153-284.

Abrial J. R. (1996); The B-Book. Cambridge University Press.

Alur R., Henzinger T., Sontag E. (eds.) (1996); Hybrid Systems III: Verification and Control. LNCS **1066**, Springer.

Back R. J. R. (1981); On Correct Refinement of Programs. J. Comp. Sys. Sci. **23**, 49-68.

Back R. J. R. (1988); A Calculus of Refinements for Program Derivations. Acta Inf. **25**, 593-624.

Back R. J. R., von Wright J. (1989); Refinement Calculus Part I: Sequential Nondeterministic Programs. *in*: Proc. REX Workshop, Stepwise Refinement of Distributed Systems, de Roever, Rozenberg (eds.), LNCS **430**, 42-66, Springer.

Cunningham J. R. (1989); Development of Computer Algorithms for Radiation Treatment Planning. Int. J. Rad. Onc. Biol. Phys., **16**, 1367-1376.

Harrison J. R. (1996); Theorem Proving with the Real Numbers. PhD. Thesis, Cambridge University Computing Laboratory, *also* Cambridge University Computing Laboratory Technical Report No. 408.

Hayes I. J. (1993); Specification Case Studies. (2nd ed.), Prentice-Hall.

Hayes I. J., Sanders J. W. (1995); Specification by Interface Separation. Form. Asp. Comp. **7**, 430-439.

Hounsell A. R., Wilkinson J. M. (1994); Dose Calculations in Multi-Leaf Collimator Fields. *in*: Proc. XIth Int. Conf. on the use of Computers in Radiation Therapy, Manchester, UK.

Huang K. (1963); Statistical Mechanics. John Wiley.

Johns, H. E., Cunningham J. R. (1976); The Physics of Radiology. Charles C. Thomas.

Jones C. B. (1990); Systematic Software Development Using VDM. (2nd ed.), Prentice-Hall.

Jones C. B., Shaw R. C. (1990); Case Studies in Systematic Software Development. Prentice-Hall.

Khan F. M. (1994); The Physics of Radiation Therapy. Williams & Wilkins.

Lano K., Haughton H. (1996); Specification in B: An Introduction Using the B-Toolkit. Imperial College Press.

Maler O. (ed.) (1997); Hybrid and Real-Time Systems. LNCS **1201**, Springer.

Morgan C. (1994); Programming from Specifications. Prentice-Hall.

Morris J. M. (1987); A Theoretical Basis for Stepwise Refinement and the Programming Calculus. Sci. Comp. Prog. **9**, 287-306.

Spivey J. M. (1993); The Z Notation: A Reference Manual. (2nd ed.), Prentice-Hall.

Wand I., Milner R. (eds.) (1996); Computing Tomorrow. Cambridge University Press.

Wordsworth J. B. (1996); Software Engineering with B. Addison-Wesley.

von Wright J. (1994); The Lattice of Data Refinement. Acta Inf. **31**, 105-135.

Synthesising Structure from Flat Specifications

Brian Matthews, Brian Ritchie, and Juan Bicarregui

Rutherford Appleton Laboratory, Chilton, Didcot, OXON, OX11 0QX, U.K.
{bmm,br,jcb}@inf.rl.ac.uk

Abstract. Within the design process, a high-level specification is subject to two conflicting tensions. It is used as a vehicle for validating the requirements, and also as a first step of the refinement process. Whilst the structuring mechanisms available in the B method are well-suited for the latter purpose, the rich type constructions of VDM are useful for the former.

In this paper we propose a method which synthesises a structured B design from a flat VDM specification by analysing how type definitions are used within the VDM state in order to generate a corresponding B machine hierarchy.

1   Introduction

Within the design process, a high-level specification is subject to two conflicting tensions. It is used as a vehicle for validating the requirements, and also as a first step of the refinement process. Whilst the structuring mechanisms available in the B method [1] are well-suited for the latter purpose, the rich type constructions of VDM [7] are useful for the former. Indeed, previous work [2] has shown that although VDM and B are equivalent in theory, in practice, VDM is used for requirements analysis, high level design and validation whereas B places more emphasis on refinement, low level design, and code generation.

Thus the kind of structuring used in the B Method, which is intended to allow compositional development from the specification, can be seen as implementation detail which can obscure the abstract behaviour.

The SPECTRUM project has investigated the benefits of combining VDM and B in the development using VDM for abstract specification and validation (as well as generation of abstract test suites) and B for development of that specification (refinement, verification and code generation). This combination requires a translation between the VDM and B notations during the development.

Typically at the early stages in the development the VDM specification has a data model employing a single module including a single state which is a monolithic value of a complex type (a composite record value whose elements themselves may consist of records, sets, maps or sequences). VDM's language of types and expressions supports the forms of data abstraction which are useful in comprehension and validation.

The required B specification will comprise a hierarchy of abstract machines, each of which contains state values of relatively simple types. This decomposition of the state may support subsequent refinement, developing an understanding of how the design can be achieved.

In other words, when translating a VDM specification to B, complexity in VDM's expression language should be replaced by complexity in AMN's state language, in order to obtain the best from both notations.

In this paper we propose a method which synthesises a structured B design from a flat VDM specification by analysing how type definitions are used within the VDM state in order to generate a corresponding B machine hierarchy.

1.1 Background

VDM and B were first used together in the MAFMETH project [3]. There, a high-level VDM specification was hand-translated into B. MAFMETH showed that using the two methods in this manner gave benefits over "traditional" development approaches. However, translation by hand was error prone: most of the few design errors were introduced at this stage.

The EC project SPECTRUM[1] has been further investigating the interoperability of VDM and B. The project has developed a design lifecycle whereby VDM is used in the early stages of design for high level design, and validation against requirements through prototype generation, and a move to B is performed for the later stages of development towards code, while referring back to the VDM as a test case oracle. Thus an important requirement of the project is an automated translation of VDM into B.

Z to B translation has been carried out in [9] and elsewhere (e.g. [4]). [9] proposed a style similar to "algebraic" specification for translating Z's free type definitions. Though feasible, the resultant B specifications were "unnatural" (in terms of B style), and were difficult to work with in practice. Nevertheless, this style formed a starting point for SPECTRUM, giving a *property-oriented* style of specification, with extensive use of **CONSTANTS** and **PROPERTIES** clauses, and few state variables.

An object-based style of B specification is developed in [8] wherein each object class is realised by a machine that "manages" a state that effectively comprises

---

[1] EC ESPRIT project 23173, SPECTRUM, is a collaboration between: Rutherford Appleton Laboratory, GEC Marconi Avionics, Dassault Electronique, B-Core UK Ltd, Institute of Applied Computer Science (IFAD), Space Software Italia and Commissariat à l'Energie Atomique. For information about this project contact Juan Bicarregui.

a set of currently-existing instances of that class. Individual objects in the set are "known" to the rest of the system via their "handles" (or object identifiers) that are created and maintained by the object manager machine. Whilst this *object-manager* approach is more natural within B and one which is more readily analysable by B tools, it can at times be overly complex, and it was not readily apparent how this could be derived from a VDM specification.

Here we propose a hybrid of these two approaches, based on a top-down analysis of the VDM specification. Where a type is used as part of the state, we follow the object based approach; a machine is created to manage the values of that type. Where a type is used only in a declarative way, say as the parameter or result of an operation, then the "algebraic" approach is followed. This translation was tested within SPECTRUM through the case study of translating a simple train control specification from Dassault Electronique ("the Metro specification").

In the remainder of this paper we discuss this translation in more detail. Section 2 gives an overview of the approach. Sections 3 and 4 give some of the technical details of the automated translation, and Section 5 discusses some extensions for further language features. Section 6 gives an example, and the paper is summed up in Section 7.

2 An Analytic Approach

The VDM-SL and B-AMN notations have broadly similar semantics[2] and address similar problem areas (specification of sequential state-based systems). However, the two notations place different emphases on state structure, and on type and value expressivity. VDM provides an expressive type definition language, and a similarly rich language of expressions and functions, but (relative to AMN) its state model is flat: in effect, the state model of a VDM-SL specification typically contains at most a small number of variables, though each variable can have a complex value (of a complex type), and operations are generally viewed as acting on the state as a whole. On the other hand, whilst AMN provides powerful constructs for state modularisation, its type and expression notations are impoverished relative to VDM-SL. The state of an AMN specification consists of a relatively large number of state variables, usually of simple types, spread across a number of machines, each of which has "local" operations.

Thus, in translating from VDM-SL to AMN, two problems must be addressed: firstly, how to represent complex types and expressions within a weaker expres-

---

[2] Whilst we recognise that VDM has a denotational semantics over a logic for partial functions, and B has a weakest precondition semantics over classical logic, and thus have some differences in interpretation, we believe that the semantics are sufficiently similar for interoperability to be meaningful and useful. A further part of our work intends to investigate any semantic differences.

sion syntax, and secondly, how to "infer" a structured state model from an unstructured model.

We propose a new approach to translation from VDM to B which attempts to use the most appropriate style of B specification for the various parts of the VDM specification, resulting in a specification with a more distributed state. A top-down analysis is undertaken to work out which approach is best for each part of the specification. We first consider the *state* in the VDM specification. Consider the state of a representative VDM specification:

> **state** S **of**
> $n : N$
> $a : A$
> **end**

where A is a user defined record type:

> $A :: a1 : A1$
> $a2 : A2$

In the property oriented approach, since the record type A is translated as an algebraic specification, it is given as the following stateless machine (truncated for brevity):

> **MACHINE** A_Type
>
> **SETS** A
>
> **CONSTANTS**
>
>> $mk\_A, inv\_A, a1, a2$
>
> **PROPERTIES**
>
>> $a1 : A \rightarrow A1 \wedge$
>> $a2 : A \rightarrow A2 \wedge$
>> $mk\_A : A1 \times A2 \rightarrow A \wedge$
>> $inv\_A : A \rightarrow BOOL \wedge$
>> $(\forall xx,yy).(xx \in A1 \wedge yy \in A1 \Rightarrow$
>>> $(a1(mk\_A(xx,yy)) = xx))$
>
>> $\cdots$
>
> **END**

And a top level state machine of the form:

> **MACHINE** S
>
> **SEES** A_Type
>
> **VARIABLES** n, a
>
> **INVARIANT**

$$n \in \mathbb{N} \land a \in A$$

END

This is a literal translation of the VDM. the *algebraic* VDM record type A is translated into a stateless "property-oriented" machine, which declares the type as a set, a new mk_A constant as the constructor function, the fields as projection functions, and a new inv_A constant as the invariant function. The behaviour of these constants is defined using properties, in effect giving an algebraic specification of the type. The properties clause soon becomes very large, with complex first-order logic and set theory expressions. Because of the relative weakness of this expression language, these become hard to read, and the support tools for B find such expressions hard to deal with.

The property oriented approach has led to a different "granularity" of the state than would be natural in a B specification. A more "natural" B approach would be to split the record A into its fields, and give a state variable for each, generating a *simple state* specification as follows:

MACHINE   *A_Obj*

VARIABLES

   a1, *a2*

INVARIANT

   $a1 \in A1 \land a2 \in A2$

...

END

And a top level state machine which includes this to represent the "inheritance" of the datatype:

MACHINE   *S*

INCLUDES *A_Obj*

VARIABLES *n*

INVARIANT

   $n \in \mathbb{N}$

...

END

If the data types *A1*, *A2* are themselves record types they can be broken down further into similar machines. Thus we build a hierarchy of machines which preserve the structure of the VDM specification, but have a finer state granularity. This specification is much clearer and easy to work with, exploiting as it does the strength of B and B tools in manipulating machine state and generalised substitutions.

If the state has an aggregate type of records, such as set or map, then the appropriate B specification is different. For example, if the state is of the form:

state S **of**
$\quad$ $n : N$
$\quad$ $a : A$-**set**
end

with A as before, then an "object manager" approach is more appropriate:

MACHINE $\quad$ A_Mgr

SETS A_Ids

VARIABLES

$\quad$ $aids, a1, a2$

INVARIANT

$\quad$ $aids \subseteq A\_Ids \wedge$
$\quad$ $a1 \in aids \rightarrow A1 \wedge$
$\quad$ $a2 \in aids \rightarrow A2$

$\ldots$

END

Typically, an object manager machine will also include some basic operations for inspecting and manipulating the variables; for example equality should be defined on the value of the attributes rather than on the identifier. In this paper, these are omitted for clarity.

A top level state machine which includes this to represent the "inheritance" of the datatype within the VDM record:

MACHINE $\quad$ S

INCLUDES A_Mgr

VARIABLES n, a

INVARIANT

$\quad$ $n \in \mathbb{N} \wedge a \subseteq aids$

$\ldots$

END

Where the attribute being modelled is a sequence or map of records, the variable a here would be a sequence or map of $aids$. Again, if either of $A1, A2$ are themselves record types, then they should themselves be made into objects. However, since they are accessed from an object manager machine, they should be implemented as object managers themselves.

In this fashion we can analyse the specification and give appropriate definitions for each record type. This is formalised in the following sections.

3 Preprocessing the VDM Specification

In this top-down analysis, the VDM spec is preprocessed to decide how to best translate each record type. Two sets are declared, *Simple* and *Manager* which represent those types which should be represented as a simple object machine, or as an object manager machine respectively. The analysis is a simple recursive procedure. First find the state, for example:

> **state** *Example* **of**
> $\quad$ $a : T$ $\qquad$ // where T contains no record type
> $\quad$ $b : R$ $\qquad$ // where R is a record type
> $\quad$ $c : S\text{-set}$ $\quad$ // where S is a record type
> **end**

T is any type which does not contain a record type, and it can be basic, user defined or an aggregate type (set, map or sequence) which do not have record types as members.

Any record types which are referenced directly, such as R, are added to the set *Simple*, and any record which is part of an aggregate, such as S, are added to the set *Manager*.

This process is repeated for each record type $R \in Simple$, and $S \in Manager$, with the additional conditions:

1. if $S \in Manager$, then $S \notin Simple$;
2. if record R occurs in a field of $S \in Manager$, then $R \in Manager$.

Thus if a record type S is added to *Manager*, it must be removed from *Simple*, and any records referenced from S must also be added to *Manager*.

4 Inferring a Structured Model

When the preprocessing is complete, then machines can be generated. All record types in *Simple* are translated as simple structured object machines, while types which are in *Manager* are translated as object manager machines. Any record types not in either of these sets are translated as property oriented stateless machines.

Thus there are three cases to consider of records to translate: a *Simple* record with a reference to a *Simple* record within it; a *Simple* record with a reference to a *Manager* record; and a *Manager* record with a reference to a *Manager* record. The final case of *Simple* within *Manager* will not occur.

In the first case, if for example, P ∈ *Simple* such that:

$$P :: r1 : T \qquad // \text{ non record type}$$
$$r2 : R \qquad // \text{ record type such that } R \in Simple$$

then we would generate the simple state machine:

MACHINE   *P_Obj*

INCLUDE *r2.R_Obj*

VARIABLES

   r1

INVARIANT

   $r1 \in T$

END

where *R_Obj* is a simple state machine as in Section 2 above. Note that the machine *R_Obj* is included into this machine with a renaming, using the convenient name *r2*. This machine may well be used elsewhere in the specification, and each including machine needs a unique copy.

For the second case, if P ∈ *Simple* such that:

$$P :: r1 : T \qquad // \text{ non record type}$$
$$r2 : S \qquad // \text{ record type such that } S \in Manager$$

then generate the simple state machine:

MACHINE   *P_Obj*

INCLUDE *S_Mgr*

VARIABLES

   r1 ,r2

INVARIANT

   $r1 \in T \wedge r2 \in sids$

   . . .

END

where *S_Mgr* is an object manager machine for the type S, as given in section 2.

Note that there is no renaming carried out here. There is only one object manager machine in the system, and all references should be to that machine. However, there is an issue here: the rules of composition in B allow a machine to be included in only one other machine. Thus if the manager record is referred to from more than one record type, this condition may be broken. The resolution of this problem would be to break down the *S_Mgr* machine into two, with a simple machine declaring the abstract set *S_Ids*, representing the object identifiers, and a manager machine. The manager machine is then included with renaming, and the set is accessed via the SEES construct. This allows the same set of object identifiers to be used across different object managers.

For the third case, if P ∈ *Manager* such that:

$$P :: r1 : T \qquad // \text{ non record type}$$
$$\quad r2 : S \qquad // \text{ record type such that S} \in Manager$$

then generate the object manager machine:

MACHINE   *P_Mgr*

INCLUDE *S_Mgr*

SETS *P_Id*

VARIABLES

   pids,r1 ,r2

INVARIANT

   pids ⊆ *P_Id* ∧
   r1 ∈ *pids* → *T* ∧
   r2 ∈ *pids* → *sids*

   . . .

END

Other types and record types, which are not accessed via the state model are treated by a property oriented translation.

It may also be necessary to give property oriented translations as well as state based ones for certain records; they are used as input/output to functions for example. The analysis of the specification can be extended to cover this eventuality.

5   Handling Further Language Constructs

The translation presented so far concentrates on the different data models of VDM and B. To present a full translation, other aspects of the languages need to be considered, especially the type and expression language, and the operation and function language. These are not the main subject of this paper, which is considering the data model, so we shall only consider them briefly.

The richness of the VDM-SL expressions and types makes direct translation to AMN difficult. Many expression constructs are not easily expressed in AMN's properties notation; and result types of operations and functions may be of compound types (e.g. tuples) which are awkward to represent and work with in AMN. On the other hand, there are reasonably obvious translations from the VDM expression syntax to AMN's generalised substitutions. Though the latter are state transformers and not functional expressions, this suggests a translation approach that wherever possible "re-interprets" VDM functions as AMN operations which do not change the state.

A VDM specification which makes heavy use of functions and expressions translates to a heavily property-oriented AMN specification which is ungainly to work with in practice, generating difficult proof obligations both for self-consistency and in subsequent refinement and implementation.

Part of the principle of our approach is to translate VDM functions into B operations as much as is practically possible. Some analysis of functions is thus required to determine which part of the state they are applied to, and which machine to enter them into. Some of these are fairly straightforward. If a function has a signature of the form:

$record\_fun1\ (rin : Record, a_1 : t_1 \ldots a_n : t_n)\ rout : Record$

pre ...

post $rout = \textbf{mk-}Record\ (P_1(rin, a_1 \ldots a_n), \ldots, P_m(rin, a_1 \ldots a_n))$;

where *Record* is a record type in the set *Simple*, then it is reasonable to translate this function as an operation in machine *Record_obj*, with the declaration of the form:

$record\_fun1(\ a\_1, \ldots, a\_n\ )\quad \widehat{=}$

    PRE

        $a\_1 \in t\_1 \wedge \ldots a\_n \in t\_n$

        ...

    THEN

        $r\_1 := P\_1(a\_1 \ldots a\_n)$

        ...

        $r\_m := P\_m(a\_1 \ldots a\_n)$

    END ;

where $r\_1, \ldots r\_m$ are the variables of the record machine. The expressions P_1, ..., P_m which give the transformation of variables may also involve the variables of the machine, and also may themselves be operations (with consequent changes in syntax), especially if the variables are themselves record types, and thus provided by an included machine.

6 A Worked Example

To illustrate the different approaches, we consider the following small example of a VDM-SL specification. This has a state *Metro*, which has a train component. The train itself is a record with two components, *motion*, representing the status of the train's motion, and the current speed of the train. The invariant on the train states that when the train is stopped, its speed is zero. We also provide a function for braking.

state

> **state** *Metro* **of**
> $\quad$ *train* : *Train*
> **end**

types

> *Train* :: *motion* : $MOTIONSTATUS$
> $\qquad\quad$ *speed* : $\mathbf{N}$
>
> **inv mk-***Train* (mm, ss) $\triangleq$
> $\quad (mm = \text{STOPPED} \Rightarrow ss = 0)$
>
>
> *brake* $(tin : Train)$ *tout* : *Train*
> **pre** $tin.motion \in \{\text{ACCELERATING}, \text{STEADY}\}$
> **post** $tout = \mathbf{mk\text{-}}Train\,(\text{DECELERATING}, tin.speed)$;

Under the property oriented translation, this becomes two machines, one with the state model:

MACHINE $\quad$ *Metro_Type*

SEES

> *Train_Type*

VARIABLES

> *train*

INVARIANT

> *train* $\in$ *Train*

END

The other machine is a stateless property-oriented specification, with the invariant represented as a complex first-order logic formula in the properties clause, and the *brake* represented as a stateless operation:

MACHINE   *Train_Type*

SETS *Train0*

CONSTANTS

  Train, mk_Train, inv_Train, motion, speed, init_Train

PROPERTIES

  $Train \subseteq Train0 \land$
  $mk\_Train \in MOTIONSTATUS \times N \to Train0 \land$
  $inv\_Train \in Train0 \to BOOL \land$
  $motion \in Train0 \to MOTIONSTATUS \land$
  $speed \in Train0 \to N \land$
  $(\forall mm,ss).(mm \in MOTIONSTATUS \land ss \in N \Rightarrow$
    $(inv\_Train(mk\_Train(mm,ss)) \Leftrightarrow ((mm = stopped) \Rightarrow (ss = 0)))) \land$
  ...

OPERATIONS

  $tout \longleftarrow brake(tin) \quad \widehat{=}$
    PRE
      $tin \in Train \land$
      $motion (tin) \in \{ accelerating , steady \}$
    THEN
      $tout := mk\_Train (decelerating , speed (tin))$
    END
END

In this latter machine, all functions are represented as stateless operations, which permits a more expressive syntax than translating them as properties. Nevertheless, this is an awkward machine to manipulate in the B-Method, and while perfectly valid in the language, is not a "natural" approach in B.

However, in the top-down method, the train record type is translated into a machine with state variables.

MACHINE   *Train_Obj*

VARIABLES

　motion , speed

INVARIANT

　motion ∈ *MOTIONSTATUS* ∧
　speed ∈ *N* ∧
　(motion = stopped) ⇒ (speed = 0)

OPERATIONS

　brake   ≙
　　PRE
　　　motion ∈ { *accelerating , steady* }
　　THEN
　　　motion : = *decelerating*
　　END

END

This machine then INCLUDEd into the top-level Metro specification, together with a renaming. This is a much more "natural" B machine, using more state variables of simple types, which are close to machine types. This machine can be easily included into a continuing B development, and resulting proof obligations more easily expressed and discharged.

7　Conclusions

We have demonstrated the feasibility of synthesizing structured B specifications from VDM. However, the translation is not yet complete. Further analysis is still required to provide an account of the translation of VDM functions and operations, and of VDM's full type and expression language. This is the subject of ongoing research.

The translation presented here automates the extraction of *design information* from the VDM-SL specification, by deriving a finer-grained state model. As the design process requires intelligent insight, the resultant design may not be in the form the user desires, and therefore an element of user judgement is still required to determine which elements of this design are appropriate. However, as the design elements have been automatically generated, the useful elements have been gained at no cost.

Acknowledgements

We would like to thank our partners on the SPECTRUM project and the Commission of the European Union for their support.

References

1. J-R. Abrial, *The B-Book: Assigning Programs to Meaning*, Cambridge University Press, 1996.
2. J.C. Bicarregui, and B. Ritchie, *Invariants, frames and preconditions: a comparison of the VDM and B notations*, in Proceedings of Formal Methods Europe'93, Lecture Notes in Computer Science, Vol. 670, ed. J. Woodcock and P G Larsen, Springer-Verlag 1993.
3. J.C. Bicarregui, A.J.J. Dick, B.M. Matthews, and E. Woods, *Making the most of formal specification through Animation, Testing and Proof*, Science of Computer Programming 29 (1-2) p.55-80 Elsevier-Science, (June 1997)
4. R.F. Docherty, *Translation from Z to AMN*, proceedings 7th International Conference on Putting into Practice Methods and Tools for Information System Design, ed. H. Habrias, ISBN 2-906082-19-8, 1995.
5. J. Draper (ed), *Industrial benefits of the SPECTRUM approach*, SPECTRUM Project External Deliverable 1.3, 1997.
6. ISO, *"ISO/IEC 13817-1 Information Technology - Programming Languages, their environments and system software interfaces - Vienna Development Method - Specification Language. Part 1:Base Language"*, 1996.
7. C.B. Jones, *Systematic Software Development Using VDM*, 2nd Edition, Prentice-Hall, 1990.
8. K. Lano, *The B Language and Method: a guide to practical formal development*, Springer-Verlag 1996.
9. B. Ritchie, J.C. Bicarregui, and H. Haughton, *Experiences in Using the Abstract Machine Notation in a GKS Case Study*, Proceeding of Formal Methods Europe '94, Naftalin, Denvir, Bertran (Eds), LNCS 873, Springer-Verlag, 1994.

An Object-Based Approach to the B Formal Method

Alexander Malioukov

Turku Centre for Computer Science (TUCS)
Åbo Akademi University, Department of Computer Science
DataCity, Lemminkäisenkatu 14 A, FIN-20520, Turku, Finland
e-mail: amaliouk@abo.fi

Abstract. In this paper, we describe an approach to the design of distributed systems that integrate object-oriented methods (OOM) and the non object-oriented B formal method. Our goal is to retain some OOM advantages and produce a flexible and reliable specification, and through the use of our example, we show how this is achieved. We prove formally that our design meets its informal specification with the help of B-Toolkit Release 3.3.1. We illustrate the approach by the B specification of A Computerized Visitor Information System (ACVIS). Using Object Modeling Technique diagrams allows us to make ACVIS more readable and open for changes.

1 Introduction

This article presents the B specification and implementation of ACVIS. B is a method for specifying, designing, and coding software systems [1]. ACVIS is *A Computerized Visitor Information System*. This system assists in managing arrangements for visitors and meetings at a large site. Our goal is to produce a reusable specification of this system. For this purpose, we use Object-Oriented Methods (OOM). We prove formally that our design meets its specification with the help of B-Toolkit Release 3.3.1 (Copyright B-Core (UK) Ltd. 1985-96) [2]. Although B is not object-oriented in nature, we still hope to retain some OOM advantages. Through the simulation of inheritance and encapsulation we integrate OOM with the not object-oriented formal method B. A B specification is generally constructed from a structure of included abstract machines. Abstract machine is a concept that is very close to certain notions well-known in programming, under the names of modules, classes or abstract data types [1]. For detailed description of ACVIS we use the Object Model Notation of Object Modeling Technique (OMT). These diagrams allow us to make ACVIS more readable and open for changes. The following steps are taken for the formal specification, design and implementation of ACVIS software:

- At an early stage in the analysis it becomes clear that ACVIS consists of several highly independent subsystems. It leads us first to define the manager of our system and then to specify the help machines (the subsystems in isolations).

- We refine the help machines into four special ones. We need to prepare the ACVIS for the implementation of a previously used dot notation.
- We implement all specifications that we are using for the system modeling.

The resulting model is bigger than the "classical" one but more robust, flexible and reliable. There are fewer numbers of proof obligations. The given solution can be changed easily according to any new task. The process of organizing new structures takes some effort.

Section 2 is a description of ACVIS problem domain. In section 3 we use our system to illustrate how an object analysis can be used to guide B developments. Section 4 is devoted to the well-commented B-Toolkit specification of our system. Sections 5 and 6 present some intermediate steps between specification and implementation. In other words, these sections show the evolution of design. Section 7 presents the implementation step. There are some concluding remarks in section 8. Appendix contains the implementation of significant operations.

2 Problem Description

The following information [5] is initially given: Visitors come to the site to attend meetings. A visitor may require a hotel reservation. Each meeting is required to take place in a conference room. A meeting may require the use of a dining room for lunch. Booking a dining room requires lunch information, including the number of places needed.

Some important properties:

1. At any time a conference room may be associated with only one meeting.
2. At any time a meeting may be associated with more than one conference room.
3. At any time a meeting may be associated with only one dining room.
4. At any time participants from several meetings can occupy the same dining room. Each dining room has a maximum capacity and unnumbered seats.
5. At any time a visitor may be associated with only one meeting.
6. At any time a meeting may involve several visitors.
7. At any time a hotel room may be associated with only one visitor.

Remark: We omit the notion of time but it can be added, if needed.

3 From the Problem Description to the Specification

At initial glance, objects and B machines have many similarities, such as inheritance or encapsulation. The B-Method and its supporting tools enforce the idea of encapsulation completely [4]. However, as noted in [10] objects are structured in order to model the real world, where machines are structured in order to encapsulate proof obligations.

We do not use polymorphism and dynamic binding because they are not supported by B-Toolkit. Thus, in practice, B-Toolkit can not even give a possibility to exploit any global variables. Nevertheless, it makes sense, because when the tool tries to prove the correctness of a machine nobody can be sure that simultaneously another machine, using the aforementioned variables has not changed their values. This causes confusion as to the correct variables to use. Finally we can state that the B-Toolkit is not object-oriented but object-based, that is why we name our system as Object-Based ACVIS (OBACVIS).

Our goal is to create a specification that meets the OBACVIS requirements. As far as OBACVIS is an object-based solution let us start from the object model. For constructing such a model we should do the following steps according to the OMT notation [6]:

- Identify classes;
- Identify associations between classes;
- Identify attributes of classes;
- Organize and simplify classes using inheritance.

1. The identification of classes consists of:

   - Extraction of all nouns from the problem statement. Presume they are the initial classes. In the OBACVIS example it is: **Visitors, Meetings, Hotel reservation, Conference rooms, Participants, Dining rooms, Lunch, Seats, Hotel rooms, Maximal capacity of a dining room, Number of places in a dining room.**
   - Additional classes that do not appear directly in the statement, but can be identified from our knowledge of the problem domain. For example, **People**.
   - Eliminating unnecessary and incorrect classes according to the following criteria:
     - Attributes. Names that primarily describe individual objects should be restated as attributes. For example, **Maximal capacity of a dining room** is a dining room's property.
     - Operations. For example, **Hotel reservation** is a sequence of actions and not an object class.
     - Irrelevant. Initial class **Lunch** has nothing in common with our visitor information system.
     - Vague. For example, **Seats** is vague. In the OBACVIS system, this is a part of **Dining rooms**.
     - Redundant. If two or more classes express the same information the most descriptive name should be kept. For instance, **Participants** and **Visitors** are redundant.

   Removing all spurious classes, we are left with the following classes:
     - **PEOPLE**
     - **MEETINGS**
     - **CONFERENCE_ROOMS**
     - **DINING_ROOMS**
     - **HOTEL_ROOMS**

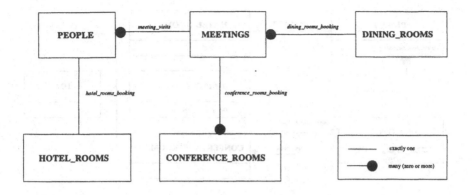

Fig. 1. OBACVIS initial class diagram

2. Now we should identify the associations between classes. Any dependency between two or more classes is an association. It can be easily done according to the task description. For example, if one considers the phrase from the problem description "At any time a conference room may be associated with only one meeting", it is obvious that between classes **MEETINGS** and **CONFERENCE_ROOMS** should be 'many-to-one' relation. By using such a simple method we find four associations between defined classes. They are designated as *meeting_visits, hotel_rooms_booking, dining_rooms_booking, conference_rooms_booking.*

Now we have the classes and associations between them. We can draw an initial class diagram by using Object Model Notation of OMT. Following the notation, all classes are described by means of rectangles and the associations among classes are defined as named arcs. Fig. 1 shows OBACVIS initial class diagram. The class diagram is an object diagram that describes classes as a schema, pattern, or template for many possible instances of data [6]. We should not forget the difference between classes and objects. **Object** is a concept, the abstraction, or thing with crisp boundaries and meanings for the problem at hand. **Class** is a description of a group of objects with similar properties, common behavior, common relationships, and common semantics [6]. In such case, **HOTEL_ROOMS** is a class but **HOTEL_ROOM** is an object.

3. Attributes are properties of individual objects, such as name, weight, velocity, or color. In the OBACVIS we define the following attributes: *register_book_for_visitors, register_book_for_meetings* and *Dining_Room_Capacity.*

Actually *register_book_for_visitors* and *register_book_for_meetings* are sets of names. The meaning of these two attributes can be explained in the following manner: having name of any visitor (meeting) one can check if this item is in the set of visitors (meetings) or not. One can use this information to avoid duplication of the registration. Attribute *Dining_Room_Capacity* is a maximal number of seats at each dining room. For the simplification of our problem we assume that all the dining rooms have an equal number of seats.

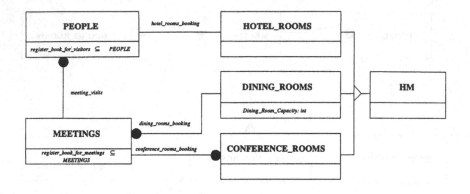

Fig. 2. OBACVIS class diagram with attributes and inheritance

4. The next step is to organize classes by using inheritance. **CONFERENCE_ROOMS**, **DINING_ROOMS** and **HOTEL_ROOMS** have similar structure, except **DINING_ROOMS** which has an attribute *Dining_Room_Capacity*. We can open a new superclass **HM** (help machine). Each subclass (**CONFERENCE_ROOMS**, **DINING_ROOMS** and **HOTEL_ROOMS**) inherits all properties from the superclass **HM**.
   Fig. 2 is a class diagram of OBACVIS with attributes and inheritance.

4 Specification

In the B-Method, specifications, refinements and implementations are presented as Abstract Machines. B is one of the few "formal methods" which has robust, commercially available tool support for the entire development life cycle from specification through to code generation [3]. Further on, we are going to show the B-code and explain the way of system modeling by using the object model of OBACVIS.

We present each class from previously defined object model as a separate abstract machine. Machine OBACVIS is the cover or manager of the system in whole. The attributes of the object model we define as two variables (*register_book_for_visitors* and *register_book_for_meetings*) and one input parameter (*Dining_Room_Capacity*).

INVARIANT should contain all information about the associations between classes, otherwise one can not be sure that a machine meets the requirements of the informal specification.

Operations can be generated according to the different scenarios (a scenario is a sequence of operations that occurs during one particular execution of a system, the scope of scenario can vary). For example, a conference:

1. A conference is arranged (operation *Create_Meeting*).
2. Conference participants are registered (*Create_Visitor*).
3. The participants need accommodations (*Book_Hotel_Room*).
4. Conference and dining rooms are needed (*Book_Dining_Room*, *Book_Conference_Room*).
5. Unused conference and dining rooms should be closed to the participants by the organizers (*Cancel_Dining_Room*, *Cancel_Conference_Room*).
6. The conference participants check out (*Cancel_Hotel_Room*, *Destroy_Visitor*).
7. The conference is over (*Cancel_Meeting*).

Finally, we specify 13 **OPERATIONS**:

- *Create_Meeting* creates a new meeting at a certain time. A meeting can not be created twice.
- *Cancel_Meeting* closes a meeting, provides no conference rooms, dining room and registered visitors are associated with the meeting.
- *Add_Visitor_To_Meeting* adds a name of registered visitor to the list of participants of an arranged meeting. The precondition of this operation checks, if there is a place for the new visitor in the already booked dining room. A visitor can not be added twice.
- *Remove_Visitor_From_Meeting* removes a name of registered visitor from the list of participants of an arranged meeting.
- *Book_Conference_Room* books a free conference room for an arranged meeting. A conference room can not be booked twice.
- *Cancel_Conference_Room* makes free a booked conference room.
- *Book_Dining_Room* books a free dining room for an arranged meeting. A dining room can not be booked twice.
- *Cancel_Dining_Room* makes free a booked dining room.
- *Cancel_Meeting_Arrangement* quits a meeting with associated conference, dining rooms and all registered visitors.
- *Create_Visitor* registers a new visitor. A visitor can not be registered twice.
- *Destroy_Visitor* removes a name of registered visitor from the registration list.
- *Book_Hotel_Room* books a hotel room for a registered visitor. A person can not book one hotel room twice. Only one person can book one hotel room.
- *Cancel_Hotel_Room* checks out a visitor.

OBACVIS manages each operation of the above-defined classes. Such managing works in the following way: OBACVIS declares the types of input parameters and after that calls the operations from the help machines. They do some actions: an initialization of variables, definition of sets and **INVARIANT**, checking preconditions of operations (the **INVARIANT** should hold for all preconditions), and finally changing sets according to the operation.

There are still some preconditions at the operations of OBACVIS. Mainly these preconditions declare the types of input parameters. That is why B-Toolkit generates only twenty-four proof obligations for the OBACVIS instead of thirty-seven for the non object-based solution ACVIS. Fifteen proof obligations were proved by the Automatic Prover (AutoProof) of B-Toolkit. Others were proved easily.

MACHINE   *OBACVIS (Dining_Room_Capacity)*

INCLUDES

HR . HM_1 ,
CR . HM_3 ,
MV . HM_2 ,
DR . HM_2

VARIABLES

register_book_for_visitors ,
register_book_for_meetings

INVARIANT

---

register_book_for_visitors is a subset of set *PEOPLE*. In other words, *register_book_for_visitors* is the list of registered visitors.

---

register_book_for_visitors $\subseteq$ *PEOPLE* $\wedge$

---

register_book_for_meetings is a subset of set *MEETINGS*.
In other words, *register_book_for_meetings* is the list of registered meetings.

---

register_book_for_meetings $\subseteq$ *MEETINGS* $\wedge$

The sum of all registered visitors from all registered meetings that associated with each dining room should be less or equal *Dining_Room_Capacity*.

$\forall d\_r . (d\_r \in DINING\_ROOMS \Rightarrow$
card $(MV . event^{-1} [DR . event^{-1} [\{ d\_r \}]]) \leq Dining\_Room\_Capacity)$

INITIALISATION

register_book_for_visitors := {} $\|$
register_book_for_meetings := {}

OPERATIONS

Create_Meeting(meeting) $\widehat{=}$
    PRE   *meeting* $\in$ *MEETINGS* $\wedge$
       meeting $\notin$ *register_book_for_meetings*
    THEN
       register_book_for_meetings := register_book_for_meetings $\cup$ *{ meeting }*
    END ;

Cancel_Meeting(meeting) $\widehat{=}$
    PRE   *meeting* $\in$ *register_book_for_meetings* $\wedge$
    meeting $\notin$ ran *(MV . event)* $\wedge$
    meeting $\notin$ ran *(CR . event)* $\wedge$
    meeting $\notin$ dom *(DR . event)*

THEN
    register_book_for_meetings := *register_book_for_meetings* − { *meeting* }
END ;

Add_Visitor_To_Meeting(*visitor* , *meeting*) ≙
    PRE   *meeting* ∈ *register_book_for_meetings* ∧
    visitor ∈ *register_book_for_visitors* ∧
    visitor ∉ dom (*MV* . *event*) ∧

Before adding a name of new *visitor* to the list of participants of the current *meeting* we want to be sure that there is as minimum one vacant place in the dining room.

---

    card (*MV* . *event* $^{-1}$ [*DR* . *event* $^{-1}$ [*DR* . *event* [{ *meeting* }]]]) <
    Dining_Room_Capacity
THEN
    MV . *Adding* (*visitor* , *meeting*)
END ;

Remove_Visitor_From_Meeting(*visitor*) ≙
    PRE   *visitor* ∈ dom (*MV* . *event*)   **THEN**
    MV . *Cancelation* (*visitor*)
END ;

Book_Conference_Room(*meeting* , *room*) ≙
    PRE   *meeting* ∈ *register_book_for_meetings* ∧
    room ∈ *CONFERENCE_ROOMS* ∧
    room ∉ dom (*CR* . *event*)
THEN
    CR . *Adding* (*room* , *meeting*)
END ;

Cancel_Conference_Room(*meeting*) ≙
    PRE   *meeting* ∈ ran (*CR* . *event*)
THEN
    CR . *Cancelation* (*meeting*)
END ;

Book_Dining_Room(*meeting* , *room*) ≙
    PRE   *meeting* ∈ *register_book_for_meetings* ∧
    meeting ∉ dom (*DR* . *event*) ∧
    room ∈ *DINING_ROOMS* ∧

Before booking the dining *room*, we want to be sure that there are enough vacant seats for all visitors of the current *meeting*.

---

    card (*MV* . *event* $^{-1}$ [*DR* . *event* $^{-1}$ [{ *room* }] ∪ { *meeting* }]) ≤
    Dining_Room_Capacity
THEN
    DR . *Adding* (*meeting* , *room*)
END ;

Cancel_Dining_Room(meeting) $\hat{=}$
    PRE   *meeting* $\in$ dom (*DR . event*)
    THEN
        DR . Cancelation (*meeting*)
    END ;

Cancel_Meeting_Arrangements(meeting) $\hat{=}$
    PRE   *meeting* $\in$ *register_book_for_meetings*
    THEN
    register_book_for_meetings := *register_book_for_meetings* $-$ { *meeting* } $\|$
        CR . Cancelation (*meeting*) $\|$
        DR . Cancelation (*meeting*) $\|$
        MV . Cancelation (*meeting*)
    END ;

Create_Visitor(person) $\hat{=}$
    PRE   *person* $\in$ *PEOPLE* $\wedge$
    person $\notin$ *register_book_for_visitors*
    THEN
        register_book_for_visitors := *register_book_for_visitors* $\cup$ { *person* }
    END ;

Destroy_Visitor(person) $\hat{=}$
    PRE   *person* $\in$ *register_book_for_visitors* $\wedge$
    person $\notin$ dom (*HR . event*) $\wedge$
    person $\notin$ dom (*MV . event*)
    THEN
        register_book_for_visitors := *register_book_for_visitors* $-$ { *person* }
    END ;

Book_Hotel_Room(person , room) $\hat{=}$
    PRE
        person $\in$ *register_book_for_visitors* $\wedge$
        person $\notin$ dom (*HR . event*) $\wedge$
        room $\in$ *HOTEL_ROOMS*
    THEN
        HR . Adding (*person , room*)
    END ;

Cancel_Hotel_Room(person) $\hat{=}$
    PRE
        person $\in$ dom (*HR . event*)
    THEN
        HR . Cancelation (*person*)
    END

DEFINITIONS
    HOTEL_ROOMS $\hat{=}$ $\mathbb{N}$;
    PEOPLE $\hat{=}$ $\mathbb{N}$;
    MEETINGS $\hat{=}$ $\mathbb{N}$;
    CONFERENCE_ROOMS $\hat{=}$ $\mathbb{N}$;
    DINING_ROOMS $\hat{=}$ $\mathbb{N}$

END

5 Help Machines

We include four help machines into system manager OBACVIS. Actually, there are only three help machines. We make our specification more elegant by using a dot notation. For instance, MV.HM_2 and DR.HM_2 are two machines with an identical structure but with different data. In other words, machines MV.HM_2 and DR.HM_2 inherit all variables and operations from the machine HM_2. If we add one element into machine MV.HM_2, it will be the same as if we would add one element into the set *MV.event* but not into the set *DR.event* or *event*. Each help machine has its own **INVARIANT**.

DR.HM_2 corresponds to the class **DINING_ROOMS**, CR.HM_3 - **CONFERENCE-_ROOMS**, HR.HM_1 - **HOTEL_ROOMS**, MV.HM_2 simulates the process of visitor registration. It is easy to note that name of each help machine consists of class name abbreviation and number of help machine's type. We keep few classes inside the system manager, for instance, **PEOPLE** and **MEETINGS**. We would like to emphasize the fact that it is not necessary to define each class as a separate abstract machine.

Each help machine includes operations to create an object (*Adding*) and to destroy all object instances (*Cancelation*). It is impossible "to send" from super-machine into sub-machines any notes about the type of operator between variables. Machines HM_1 and HM_2 are absolutely identical but variable *event* at HM_1 is a set of partial injections (also known as 'one-to-one relation'). Unlike variable *event* at HM_2 is a set of partial function (also known as 'many-to-one relations'). The difference between HM_3 and HM_1 or HM_2 is that at operation *Cancelation* of machine HM_2 the result is an anti-restriction (also known as domain subtraction) but at other help machines it is anti-co-restriction (also known as range subtraction).

MACHINE *HM_2*

VARIABLES

   event

INVARIANT

   $event \in XX \nrightarrow YY$

INITIALISATION

   $event := \{\}$

OPERATIONS

   Adding(*xx* , *yy*) $\hat{=}$
      PRE $xx \in XX \wedge$
         $xx \notin \text{dom} \, (\, event \,) \wedge$
         $yy \in YY$
      THEN $event := event \cup \{ \, xx \mapsto yy \, \}$
      END ;

   Cancelation(*xx*) $\hat{=}$
      PRE $xx \in XX$
      THEN $event := \{ \, xx \, \} \vartriangleleft event$
      END

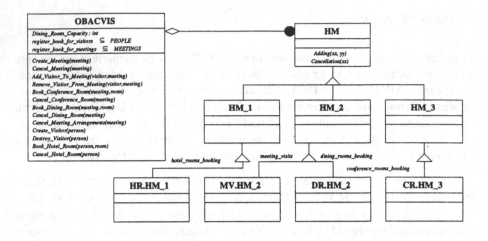

Fig. 3. General structure of the OBACVIS.

DEFINITIONS

$XX \,\,\hat{=}\,\, N;$
$YY \,\,\hat{=}\,\, N$

END

The B-Toolkit generates nine proof obligations for the help machines. All of them can be easily proved by the AutoProof.

6 From the Specification to the Implementation

All advantages that we had on the previous level, we lose on the level of implementation. Unfortunately, it is almost impossible to implement the dot notation in B-Toolkit. We simulate it in the following manner. To make the help machines different we change the names of variables to prevent B-Toolkit from generating errors. On the previous level we have three help machines with the similar structures and one of them was used twice with different prefixes. Now we have four help machines with different names without any prefixes. You can clearly identify which one corresponds to the help machine on the previous level because of the information within the machine's name. For example, machine HRHM1 is the machine HR.HM_1 which is submachine for machine HM_1 in its turn. Fig. 3 shows general structure of the OBACVIS.

The following example demonstrates how the system works. If one needs to book a hotel room he (she) should call operation *Book_Hotel_Room* from machine OBACVIS which calls operation Adding_HR from HRHM1. Machine OBACVIS checks types of input parameters (name of visitor and number of room). The help machine checks if the visitor is previously registered and if the room is vacant. If successful, it will proceed to add the tuple (name, number) to *hotel_rooms_booking*.

MACHINE *MVHM2*

VARIABLES

  MVevent

INVARIANT

  $MVevent \in XX \nrightarrow YY$

INITIALISATION

  $MVevent := \{\}$

OPERATIONS

  $Adding\_MV(xx, yy) \quad \hat{=}$
  PRE $xx \in XX \land$
    $xx \notin \text{dom}(MVevent) \land$
    $yy \in YY$
  THEN $MVevent := MVevent \cup \{xx \mapsto yy\}$
  END;

  $Cancelation\_MV(xx) \quad \hat{=}$
  PRE $xx \in XX$

The result of this operation will be anti-restriction of *MVevent* by *xx* (also known as domain subtraction).

  THEN $MVevent := \{xx\} \lhd MVevent$
  END

DEFINITIONS

  $XX \quad \hat{=} \quad \mathbb{N};$
  $YY \quad \hat{=} \quad \mathbb{N}$

END

7 Implementation

In B, an implementation is an abstract machine from which data declaration and executable statements can be generated. The implementation has no **VARIABLES** clause. Instead, it has **IMPORTS** clause. The B-Toolkit provides a library of machines with concrete data types. In our example, OBACVISI is an implementation of the system manager. HRHM1I, MVHM2I, CRHM3I and DRHM2I are implementations of the help machines (subsystems). They are imported into the OBACVISI. Bool_TYPE, basic_io, String_TYPE are machines from library.

The specification's variables are encapsulated in the machines from the standard library. The preconditions of operations are presented as error messages. After these changes

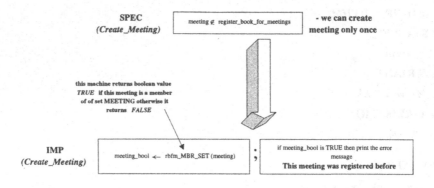

Fig. 4. Example of implementation of a logical sentence

the model of the OBACVIS system looks like a C program. There are some typical situations:

– when we try to book something (for example, *Create_Meeting*);
– when we try to cancel/destroy something/somebody (*Cancel_Meeting*).

Fig. 4 shows an example of a translation of one logical sentence of the precondition's operation *Create_Meeting*:

– At the specification there was the line "a meeting is not a member of operation *register_bool_for_meetings*". It means that we can create a meeting only once.
– At the implementation this line is translated into the following sequential composition:
  1. Run the machine *rbfm_MBR_SET* with an input parameter *meeting*. This machine checks if the current *meeting* is in the set *register_book_for_meetings* or not. The result is the value of Boolean variable *meeting_bool*. An abbreviation *rbfm* corresponds to the variable *register_book_for_meetings*.
  2. If *meeting_bool* is *TRUE* then the error message *"There is no use to register this meeting, it has already been registered."* says on the screen of the monitor.

The implementation of six significant operations (e.g. *Create_Meeting, Cancel_Meeting, Add_Visitor_To_Meeting, Remove_Visitor_From_Meeting, Book_Conference_Room and Cancel_Conference_Room*) is available as an Appendix.

8 Conclusions

There is an advantage in object-based solution ACVIS (*A Computerized Visitor Information System*) problem:

- Decrease a quantity of proof obligations. There are 24 proof obligations for the main machine OBACVIS and 9 for the sub-machines. However, about 80 % of the proof obligations are proved by AutoProof.
- The new system is quite flexible. If one needs a new kind of room he (she) should include one of the submachines, which meets the requirements of the selected type, call some operations of this submachine from OBACVIS or if it makes sense, add a new submachine. He (she) should not add any new variables or lines into the **INVARIANT**.
- A beneficial side effect for practitioners writing such documents is that their understanding of the system in OMT diagrams is greatly helped by the process of constructing formal specifications. Such diagrams can be useful for presentations.

Acknowledgment

I would like to thank my supervisor Ralph-Johan Back, Emil Sekerinski, Kaisa Sere and Ib Sørensen who readily responded to my questions and also to express gratitude to Philipp Heuberger whose critical comments were very useful.

References

1. Abrial, J.-R.: The B-Book. Cambridge University Press (1996)
2. B-Core. B-Toolkit Release 3.2. Manual. Oxford, U.K. (1996)
3. Lano, K.: The B Language and Method. A guide to Practical Formal Development. Springer-Verlag (1996)
4. Wordsworth, J.B.: Software Engineering with B. Addison-Wesley (1996)
5. Flinn, B., Sørensen, I.H.: CAVIAR: a case study in specification. In I.Hayes (editor) Specification Case Studies, Prentice-Hall International (1987)
6. Rumbaugh, J., Blaha, M., Premerlani, W., Eddy, F., Lorensen W.: Object-Oriented Modeling and Design. Prentice-Hall International (1991)
7. Seidewitz, E., Stark., M.: Reliable Object-Oriented Software. SIGS Books (1995)
8. Meyer, B.: Object-oriented Software Construction. Prentice-Hall International (1988)
9. Shore, R.: An Object-Oriented Approach to B. "First B Conference", Nantes, France, November, 24-26 (1996)
10. Facon, P.: Mapping object diagrams into B specifications. In Methods Integration Workshop (1996)

Appendix

IMPLEMENTATION *OBACVISI*
REFINES
   OBACVIS
SEES
   Bool_TYPE , *basic_io* , *String_TYPE* , *HRevent_Nfnc* , *CRevent_Nfnc* ,

DRevent_Nfnc , *MVevent_Nfnc*

IMPORTS

    HRHM1 , *MVHM2* , *CRHM3* , *DRHM2* ,
    rbfv_set (*PEOPLE* , *n_of_visitors*) ,
    rbfm_set (*MEETINGS* , *n_of_meetings*) ,
    STORAGE_Varr ($\mathbb{N}$, *for_storage*) ,
    OBLOOPS

INVARIANT

    rbfv_sset = *register_book_for_visitors* $\wedge$
    rbfm_sset = *register_book_for_meetings*

OPERATIONS

    Create_Meeting(*meeting*) $\widehat{=}$
      VAR
        meeting_bool
      IN
        IF   *meeting* $< 0 \vee$ *meeting* $>$ *n_of_meetings*
        THEN
          PUT_STR ("This meeting is not a member of the set
          MEETINGS. ");
          NWL (*1*)
        ELSE
          meeting_bool $\longleftarrow$ *rbfm_MBR_SET* (*meeting*);
          IF   *meeting_bool* = *TRUE*
          THEN
            PUT_STR ("There is no use to register this meeting,   ");
            PUT_STR ("it has already been registered.");
            NWL (*1*)
          ELSE
            rbfm_ENT_SET (*meeting*)
          END
        END
      END ;

    Cancel_Meeting(*meeting*) $\widehat{=}$
      VAR
        meeting_bool , *mv* , *check* , *def_mv*
      IN
        meeting_bool $\longleftarrow$ *rbfm_MBR_SET* (*meeting*);
        IF   *meeting_bool* = *FALSE*
        THEN
          PUT_STR ("It is unregistered meeting.");
          NWL (*1*)
         ELSE
          mv := *0* ;
          check := *FALSE* ;
          WHILE   *mv* $\leq$ *n_of_meetings* $\wedge$ *check* = *FALSE*   **DO**
            def_mv $\longleftarrow$ *MVevent_DEF_NFNC* (*mv*);
            IF   *def_mv* = *TRUE*

```
            THEN
                check ←— MVevent_EQL_NFNC ( mv , meeting )
            END ;
            mv := mv + 1
        INVARIANT
            ( check = FALSE ⇒ meeting ∉ MVevent_Nfnc [ 1 .. mv − 1 ] ) ∧
            ( check = TRUE ⇒ meeting ∈ ran ( MVevent_Nfnc ) ) ∧
            mv ∈ 0 .. n_of_meetings + 1 ∧
            meeting ∈ 0 .. n_of_meetings
        VARIANT
            n_of_meetings − mv
        END ;
        IF    check = TRUE
        THEN
            PUT_STR ( "Still, there are some registered visitors of
            meeting number" );
            PUT_NAT ( meeting );
            NWL ( 1 )
        ELSE
            check ←— loop_cr ( meeting );
            IF    check = TRUE
            THEN
                PUT_STR ( "Still, there are some conference rooms
                for meeting number" );
                PUT_NAT ( meeting );
                NWL ( 1 )
            ELSE
                check ←— DRevent_DEF_NFNC ( meeting );
                IF    check = TRUE
                THEN
                    PUT_STR ( "Still, there are some dining rooms
                    for meeting number" );
                    PUT_NAT ( meeting );
                    NWL ( 1 )
                ELSE
                    rbfm_RMV_SET ( meeting )
                END
            END
        END
    END
END ;

Add_Visitor_To_Meeting( visitor , meeting )   ≘
    VAR
        meeting_bool , visitor_bool , check , aa , def_aa , bb , def_bb , room , sum , ii
    IN
        meeting_bool ←— rbfm_MBR_SET ( meeting );
        IF    meeting_bool = FALSE
        THEN
            PUT_STR ( "It is unregistered meeting." );
            NWL ( 1 )
```

ELSE
  visitor_bool ⟵ *rbfv_MBR_SET* (*visitor*) **;**
  IF   *visitor_bool* = *FALSE*
  THEN
    PUT_STR (" It is unregistered visitor. ") **;**
    NWL (*1*)
  ELSE
    check ⟵ *MVevent_DEF_NFNC* (*visitor*) **;**
    IF   *check* = *TRUE*
    THEN
      PUT_STR (" Visitor can not be at two meetings
      simultaneously ") **;**
      NWL (*1*)
    ELSE
      aa := *0* **;**
      def_aa := *TRUE* **;**
      room := *0* **;**
      WHILE   *aa* ≤ *n_of_meetings* ∧ *def_aa* = *TRUE*   **DO**
        def_aa ⟵ *DRevent_DEF_NFNC* (*aa*) **;**
        IF   *def_aa* = *TRUE*
        THEN
          IF   *aa* = *meeting*
          THEN
            room ⟵ *DRevent_VAL_NFNC* (*aa*)
          END
        END ;
        aa := *aa* + *1*
      INVARIANT
        (*def_aa* = *FALSE* ⇒ *meeting* ∉ *DRevent_Nfnc* [*1* .. *aa* − *1*]) ∧
        (*def_aa* = *TRUE* ⇒ *meeting* ∈ dom (*DRevent_Nfnc*)) ∧
        aa ∈ *0* .. *n_of_meetings* + *1* ∧
        meeting ∈ *0* .. *n_of_meetings*
      VARIANT
        n_of_meetings − *aa*
      END ;
      sum := *0* **;**
      aa := *0* **;**
      ii := *0* **;**
      check := *FALSE* **;**
      def_aa := *TRUE* **;**
      loop_dr **;**
      bb := *0* **;**
      aa := *0* **;**
      check := *FALSE* **;**
      def_bb := *TRUE* **;**
      WHILE   *bb* ≤ *n_of_visitors* ∧ *def_bb* = *TRUE*   **DO**
        def_bb ⟵ *MVevent_DEF_NFNC* (*bb*) **;**
        IF   *def_bb* = *TRUE*
        THEN
          aa ⟵ *DRevent_VAL_NFNC* (*bb*) **;**

```
                check ⟵ STORAGE_EQL_ARR ( ii , aa )
              END ;
              IF    check = TRUE
              THEN
                 sum := sum + 1
              END ;
              bb := bb + 1
           INVARIANT
              ( def_bb = FALSE ⟹ visitor ∉ MVevent_Nfnc [ 1 .. bb − 1 ] ) ∧
              ( def_bb = TRUE ⟹ visitor ∈ dom ( DRevent_Nfnc ) ) ∧
              bb ∈ 0 .. n_of_visitors + 1
           VARIANT
              n_of_visitors − bb
           END ;
           IF    sum < Dining_Room_Booking
           THEN
              Adding_MV ( visitor , meeting )
           ELSE
              PUT_STR ( " There is no empty seats in the dining
              room that " );
              PUT_STR ( " has been booked for meeting " );
              PUT_NAT ( meeting );
              NWL ( 1 )
           END
         END
       END
     END
   END ;
Remove_Visitor_From_Meeting( visitor )   ≙
   VAR
      check
   IN
      check ⟵ MVevent_DEF_NFNC ( visitor );
      IF   check = FALSE
      THEN
         PUT_STR ( " There is no visitor with such name. " );
         NWL ( 1 )
      ELSE
         Cancelation_MV ( visitor )
      END
   END ;
Book_Conference_Room( meeting , room )   ≙
   VAR
      meeting_bool
   IN
      meeting_bool ⟵ rbfm_MBR_SET ( meeting );
      IF   meeting_bool = FALSE
      THEN
         PUT_STR ( " It is unregistered meeting. " );
```

```
            NWL ( 1 )
      ELSE
          IF     room < 0 ∨ room > n_of_crs
          THEN
              PUT_STR ("This conference room is not a member of
              the set CONFERENCE_ROOMS. ");
              NWL ( 1 )
          ELSE
              Adding_CR ( room , meeting )
          END
      END
    END ;
Cancel_Conference_Room( meeting )   ≙
    VAR
        check
    IN
        check ⟵ loop_cr ( meeting ) ;
        IF    check = FALSE
        THEN
            PUT_STR ("For this meeting no conference
            rooms were booked. ");
            NWL ( 1 )
        ELSE
            Cancelation_CR ( meeting )
        END
    END ;


DEFINITIONS
    for_storage  ≙  50 ;
    Dining_Room_Booking  ≙  20 ;
    n_of_visitors  ≙  50 ;
    n_of_meetings  ≙  50 ;
    n_of_hrs  ≙  100 ;
    n_of_drs  ≙  100 ;
    n_of_crs  ≙  100 ;
    HOTEL_ROOMS  ≙  ℕ ;
    PEOPLE  ≙  ℕ ;
    MEETINGS  ≙  ℕ ;
    CONFERENCE_ROOMS  ≙  ℕ ;
    DINING_ROOMS  ≙  ℕ ;
    HELP_SET  ≙  ℕ ;
    loop_dr  ≙  WHILE    aa ≤ n_of_meetings ∧ def_aa = TRUE   DO
        def_aa ⟵ DRevent_DEF_NFNC ( aa ) ;
        IF    def_aa = TRUE
        THEN
            check ⟵ DRevent_EQL_NFNC ( aa , room )
        END ;
        IF    check = TRUE
        THEN
```

```
        STORAGE_STO_ARR ( ii , aa ) ;
        ii := ii + 1
    END ;
    aa := aa + 1
INVARIANT
    ( def_aa = FALSE ⇒ meeting ∉ DRevent_Nfnc [ 1 .. aa − 1 ] ) ∧
    ( def_aa = TRUE ⇒ meeting ∈ dom ( DRevent_Nfnc ) ) ∧
    aa ∈ 0 .. n_of_meetings + 1 ∧
    meeting ∈ 0 .. n_of_meetings
VARIANT
    n_of_meetings − aa
END
END
```

Graphical Design of Reactive Systems

Emil Sekerinski

McMaster University, Department of Computing and Software
Hamilton, Ontario, Canada, L8S 4K1
emil@mcmaster.ca

Abstract. Reactive systems can be designed graphically using statecharts. This paper presents a scheme for the translation of statecharts into the Abstract Machine Notation (AMN) of the B method. By an example of a conveyor system, we illustrate how the design can be initially expressed graphically with statecharts, then translated to AMN and analysed in AMN, and then further refined to executable code.

1 Introduction

Reactive systems are characterised as having to continuously react to stimuli from their environment, rather than having to produce a single outcome. Distributed systems, embedded systems, and real-time systems are examples of reactive systems.

Statecharts are a visual approach to the design of reactive systems [6]. Statecharts extend finite state diagrams, the graphical representation of finite state machines, by three concepts: hierarchy, concurrency, and communication. These three concepts give enough expressiveness for the specification of even complex reactive systems. Because of the appeal of the graphical notation, statecharts have gained some popularity. For example, statecharts are also part of object-oriented modelling techniques [11, 7].

This paper presents a scheme for the translation of statecharts to the Abstract Machine Notation (AMN) of the B method [1]. This translation scheme allows the design of reactive systems to be

1. initially expressed in the graphical notation of statecharts,
2. translated to AMN and analysed in AMN, e.g. for safety properties, and
3. further refined to AMN machines which can be efficiently executed.

By this translation scheme, statecharts are given a formal semantics in terms of AMN. Several other definitions of the semantics of statecharts were proposed [4]. Although we largely follow the (revised) original definition [8], our goal is a semantic which harmonises well with the refinement calculus in general and with AMN in particular.

Sections 2 – 5 give the translation schemes for state diagrams, hierarchical state diagrams, state diagrams with concurrency, and state diagrams with broadcasting, respectively. Section 6 illustrates the approach by an example of a conveyor system. Section 7 compares this approach with other definitions of statecharts and other approaches to modelling reactive systems with AMN

2 State Diagrams

A state diagram is a graphical representation of a finite state machine. State diagrams, the simplest form of statecharts, consists of a finite number of *states* and *transitions* between those state. Upon an *event*, a system (state machine) may evolve from one state into another. In statecharts, states are symbolised by (rounded) boxes. In AMN, the states of a state diagram are represented by a variable of an enumerated set type:

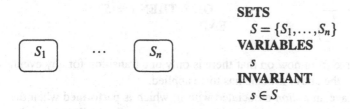

SETS
$$S = \{S_1, \ldots, S_n\}$$
VARIABLES
$$s$$
INVARIANT
$$s \in S$$

A system must have an initial state. In statecharts, an arrow with a fat dot points to the initial state. In AMN, this corresponds to initialising the state variable with that state:

INITIALISATION
$$s := S_1$$

A system can have several initial states, which leads to a nondeterministic initialisation:

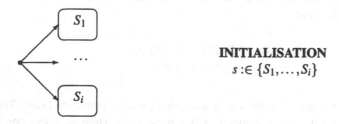

INITIALISATION
$$s :\in \{S_1, \ldots, S_i\}$$

Events cause transitions from one state to another. Events may be *generated* by the environment. In statecharts, transitions are visualised by an arrow between two states, where the arrow is labelled with the event which triggers this transition. In AMN, events are represented by operations, which may be called by the environment. Upon an event, a transition takes only place if in the current state there is a transition on this event. Otherwise, the event is ignored. Suppose only one transition in the system for event E exists:

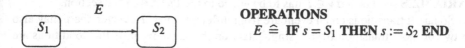

OPERATIONS
$$E \mathrel{\widehat{=}} \textbf{IF } s = S_1 \textbf{ THEN } s := S_2 \textbf{ END}$$

In case there are several transitions labelled with E, the one starting from the current state is taken, if any transition is taken at all. Let $\{S'_1, \ldots, S'_i\} \subseteq S$, where $S'_1, \ldots, S'_i$ do not have to be distinct:

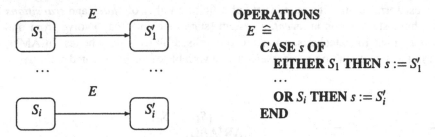

OPERATIONS

$E \;\widehat{=}\;$
  CASE s OF
    EITHER S_1 THEN $s := S'_1$
    ...
    OR S_i THEN $s := S'_i$
  END

For simplicity, we assume from now on that there is only one transition for any event. In case there are several, the above scheme has to be applied.

A transitions may have an *action* associated with it, which is performed when the transition takes places. Actions are assumed to be instantaneous. Typically, actions involve setting actuators or modifying global variables. With the ability to have global variables of arbitrary types, statecharts are not restricted to a finite state space. Here we allow actions to be statements of AMN. In statecharts, an action (or its name) is written by preceding it with a slash:

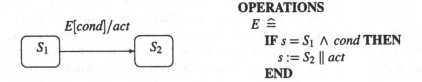

OPERATIONS

$E \;\widehat{=}\;$ IF $s = S_1$ THEN $s := S_2 \;\|\; act$ END

An action may also be performed when setting an initial state. Here we give only the rule if there is one initial state:

/act

  S_1

INITIALISATION

$s := S_1 \;\|\; act$

Transitions may be restricted to be taken only when an additional condition holds. Typically, conditions depend on sensor values and global variables. Here we allow conditions to be predicates of AMN. In statecharts, a condition is written in square brackets:

$E[cond]/act$

$S_1 \longrightarrow S_2$

OPERATIONS

$E \;\widehat{=}\;$
  IF $s = S_1 \wedge cond$ THEN
    $s := S_2 \;\|\; act$
  END

If an action or a condition mentions variable v of type T, then v has to be added to the **VARIABLES** section and $v \in T$ has to be added to the **INVARIANT** section.

So far all transitions on an event are from different states. However, there may also be two or more transition from a single state on the same event. If the conditions are disjoint, then at most one transition can be enabled. If the conditions are overlapping, an enabled transition is chosen nondeterministically:

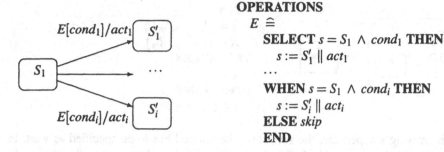

OPERATIONS
$E \; \widehat{=}$
    SELECT $s = S_1 \wedge cond_1$ **THEN**
        $s := S_1' \parallel act_1$
    ...
    WHEN $s = S_1 \wedge cond_i$ **THEN**
        $s := S_i' \parallel act_i$
    ELSE *skip*
    END

Finally, a transition may have parameters, which are supplied by the environment which generates the event. These parameters may be used in the condition and the action of the transition:

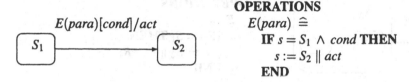

OPERATIONS
$E(para) \; \widehat{=}$
    IF $s = S_1 \wedge cond$ **THEN**
        $s := S_2 \parallel act$
    END

As a special case, a transition can be without an event, known as a *spontaneous* transition. In this case the transition leading to a state with a spontaneous transition needs to be continued immediately by this transition, if the condition is true. Spontaneous transitions allow sharing of a condition and an action if several transitions lead to the starting state of a spontaneous transition:

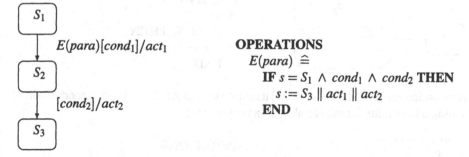

OPERATIONS
$E(para) \; \widehat{=}$
    IF $s = S_1 \wedge cond_1 \wedge cond_2$ **THEN**
        $s := S_3 \parallel act_1 \parallel act_2$
    END

For brevity, we continue to consider transitions labelled only by an event. Parameters, conditions, and actions can be added as given above.

3 Hierarchy

States can have substates. If the system is in a state with substates, it is also in exactly one of those substates. Conversely, if a system is in a substate of a superstate, it is also in that superstate. In statecharts, a superstate with substates is drawn by nesting. In AMN, we model the substates by an extra variable for each superstate containing substates. This generalises to substates which again contain substates:

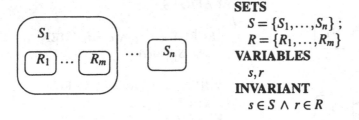

SETS
$S = \{S_1, \ldots, S_n\}$;
$R = \{R_1, \ldots, R_m\}$
VARIABLES
s, r
INVARIANT
$s \in S \land r \in R$

When entering a superstate, the substate to be entered has to be specified as well. In statecharts this is expressed by letting the transition arrow point to a specific substate. In AMN this corresponds to setting the variable for both the superstate and the substate(s) appropriately:

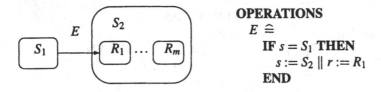

OPERATIONS
$E \cong$
    IF $s = S_1$ THEN
        $s := S_2 \parallel r := R_1$
    END

If a transition arrow points only to the contour of a superstate, then an initial substate must be marked as such. This is identical to letting the transition arrow point directly to that initial state. This is useful if the superstate is referred to only by its name and is defined separately:

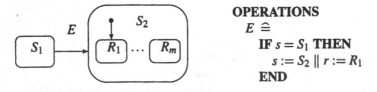

OPERATIONS
$E \cong$
    IF $s = S_1$ THEN
        $s := S_2 \parallel r := R_1$
    END

A transition can leave both a state and its superstate. In AMN, this corresponds to simply setting a new value for the variable of the superstate:

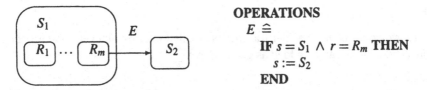

OPERATIONS
$E \cong$
    IF $s = S_1 \land r = R_m$ THEN
        $s := S_2$
    END

If a transition arrow starts at the contour of a superstate, then this is like having an arrow starting from each of the substates, going to the same state on the same event. This is one of the ways statecharts economise on drawing arrows. In AMN, this corresponds to simply setting a new value of the variable of the superstate, irrespective of the current substate. Note that the basic schema for the transition between two simple states is a special case of this:

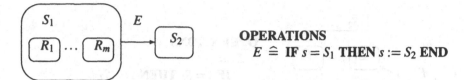

OPERATIONS
$E \mathrel{\hat{=}} \mathbf{IF}\ s = S_1\ \mathbf{THEN}\ s := S_2\ \mathbf{END}$

In statecharts, a transition can point from the contour of a superstate inside to one of the substates. This is like having a transition from all of the substates on that event to this substate. It is again a way statecharts economise on drawing arrows. In AMN, this corresponds to going to that substate irrespective of the value of the variable for the substate:

OPERATIONS
$E \mathrel{\hat{=}} \mathbf{IF}\ s = S_1\ \mathbf{THEN}\ r := R_1\ \mathbf{END}$

The schema for multiple transitions on an event and for multiple transitions starting from the same state apply to hierarchical states as well. However, it should be pointed out that if there is a transition on an event between two substates and between the superstate of those substates and another state, then the schema for multiple transitions from the same state applies, which gives rise to nondeterminism.

4 Concurrency

Reactive systems are naturally decomposed into concurrent activities. In statecharts, concurrency is expressed by orthogonality: a system can be in two independent states simultaneously. This is drawn by splitting a state with a dashed line into independent substates, each of which consists of a number of states in turn. In AMN, this corresponds to declaring a variable for each of the (two or more) concurrent states. These variables are only relevant if the system is in the corresponding superstate:

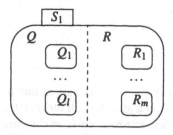

SETS
$S = \{S_1, \ldots, S_n\}$;
$Q = \{Q_1, \ldots, Q_l\}$;
$R = \{R_1, \ldots, S_m\}$
VARIABLES
s, q, r
INVARIANT
$s \in S \wedge q \in Q \wedge r \in R$

A state with concurrent substates is entered by a fork into states in each of the concurrent substates. In AMN, this corresponds to setting the variables for all the concurrent states:

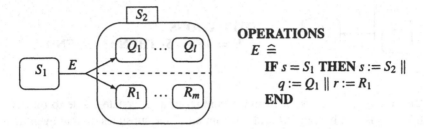

OPERATIONS

$E \ \widehat{=}$

    IF $s = S_1$ **THEN** $s := S_2 \ \|$

       $q := Q_1 \ \| \ r := R_1$

END

If a transition arrow points only to the contour of a state with concurrent substates, then an initial state must be marked as such in all of the concurrent states. This is identical to a fork of the transition arrow to all those initial states. This is useful if the state is referred to only by its name and is defined separately:

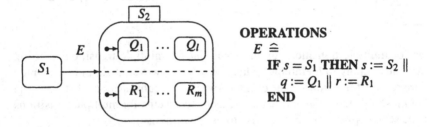

OPERATIONS

$E \ \widehat{=}$

    IF $s = S_1$ **THEN** $s := S_2 \ \|$

       $q := Q_1 \ \| \ r := R_1$

END

A state with concurrent substates is exited by a join from all the concurrent states. Such a transition can only be taken if all concurrent states are in the substate from where the transition arrow starts. In AMN, this implies testing all substates before making the transition:

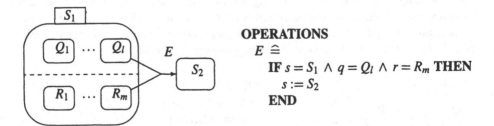

OPERATIONS

$E \ \widehat{=}$

    IF $s = S_1 \ \wedge \ q = Q_l \ \wedge \ r = R_m$ **THEN**

       $s := S_2$

END

If a transition arrow for exiting a state with concurrent substates starts only at one of the states in the concurrent substates, then this is like having a join from all other states of the concurrent state. Again, this is one of the ways statecharts economise on drawing arrows. In AMN, this corresponds to simply setting a new value of the variable of the superstate, irrespective of the concurrent substate:

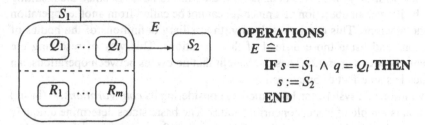

OPERATIONS
$E \cong$
  IF $s = S_1 \wedge q = Q_l$ THEN
    $s := S_2$
  END

Two concurrent states may have transitions on the same event. In case this event occurs, these transitions are taken simultaneously. In AMN, this corresponds to the parallel composition of the transitions. Note that this has implications on the global variables which can occur in the conditions and the actions, a variable can only be assigned by one action:

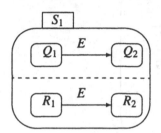

OPERATIONS
$E \cong$
  BEGIN
    IF $q = Q_1$ THEN $q := Q_2$ END $\parallel$
    IF $r = R_1$ THEN $r := R_2$ END
  END

5 Communication

Communication between concurrent states is possible in three ways: First, concurrent states can communicate by global variables. These can be set in actions and read in actions and conditions, following the rules for variables given earlier. Secondly, the condition or the action of a transition may depend on the current substate of a concurrent state. The test whether state S is in substate S_i is written *in S_i*. In AMN, this corresponds to comparing the state variable to S_i:

    in S_i $s = S_i$

Thirdly, concurrent states can communicate by broadcasting of events. On a broadcast of an event, all concurrent states react simultaneously. Events are either generated internally through a broadcast or externally by the environment. Broadcasting of events is associated to transitions and is drawn the same way as an action. In AMN, broadcasting an event corresponds to calling the operation for that event:

           E_1/E_2

$\boxed{S_1} \longrightarrow \boxed{S_2}$

OPERATIONS
$E \cong$ IF $s = S_1$ THEN $s := S_2 \parallel E_2$ END

As calling an operation is a statement, which can appear as an action, the above schema is just a special case of the schema for translating actions. In general, broadcasting of an event may occur anywhere within an action. Care has to be taken since the resulting code may be illegal: an operation of a machine cannot be called from another operation of the same machine. This can be resolved with auxiliary definitions of the bodies of the operations and using those instead of the operations. This way of resolving the dependencies between operations has the benefit that no cycles between operations can be introduced as an effect of broadcasting.

The evolution of a system can be studied by considering its *configurations*. A (basic) configuration is a tuple of basic, concurrent states. The basic states determine uniquely the superstates in which the system is and hence a configuration gives the complete information about the current states of a system. We denote the fact that a system makes a transition from configuration C to C' on event E by $C \xrightarrow{E} C'$.

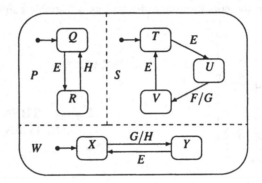

Fig. 1. Statechart with simultaneous transitions on event E and a chain reaction on event F.

In the statechart of Fig. 1, the initial configuration is (Q,T,X). On external event E, states P and S change from Q to R and T to U, respectively, and W remains in X:

$$(Q,T,X) \xrightarrow{E} (R,U,X)$$

If external event F follows, then event G is generated in S on the transition from U to V, which in turn generates event H in W on the transition from Y to Z. This causes the transition from R to Q in P:

$$(R,U,X) \xrightarrow{F} (Q,V,Y)$$

Figure 2 gives the code which results from the translation. It exhibits the above behaviour.

6 Example

We illustrate the technique by an example of a conveyor system. A conveyor belt and an elevating and rotation table are placed next to each other (see Fig. 3). The conveyor belt

```
MACHINE M
SETS
    P = {Q,R} ;
    S = {T,U,V} ;
    W = {X,Y}
VARIABLES
    p,s,w
INVARIANT
    p ∈ P ∧ s ∈ S ∧ w ∈ W
INITIALISATION
    p := Q ∥ s := T ∥ w := X
DEFINITIONS
    HH == (IF p = R THEN p := Q END) ;
    GG == (IF w = X THEN w := Y ∥ HH END)
OPERATIONS
    E =
    BEGIN
        IF p = Q THEN p := R END ∥
        CASE s OF
            EITHER T THEN s := U
            OR V THEN s := T
            END
        END ∥
        IF w = Y THEN w := X END
        END ;
    F =  IF s = U THEN s := V ∥ GG END ;
    G = GG ;
    H = HH
END
```

Fig. 2. AMN machine which corresponds to the statechart of Fig. 1

has to transport objects which are placed on the left of the conveyor belt to its right end and then on the table. The table then elevates and rotates the object to make it available for processing by further machines.

The conveyor belt has a photo-electric cell which signals when an object has arrived at the right end or has left the belt (and thus has moved onto the table). The motor for the belt may be switched on and off: it has to be on while waiting for a new object and has to be switched off when an object is at the end of the belt but cannot be delivered onto the table because the table is not in proper position.

The table lifts and rotates an object clockwise to a position for further processing. The table has two reversing electric motors, one for elevating and one for rotating. Mechanical sensors indicate whether the table is at its left, right, upper, and lower end position, respectively. The table must not move beyond its end position. We assume that initially the table is in its lower left position.

Both machines run in parallel, thus allowing several objects to be transported simultaneously. The program has to ensure that all objects are transported properly, i.e. objects leave the conveyor belt only if the table is in lower left position.

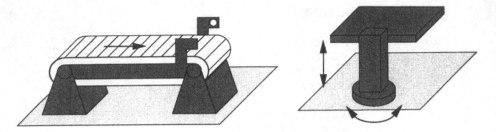

Fig. 3. The conveyor belt on the left and the elevating and rotating table on the right

Statechart of the Conveyor System

The statechart of the conveyor system is given in Fig. 4. We assume that the events *SensorOff* and *SensorOn* for the conveyor belt and the events *UpReached*, *DownReached*, *RightReached*, *LeftReached*, and *ObjectTaken* for the Table are generated by the environment (hardware). The events *ContinueDelivery* and *ObjectPlaced* serve internally for the communication between the concurrent *ConveyorBelt* and *Table* states. At this stage, we consider only the abstract states of the system, like the table being in loading position, rather than the detailed states of the actuators and sensors. As common in statecharts, some states are not given names.

AMN Specification

An AMN machine of the conveyor system is given in Fig. 5. Note that the names *MovingToUnloading* and *MovingToLoading* for the two unnamed states of *Table* and the

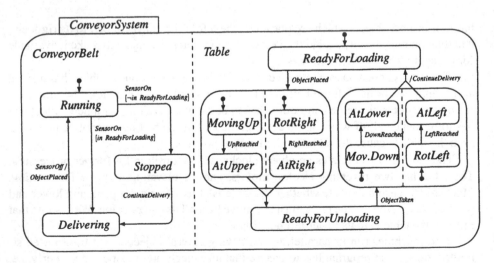

Fig. 4. The statechart of the conveyor system

sets *ToUpper*, *ToRight*, *ToLower*, *ToLeft* for their concurrent substates are introduced. As the events *ObjectPlaced* and *ContinueDelivery* are generated only internally, they are defined only in the **DEFINITIONS** section.

```
MACHINE ConveyorSystem
SETS
    ConveyorBelt = {Running, Stopped, Delivering} ;
    Table = {ReadyForLoading, MovingToUnloading, ReadyForUnloading, MovingToLoading} ;
    ToUpper = {MovingUp, AtUpper} ;
    ToRight = {RotRight, AtRight} ;
    ToLower = {MovingDown, AtLower} ;
    ToLeft = {RotLeft, AtLeft}
VARIABLES
    conveyorBelt, table, toUpper, toRight, toLower, toLeft
INVARIANT
    conveyorBelt ∈ ConveyorBelt ∧ table ∈ Table ∧
    toUpper ∈ ToUpper ∧ toRight ∈ ToRight ∧ toLower ∈ ToLower ∧ toLeft ∈ ToLeft
INITIALISATION
    conveyorBelt := Running ‖ table := ReadyForLoading ‖
    toUpper :∈ ToUpper ‖ toRight :∈ ToRight ‖ toLower :∈ ToLower ‖ toLeft :∈ ToLeft
DEFINITIONS
    ObjectPlaced ==
        (IF table = ReadyForLoading THEN table := MovingToUnloading ‖
            toUpper := MovingUp ‖ toRight := RotRight
        END) ;
    ContinueDelivery ==
        (IF conveyorBelt = Stopped THEN conveyorBelt := Delivering END)
OPERATIONS
    SensorOn ≙
        SELECT conveyorBelt = Running ∧ table = ReadyForLoading THEN
            conveyorBelt := Delivering
        WHEN conveyorBelt = Running ∧ table ≠ ReadyForLoading THEN
            conveyorBelt := Stopped
        ELSE skip
        END ;
    SensorOff ≙
        IF conveyorBelt = Delivering THEN ObjectPlaced ‖ conveyorBelt := Running END ;
    ObjectTaken ≙
        IF table = ReadyForUnloading THEN table := MovingToLoading ‖
            toLower := MovingDown ‖ toLeft := RotLeft
        END ;
    UpReached ≙
        IF table = MovingToUnloading ∧ toUpper = MovingUp THEN toUpper := AtUpper ‖
            IF toRight = AtRight THEN table := ReadyForUnloading END
        END ;
    RightReached ≙
        IF table = MovingToUnloading ∧ toRight = RotRight THEN toRight := AtRight ‖
            IF toUpper = AtUpper THEN table := ReadyForUnloading END
        END ;
    DownReached ≙
        IF table = MovingToLoading ∧ toLower = MovingDown THEN toLower := AtLower ‖
            IF toLeft = AtLeft THEN table := ReadyForLoading ‖ ContinueDelivery END
        END ;
    LeftReached ≙
        IF table = MovingToLoading ∧ toLeft = RotLeft THEN toLeft := AtLeft ‖
            IF toLower = AtLower THEN table := ReadyForLoading ‖ ContinueDelivery END
        END
END
```

Fig. 5. AMN specification of the conveyor system

Safety Properties

Given an AMN machine of the conveyor system, safety properties can be expressed as invariants. For example, the condition that the conveyor belt must be *Delivering* only if the table is *ReadyForLoading* can be proved by adding following implication to *ConveyorSystem*:

INVARIANT
$$(conveyorBelt = Delivering \Rightarrow table = ReadyForLoading)$$

Note that for this safety property to hold, it is essential that the events *ObjectPlaced* and *ContinueDelivery* are considered to be internal events. If they were operations rather than definitions in *ConveyorSystem*, they could be called from the environment at any time and would violate this safety property.

Implementation

An implementation has to set the actuators. Assuming that following types are given,

SETS
$$MOTOR = \{RUN, HALT\} \; ;$$
$$REVMOTOR = \{FWD, BACK, STOP\}$$

variables for the conveyor belt motor and the two table motors can be introduced and related to the original states:

VARIABLES
$$beltMotor, elevMotor, rotMotor$$
INVARIANT
$$beltMotor \in MOTOR \land elevMotor \in REVMOTOR \land rotMotor \in REVMOTOR \land$$
$$(conveyorBelt \in \{Running, Delivering\} \Rightarrow beltMotor = RUN) \land$$
$$(conveyorBelt = Stopped \Rightarrow beltMotor = HALT) \land$$
$$(table = MovingToUnloading \land toUpper = MovingUp) \Leftrightarrow (elevMotor = FWD) \land$$
$$(table = MovingToLoading \land toLower = MovingDown) \Leftrightarrow (elevMotor = BACK) \land$$
$$(table = MovingToUnloading \land toRight = RotRight) \Leftrightarrow (rotMotor = FWD) \land$$
$$(table = MovingToLoading \land toLeft = RotLeft) \Leftrightarrow (rotMotor = BACK)$$

The implementation then needs to update these variables accordingly. The implementation could also reduce the state space of the specification since not all the information in there is necessary for controlling the conveyor system. Finally, the implementation has to replace parallel composition by compilable constructs like sequential composition. These are all standard refinement steps in AMN but are not common for statecharts.

An alternative to this refinement approach is to provide the information about the actuators and how they are updated in the original statechart itself. We believe this is an unnecessary overloading of the statechart since it is not needed for an abstract understanding of the system. This information can be better presented separately and related to the statechart and checked for consistency via refinement relations.

7 Discussion

We briefly compare our semantics with the (revised) original definition [8]. One difference is that we currently do not give priorities to transitions. If there is the possibility of either a transition between two substates within a superstate or from one of the substates out of the superstate to another state, then we leave this choice nondeterministic. In the original statechart semantics, priority is given to the transitions which leave the superstate.

The other major difference comes from our use of parallel composition for the combination of all actions in concurrent states which are triggered by the same event. Two or more concurrent actions must not modify the same variables. This eliminates any nondeterminism which would be otherwise present. However, it also disallows that any two actions which are taken simultaneously may generate the same event (since this corresponds to a parallel call of the same operation, which inevitably causes a read/write conflict).

A number of useful features of statecharts have been left out [6]:

1. activities which take time (in contrast to actions which don't);
2. entry and exit actions in states for all incoming and outgoing transitions, resp.;
3. internal actions which leave the system in the substates is was;
4. timing, e.g. by an event $timeout(E, d)$ which is generated exactly d time units after event E is generated;
5. transitions with multiple targets depending on a condition;
6. histories, for returning to the same substates from which a superstate was left;
7. overlapping states;
8. boolean expressions for events, e.g. $E \wedge \neg F$.

These remain the subject of further research. We believe that most can be treated by straightforward extensions, possibly with the exception of the last one. Also, as soon as the interaction between statechart features gets more involved, a more rigorous definition of the translation to AMN becomes desirable.

The use of statecharts as well as other graphical, object-oriented techniques in the formal program development with AMN is studied in [9]. There, the more general situation is studied when statecharts describe the behaviour of a set of objects, rather than a single object as here. Statechart events are translated to operations in AMN, as here, but with the initial state of a transition being part of the precondition of the corresponding operation. However, this implies that during refinement this precondition can be weakened and more transitions become possible, which is not the case here.

The theory of action systems can also be applied to the refinement of reactive systems in AMN [5, 13]. Although action systems can be naturally expressed in AMN, with each action becoming an AMN operation with a guard (rather than a precondition), an additional proof obligation (for the exit condition) is necessary, which is not part the AMN refinement rule. With the modelling of reactive systems by statecharts in AMN as studied here, the AMN refinement rule is sufficient. However, the reason for this is that action systems describe reactive behaviour in terms of actions, which are not called but become enabled, whereas the reactive behaviour of statecharts in AMN is in terms of operations, which are called. Hence, the operations here correspond to procedures rather than actions [3]. These serve different purposes: AMN operations as procedures describe 'abstract machines', whereas AMN operations as actions describe 'abstract systems' [2].

Statecharts have also been combined with the Z specification language in various ways, for example for formalising different aspects of a reactive system in Z and statecharts and then checking the consistency of these views [12, 14], or by extending the statechart semantics to include Z data types and operations [10]. By comparison, here we embed statecharts in AMN. In all cases, this gives similar possibilities of specifying the state space with data types and the modification of the state space in actions with operations of Z and AMN, respectively. The embedding of statecharts in AMN offers the further possibility of subsequent refinement: the statechart specification may give a concise, abstract view of the system; implementation details can be introduced gradually in refinement steps.

Acknowledgement. We are grateful to the reviewers for their careful reading and for pointing out related literature.

References

1. J.-R. Abrial. *The B Book: Assigning Programs to Meaning.* Cambridge University Press, 1996.
2. J.-R. Abrial. Extending B without changing it. In H. Habrias, editor, *First B Conference*, pages 169–170, Nantes, France, 1996. Institut de Recherche en Informatique de Nantes.
3. R. J. R. Back and K. Sere. Action systems with synchronous communication. In E.-R. Olderog, editor, *IFIP Working Conference on Programming Concepts, Methods, Calculi*, pages 107–126, San Miniato, Italy, 1994. North-Holland.
4. M. von der Beck. A comparison of statechart variants. In H. Langmaack, W.-P. deRoever, and J. Vytopil, editors, *Formal Techniques in Real-Time and Fault-Tolerant Systems*, Lecture Notes in Computer Science 863, pages 128–148. Springer Verlag, 1994.
5. M. Butler and M. Walden. Distributed system development in B. In H. Habrias, editor, *First B Conference*, pages 155–168, Nantes, France, 1996. Institut de Recherche en Informatique de Nantes.
6. D. Harel. Statecharts: A visual formalism for complex systems. *Science of Computer Programming*, 8:231–274, 1987.
7. D. Harel and E. Gery. Executable object modeling with statecharts. *IEEE Computer*, 30(7):31–42, 1996.
8. D. Harel and A. Naamad. The statemate semantics of statecharts. *ACM Transactions on Software Engineering and Methodology*, 5(5):293–333, 1996.
9. K. Lano, H. Haughton, and P. Wheeler. Integrating formal and structured methods in object oriented system development. In S. J. Goldsack and S. J. H. Kent, editors, *Formal Methods and Object Technology*. Springer-Verlag, 1996.
10. C. Petersohn. *Data and Control Flow Diagrams, Statecharts and Z: Their Formalization, Integration, and Real-Time Extension.* Doctoral thesis, Christian-Albrecht Universität, 1997.

11. J. Rumbaugh, M. Blaha, W. Premerlani, F. Eddi, and W. Lorensen. *Object-Oriented Modelling and Design*. Prentice-Hall, 1991.
12. F. G. Shi, J. A. McDermid, and J. M. Armstrong. An introduction to ZedCharts and its application. Research Report YCS-96-272, University of York, Department of Computer Science, 1996.
13. M. Walden and K. Sere. Refining action systems within B-Tool. In M.-C. Gaudel and J. Woodcock, editors, *FME'96: Industrial Benefit and Advances in Formal Methods*, Lecture Notes in Computer Science 1051, pages 85–104. Springer-Verlag, 1996.
14. M. Weber. Combining statecharts and Z for the design of safety-critical control systems. In M.-C. Gaudel and J. Woodcock, editors, *FME '96: Industrial Benefits and Advances in Formal Methods*, Lecture Notes in Computer Science 1051, pages 307–326. Springer Verlag, 1996.

Process Control Engineering: Contribution to a Formal Structuring Framework with the B Method

Jean-François Pétin[1], Gérard Morel[2], Dominique Méry[1], Patrick Lamboley[2]

[1] LORIA UMR 7503, CNRS & Université Henri Poincaré Nancy 1,
email: petin@loria.fr
[2] CRAN UPRES-A 7039, CNRS & Université Henri Poincaré Nancy 1

Abstract. This paper explores the use of the B method as a formal framework for structuring and verifying process control systems engineering. In particular, it is shown how the B method can be used to define implementation independent modular specifications. Benefits are related to the re-use of verified and perennial specifications for control systems facing a fast evolution of implementation technologies. Limits are related to the compliance of formal methods with the other methods or methodologies involved in the development of a production system. This justifies the methodological framework needed for representing, reasoning and verifying the control system as interacting with other technological or human systems. The approach is illustrated and discussed using a level control system example.

1 Introduction

The paper shows how to use a formal framework, such as the B method, to improve the competitiveness of process control engineering, in terms of design re-use and safety. Indeed, facing fast technology evolution, control engineering could benefit from promoting the re-use of implementation independent and modular specifications. Re-use implies, first, that specifications result from a structuring framework ensuring their modularity and perenniality with regards to new distributed technologies and, second, that these specifications are fully validated and compliant with users' requirements.

Current practice in industrial control engineering is based on the standardisation process. In this way, IEC 1131-3 standard [8] constitutes an implementation standard which provides basic building blocks for programmable logic controllers (P.L.C.). Proposal IEC 1499 [14] evolves from this implementation standard, which suffers from a serious lack of semantics, to a designing standard which provides functional blocks described by data-flow diagrams and state-transitions structures to be used in the process control specification.

Another step would be to complete these normative approaches by a formal framework allowing us to define semantics for a structured control system specification using function blocks and to prove their correctness with regards to users' requirements.

Section 2 briefly introduces control engineering practice and requirements. Section 3 presents what process control engineering could expect from using formal methods borrowed from software engineering. Section 4 illustrates the use of a B formal framework using the level control system example.

2 Control Engineering Requirements

The definition of a control system depends on the process being controlled (whose representation stands on scientific foundations such as mathematics, physics or chemistry) and on the activities assigned to control operators [11].

In this context, a control system is expected to schedule commands to actuators and sensors according to predetermined control laws in order to achieve the desired states of a process system in a safe manner.

Traditionaly, methods and models taken from control engineering provides materials for specifying a global constrained system behaviour, commonly represented as a closed control loop, which supports more or less complex control algorithms. Validation of this behaviour is obtained via simulation techniques which provide a global view of the plant functioning (including simulation of control and process systems) and allow us to minimise the bad-functioning states.

Fast technology (from P.L.C. towards integrated circuits for intelligent field-devices) and architecture evolution (from rigid centralised architecture towards open distributed ones) provides the control engineers with a double challenge.

Firstly, we have to minimise the impact of technology evolution in the engineering process, by encouraging the re-use of implementation independent specifications. Specific attention shall be paid to the validation and verification of re-usable, or even standardised, functional control blocks [21]. This requires to define systematic methodology for testing control blocks with the aim of detecting specification errors and to formally prove that some safety critical properties are satisfied.

Secondly, we have to minimise the impact of architecture evolution, by promoting a modular structure for control systems which can be distributed among different computing devices. A structuring framework, as defined in [7], advocates the control architecture to be based on the process structure, which can be considered as the most stable element of the process control, by defining tightly coupled automation and mechanical specifications [16].

3 Expected Benefits of Formal Methods for Control Engineering

Formal methodologies borrowed from software engineering could be suitable for re-usable control specifications by providing descriptions at a very high level of abstraction, as required by implementation independent issues, and formal proofs of some behavioural properties, as required by validation issues.

However, specific attention shall be paid to avoid hiding automation criteria behind formal notations.

First of all, validation of control studies aims to secure the correct plant functionality. The objective is not limited to safely control the production system but rather to product in a safe manner, i.e. to ensure the safety of a discrete event control system tightly coupled with a continuous process systems [11]. Thus, proving control system properties, without reasoning about their impact on the controlled system, assumes that the physical process functioning (event reactions to/from actuators/sensors) is perfect. Taking into account the process reality, which is far from perfect, properties proofs should be more significant if the formal specification of the discrete control system is completed, as suggested by [15], using a formal representation of the continuous system model.

A second difficulty is linked to the interaction of control engineering with other related activities - mechanical engineering, control display, etc - involved in the development cycle of a production system. This requires a methodological framework for integrating formal methods in the industrial development processes, in order: first, to keep the control specifications in line with the other engineering studies and, second, to master, from an end-user point of view, the difficulties linked to the notation complexity.

Such a methodological framework has been widely discussed for software engineering. For instance, we mention methodological frameworks for specifying B machines from textual description [17], from object OMT semi-formal models [9], from NIAM specifications [13]; or for structuring VDM modules from functional analysis with SART [19]. The key idea is to provide the designer with semi-formal or graphical notations used as an intermediate step allowing the pre-formalisation of the users' textual requirements.

However, considering the widely agreed hypothesis that the control functions of a production system are defined from the mechanical studies, the methodological framework would benefit from being based on the structure of the physical process with automation engineering criteria rather than on an abstract analysis based on software engineering criteria [1]. The advantage is to provide re-usable and modular specifications of quite autonomous automation objects associating their control and mechanical resources.

Finally, implementation of the formal specification has to be compliant with the implementation or designing standards used in an industrial context, such as the IEC 1131-3 [8] for P.L.C. programming or the IEC 1499 proposal [14] related to function blocks for process control specification. Indeed, these standards are needed to ensure the consistency and the interoperability of the distributed process applications, that is to say the ability for heterogeneous devices to communicate and to provide complementary services. However, semantics of this standards is very poor and need to be enriched [22] or defined as a final step of a formal development.

Our application of the B formal method on the level control system case study is an attempt to provide elements of solutions for these problems.

4   Level Control System Case Study

Our case study is the simplified level control system shown in figure 1. It consists of the following process items: the water level in a constant section tank is obtained by modifying the output flow rate through a modulating motorised valve in presence of an external perturbation represented by the input flow of the tank. The control architecture is distributed on different heterogeneous processing devices, such as P.L.C. or computer, communicating via field-bus, as promoted by the new generation of intelligent field-devices [12].

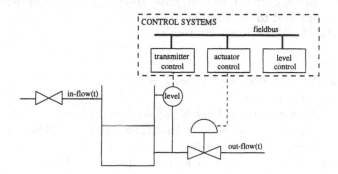

Fig. 1. Level control system

The objective of the exercise is to prototype and test a structuring framework of B machines allowing us to map the functional view of the end-users to the technological description of the process. Indeed, from an end-user point of view, what is expected to be proved is not limited to the level control software but should include the functioning of the whole system (control and process systems).

This problem can be modelled as an interaction between functional agents (human operators and/or control systems), operating in the world of information in order to reach the system goal, and technological objects having to be physically modified. The B structure of the level control system is expected to provide modular specifications based on process / control elementary interaction, capable of being implemented, in terms of process control function blocks, as interoperable but heterogeneous processing devices.

4.1   Structured Modelling of the Level Control System

The functionality of the level control system is to maintain a tank level *(Phy_level)* at a requested value *(Level_Rq)* within a certain tolerance *(tol)*. It is represented by the invariant of the *Mach_Level_Control_System* machine as following:

INVARIANT

/* *information and physical variables associated to the level control* */
(Phy_Level ∈ PhyLevel) ∧ (Inf_Level ∈ InfLevel) ∧ (Phy_Flow ∈ Ph-Flow) ∧ (tol ∈ NAT1)
/* *type of request for control system* */
∧ (Level_Rq ∈ Rlevel) ∧ (Flow_Rq ∈ Rflow)
/* *finality of the level control* */
∧ ((Phy_Level ≤ Level_Rq + tol) ∧ (Phy_Level ≥ Level_Rq - tol)

This functionality is expected to be maintained thanks to :

− a physical process, which is able to store and to modify a level quantity. The operation *Level_Process* describes how the level of the tank *(level)* evolves according to the output flow *(out_flow)* and to the section of the tank *(Sec)*, which is supposed to be constant.
MACHINE Mach_Level_Process

....

OPERATIONS

level ← Level_Process(out_flow) =
PRE out_flow ∈ NAT
/* *integral calculus of the level of the tank with a dt sampling period* */
THEN level := (1/Sec) × (((out_flow_pre - in_flow_pre) × dt) + ((out_flow - in_flow) × dt)))
|| out_flow_pre := out_flow || in_flow_pre := in_flow
END

− a control system for managing the previous physical transformation, that is to say to process a level request *(level_setpoint)* in order to produce a flow variation request *(flow_setpoint)* according to the measured level of the tank *(level_meas)*.
Note that our example focuses on the event control processing but could be extended to describe mode management or monitoring functions associated to the controller.
MACHINE Mach_Level_Controller

....

OPERATIONS

flow_setpoint ← level_controller (level_setpoint, level_meas) =
PRE (level_meas ∈ NAT) ∧ (level_setpoint ∈ NAT)
THEN IF level_meas ≠ level_setpoint
THEN ∃ fl . (level_meas ≠ level_meas_pre); flow_setpoint := fl
ELSE flow_setpoint := 0 /* *no output flow variation if requested level is reached* */
END ;
level_meas_pre := level_meas
END

These "process" and "control" operations are performed in two dedicated machines which are included in the machine which describes the higher level of abstraction of our case study as follows:

MACHINE Mach_Level_Control_System

....

INCLUDES Mach_Level_Process, Mach_Level_Controller
OPERATIONS   Level_System=
    PRE Phy_Level $\neq$ Level_Rq
    THEN Phy_Level $\leftarrow$ level_process(Phy_Flow)
        || Flow_Rq $\leftarrow$ level_control(Level_Rq, Inf_Level)
    END

Solving the process / control interaction is based on the emergence mechanism [6] which considers that interactions between two entities define additional properties which are not included in the own properties of each entity.

This mechanism, often used to describe emerging behaviour of complex systems, especially in the field of distributed artificial intelligence or multi-agents Systems [10], has been proposed by [18] to describe an emerging engineering process for the production systems. It leads to define, from each process / control interaction, emerging actuation and measurement operators which support the interface between the symbolic and physical worlds (respectively by transforming control requests into physical effects and physical effect into significant information) and their related mechanical and automation know-how.

The emergence mechanism is represented in B with the help of a refinement mechanism which allows us to introduce new machines (and operations) as required for solving the process / control interaction and satisfying its invariant. It means that the proof failures encountered by the B prover are used not only to enrich the specifications (detection of particular control states in which the invariant cannot be maintained due to process functioning in limit conditions) but also to systematically and progressively define the control system structure thanks to the emergence mechanism.

Application to the level control problem leads us to identify: an actuation operation *(flow_actuation)* which transforms a flow variation informational request into physical variation of the output flow and a measurement operation *(level_measurement)* which transforms the tank level into significant information. These new operations are described in B machines, respectively dedicated to flow modification and level measurement. They can be considered as quite autonomous with regards to the first set of machines related to the level modification. Indeed, this set described their own level control goals and the process and control resources needed to reach it. In the same way, the new actuation and measurement machines describe other sub-goals also including their own process and control resources. For instance, the actuation machine *(Mach_Flow_Actuation)* focuses on the output flow control by modifying the percentage of the valve opened due to process *(flow_process)* and control *(flow_control)* operations.

MACHINE Mach_Flow_Actuation
INCLUDES Mach_Flow_Process,Mach_Flow_Control
....
INVARIANT
   (Phy_Opening ∈ PhOP) ∧ (outflow ∈ PhFl)
   ∧ (Opening_Rq ∈ RqOP) ∧ (Inf_Flow ∈ InfFlow)
   /* finality of flow control module */
   ((outflow ≤ Flow_SP + ftol) ∧ (outflow ≥ Flow_SP - ftol))
OPERATIONS *Flow actuation(Flow_SP)* =
   PRE Flow_SP ∈ NAT
   THEN outflow ← flow_process(Phy_Opening, Phy_Level)
   ‖ Opening_Rq ← flow_control(Flow_SP, Inf_Flow)
   ‖ Flow := outflow
   END

REFINEMENT Ref_Level_Control_System
REFINES Mach_Level_Control_System
IMPORTS Mach_Flow_Actuation, Mach_Level_Measurement
....
OPERATIONS Level_System=
   PRE Phy_Level ≠ Level_Rq
   THEN Phy_Level ← level_process(Phy_Flow);
      Phy_Flow ← actuation(Flow_Rq);
      Inf_Level ← measurement(Phy_Level);
      Flow_Rq ← level_control(Level_Rq,Inf_Level)
   END

Applying again the same structuring concept leads us to identify several refinements of product/process interactions characterised by automation engineering quantities to be modified - from water volume in the tank towards a servo-motor position through a flow rate, an opening percentage of the valve and a position of the valve stem - and their associated mechanical objects performing the considered modification (figure 2).

These B machines can be considered as non divisible according to distribution criteria because they are associated to a mechanical device supporting elementary physical transformation. Thus, the resulting B specifications of the controllers machines have the same structure as the process controlled one. Furthermore, they can be refined and implemented into different heterogeneous processing devices as shown in next section.

4.2   Refinement and Implementation

Control design has now to focus on the behavioural description of the controllers, previously identified for managing the level, flow, valve position, stem position and servo-motor position. Indeed, each controller needs to be refined in order to complete the description of its functionality by the algorithm used to achieve it.

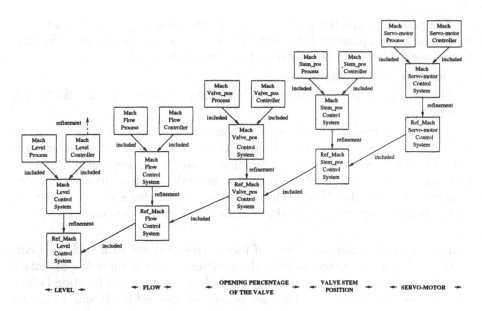

Fig. 2. Architecture of the level control system specification

For instance, the previously described level controller only specifies that the modification of the tank will be obtained by a modification of the output flow while the refined operation describes how the output flow has to be decreased or increased in order to reach the requested level:

REFINEMENT Ref_Level_Controller
REFINES Mach_Level_Controller
...
OPERATIONS
    flow_setpoint ← level_controller(level_setpoint, level_meas) =
    PRE level_setpoint ≠ level_meas
    THEN IF level_setpoint > level_meas THEN
        fl:(fl<fl$0); /* output has to be decreased */
        Tstate := filling;
        flow_setpoint := fl
      ELSIF level_setpoint < level_meas THEN
        fl:(fl>fl$0); /* output flow has to be increased */
        Tstate := emptying;
        flow_setpoint := fl
      ELSE Tstate := ok;
        flow_setpoint := 0 /* output flow is maintened at its current
                        value,e.d. flow variation equal to zero */
  END
END

The property expected to be proved for this elementary control machine is related to liveness property : the level control process must eventually terminate. Such a constraint could be represented in linear temporal logic by [2] :

(tstate $\neq$ Ok) $\rightsquigarrow$ (tstate = ok)

(tstate = ok means that the tank is not filling or emptying when the level is as requested)

This kind of property is defined in [15] as a variant function of the controller state. This function is such that whenever the level is not reached, each action of the controller decreases the variant function. However, the proof of such a property requires an extension of the B model. Several work has already suggested alternatives approaches [3][20]. The importance of proving such a property for control engineering problems justifies further work in this domain.

Considering the needed compliance of formal specifications with standards currently used in an industrial context, the structure of our B controller operation can be viewed as close to a control loop including a comparator function (which delivers the gap between the level set point and the real level) and a transfer function controlling the variation of the flow set-point in order to reduce this gap (most of the time by applying a Proportional-Integrative-Derivative P.I.D. algorithm). Consequently, this B operation could be implemented using the required function blocks provided by the IEC 1131-3 standard (figure 3). The benefit is that B machines represent a proved formalisation of the control architecture which can be considered as a first step to compensate for the lack of semantics of implementation standards. A more complete approach, allowing a safe implementation of reusable and standardised function blocks, needs to solve the two following problems.

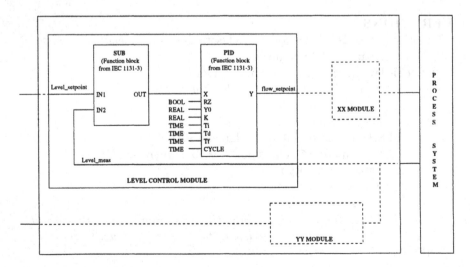

Fig. 3. Implementation of level controller using 1131-3 standard

Firstly, we must consider the semantic break between the specification and implementation steps which can cause trouble. Indeed, even if the B specification can be trusted thanks to the prover, its implementation through industrial standards is not guaranteed to maintain the properties already proved. However, taking into account the current practice in industrial world, and the fact that the use of implementation standards (IEC 1131-3) or designing standards (in progress IEC 1499) is currently the only way towards interoperability of distributed process applications, the work to be done is to define formal links between the used standards and formal approaches, such as suggested by [22], allowing automatic generation of standardised function blocks from formal specifications.

The second problem is related to the choice of interpretation algorithm required for implementation as processing devices. Indeed, implementation of these blocks requires us to schedule the execution of each block according to real process events and to data flow structure, in order to ensure the determinism property of the reactive systems. This criteria can be applied in B by defining a synchronous polling cycle which processes internal states of operations according to a fixed image of the input and output events. Note that this approach is very close to the one used in discrete event control theory, in particular with synchronous languages [4] and Grafcet [5].

5   Conclusion

This paper is an attempt to show how the B method can be used for process control engineering. The benefits have been shown in terms of description at a high abstraction level which favours the re-usability of control studies by providing safe implementation independent specifications. However, pragmatic use in the industrial context of control engineering requires defining structuring framework which allow us to ensure re-use of modular specifications able to be implemented on a distributed architecture and to be compliant with the implementation standards.

Our level control system case study has shown how the B method can used to support the emergence mechanism in order to fulfill this structuring requirement. This mechanism allows us to avoid having the structure of modular B specifications depend on the designer intuition, but results in a methodological framework which systematically leads to modular machines representing process / control interactions to be implemented on different processing devices according to the required standards.

In this context, the B method provides materials to progressively, but systematically, refine the initial specification by considering a proof failure as a means to enrich the specifications. In a complementary way, liveness properties have been shown as interesting for process control engineering but difficult to prove in the current B model. This point motivates further research in this area.

Even if these preliminary results highlight the scientific benefit of formal approaches for process control engineering and the work still to be done, the real benefit for industrial use will be demonstrated only when applied on real production systems with higher complexity than the case studies presented up to now. In this way, our structuring approach is expected to be validated as a practicale methodological approach for the European Intelligent Actuation and Measurement pilot developed in the framework of Esprit IV-23525 IAM-Pilot.

References

1. J.R. Abrial. *The B book - Assigning programs to meanings*. Cambridge University Press, 1996.
2. J.R. Abrial. Extending B without changing it (for developing distributed systems. In *1st International Conference on the B method*, pages 169–190, Nantes, France, November 1996.
3. J.R. Abrial and L. Mussat. Specification and design of a transmission protocol by successive refinement using B. STERIA Meeting on Protocol, May 15 1997.
4. A. Benveniste and G. Berry. Another look at real time programming. *Special session of the Proceedings of the IEEE*, 79(9):1268–1336, September 1991. ISSN 0018-9219.
5. E. Bierel, O. Douchin, and P. Lhoste. Grafcet : from theory to implementation. *European Journal of Automation*, 31(3):534–559, 1997. ISSN 0296-1598.
6. E. Bonnabeau, E. Desalge, and A. Grumbach. Characterising emergence mechanism phenomena: a critical review. *International Review of Systemic*, Vol 9(3), 1995. ISSN 0980-1472, Dunod Publishing.
7. M. Combacau and M. Courvoisier. A hierarchical and modular structure for F.M.S. control and monitoring. In *First IEEE International Conference on A.I., Simulation and Planning in High Autonomy Systems*, pages 80–88, Tucson (USA), March 26-27 1990.
8. International Electrotechnical Commission. *IEC 1131-3 on Programmable controllers, part 3: programming languages*, 1993.
9. P. Facon, R. Laleau, and P. Nguyen. Dérivations de spécifications formelles B à partir de spécifications semi-formelles de systèmes d'informations. In *1st B International Conference*, pages 271–290, Nantes (France), November 1996.
10. J. Ferber and P. Carle. Actors and agents as reflective objects: a Mering IV perspective. *IEEE Transactions on Systems, Man and Cybernetics*, 21(6), 1991.
11. D. Galara and J.P. Hennebicq. The gap from scientific system approach down to industrial power plant control engineering. In D. Dubois, editor, *1st International Conference on Computer Anticipating Systems (CASYS'97)*, Liege (Belgium), August 11-15 1997. CHAOS.
12. D. Galara, F. Russo, G. Morel, and B. Iung. Update on the european state of the art of intelligent field-devices. In *International Conference on Intelligent Systems in Process Engineering*, pages 339–342, Volume 2, Snow Mass (USA), 1996. AIChE symposium series.
13. N. Hadj-Rabia and H. Habrias. Formal specification from NIAM model: a bottom-up approach. In *XI International Symposium on Computer and Information Sciences*, Antalya (Turkey), November 6-8 1996.

14. TC65/WG6 International Electrotechnical Commission. *Committee Draft for IEC 1499 on Function Blocks for Industrial Process Measurement and Control systems, Part 1: Architecture*, May 1997.

15. K. Lano, J. Bicarregui, P. Kan, and A. Sanchez. Using B to design and verify controllers for chemical processing. In *1st B International Conference*, pages 237–269, Nantes (France), November 1996.

16. P. Lhoste and G. Morel. From discrete event behavioural modelling to intelligent actuation and measurement modelling. In *ESPRIT Advanced Summer Institute (ASI) in Life Cycle Approaches to Production Systems*, pages 75–83, Toulouse (France), June 1996.

17. N. Lopez. Construction de la spécification formelle d'un système complexe. In *1st B International Conference*, pages 63–119, Nantes (France), November 1996.

18. F. Mayer, G. Morel, and P. Lhoste. Towards manufacturing engineering based on semi-formal systemic engineering. In *14th International congress on Cybernetic*, Namur (Belgium), August 21-25 1995.

19. R. Mhrailaf and A.E.K. Sahraoui. A formal specification of manufacturing system: a case study on manufacturing cell with VDM method. In *CESA'96 IMACS Multiconference*, Lille (France), July 1996.

20. D. Méry. Machines abstraites temporelles:analyse comparative de B et TLA+. In *1st International Conference on the B method*, pages 191–220, Nantes (France), November 1996.

21. J.F. Pétin, D. Méry, H. Panetto, and B. Iung. Validation of software components for intelligent actuation and measurement. In *Sixth International Symposium on Robotics And Manufacturing, ISRAM'96 in the second World Automation Congress*, pages Volume 3, 631–637, Montpellier, France, May 27-30 1996. TSI Press,ISBN 1-889335-00-2.

22. A.H. Wolfgang and B.J. Kramer. Achieving high integrity of process control software by graphical design and formal verification. *Software Engineering Journal*, pages 53–64, January 1992.

Designing a B *Model*
for Safety-Critical Software Systems

Souâd Taouil-Traverson[1] and Sylvie Vignes[2]

[1] CR2A-DI,19 Av Dubonnet, F - 92411 Courbevoie Cedex
email: straverson@cr2a-di.fr
[2] ENST, 46 rue Barrault,F - 75634 Paris-Cedex 13
email: Sylvie.Vignes@enst.fr

Abstract. The observations described in this paper are based on the experience we gained in applying the B method to a realistic safety-critical case study. The main goal was to integrate the B method into the heart of the development cycle, particularly for such applications. We outline a framework to reason about control process systems in order to capture functional and safety-related properties and to organize the conceptual architecture of these systems.

Thus, we describe how a B Model can be designed both with respect to safety constraints and in terms of software architecture abstractions. We use the B method to support architectural abstractions, codifying the interactions of components. Finally, we present essential results of the case study and we show the significant impact of such a B formal development on the development process by giving some metrics.

1 Introduction

The main concern in the development process is to identify the characteristics of the application domain. These vary with the physical phenomena being modeled, the computational model (i.e. sequential, distributed, distributed and concurrent, and real time dependent) and the constraints to be hold (i.e., safety-related, embedded, and cost-critical). These characteristics determine the methodological choices at each step of the development process. For instance, in the specific domain of control process, cyclic software systems can be modeled in a sequential way. Usually, they must respect safety constraints. An appropriate analysis method must be based on state machines.

Considering the characteristics of control processes, the B method seems to be a suitable support. At the present time, when standards recommend the integration of formal methods within the safety critical development process, Z and VDM are mentioned. However, the B method could be similarly used. Nevertheless, as the B method covers most of the life-cycle phases, there are some pitfalls when it comes to completely integrating it. In the rest of this paper, we will present a strategy to overcome these problems and we will describe the architecture phase in more detail.

Recently, software architecture has begun to emerge as an important field of study for software developers and researchers alike. The architecture of a software system defines the system in terms of components and interactions among those components.

Different trends can be observed in this domain. One is the recognition of well-known patterns and idioms for structuring complex software systems [Cop95]. Another trend consists in exploring a specific domain to provide reusable frameworks for product families and thus for capturing an architectural style (cf. [Sha96b]).

In addition to specifying the structure and topology of the system, the architecture must show the intended correspondence between the system requirements and elements of the system constructed. Thus, it can deal with system-level properties. Such of a *conceptual architecture* must evidently be described independently of the implementation. The corresponding step of life-cycle is not clearly outlined. In most systems, conceptual architectures are implicit, and hidden within the documentation.

The use of computers to automate various applications has increased and concern about the safety of those systems has also grown. In this paper, we focus on software components of *control process systems*. Some common aspects can be extracted from these software systems, so that an architectural style can be inferred[Sha96a].

In a global approach [Sae90], the physical process may be modeled by a single component. Disturbances from the environment require the introduction of a controller. The whole system forms a control loop (see Figure-1). Data

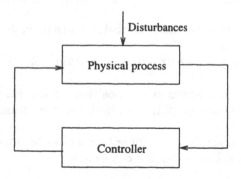

Fig. 1. Control process system.

consist of parameters, inputs, outputs of the physical process, and disturbances. Transformations are physical laws and alterations which are a consequence of the controller action. We are not interested in the real-time behavior of the controller. We assume that any transformation can happen in a time interval that the designer can determine. We take a static view of its behavior including all different states of the system.

Usually, the design of a reactive system begins with the specification of the system behavior. In the design of a control process system, this specification must be derived both from functional requirements and from safety-related requirements. Experts of the application domain describe the physical process, the disturbances expected from the environment and the behavior of the system under hazardous circumstances.

In this paper, we outline our methodology to design a B model. Our approach focuses on traceability of safety-related constraints. The remainder of the paper is organized as follows. Section 2 presents our experience with the B development process. We further describe our main methodological contribution: Section 3 explains how to link the user's requirements with system safety analysis in a new structured informal statement. Section 4 presents our preliminary analysis cycle at the end of which a formal statement of the critical requirements is produced. Section 5 deals with the architectural conception phase. Finally, in Section 6 we report the results of our experience gained from the development of a case study in the railways domain.

2   B development process

In this section we summarize the essential features of the B method which will be useful to us.

2.1   Our terminology

First, let us recall some B terminology in relation with structuring concepts:

- **A component** denotes either an abstract machine, one of its refinements, or its implementation.
- **A module** puts together an abstract machine, all its refinements and its implementation.
- **Links** denote shared access or composition mechanisms.
- **A model** is composed of all the modules and their links.

We use conventional software architecture notations : modules represent *software components* and links represent *connectors*.

2.2   Development activities

The main B development activities are type checking, refinement engineering and verification engineering. The interaction between these activities is shown in figure 2. Refinement and verification activities have a *trial and error* nature, reflecting some *invention* and *verification* aspects.

Each refinement step is an iteration from the refinement first to the type checking, then to the verification. The modeling process and the construction of the verification must be performed concurrently.

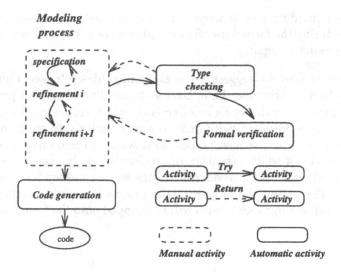

Fig. 2. B development activities.

2.3 Module and model elaboration

Construction of a module entails a number of refinement steps, each introducing a few specification details or design decisions, so that the induced properties can be easily proved. Module elaboration involves a *layered architecture*. Proof is constructed to verify the consistency between each level and the previous one.

Simple enough problems can be modeled in a single module. In more complex problems, the development process begins at a very abstract level. A formal high-level design which describes the mapping of the requirements onto specification must be constructed. This high-level design describes how specification-level information is to be implemented in software structures. Consistency between the specification and this high-level design can be formally proved.

At each step of module construction, the B method provides links allowing shared and compositional specification. Thus, when designing a B model, modules may exist and interact while at different development stages. While the entire B-development process can be conducted in a process of systematic stepwise refinement, it is practically conducted more on intuition than on process framework.

2.4 Life-cycle phases

The B method covers the central aspects of the software life-cycle from specification to code generation. The requirements analysis phase is not addressed, thus we have to assume that functional and safety properties have been captured. However, the development process does not respect the usual sequencing of the phases. The designer must wait until the end of the development to bring out a very clear dividing line between specification concerns and design decisions. Moreover, during the formal specification phase, the organization of the B model must be questioned again.

To fill this void we suggest a corresponding life-cycle (see Figure-3), each phase of which we will describe in later sections. The integrated process begins with a restatement of the user's requirements (which are informally expressed) in a new structured document with links to safety analysis. In order to extract the software requirements, we have proposed elsewhere a Preliminary Analysis Cycle [Tao96], the aim of which is to draw out a detailed analysis of the requirements. Our aim is to help both the developer and the verifier to keep track of the desired properties. The output of this part of the process is mainly a formal statement of the 'critical requirements' which will be mapped onto the formal specification.

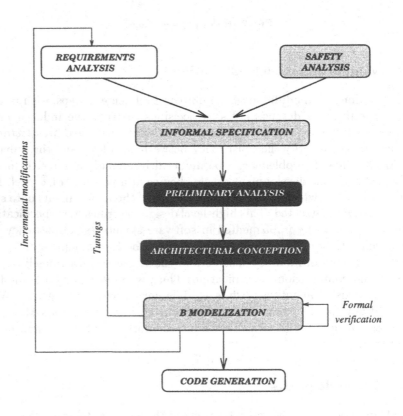

Fig. 3. Life-cycle model.

3 Safety analysis

In order to ensure a given level of safety a hazard analysis should be performed. Its process is continuous and iterative (see Figure-4). This analysis should be started early in the process development of the system.

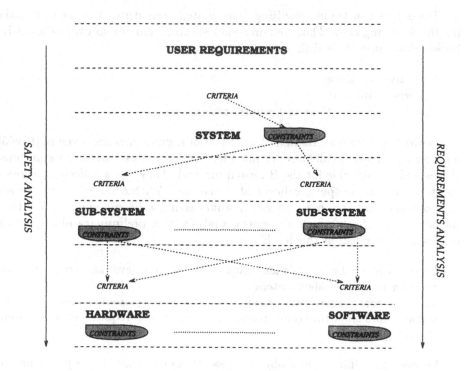

Fig. 4. Safety analysis.

Standards describe the analysis process in four steps:

– Preliminary hazards analysis : The scope of this step is to highlight critical functions and identify hazards. This step yields a set of functional and safety criteria for the whole system. It is the input for the next step.
– Hazards at the system level : This step starts as soon as the design activity is stabilized and continues while the design is being modified. The scope of this step is to identify hazards introduced by interfaces between sub-systems and to deduce a set of constraints on system design. The result of this step is the input for the following step.
– Hazards at the sub-system level : The system analysis has decomposed the system into several sub-systems, at the same time decomposing these sub-systems into functions. The safety analysis consists in translating constraints which result from the previous step into criteria for the sub-systems. At this

step, each sub-system is analyzed according to its safety criteria in order to identify hazards introduced by the relation between sub-systems and equipment and to determine safety inputs and outputs.

– Hazards at the operational level : The scope of this level is to identify hazards due to the support and operation of the system. This notably applies to the human interface with the machine.

The set of constraints resulting from a step constitutes the set of criteria for the following step. Thus, requirements specification for software should be broken down into three definitions :

– Objective definition;
– Criteria definition;
– Priorities on objectives and criteria assignment.

In order to ease construction of specifications, guidelines are given in [Lev95] and [Sae90]. These guidelines are intended for an analysis based on state machines and are suitable for the B formal method. They are a collection of rules on states, inputs, outputs, values and transitions. Within the software process development, the continuity of safety analysis must be maintained. We thus introduce into the life-cycle the safety analysis as a preliminary phase, which means that we must, at this level:

– keep record of the hazards identified at the system level and translate software hazards into safety criteria.
– show the consistency between safety criteria and requirements related to the software and show the completeness of the functional requirements regarding the safety criteria.

In order to fulfill the first objective, safety analysis should be performed in a top-down approach from the system down to sub-system. This phase must start early in the system analysis. We feel that inputs to the system process development should be requirements and safety objectives. The safety analysis takes these goals as inputs and then deduces the criteria in order to fulfill them. The criteria are identified at the system level. Criteria documentation must give means to verify that safety criteria and objectives are satisfied. Moreover, as the software can make more or less than the requirements the generated code must be verified in order to show that safety criteria are held or to highlight vulnerabilities to be circumvented by other means.

4 Preliminary analysis cycle

Keeping in mind the objective of traceability in terms of both software engineering and safety, we introduce a preliminary analysis phase before the formal specification phase. The scope of this phase is the analysis of requirements, first their semi-formal expression, and finally, their formal expression.

Our approach takes into account three points : type of application, formal method for the specification, and constraints of safety design. Each of these points contributes toward this method :

- the type of application provides a well-defined structure where the main relation between modules is well established ;
- the B formal method is model-oriented and its basic concept is the abstract machine. This concept allows us to classify this method among state machine oriented ones.
- safety analysis imposes rules on the specification in order to ensure safety constraints.

This approach constitutes a preliminary analysis of the informal specifications to construct the formal specifications. It is a mean to keep track of the safety criteria deduced from the analysis at the system level. The system being modeled is studied module by module. For each module, the question is to identify its function and the criteria it ensures. Each module is described by a set of variables, by relations with the other modules and then by the whole behavior. For this analysis, we define a four-step framework:

- Determination of elementary time for the analysis. The objective is to determine the relevant interval of time to observe the system behavior. *E.g.*, for the cyclic system the basis time will be the cycle ;
- Static analysis for module description. This phase allows the specification of constraints on behavior without detailing them. The analysis may be performed in three steps:
  - Modules characterization: At first, one must identify all modules, then for each module, one must determine variables useful to its description.
  - Static relationships : At this time, we have to determine all static relationships between these variables. These relationships constitute a part of the constraints on behavior; they could be constraints induced by equipment design or physical laws. At this step, results by domain experts should be mandatorily introduced, because these constraints typically cannot be formally verified.
  - State variables: The question is to bring out state variables, which are used to describe behavior according to the elementary time, *e.g*, at the beginning and the end of cycle. To this end, the first task is to determine the relevant properties to be considered, then to identify useful variables to express them.
- Dynamic analysis to describe desired behavior: This phase is concerned with behavior description using state transformation relationships. A deductive analysis is adopted, its input being the set of state variables. For each variable, one must determine all the relationships working towards its transformations. Performing analysis in this way, we ensure that all transformations will be identified and described.

– Safety analysis to identify safety constraints. Inputs for this task are criteria resulting from the safety analysis at the system level. One must first express these criteria using software variables. At this point, it is interesting to observe that not all criteria could be translated in this manner. Instead, verification of the non expressed criteria should be done statically.

In order to help domain experts verify the completeness of the specifications and to help designers understand the requirements, results of each phase are expressed in a semi-formal language, and then in a formal language. Complete results of the preliminary analysis constitute inputs for formal specifications.

5 Architectural conception

To cope with mandatory requirements, it seems important to underline that this architectural conception must be clearly identified.

5.1 Specific concerns of control process design

In the global approach mentioned in section 1, modeling of control process systems is based on data abstraction of the physical process and state transformations of the system. The main concern in modeling such systems is to keep a general relation between components of the control loop. The architectural style must be related to abstract data encapsulation. However, it is not compatible with the philosophy of objet-oriented organization. When developing an object-oriented system, designers must identify and create software objects corresponding to real-world objects. When developing a control process system, their main concerns must be to keep a global link between components in relation with the safety properties. Sometimes, objects may appear just as iconic classes of interface. Usually, designers think of software as algorithmic transformation. This model breaks down when the system operates a physical process with external disturbances because values appear somehow to change spontaneously. Thus, the architectural style is not either compatible with functional design. The organization is a particular kind of dataflow architecture which assumes that data are updated continuously and which requires a cyclic topology.

Observing software products for various control process applications, a control paradigm and some useful definitions have been highlighted:

– Process variables are properties of the process that can be measured.
– Controlled variables are process variables the values of which the system is intended to control.
– Input variables are process variables which measure an input to the process.
– Manipulated variables are process variables the value of which can be changed by the controller.
– A set point is the desired value for a controlled variable.

The essential parts of the software system are:

- Computational elements which logically partition the process of the control policy.
- Data elements which update process variables and give set points.
- The control loop paradigm which establishes the relation that the control algorithm exercises.

The design methodology requires an explicit identification of each kind of variable and element of the control loop. An example is described later in subsection 6.2.

5.2 B designing features

To build a software architecture of modules, designers have a single connector composed of SEES and IMPORTS links. The SEES link provides a *shared data access*. SEES and IMPORTS together provide a *full-hiding interaction* and support independent development. In order to encourage reuse and to aid large system construction, designers have at their disposal, among others links, INCLUDES link. To clarify structural properties of modules interactions, we recommend designers to merely use *independent INCLUDES* link as described in [Ber96]. Thus, this INCLUDES link provides an *exclusive data access* as well as a *semi-hiding interaction*. The refinement of the including module can be done independently. Proof obligations for a machine Y including a machine X are simpler to manage than when considering them as a single component.

5.3 Design methodology

In this section we introduce our methodology to design an architecture according to formal specifications. This methodology is heterogeneous because it is based on process-control style [Sha95] and a development organization using the B method. At first, the architecture design achieved using a process control style constitutes an architecture abstraction, which will be refined using our methodology. The proposed methodology takes into account three points:

- Use of invariants to express safety constraints in order to formally verify that they have been taken into consideration. It is important to organize the expression of the safety criteria into modules in accordance with the following objectives: consistency of state components and use of appropriate links.
- Formal demonstration that the constraints have been taken into account.
- Keeping track of constraints.

The abstraction of the architecture could then be formulated from three points of view:

- Consistent states point of view: dependency links are listed in order to enable a classification of variables according to the criteria of strong connection. This classification brings out a set of consistent states to be modeled by abstract machine.

– Sharing data point of view: in this task one must build a graph where nodes are consistent states identified in the previous state and links visualize data sharing. This graph is used during formal specification to organize data and control.

– Constraints point of view: at this step we have to construct a set of graphs. Each graph modelizes for each variable its links with other variables and constraints. This graph will be used during specification elaboration to integrate safety constraints and to validate that they have been taken into account.

5.4 Formal specification

According to our approach, at this stage we shall use the software architecture paradigm together with the results of the preliminary analysis. Indeed this paradigm just suggests a framework. In order to build the formal specifications, we develop each component using results of preliminary analysis to specify the abstract machine and its refinements. During this specification, at each step we can introduce new components or we can converge on an existing component. This allows us to emphasize the fact that the results of architecture design only give a framework and that there are not the final architecture.

6   Results and perspectives

In this section, we illustrate the framework presented in previous sections with the example which is given in its entirely in [Tao97a]. This case study, called KLV [1], concerns a critical software system whose aim is to control the speed of a train. This KLV system carries out a specific function of the real system which is in service in the French railway system (the KVB System [2]).

6.1   Simplified behavior of KLV

The KLV functions are restricted to control the temporary speed limitations which are applied near a construction area. We only present a simplified description of the KLV behavior. The KLV system is cyclic and the cycle is determined by a time interval which is unsplittable. At the beginning of each cycle, the system receives information on:

– the distance covered by the train during the previous cycle;
– complex and composed informations concerning signalling;
– the train location.

During a cycle, according to the inputs, the system carries out the following controls:

---

[1] KLV means Limited Speed Control.
[2] KVB means Speed Control with signalling informations given by Beacons.

221

- If the train respects all the speed controls given by the signals, the system does nothing. The states of warning and emergency braking do not change;
- If the speed becomes higher than the warning level, the system informs the driver with the warning 'tell-tale ' lamp;
- If the speed becomes higher than the emergency level, the system commands the emergency braking [3]. This command cannot be terminated until the train stops.

Disturbances can come from erroneous signalling informations (for instance, bad transmission). The warning level does not influence the safety, but provides for a better availability. In order to observe the efficiency of our design methodology when it comes to maintenance, we develop the system without the warning speed level at first.

6.2 Software architecture paradigm for KLV

The KLV system is analyzed considering it in accordance with control process paradigm. The essential parts of the software system are (see figure-5):

- Function: The description of the physical process takes two elements into account: the train and the driving instructions. The train is described by equations which modelizes its kinematic behavior. The driving instructions are also described by equations based on signalling informations. The speed ordered by the driver must respect both sets of equations. If the emergency braking has been commanded, the driver should not be able to do anything.
- Control loop : The paradigm corresponds to a feed-forward control system. Future effects of the speed are anticipated. The controller raises the emergency braking if the speed becomes too high.

  Different kinds of variable are identified:

- The process variable which concerns the measured speed of the train;
- The controlled variable which is the computed speed of the train;
- Input variables which are signalling information and command from the controller;
- The manipulated variable which are the emergency braking and the tell-tale lamp when considering the warning level;
- Set point which is a technical data. It concerns the maximum authorized speed of the train.

The relations between variables are not only established by equations but also expressed with pre-conditions and post-conditions to express a residual state through successive cycles.

---

[3] Moreover, the system informs the driver with the emergency 'tell-tale ' lamp.

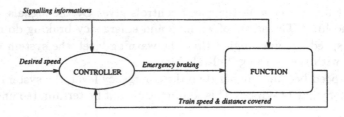

Fig. 5. KLV control loop.

6.3 B architectural model

The results of the preliminary analysis for the KLV case study have been presented elsewhere [Tao97b]. From this analysis, we outline a graph of shared data (see figure-6). This graph and the control process outline the same elements.

This B model corresponds to an abstract system as described in [Abr96]. It describes in a hierarchical way the global vision of the safety-related properties of the system. The role of the abstract machine of each module will be to express in its invariant a part of these global properties. The corresponding data are 'encapsulated' into the module and gradually introduced following the graphs of the preliminary analysis.

To manage an incremental modification, designers can choose between two options: modify the operation or add a new one. The latter choice minimizes the effort in developing the proof. The results of the high-level design are presented in both cases. Figure-6 represents the B model of the system without the warning level while figure-7 represents the B model after the incremental modification. A new module named *WARNING* has been added; its state corresponds to the modelization of the tell-tale lamp. This *WARNING* module and the *BRAKING* module are sharing the same data, and their states are strongly consistent. Introducing the *WARNING* state with a new module allows to provide a separated proof.

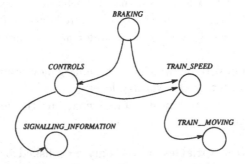

Fig. 6. KLV B model.

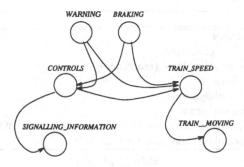

Fig. 7. KLV B model after modification.

6.4 Observations

This section presents the results of the observations made across the project. The table 1 shows how the effort expended on the project was distributed. It is a typical profile of formal development practice. The most important effort is in the early activities where the requirements are being analyzed.

Phases	Effort given in person-month
Theoretical training for modeling	1
Practical training for safety of specific domain	2
Restatement of informal specification	1
Preliminary analysis	1
Architectural Design	1/2
Formal modelization	2

Table 1. Distribution of time within each activity

The results presented in table 2 are very similar to metrics given in [Hab97] for the development of the Calcutta subway.

6.5 Conclusion

In this paper, we present ideas to provide a methodological guideline, emphasizing safety-related traceability through the life-cycle. As a demonstration of the feasibility of our approach, a real case study has been entirely developed. From this experience, we draw some remarks:

It is well-known that without any guideline, there is a risk that a B model will be difficult to prove and also to refine until the code generation phase. The main advantage of our approach is to provide a framework which overcomes these problems, in a way easily understood by domain experts. This framework

Comments	Measure
Number of modules	18
Number of C lines generated	3261
Number of specification lines (machines)	1017
Number of B0 lines	1083
Number of proof obligations	1638
Ratio for automatic proof	92%
Number of proof obligations per specification lines and BO lines	1.7
Number of proof obligations per lines of code	2

Table 2. Metrics

has a significant impact on the software development process as well as its documentations.

The validation process cannot be formalized, since the original system description is provided informally; experts must convince themselves that the formal description accurately reflects the intended system behavior. The traceability of the safety-related properties is helpful to conduct this process. This traceability will be reinforced by a tool, the role of which could be to produce *before-after predicates* derived from substitutions. The resulting document should allow to perform down-up trace from the B model to the formalization of the preliminary analysis.

To efficiently use the B method, one must follow methodological heuristics. Currently, there is no general solution. However, various proposals have been put forward in specific application domains (*e.g.* [Abr97]). They all have in common the outline of architectural concepts based on an abstract system. More work needs to be done in this direction to bring closer Software Architecture and B formal development.

6.6 Acknowledgments

We wish thank P. Ozello (SNCF) for his suggestive comments during the real case study development and for discussions on the safety methodology.

References

[Abr96] Abrial, J.R. Extending B without changing it. In Henri Habrias, editor, *First Conference on the B method*, Nantes, 1996.

[Abr97] Abrial, J.R. and Mussat, L. Specification and design of a transmission protocol by successive refinements using B. In *Marktoberdorff Summer School*, LNCS, to appear 1997.

[Ber96] Bert, D., Potet, M.L. and Rouzaud, Y. A study on Components and Assembly Primitives in B. In Henri Habrias, editor, *First Conference on the B method*, Nantes, 1996.

[Cop95] Coplien, J. O. *Pattern Languages of Program Design*. Addison Wesley, 1995.

[Hab97] H. Habrias. *Dictionnaire encyclopédique du génie logiciel*. Masson, 1997.

[Lev95] Levenson, N. G.. *Safeware - System Safety and Computers*. Addison-Wesley Publishing Company, 1995.

[Sae90] Saeed, A., Anderson, T. and Koutny, M. A formal model for safety-critical computing systems. SAFECOMP'90, 1990.

[Sha95] M. Shaw. Beyond objects : A software design paradigm based on process control. *ACM Software Engineering Notes*, 20(1), January 1995.

[Sha96a] Shaw, M. and Clements, P. A field guide to boxology: Preliminary classification of architectural styles for software systems. Site Web de Mary Shaw, Avril 1996.

[Sha96b] Shaw, M. and Garlan, D. *Software Architecture, Perspectives on an Emerging Discipline*. Prentice-Hall, 1996.

[Tao96] Taouil-Traverson, S. and Vignes, S. A preliminary analysis cycle for B development. In *Beyond 2000: Hardware and Software Design Strategies*, pages 319–325. EUROMICRO 96, Prague, Czech Republic, Septembre 2-5 1996.

[Tao97a] Taouil-Traverson, S. *Stratégie d'intégration de la méthode B dans la construction du logiciel critique*. PhD thesis, ENST, July 1997.

[Tao97b] Taouil-Traverson, S., Ozello, P. and Vignes, S. Développement formel de logiciel de sécurité dans le domaine ferroviaire : utilisation de la méthode B à la SNCF. *TSI*, to appear in december 1997.

Abstract State Machines: Designing Distributed Systems with State Machines and B

Bill Stoddart, Steve Dunne, Andy Galloway[*], Richard Shore

School of Computing and Mathematics, University of Teesside, U.K.

Abstract. We outline a theory of communicating "Abstract State Machines". The state of an Abstract State Machine has two components: a behavioural state and a data state. The behavioural states are shown on a state diagram, whose transitions are labelled with an "event" and a B operation. The firing of a transition is synonymous with the occurrence of its associated event. We use a synchronous model of communication based on shared events which simultaneously change the state of each participating machine. The B operation associated with a transition generally has the form $G \implies S$, where a necessary condition for the transition to fire is that G is true, and where S describes any resulting changes in the data state of the Abstract Machine. The paper includes simple examples, the translation of Abstract State Machines to B Action Systems, the translation of Abstract State Machines into "primitive" Abstract State Machines which have only behavioural state, the parallel combination of high level Abstract State Machines, and short notes on choice and refinement.

1 Introduction

Recently there has been a considerable interest in modelling reactive and distributed systems in B. [1] [3] [4] [6]. In such cases, we are interested in describing a system in terms of its interacting subsystems, and in the closely connected issue of describing how a system behaves with respect to its environment. The most popular approach [1] [3] [4] is to use a B representation of the Action System formalism. Within this formalism it is possible to use approaches which communicate via shared variables, or via shared events.

An action system in B consists of an abstract machine whose operations are *guarded* rather than pre-conditioned. Whereas the operations of a classical B Abstract Machine can be thought of as specifying procedures, whose pre-conditions provide us with information on when they may be safely used, the operations of an Action System describe transitions. These transitions are thought of as being enabled if their guard is true. The life cycle of an action system consists of seeing which of its operations have true guards, and non deterministically choosing one such operation to fire. This process is repeated indefinitely.

In this paper we present an approach based on a related formalism which we call "Abstract State Machines". An Abstract State Machine resembles an

---

[*] High Integrity System Group, Dept. of Computer Science, University of York

Action System whose state is factored into two components, a data state, and a behavioural state. This factoring does not increase our expressive power in a mathematical sense, but we believe it allows us to present our distributed system models in a more accessible way. The behavioural aspects of an Abstract State Machine can be presented in pictorial form, using state machine diagrams.

We begin by presenting "primitive" Abstract State Machines, which have only behavioural state, and we give rules of communication between such machines based on the idea of the simultaneous change of state of machines on the occurrence of a shared event. We show how communicating primitive state machines can be described in terms of Action Systems.

We then present an example of an Abstract State Machine which has an internal data state. We show how the description of such a machine is structured in terms of a data machine, which provides operations that act on the data state, together with a state machine diagram which adds a behavioural layer. We give the machine's translation into a B action system.

After these initial examples we outline a semantics for Abstract State Machines, based on the translation of Abstract State Machines into primitive Abstract State Machines.

We then consider the parallel composition of Abstract State Machines. The ability to perform such composition is of primary importance because it enables us to build a mathematical model of system behaviour[2] and to state any global invariant properties we feel are important. The techniques for checking that our model does not violate the global invariant is then identical to verifying the invariant of a B Action System (or indeed a B Abstract Machine, since the replacement of pre-conditions by guards leaves us with exactly the same proof obligations.[2])

The above discussions equip us to look more closely at the translation of Abstract State Machines into B Action Systems, and we return to this topic with another example which shows our general approach to handling i/o.

We follow this with some remarks of the different forms of choice that can be expressed in our formalism: provisional (with backtracking), irrevocable and clairvoyant.

We have previously explored communicating state machines in the "Event Calculus", a theory of communicating state machines described in Z [9]. Some of the ideas have also evolved through our work on process algebras, in particular ZCCS, a dialect of CCS which uses Z as its value calculus [5]. What is new in this paper is the re-expression of these ideas in B, which is important because it may improve our ability to compartmentalise proof. It also gives us the opportunity to work with predicate transformers, a formalism that is very amenable to mechanical manipulation through the idea of a generalised substitution.

1.1 Primitive Abstract State Machines

We use a simple formulation of the idea of a "state machine". A machine has a number of states, and changes state on the occurrence of an "event". Only one event can occur at a time. Communication between machines, including the passing of data, is expressed in terms of shared events that simultaneously change the state of two or more machines

We assume three primitive sets, *MACHINE*, *STATE* and *EVENT*, and a function ψ which maps each machine to its behaviour, expressed as a next state relation. So that $\psi \in MACHINE \longrightarrow ((STATE \times EVENT) \longleftrightarrow STATE)$.

As a first example we consider a vending machine V that sells chocolate bars at two pounds each, and a customer C. Their next state relations, which are denoted by ψV and ψC, are shown in Fig. 1.

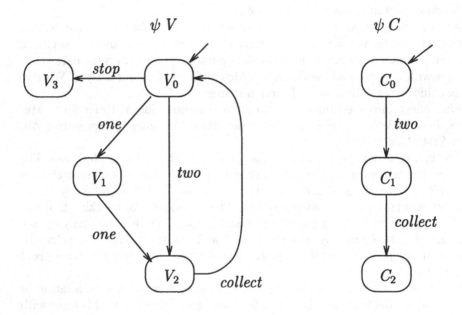

$$one \in \operatorname{dom} C$$

Fig. 1. Vending Machine and Customer

First consider the vending machine V without reference to the customer. Suppose it starts in initial state V_0. The machine can accept one pound and two pound coins, and after insertion of two pounds allows a customer to collect his chocolate bar. The machine may also stop accepting coins and dispensing chocolate bars, perhaps because it is empty.

Next consider the vending machine with its customer, starting in the initial composite state $\{V_0, C_0\}$. The basic rule of synchronisation is that events which are common to more that one machine only occur as shared events.

From initial state $\{V_0, C_0\}$ the possible events that may occur are *two* or *stop*. The event *two* is a shared event: the vending machine has a two pound coin inserted, and the customer inserts the coin. This results in a simultaneous change of state in both machines, from $\{V_0, C_0\}$ to $\{V_2, C_1\}$.

The event *stop* concerns machine V only, and results in a change of state from $\{V_0, C_0\}$ to $\{V_3, C_0\}$.

We do not want the rules of our calculus to allow the event *one* to occur from state $\{V_0, C_0\}$, since the customer has no intention of inserting a one pound coin. But how should we frame these rules to differentiate between *one* and *stop*, since these are both events which the customer is not prepared to take part in? We associate with each machine a set of events known as its *repertoire*. This set will contain all the events evident in the machines behaviour (i.e. all events used in forming its next state function) but may also include additional events. We include *one* in the repertoire of C.

We can now give an informal set of rules for the behaviour of a set of state machines (a formal version of these rules is given in [8])

- An event can only occur when all machines that have that event in their repertoire are ready to take part in it.

- When an event occurs each machine that has that event in its repertoire changes according to one of the possibilities offered by its next state relation. Other machines are unaffected.

These rules allow us to derive the behaviour of a composed machine from the behaviour of its constituent machines.

For each Abstract State Machine there is a corresponding B Action System with isomorphic behaviour. The isomorphism consists of there being a one to one correspondence between event traces of the Abstract State Machine, and operation traces of the Action System. We now give a translation of our example machines into corresponding B Action Systems. For reasons of space we use a notation based on GSL (the Generalised Substitution Language).

Machine V
Sets $STATE = \{V_0, V_1, V_2, V_3\}$
Variables *state*
Invariant *state* $\in STATE$
Initialisation *state* $:= V_0$
Operations
$\quad stop \mathrel{\widehat{=}} state = V_0 \implies state := V_3$
$\quad one \mathrel{\widehat{=}} state = V_0 \implies state := V_1 \, [\!] \, state = V_1 \implies state := V_2$
$\quad two \mathrel{\widehat{=}} state = V_0 \implies state := V_2$
$\quad collect \mathrel{\widehat{=}} state = V_2 \implies state := V_0$

Machine C
Sets $STATE = \{C_0, C_1\}$
Variables $state$
Invariant $state \in STATE$
Initialisation $state := C_0$
Operations
$\quad two \;\widehat{=}\; state = C_0 \Longrightarrow state := C_1$
$\quad collect \;\widehat{=}\; state = C_1 \Longrightarrow state := C_2$
$\quad one \;\widehat{=}\; false \Longrightarrow skip$

The combined behaviour of the machines V and C, in accordance with the rules of synchronisation given above, is isomorphic to the following action system.

$Machine\,V with C$
Includes $V.V, C.C$
Operations
$stop \;\widehat{=}\; V.stop$
$one \;\widehat{=}\; V.one \parallel C.one$
$two \;\widehat{=}\; V.two \parallel C.two$
$collect \;\widehat{=}\; V.collect \parallel C.collect$

1.2 Abstract State Machines with Internal Data States

We extend our model to one in which the vending machine has an internal data state. We first define some constants to detail the price of a bar and the set of coins accepted by the machine.

Machine $VMDetails$
Constants $coins, price, maxbars$
Properties $coins = \{1, 2\}$, $price = 2$

The data state of our vending machine details the number of chocolate bars it holds and the value of coins input so far for the present transaction. We define a "data machine" to describe this internal data and the effect of operations which are invoked on the input of a coin, on completion of payment, and on the sale of a chocolate bar.

Machine $VMData$
Uses $VMDetails$
Variables $numbars, coins\_in$
Invariant $numbars \in 0\,..\,maxbars \land coins\_in \in 0\,..\,price$
Initialisation $numbars := maxbars \parallel coins\_in := 0$
Operations
$\quad In(coin) \;\widehat{=}\; numbars > 0 \land coin + coins\_in \leq price \Longrightarrow$
$\qquad coins\_in := coins\_in + coin$
$\quad Paid \;\widehat{=}\; coins\_in = price \Longrightarrow skip$
$\quad Sale \;\widehat{=}\; numbars > 0 \Longrightarrow numbars := numbars - 1$

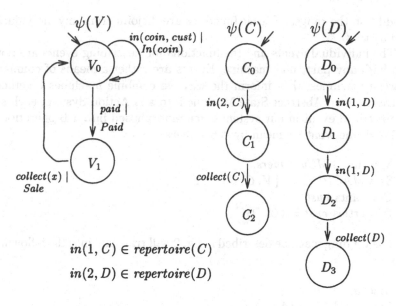

Fig. 2. Vending machine with internal state

The complete description of the vending machine is obtained by adding a behavioural layer, which is provided in diagrammatic form in figure 2). The figure also describes the behaviour of two customers. Note that the transitions of the vending machine have labels of the form $e \mid Op$ where e is an event, and Op is an operation from the associated data machine. The function of the operation is to impose any guard required to limit when the transition can occur, and to describe the change in data state when the transition does occur. For example consider the system in its initial state. That is in behavioural state $\{V_0, C_0, D_0\}$ and with data state of V as given by the initialisation clause of *VMData*. Then the transition labelled *paid* | *Paid* cannot occur because the guard of *Paid* is false. On the other hand the guard of the transition labelled $in(coin, cust) \mid In(coin)$ is true for suitable values of *coin* and *cust*. Input of a coin is a shared event so for this transition to occur we also need to satisfy the rules of synchronisation. In this case there are two ways for this to occur: the vending machine can synchronise with either machine C or machine D. If it synchronises with C the event is $in(2, C)$; *cust* becomes instantiated to C, *coin* becomes instantiated to 2, and the change to the data state of the vending machine is described by the operation $In(2)$. A formal semantics will be given in the next section.

We use descriptive functions to refer to events. For example the expression $in(2, C)$ is used to refer to the event that customer C inserts a ten pence coin. These descriptive functions are injections (which ensures, for example, that $collect(C)$ and $collect(D)$ are different events) with mutually disjoint ranges (which ensures, for example, that $collect(C)$ is a different event from $in(2, C)$).

In addition the ranges of these functions are disjoint from any individual events, such as *paid*.

The individual events and the functions for describing events are not associated with any particular machine. Events are rather a means of communication between machines; they inform the way we combine machines together. When we translate an Abstract State Machine into a B Action System, each simple or parametrized event in our system is metamorphosed into a B operation.

We define what we mean by "customers".

Machine *VMCustomers*
Sets $MACHINE = \{V, C, D\}$
Constants *cust*
Properties $cust = \{C, D\}$

The vending machine described in fig. 2 will translate into the following Action System:

Machine *VM*
Includes *VMDATA*
Uses *VMCustomers*
Sets $STATE = \{V_0, V_1\}$
Variables *state*
Invariant $state \in STATE$
Initialisation $state := V_0$
Operations
  $in(coin, cust) \mathrel{\hat{=}} state = V_0 \land coin \in coins \land$
    $cust \in customers \implies skip \parallel In(coin)$
  $paid \mathrel{\hat{=}} state = V_0 \implies state := V_1 \parallel Paid$
  $collect(cust) \mathrel{\hat{=}} state = V_1 \land cust \in customets \implies state := V_0 \parallel Sale$

2 A Semantics for Abstract State Machine Transitions

In our first example we introduced some simple state machines diagrams. We can think of these as next state relations, which map a current primitive state and a primitive event to a next primitive state. Each element of these relations may be thought of as a primitive transition. The purpose of this section is to interpret the possibly parametrized labelled transitions of Abstract State Machines with an internal data state in terms of primitive transitions.

In the following discussion we consider an Abstract State Machine A whose associated data state machine has a state space D. We take A_0 and A_1 to be two arbitrary behavioural states of A, such that there is some high-level transition from A_0 to A_1. It will be convenient to consider behavioural states as total injective functions from D, the set of data states, to the set of primitive states. This is to provide a convenient way of combining a behavioural state and a data state into a primitive state (or alternatively of factoring a primitive state into a behavioural state and a data state). Thus if A is in behavioural state A_0 and data state d (where necessarily $d \in D$) it is in the primitive state $A_0(d)$.

Suppose the transition from A_0 to A_1 has the form:

$$A_0 \xrightarrow{\ e \mid Op\ } A_1$$

where e is a primitive event. Then our high level transition denotes the set of all primitive transitions from A_0 with some data state d to $A1$ in some data state d', where the change of data state from d to d' is one of the possibilities offered by Op. i.e.

$$\{t \mid \exists\, d, d' \bullet (d, d') \in rel(Op) \wedge t = (A_0(d), e) \mapsto A_1(d')\}$$

where

$$rel(Op) = \{d, d' \mid (d, d') \in D \times D \wedge \neg ([Op]d \neq d')\}$$

This idea extends in an obvious way to the form in which e is parametrized by the input parameter of Op.

$$A_0 \xrightarrow{\ e(x) \mid Op(x)\ } A_1$$

Now our parametrized transition denotes the following set.

$$\{t \mid \exists\, d, d', x \bullet x \in \mathrm{dom}(e) \wedge (d, d') \in rel(Op(x)) \wedge$$
$$t = (A_0(d), e(x)) \mapsto A_1(d')\}$$

Handling of output parameters is rather different, since instantiating an output parameter with a value gives an invalid substitution. This is because output parameters occur on the left side of assignments, which is not a suitable place for a value! Consider the parametrized transition:

$$A_0 \xrightarrow{\ e(y) \mid y \leftarrow Op\ } A_0$$

To know if $e(y)$ can occur for some given value of y, we need to know if Op could yield that value as its output. We achieve this by placing the operation in a context which renders is non-feasible unless it yields the result we require. To do this we provide a local variable y' in which Op will deposit its result, and then we impose a guard that will only allow through a value y' that is equal to y. The denoted set in this case is:

$$\{t \mid \exists\, d, d', y \bullet y \in \mathrm{dom}(e) \wedge$$
$$(d, d') \in rel\,(var\ y' \bullet y' \leftarrow Op;\, y' = y \implies skip)\}$$

A transition with both inputs and outputs is a straightforward combination of the previous two cases. It is also possible for the event function e to involve parameters which are not related to the associated operation. E.g. in our vending machine some events are parametrized with a variable that becomes instantiated to the identity of the customer, and are used to specify where input comes from or output goes to. Such cases are also a straightforward extension of the above.

Along with the rules for the firing of transitions given in section 1.1, these rules give us the entire behaviour of an Abstract State Machine model. This can be of practical use with model checking techniques, or when the state space of the machine is small enough to permit exhaustive search methods to be used to investigate its properties. It also provides the definitive meaning of our event calculus, against which we can judge the correctness of techniques for the high level combination of parametrized machines. Such techniques are introduced in the next section.

3   The High Level Combination of Synchronized Transitions

The rules given so far enable us to translate high level abstract state machines into primitive abstract state machines, and to combine such primitive machines into primitive systems. Although this provides the theoretical basis of our calculus, it is much more useful to be able to combine high level systems directly. We will be able to do this if we can combine pairs of high level transitions.

We will consider transitions from two disjoint systems A and B, where A and B are said to be disjoint if no component machine of A is also a component machine of B.

3.1   Combining Transitions which Synchronise on a Primitive Event

Suppose that in systems A and B we have the transitions:

$$A_0 \xrightarrow{\ e\ |\ Op1\ } A_1$$

$$B_0 \xrightarrow{\ e\ |\ Op2\ } B_1$$

then this gives us the following single transition in the combined system $A \parallel B$:

$$A_0, B_0 \xrightarrow{\ e\ |\ Op3\ } A_1, B_1$$

where:

$$Op3 \cong Op1 \parallel Op2$$

3.2 Combining Transitions which Synchronise on a Parametrized Events

We consider events described by a total injective function e. For the moment we will restrict ourselves to the case in which $ran(e) \subseteq repertoire(A)$ and $ran(e) \subseteq repertoire(B)$. This ensures, by the rules of our primitive calculus, that the transitions can only fire together.

We will be rather informal with respect to describing the necessary side conditions to avoid variable capture, simply assuming that if this occurs when applying one of our rules, then this renders the application of the rule invalid.

Shared Input Suppose that in systems A and B we have transitions:

$$A_0 \xrightarrow{\quad e(x) \mid Op1(x) \quad} A_1$$

$$B_0 \xrightarrow{\quad e(y) \mid Op2(y) \quad} B_1$$

Then we obtain the following transition in $A \parallel B$.

$$A_0, B_0 \xrightarrow{\quad e(x) \mid Op3(x) \quad} A_1, B_1$$

where:

$$Op3(u) \mathrel{\widehat{=}} Op1(u) \parallel Op2(u)$$

One way Transfer of Data Suppose in systems A and B we have transitions:

$$A_0 \xrightarrow{\quad e(y) \mid y \leftarrow Op1 \quad} A_1$$

$$B_0 \xrightarrow{\quad e(x) \mid Op2(x) \quad} B_1$$

This will give us the following transition in $A \parallel B$.

$$A_0, B_0 \xrightarrow{\quad e(x) \mid x \leftarrow Op3(x) \quad} A_1, B_1$$

where:

$$v \leftarrow Op3(u) \mathrel{\widehat{=}}$$
$$var\ v' \bullet v' \leftarrow Op1; v' = u \implies (v := u \parallel Op2(u))$$

The combined transition accepts an input and offers the same value as output. By still offering an output, we can combine with a further transitions that require input, and thus model broadcast communications. By still accepting an input we can combine with further transitions that provide output, but what would that mean? In fact if we combine several transmitters with a single receiver the transmitters must agree on the value to be transmitted. This is obviously a less likely scenario than a broadcast transmission, and in the approach of [4] it is not allowed. We include it for two reasons. Firstly, our policy for high level combination of systems is to include anything that is allowed by the underlying semantics. Secondly, we have found that models that do not match what we expect from implementations can nevertheless be used to give an abstract conceptual description of a system. For example if we are modelling a system in which a critical calculation is duplicated on several different bits of hardware; the event that identical results are transmitted could be modelled by combining the transmissions into a single event.

If we know that *only* A and B are involved in the communication, we can simplify the resulting transition to:

$$A_0, B_0 \xrightarrow{\quad e(x) \mid Op3(x) \quad} A_1, B_1$$

Since the communication is now internal to the combined system made up of A and B, there is no notion of "input" required for this transition. The value of x serves purely to parametrize Op3, which is defined as:

$$Op3(u) \triangleq var \ v' \bullet v' \leftarrow Op1; \ v' = u \implies Op2(u).$$

Two way Exchange of Data It is possible to combine operations which both involve both input and output. Suppose we have the transitions:

$$A_0 \xrightarrow{\quad e(w, x) \mid x \leftarrow Op1(w) \quad} A_1$$

$$B_0 \xrightarrow{\quad e(y, z) \mid y \leftarrow Op2(z) \quad} B_1$$

This will give us the following transition in $A \parallel B$

$$A_0, B_0 \xrightarrow{\quad e(x, y) \mid x, y \leftarrow Op3(x, y) \quad} A_1, B_1$$

where:

$$
\begin{aligned}
s, t \leftarrow Op3(u, v) &\triangleq var \ a, b \bullet \\
&\quad (a \leftarrow Op1(u) \parallel b \leftarrow Op2(v)); \\
&\quad (u = b \wedge v = a) \implies (s := u \parallel t := v)
\end{aligned}
$$

If the exchange involves only A and B we can suppress the output parameters, and express the combined transition as:

$$A_0, B_0 \xrightarrow{\quad e(x, y) \mid Op3(x, y) \quad} A_1, B_1$$

where:

$$Op3(u, v) \mathrel{\widehat{=}} var\ a, b \bullet (a \leftarrow Op1(u) \parallel b \leftarrow Op2(v));$$
$$(u = b \wedge v = a) \Longrightarrow skip;$$

To model an exchange of data we have used our parametrized events to positionally match the output of each transition with the input of the other. i.e. in machine A's transition we have the event $e(w, x)$ where w is an input and x an output, and in B's transition we have $e(y, z)$ where y is an output and x an input. We needed to call upon the parametrization of the event e to match A's input with B's output and vice-versa. Note that there is another, possibly less useful, scenario allowed by our semantics, which matches up the inputs of the two transitions with each other, and matches the outputs with each other. The parametrizations of the operations themselves are insufficient to distinguish the two scenarios, because the B syntax for representing inputs and outputs of operations loses the required positional information. This is one reason for distinguishing events from operation names. Another is that events are semantic objects in our universe of discourse, whereas operation names appear to exist at a meta level, as part of the language with which we describe that universe. For an approach that does not make this distinction see [4].

3.3 Other Cases

We have only considered transitions for events described by some function e and systems A and B such that $ran(e) \subseteq repertoire(A)$ and $ran(e) \subseteq repertoire(B)$. This will not be the case where we parametrize events with the identity of the machine they are associated with, as we did with $in(2, C)$ (C inserts £2) and $in(1, D)$ (D inserts £1) in our second vending machine example. Here the parameters C and D are introduced precisely to distinguish the events of machine C from those of machine D. Such cases do not introduce any significant complications, but we do not have space to consider them here.

4 The Treatment of Output Operations when Translating Abstract State Machines to B Action Systems

In our initial example machines we avoided any mention of output operations. In the previous two sections we have considered the translation of high level Abstract State Machine transitions into sets of primitive transitions, and the combination of high level Abstract State Machines by combining pairs of transitions. In both cases the treatment of output operations involved us in assigning a value and then attempting to execute a guarded operation which not fire unless the previous assignment caused its guard to be true. Operationally, we could think of such an arrangement in terms of *backtracking*. if the wrong assignment is made, the operation in question will back track to the point the assignment was made and try another value if it can.

238

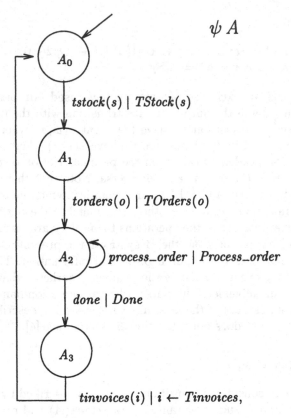

ψA

$tstock(s) \mid TStock(s)$

$torders(o) \mid TOrders(o)$

$process\_order \mid Process\_order$

$done \mid Done$

$tinvoices(i) \mid i \leftarrow Tinvoices,$

Fig. 3. Invoice Clerk

We now show how output operations are handled when translating an Abstract State Machine into an Action System. We use an example machine taken from an invoicing system. The particular machine we will consider performs the duties of an invoicing clerk. The Abstract State Machine diagram is shown in figure 3.

The invoice clerk receives details of stock and details of orders, and then processes the orders until all orders have either been converted into invoices, or have become failed orders (unable to be met from current stock). He then outputs details of the invoiced orders and becomes ready to process the next batch.[2] We will assume, without giving further details, a data machine *InvoiceClerkData*

---

[2] This machine provides two nice examples of how the ability to express behaviour can simplify system specification. Firstly, to specify the processing of a batch of orders we are able to make use of *Process_order*, the specification of an operation to process a single order. Secondly, we can use the outer loop to specify, within the operation *Tinvoices*, that failed orders will be re-queued as pending orders to be retried next time round.

which describes the internal data held by the invoice clerk and provides the operations *Tstock* (transfer stock), *Torders* (transfer orders), *Process_order* and *Tinvoices* (transfer invoices).

The B Action System corresponding to the data clerk machine is:

> Machine *InvoiceClerk*
> Includes *InvoiceClerkData*
> Sets *State* = $\{A_0, A_1, A_2, A_3\}$
> Variables *state*
> Invariant *state* $\in$ *STATE*
> Initialisation *state* := A_0
> Operations
> *tstock*(*s*) $\widehat{=}$ *state* = A_0 $\Longrightarrow$ *state* := A_1 $\parallel$ *Tstock*(*s*)
> *torders*(*o*) $\widehat{=}$ *state* = A_1 $\Longrightarrow$ *state* := A_2 $\parallel$ *Torders*(*o*)
> *process_order* $\widehat{=}$ *state* = A_2 $\Longrightarrow$ *skip* $\parallel$ *Process_order*
> *tinvoices*(*i*) $\widehat{=}$
>   *state* = A_3 $\Longrightarrow$ *state* := A_0 $\parallel$
>   *var* i' $\bullet$ i' $\leftarrow$ *Tinvoices*; $i = i'$ $\Longrightarrow$ *skip*

In the Abstract State Machine, to see that the parameter *i* in the *event* *tinvoices*(*i*) represents an output, we have to refer to the associated B operation $i \leftarrow Tinvoices$. We mirror this approach in the corresponding Action System. The *operation tinvoices*(*i*) can only fire with a value of *i* which corresponds to the value that will be output by the data level operation $i \leftarrow Tinvoices$. Any other value will cause the operation to be disabled, because the guard $i = i'$ will be false.

By means of this approach, we encapsulate the distinction between input and output at the inner level of the data machine. Operations that mimic events have no outputs, but only inputs. Freeing ourselves from outputs, which cannot be considered as true parameters, enables us to extend the correspondence between the events of Abstract State Machines and the operations of the isomorphic B action system to cover parametrized as well as primitive events.

It also makes it very easy to combine our Action Systems in parallel. For example, the invoicing system of which the *InvoiceClerk* Action System is a part will include *InvoiceClerk.InvoiceClerk* and *InventoryClerk.InventoryClerk*, where the inventory clerk machine also includes an operation *tinvoices*(*i*) which will receive the invoices output by the invoice clerk. In the combined system the operation will appear as:

> *tinvoices*(*i*) $\widehat{=}$ *InvoiceClerk.tinvoices*(*i*) $\parallel$ *InventoryClerk.tinvoices*(*i*)

4.1 Choice

Our theory allows us several different kinds of choice, which we might term *provisional*, *irrevocable* and *clairvoyant*.

Provisional choice arises when we combine choice and sequence at the GSL level. For example consider:

$(x := 1 \,[\!]\, x := 2); \; x = 1 \Longrightarrow skip$

Here we have a sequence of two commands in which the first appears to give us a choice of assigning either 1 or 2 to x. However, B's predicate transformer calculus tells us the sequence terminates with $x = 1$. Note that if we assign 2 to x, the guard of the following command becomes false. As Nelson has remarked in the context of his own abstract command language,[7] an operational interpretation would be to think of a false guard as forcing a sequence to backtrack and make a different choice. We have used a similar technique when dealing with output "parameters".

The kind of choice we exercise in making Abstract State Machine transitions, on the other hand, is irrevocable. Once a transition has been made at the state machine level it cannot be reversed. If all further transitions are inhibited by false guards the system is deadlocked.

For an example of clairvoyant choice, suppose machine A has a transition:

$$A_0 \xrightarrow{\quad in(x) \mid Op(x) \quad} A_1$$

where $Op(u) \; \widehat{=} \; (u = 3) \Longrightarrow S$. When machine A is in state A_0 it is expecting an input value, but is fussy about the input it will accept. The transition which accepts the input will only fire if the offered input has the value of 3. Thus in our calculus an Abstract State Machine can see an input value before it arrives, and decide to ignore it if it considers the value to be invalid. This is very useful in modelling the event driven interfaces generated by visual programming environments. Consider, for example, a delete file operation. At the implementation level the application presents the user with a list of files that are available for deletion. The user selects a file from the list, and when satisfied with his choice presses an "ok" button. The file is than deleted. Most of this detail can be abstracted away at the specification level, and we only model the operation that occurs when the user activates the "ok" button after having selected a valid choice of file.

5 Refinement

As with B Abstract Machines, our intuitive concept of refinement is based on the idea of an observer, armed with the specification of an abstract system A and actually observing a system that conforms to a more concrete specification C. We say that C is a refinement of A if C does not allow any behaviour that would lead the observer to conclude the machine did not conform to the specification of A.

With Abstract Machines, operational refinement allows us to strengthen guards and weaken pre-conditions. By strengthening guards we reduce the possible responses of the system, but those that remain still accord with the abstract specification. In fact we can strengthen guards to the point at which an operation becomes non-feasible. The ultimate refinement of all operations is *magic*, which can be defined as *false* $\Longrightarrow$ *skip*. All states existing after the execution of *magic* satisfy any post condition we care to formulate, which is equivalent to saying there are no such states.

Strengthening guards in the operations of an Abstract State Machine also reduces non-determinism, and if pursued beyond a certain point will lead to deadlock. Just as *magic* is the ultimate refinement of any abstract machine operation, so the deadlocked Abstract State Machine is the absolute refinement of any Abstract State Machine. Also, just as refinement of AMN operations incurs the obligation to prove feasibility if we want to obtain an operation that can be implemented, so the refinement of Abstract State Machines incurs proof obligations concerning freedom from deadlock. Note however that, unlike *magic*, the deadlocked Abstract State Machine is possible to implement.

The operations of a B Abstract Machine have pre-conditions which inform as when the operations are safe to use (in the sense that they will be sure to terminate). In an Abstract State Machine, we are actually using the operations, and we have the obligation to check that the behavioural context we impose on an operation will ensure its pre-condition. Once this is established, we are free to widen pre-conditions as we normally are able to do in operational refinement. We know, of course, that these wider conditions will never be exercised.

The operations of a B Abstract Machine should be feasible to allow their implementation. In a B Action System, the individual operations may be partial (not everywhere feasible) as the guard is now interpreted as a firing condition. We similarly make use of partial operations in Abstract State Machines.

The parallel composition of Abstract State Machines is monotonic with respect to refinement. This allows us to implement an Abstract State Machine System by implementing its individual component machines. Freedom from deadlock, however, cannot be assured by proving freedom from deadlock in all constituent machines. It must be considered globally.

The theory of "time refinement"[1] is applicable to Abstract State Machines. In this theory we allow refinements to introduce new events not seen in the abstract system. Our observer, armed with the abstract system specification, ignores these extra events when observing the concrete system. He merely verifies that the events detailed in his abstract specification occur as required.

6 Time

We have not found space to include examples involving time, but in [9] we use a Z based version of this formalism to specify a distributed ticket booking system with timeouts. The basic technique for handling time is to introduce an event, *tick*, supposed to occur at regular time intervals. Introduction of the *tick* event incurs the "King Canute proof obligation" (time and tide wait for no man). I.e. for any system with *tick* in its repertoire it must always be possible for another *tick* to occur at some future point in the systems behaviour.

7 Conclusions

We have sketched some ideas for a calculus of Abstract State Machines. These provide an expressive means of specifying and modelling distributed and reactive systems.

We can use multiple Abstract State Machines to model distributed systems. Such machines may be combined into a single Abstract State Machine. The motivation for combining machines in this way is not to aid implementation, but rather to provide an overall mathematical model of system behaviour.

To make use of the B Toolkit in analysing such a model, we can translate Abstract State Machines into B Action Systems. These Action Systems are very simple to combine together, but their operations necessarily involve sequencing, which is not traditionally available at the B Abstract Machine level.

The need for sequencing arises from our desire to forge a correspondence between parametrized events in Abstract State Machines, and parametrized operations in Action Systems. Events may be freely parametrized, but the parametrization of operations is more restricted; for example we cannot replace an output parameter by a constant, as this could yield an invalid substitution. We have reconciled events and operations by making use of the GSL's ability to express backtracking and clairvoyant choice.

References

1. J R Abrial. Extending B without Changing it (for Developing Distributed Systems). In H Habrias, editor, *The First B Conference, ISBN : 2-906082-25-2*, 1996.
2. Jean-Raymond Abrial. *The B Book*. Cambridge University Press, 1996.
3. M Butler and M Waldén. Distributed System Development in B. In H Habrias, editor, *The First B Conference, ISBN : 2-906082-25-2*, 1996.
4. M J Butler. An approach to the design of distributed systems with B AMN. In J P Bowen, M J Hinchey, and Till D, editors, *ZUM '97: The Z Formal Specification Notation*, number 1212 in Lecture Notes in Computer Science, 1997.
5. A J Galloway and Stoddart W J. An Operational Semantics for ZCCS. In M J Hinchey, editor, *Proc of ICEEM*, 1997.
6. K Lano. Specifying Reactive Systems in B AMN. In J P Bowen, M J Hinchey, and Till D, editors, *ZUM '97: The Z Formal Specification Notation*, number 1212 in Lecture Notes in Computer Science, 1997.
7. Greg Nelson. A Generalization of Dijkstra's Calculus. *ACM Transactions on Programming Languages and Systems, Vol 11, No. 4*, 1989.
8. W J Stoddart. The Event Calculus, vsn 2. Technical Report tees-scm-1-96, University of Teesside, UK, 1996.
9. W J Stoddart. An Introduction to the Event Calculus. In J P Bowen, M J Hinchey, and Till D, editors, *ZUM '97: The Z Formal Specification Notation*, number 1212 in Lecture Notes in Computer Science, 1997.

Layering Distributed Algorithms within the B-Method

M. Waldén

Åbo Akademi University, Department of Computer Science,
Turku Centre for Computer Science (TUCS),
Lemminkäineng. 14 A, FIN-20520 Turku, Finland,
e-mail: Marina.Walden@abo.fi

Abstract. *Superposition* is a powerful program modularization and structuring method for developing parallel and distributed systems by adding new functionality to an algorithm while preserving the original computation. We present an important special case of the original superposition method, namely, that of considering each new functionality as a *layer* that is only allowed to read the variables of the previous layers. Thus, the superposition method with layers structures the presentation of the derivation. Each derivation step is, however, large and involves many complicated proof obligations. Tool support is important for getting confidence in these proofs and for administering the derivation steps. We have chosen the B-Method for this purpose. We propose how to extend the B-Method to make it more suitable for expressing the layers and assist in proving the corresponding superposition steps in a convenient way.

1 Introduction

Superposition is a powerful program modularization and structuring method for developing parallel and distributed systems [4, 11, 13]. In the superposition method some new functionality is added to an algorithm in the form of additional variables and assignments to these while the original computation is preserved. The superposition method has been formalized as a program refinement rule for *action systems* within the *refinement calculus* and has succesfully been used for constructing distributed systems in a stepwise manner [5]. We use action systems extended with procedures [14] to be able to represent them as distributed systems where the communication is handled by remote procedure calls.

Since the distributed algorithms are often large and complicated, we need a good way to represent them. In the superposition method a new mechanism is added to the algorithm at each step. We can consider each new mechanism as a new *layer* of the algorithm. The resulting distributed algorithm will, thus, be of a structured form consisting of a basic computation and a set of layers.

The derivation using layers is in fact an important special case of the original superposition refinement for action systems [4, 5]. It is, however, powerful enough for deriving interesting distributed algorithms [15]. Even if the super-position refinement with layers is easier to prove than the original superposition refinement rule [5], it still yields large refinement steps with many complicated proof obligations, and tool support is important for getting confidence in these proofs and for administering the derivation steps. Recently, Waldén et al. [8, 17, 18] have shown how to formalize action systems in the B-Method [1]. We use this work as a basis for providing tool support for our method. In order to be able to represent the layers as well as to prove the corresponding superposition steps in a more convenient way, we propose an extension to the B-Method. This extension is in line with the previously proposed extensions by Abrial [2] and Butler et al. [7, 8] to make it possible to derive distributed algorithms within the B-Method.

Hence, in this paper we will present the superposition derivation in a structured way with layers and propose how to extend the B-Method to handle these layers when deriving distributed algorithms. We put special emphasis on showing how to represent procedures within the layering method. Thereby, we are able to handle the communication within the distributed algorithms using remote procedure calls in a uniform manner. Furthermore, we show how to provide tool support for proving the correctness of the refinement steps within the superposition method with layers. An example of the layering method is given in [15]. We assume familiarity with the B-Method.

Overview: In section 2 we describe the action system formalism within the B-Method extending our previous work with procedures. In section 3 we describe how these action systems are refined into distributed systems using superposition refinement with layers. We also show how this refinement could be performed within the B-Method and propose the needed machines and operations on these. Finally, we end with some concluding remarks in section 4.

2 Action Systems

We use the action systems formalism [4, 6, 14] as a basis for constructing distributed algorithms. We first give a brief overview of action systems representing them within an extended B-notation. Special emphasis is put on the procedure mechanism. The ideas within the original B-Method are used as far as possible.

2.1 The Action Systems Formalism

An *action system* $\mathcal{A}$ is a machine of the form:

```
MACHINE  A

INCLUDES
  GlobalVar_z,

  GlobalProcA_p1, ..., GlobalProcA_pm,
  GlobalProcE_r,
  LocalProcsA_q
VARIABLES
  x
INVARIANT
  I(x, z)
INITIALISATION
  x := x0


ACTIONS
  a1  ≙  A1;
  ...
  an  ≙  An
END
```

on the *state variables* x and z. Each variable is associated with some domain of values. The set of possible assignments of values to the state variables constitutes the *state space*. The *local* variable x is declared and initialised within the *variables-* and *initialisation*-clauses. It is referenced only within the actions and procedures of A. The variable z is the *global* variable of A and is unlike x assumed to be referenced in several action systems. Therefore, following the B-Method it is declared in a separate machine *GlobalVar_z* which is then included in machine A. The global and the local variables are assumed to be distinct. The invariant $I(x,z)$ of the action system gives the domain of the local variable x and states the relation between the variables x and z in the *invariant*-clause.

The procedures $p_1, \ldots, p_m$ in A are the exported global procedures and are declared in the machine *GlobalProcA_p*. These procedures are also called from an environment $\mathcal{E}$, i.e. from another action system than A. The way the environment $\mathcal{E}$ and the action system A are composed is, however, not a topic of this paper. We refer to Sere and Waldén [14] for more information. The local procedures q of A are called only from A. Since a procedure and the statement calling it should be in different machines according to the B-Method, we also declare the local procedures in a separate machine *LocalProcsA_q*. The imported global procedure r is declared within the environment $\mathcal{E}$ in the machine *GlobalProcE_r*, but is also called from A and is included in A via this machine. The global procedures r and p are assumed to be distinct from the local procedures q.

The actions A_i of A are given in the *actions*-clause. Each action A_i in this clause is named a_i and is of the form **SELECT** gA_i **THEN** sA_i **END**, where the *guard* gA_i is a boolean expression on the state variables x and z and the *body*

sA_i is a statement on these state variables. We say that an action is enabled in a state when its guard evaluates to *TRUE* in that state.

The behaviour of an action system is that of Dijkstra's guarded iteration statement [9] on the state variables: the initialisation statement is executed first, thereafter, as long as there are enabled actions, one action at a time is non-deterministically chosen and executed. When none of the actions are enabled the action system terminates. The procedures in the action system are executed via the actions.

The global variable z in $\mathcal{A}$ is declared in a separate machine *GlobalVar_z*. This machine is of the following form:

MACHINE   *GlobalVar_z*

VARIABLES
z
INVARIANT
$P(z)$
INITIALISATION
$z := z_0$
OPERATIONS
$assign\_z(y) \; \widehat{=} \;$ **PRE** $P(y)$ **THEN** $z := y$ **END**
END

It gives the domain of the variable z in $P(z)$. Furthermore, the variable z is assigned merely via procedure calls. For example, in machine $\mathcal{A}$ a new value y is assigned to z via the procedure call *assign_z(y)*.

Procedures Within Action Systems. The procedures of an action system are, like the global variables, declared in separate machines. Before we look at the machines declaring the procedures, let us first study the procedures in general.

A procedure is declared by giving a *procedure header*, p, as well as a *procedure body*, P. The header gives the name of the procedure while the body consists of statements on the state variables of the action system in which the procedure is declared as a local or an exported global procedure. The call on a parameterless procedure $p \; \widehat{=} \; P$ within the statement S is determined by the substitution:

$$S \; = \; S[P/p].$$

Thus, the body P of the procedure p is substituted for each call on the procedure in the statement S, i.e. the statement is expanded.

The procedures can also pass parameters. There are three different mechanisms of parameter passing for procedures in an action system: *call-by-value*, *call-by-result* and *call-by-value-result*. Call-by-value is denoted as $p(f)$, call-by-result as $f \leftarrow p$ and call-by-value-result as $f \leftarrow p(f)$, where p is a procedure and f is a formal parameter.

Procedures with parameters can be expanded in the same way as procedures without parameters. Let $y', z \leftarrow p(x, y) \mathbin{\hat{=}} P$ be a procedure declaration, where x, y and z are formal parameters. We note that due to B restrictions the value-result parameter y is renamed to y' on the lefthand side in the declaration. Then a call on p with the actual parameters a, b and c can be expanded in the following way

$$ S \;=\; S[P'/b, c \leftarrow p(a, b)], $$

where P' can be interpreted as the statement

$$ \mathbf{VAR}\ x, y, y', z\ \mathbf{IN}\ x := a; y := b; P; b := y'; c := z\ \mathbf{END}. $$

Thus, the formal parameters x, y and z in P are replaced by the actual parameters a, b and c, respectively, when substituting the procedure body P for the call $b, c \leftarrow p(a, b)$.

We also permit the procedure bodies to have guards that are not equivalent to $TRUE$. If an action calls a procedure that is not enabled, the system acts as if the calling action never was enabled. Thus, the enabledness of the whole statement is determined by the enabledness of both the action and the procedure. The calling action and the procedure are executed as a single atomic entity. This can easily be seen by an example. Let us consider the action

$$ A \mathbin{\hat{=}} \mathbf{SELECT}\ gA\ \mathbf{THEN}\ sA\ \|\ P\ \mathbf{END} $$

and the procedure declaration

$$ P \mathbin{\hat{=}} \mathbf{SELECT}\ gP\ \mathbf{THEN}\ sP\ \mathbf{END}. $$

The statements sA and sP are assumed to be non-guarded statements. Expanding the action A then gives the following action:

$$ \mathbf{SELECT}\ gA \wedge gP\ \mathbf{THEN}\ sA\ \|\ sP\ \mathbf{END}, $$

when sA terminates. Thus, the guard of the action A is $gA \wedge gP$. In case we allow sequential composition within the action A, we have to take the substitution sA into account when forming the guard. The action A is then of the form:

$$ \mathbf{SELECT}\ gA \wedge \neg\mathrm{wp}(sA, \neg gP)\ \mathbf{THEN}\ sA;\ sP\ \mathbf{END}, $$

where wp denotes the *weakest precondition* predicate transformer [9]. Hence, the action calling a procedure and the procedure itself are synchronized upon execution.

The procedure declaration can be interpreted as receiving a message, while the procedure call in an action models the sending of a message, i.e., the procedure is executed upon 'receiving' a call with the actual parameters 'sent' from the action. Procedures in action systems are described in more detail by Sere and Waldén [14].

Let us now return to the procedure declarations of the action system $\mathcal{A}$. The exported procedure p_i of $\mathcal{A}$ is included via the machine $GlobalProcA\_p_i$:

```
MACHINE   GlobalProcA_pi

GLOBAL PROCEDURES
    pi ≙ Pi
END
```

This procedure is declared in the *global procedures*-clause. Each exported global procedure is included via a separate machine, so that another action system calling such a procedure can include exactly the procedures that it needs. Since the machine $GlobalProcA\_p_i$ does not have a state space of its own, we here postulate that the procedure p_i refers to the state space of $\mathcal{A}$ by giving $\mathcal{A}$ within the machine name. Considering the B restrictions this state space problem can for example be solved by allowing the procedure p_i to change the state space of $\mathcal{A}$ via its parameters [16].

Also each imported global procedure of $\mathcal{A}$ is included in $\mathcal{A}$ via a separate machine. The imported global procedure r is declared within the *global procedures*-clause in the machine $GlobalProc\mathcal{E}\_r$:

```
MACHINE   GlobalProcE_r

GLOBAL PROCEDURES
    r ≙ ...
END
```

It is only the headers of the imported procedures that are of interest to us. The bodies of the imported procedures can, therefore, be given as *SKIP* or remain undefined. The imported global procedures are considered to be declared in the environment $\mathcal{E}$ and to reference the state variables of $\mathcal{E}$ as indicated in the machine name.

The local procedures can all be declared in the same machine, $LocalProcsA\_q$, since they are all called within $\mathcal{A}$ and only within $\mathcal{A}$. These procedures are declared in the *local procedures*-clause as follows:

```
MACHINE   LocalProcsA_q

LOCAL PROCEDURES
    q1 ≙ Q1;
    ...
    ql ≙ Ql
END
```

and reference the state variables, x and z, of $\mathcal{A}$.

Notation: We use the standard B-notation with the exception of the clauses **ACTIONS**, **GLOBAL PROCEDURES** and **LOCAL PROCEDURES**. These clauses are used for representing the corresponding constructs of the action systems. They are merely renamings of the clause **OPERATIONS** in order to separate the different constructs of the action systems.

2.2 Distributed Action Systems

An action system can be considered to have a process network associated to it. This can be done either by assigning each action to a process or by assigning each state variable to a process. The processes execute the actions concurrently guaranteeing the atomicity of the actions.

Let us consider an example where we assign variables to processes. We assume that a variable $load\_i$ is assigned to the process i. For example, if an action A has a guard of the form $load\_i < T \wedge load\_j \geq T$, where T is a constant, then action A refers to variables of both the processes i and j. The action A is, thus, shared by these processes and they need to co-operate to execute A. In case action A would refer merely to variables that are assigned to process i, only process i is needed to execute action A and we consider action A to be local to this process i. An action system is considered to be *distributed*, if all its actions are local to some process. The values of the variables assigned to other processes are then communicated to the process, e.g., via remote procedure calls between the processes.

If two actions are independent, i.e. they do not have any variables in common, they can be executed in parallel. Their parallel execution is then equivalent to executing the actions one after the other, in either order. A distributed action system with merely local actions has many independent actions and, thus, also a high degree of parallelism.

We introduce procedures into an action system in order to distribute it. Let us, for example, consider the action system $\mathcal{A}$ containing only action A shared by the processes i and j:

$$A \triangleq \textbf{SELECT } load\_i < T \wedge load\_j \geq T$$
$$\textbf{THEN } load\_j := load\_i \parallel load\_i := load\_i + 1 \textbf{ END}.$$

We can rewrite A as the action A':

$$A' \triangleq \textbf{SELECT } load\_i < T \textbf{ THEN } P(load\_i) \parallel load\_i := load\_i + 1 \textbf{ END},$$

calling the procedure $P(e)$:

$$P(e) \triangleq \textbf{PRE } e \geq 0 \textbf{ THEN } (\textbf{SELECT } load\_j \geq T \textbf{ THEN } load\_j := e \textbf{ END}) \textbf{ END}.$$

The procedure $P(e)$ is located in another machine than A' and is included in the machine of A' as explained previously. Let us denote the action system containing A' and P with $\mathcal{A}'$. This action system is equivalent to $\mathcal{A}$, since introducing procedures into an action system only involves rewriting of this action system. Furthermore, $\mathcal{A}'$ is a distributed action system, since the action A' is local to process i and the procedure P is local to process j.

3 Refinement Using Layers

When deriving distributed systems we rely on the superposition method, which is a modularization and structuring method for developing parallel and distributed systems [4, 5, 11, 13]. At each derivation step a new functionality is added to the algorithm while the original computation is preserved. The new functionality could, for example, be an information gathering mechanism that replaces the direct access to shared variables. Thus, by applying the superposition method to a program, we can increase the degree of parallelism of the program and distribute the control in the program.

Since the superposition refinement is a special form of data refinement, we first describe the data refinement of action systems generally and then concentrate on the superposition refinement with layers.

3.1 Data Refinement

The superposition method has been formalized as a rule within the refinement calculus, which provides a general formal framework for refinements and for verifying each refinement step. However, it has been shown [7, 8, 17, 18] how the data refinement within the refinement calculus, and in particular the superposition refinement rule, correspond to the rules within the B-Method.

Let S be a statement on the abstract variables x, z and S' a statement on the concrete variables x', z. Let the invariant $R(x, x', z)$ be a relation on these variables. Then S is *data refined* by S' using the data invariant R, denoted $S \sqsubseteq_R S'$, if for any postcondition Q

$$R \wedge \mathrm{wp}(S, Q) \Rightarrow \mathrm{wp}(S', (\exists x.R \wedge Q))$$

holds.

Data refinement of actions can now be defined, considering that the weakest precondition for an action A [5] of the form **SELECT** gA **THEN** sA **END** is defined as:

$$\mathrm{wp}(A, R) \;\hat{=}\; gA \Rightarrow \mathrm{wp}(sA, R).$$

Let A be an action on the program variables x, z and A' an action on the program variables x', z. Let again the invariant $R(x, x', z)$ be a relation on these variables. Then A is data refined by A' using R, denoted $A \sqsubseteq_R A'$, if

(i) $\{gA'\}; sA \sqsubseteq_R sA'$ and
(ii) $R \wedge gA' \Rightarrow gA$.

Intuitively, (i) means that A' has the same effect on the program variables that A has when R holds assuming that A' is enabled, and moreover, A' preserves R. The condition (ii) requires that A is enabled whenever A' is enabled provided R holds.

The data refinement of statements can be extended to the data refinement of procedures [14]. Let us consider the procedure header $v \leftarrow p(u)$ with the value parameter u and the result parameter v for the procedure P, as well as the abstraction relation $R(x, x', z, u, v)$, where x, z are the variables in the procedure P and x', z are the variables in the refined procedure P', such that $P \sqsubseteq_R P'$. It then follows that the call $b \leftarrow p(a)$ on the original procedure P is refined by the call $b \leftarrow p(a)$ on the refined procedure P', due to:

$$\textbf{VAR } u, v \textbf{ IN } u := a; P; b := v \textbf{ END } \sqsubseteq_R \textbf{ VAR } u, v \textbf{ IN } u := a; P'; b := v \textbf{ END}.$$

3.2 Superposition Refinement with Layers

The superposition refinement is a special form of refinement where new mechanisms are added to the algorithm without the computation being changed [4, 5, 11, 13]. The new functionality that is added involves strengthening of the guards by taking into consideration the auxiliary variables and including assignments to these variables in the bodies of the actions and procedures. Therefore, when representing the superposition refinement we only need to introduce the new mechanism, i.e., the auxiliary variables and the computation on them, as a layer at each refinement step instead of the whole new algorithm.

The Layer. Let us consider the action system $\mathcal{A}$ and the new mechanism added to $\mathcal{A}$ only by strengthening the guards of the procedures and actions in $\mathcal{A}$, as well as adding some statements to them. The new mechanism is given as the *layer* machine $\mathcal{M}$. Let $\mathcal{A}$ and $\mathcal{M}$ be as follows:

MACHINE $\mathcal{A}$	LAYER $\mathcal{M}$
	SUPERPOSES $\mathcal{A}$
INCLUDES	INCLUDES
$\quad GlobalVar\_z,$	
$\quad GlobalProcA\_p_1, \ldots, GlobalProcA\_p_k,$	$\quad GlobalProcA\_p_1^+, \ldots, GlobalProcA\_p_k^+,$
$\quad GlobalProc\mathcal{E}\_r,$	
$\quad LocalProcsA\_q$	$\quad LocalProcsA\_q^+$
VARIABLES	**VARIABLES**
$\quad x$	$\quad y$
INVARIANT	**INVARIANT**
$\quad I(x,z,f)$	$\quad R(x,y,z,f)$
INITIALISATION	**INITIALISATION**
$\quad x := x0$	$\quad y := y0$
ACTIONS	**ACTIONS**
$\quad a_1 \;\hat{=}\; \textbf{SELECT } gA_1$	$\quad a_1 \;\hat{=}\; \textbf{SELECT } gA_1^+$
$\qquad\qquad \textbf{THEN } sA_1 \textbf{ END};$	$\qquad\qquad \textbf{THEN } sA_1^+ \textbf{ END};$
$\quad \ldots$	$\quad \ldots$
$\quad a_m \hat{=} \textbf{ SELECT } gA_m$	$\quad a_m \hat{=} \textbf{ SELECT } gA_m^+$
$\qquad\qquad \textbf{THEN } sA_m \textbf{ END}$	$\qquad\qquad \textbf{THEN } sA_m^+ \textbf{ END}$
	AUXILIARY ACTIONS
	$\quad b_1 \;\hat{=}\; \textbf{SELECT } gB_1$
	$\qquad\qquad \textbf{THEN } sB_1 \textbf{ END};$
	$\quad \ldots$
	$\quad b_n \;\hat{=}\; \textbf{SELECT } gB_n$
	$\qquad\qquad \textbf{THEN } sB_n \textbf{ END}$
END	**END**

In the layer $\mathcal{M}$ the *superposes*-clause states that the mechanism is to be added to the action system $\mathcal{A}$. Only the auxiliary variables y and the new guards and statements on these, which form the mechanism, are given in this layer. The layer can, however, read the previously declared variables. The invariant $R(x,y,z,f)$ gives the relation between the auxiliary variables y in $\mathcal{M}$ and the previously declared variables x,z in $\mathcal{A}$, as well as the formal parameters f. In the actions A_i the parts of the guards and the bodies that concern the auxiliary variable y are given as gA_i^+ and sA_i^+, respectively. The auxiliary actions B of the layer are presented for the first time in the derivation and are given in the *auxiliary actions*-clause. This clause is an *operations*-clause for actions with no corresponding actions in the superposed action system $\mathcal{A}$. In the next derivation step these actions will not be considered auxiliary anymore, since they will then already exist from the previous step.

The new functionality is also considered in the global procedures p_i and the local procedures q_i in the same way as in the actions A_i. In the procedure

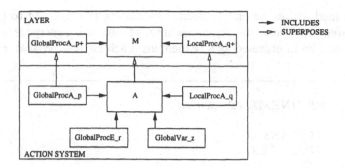

Fig. 1. Overview of the machines and their relations in a layered action system.

layers we state that the procedure layer $GlobalProcA\_p_i^+$ is superposed on the previously given global procedure $GlobalProcA\_p_i$. The global procedure p_i in $GlobalProcA\_p_i$ and its additions in $GlobalProcA\_p_i^+$ are given as follows:

MACHINE $GlobalProcA\_p_i$	**LAYER** $GlobalProcA\_p_i^+$
	SUPERPOSES $GlobalProcA\_p_i$
GLOBAL PROCEDURES	**GLOBAL PROCEDURES**
$p_i \; \hat{=} \;$ **SELECT** gP_i	$p_i \; \hat{=} \;$ **SELECT** gP_i^+
THEN sP_i **END**	**THEN** sP_i^+ **END**
END	**END**

The local procedures q_i in $LocalProcsA\_q$ and their additions in the layer machine $LocalProcsA\_q^+$ are given in the same way:

MACHINE $LocalProcsA\_q$	**LAYER** $LocalProcsA\_q^+$
	SUPERPOSES $LocalProcsA\_q$
LOCAL PROCEDURES	**LOCAL PROCEDURES**
$q_1 \; \hat{=} \;$ **SELECT** gQ_1	$q_1 \; \hat{=} \;$ **SELECT** gQ_1^+
THEN sQ_1 **END**;	**THEN** sQ_1^+ **END**;
...	...
$q_l \; \hat{=} \;$ **SELECT** gQ_l	$q_l \; \hat{=} \;$ **SELECT** gQ_l^+
THEN sQ_l **END**	**THEN** sQ_l^+ **END**
END	**END**

In Figure 1 we give an overview of the action system A, the layer M as well as their included variables and procedures and show how they are related. We have chosen to include only one exported global procedure ($k = 1$), in order to reduce the amount of detail in the figure.

The refined action system is attained by adding the layer $\mathcal{M}$ to the original action system $\mathcal{A}$. Thus, the layer machine $\mathcal{M}$ and the *superposes*-clause containing $\mathcal{A}$ can be interpreted as a refinement machine $\mathcal{A} + \mathcal{M}$ that *refines* $\mathcal{A}$ as follows:

REFINEMENT $\mathcal{A} + \mathcal{M}$

REFINES $\mathcal{A}$
INCLUDES
  $GlobalVar\_z'$,
  $GlobalProcA\_p'_1, \ldots, GlobalProcA\_p'_k$,
  $GlobalProc\mathcal{E}\_r'$,
  $LocalProcsA\_q'$

VARIABLES
  x, y
INVARIANT
  $I(x, z, f) \ \wedge \ R(x, y, z, f)$
INITIALISATION
  $x := x0 \ \| \ y := y0$

ACTIONS
  $a_1 \ \hat{=} \ \textbf{SELECT} \ gA_1 \wedge gA_1^+ \ \textbf{THEN} \ sA_1; sA_1^+ \ \textbf{END};$
  $\ldots$
  $a_m \ \hat{=} \ \textbf{SELECT} \ gA_m \wedge gA_m^+ \ \textbf{THEN} \ sA_m; sA_m^+ \ \textbf{END}$

AUXILIARY ACTIONS
  $b_1 \ \hat{=} \ \textbf{SELECT} \ gB_1 \ \textbf{THEN} \ sB_1 \ \textbf{END};$
  $\ldots$
  $b_n \ \hat{=} \ \textbf{SELECT} \ gB_n \ \textbf{THEN} \ sB_n \ \textbf{END}$
END

The variables of the refined action system $\mathcal{A} + \mathcal{M}$ are the variables of $\mathcal{A}$ and $\mathcal{M}$. The invariant R in $\mathcal{A} + \mathcal{M}$ is the conjunction of the invariants of $\mathcal{A}$ and $\mathcal{M}$. Furthermore, by parallel composition of the initialisations in $\mathcal{A}$ and $\mathcal{M}$ we form the initialisation of $\mathcal{A} + \mathcal{M}$. In order to get the guard of the refined action A_i we join the guards gA_i in $\mathcal{A}$ and gA_i^+ in $\mathcal{M}$ using conjunction, i.e., $gA_i \wedge gA_i^+$. By adding the statements sA_i in $\mathcal{A}$ and sA_i^+ in $\mathcal{M}$ using sequential composition we get the refined statement $sA_i; sA_i^+$. We have chosen to model the adding of statements with sequential composition for purity. The composition could equally well be modelled with parallel composition [3].

The procedures p_i and q_j of $\mathcal{A} + \mathcal{M}$ are generated in the same way as the actions. The refined global procedures p_i are included via the machine $GlobalProcA\_p'_i$ and the refined local procedures q_j via $LocalProcsA\_q'$. We note that the imported global procedure r as well as the global variable z in $\mathcal{A} + \mathcal{M}$ remain the same as in $\mathcal{A}$. However, following the B restrictions the machines $GlobalVar\_z$ and $GlobalProc\mathcal{E}\_r$ are renamed to $GlobalVar\_z'$ and $GlobalProc\mathcal{E}\_r'$ in the refinement.

The Rule. We will now study the correctness of this superposition refinement with layers. Let us consider the action system $\mathcal{A}$ and the layer $\mathcal{M}$ given above. Furthermore, let $g\mathcal{A}$ be the disjunction of the guards of the actions A_i in $\mathcal{A}$ and $g\mathcal{A}^+$ and $g\mathcal{B}$ the disjunctions of the guards of the actions A_i and B_j in $\mathcal{M}$. The action $A_i + A_i^+$ is the result of adding action A_i in $\mathcal{A}$ and A_i^+ in $\mathcal{M}$. Then the action system $\mathcal{A}$ is correctly data refined by the action system $\mathcal{A} + \mathcal{M}$, $\mathcal{A} \sqsubseteq_R \mathcal{A} + \mathcal{M}$, using $R(x, y, z, f)$, where f denotes the formal parameters of the exported global procedures P_i, if

(1) the initialisation in $\mathcal{A} + \mathcal{M}$ establishes R for any initial value on f,
(2) each refined global procedure, $P_i + P_i^+$ in $\mathcal{A} + \mathcal{M}$, preserves the data invariant R,
(3) if a global procedure P_i is enabled in $\mathcal{A}$, so is $P_i + P_i^+$ in $\mathcal{A} + \mathcal{M}$ or then some actions in $\mathcal{A} + \mathcal{M}$ will enable $P_i + P_i^+$,
(4) every refined action $A_i + A_i^+$ in $\mathcal{A} + \mathcal{M}$ preserves the data invariant R,
(5) every auxiliary action B_i is a data refinement of the empty statement $SKIP$ using R,
(6) the computation denoted by the auxiliary actions $B_1, \ldots, B_n$ terminates provided R holds, and
(7) the exit condition $\neg(g\mathcal{A}^+ \vee g\mathcal{B})$ of $\mathcal{M}$ implies the exit condition $\neg g\mathcal{A}$ of $\mathcal{A}$ when R holds.

If action system $\mathcal{A}$ occurs in some environment $\mathcal{E}$, we have to take this environment into account with an extra condition on the refinement. Thus, for every action in $\mathcal{E}$:

(8) the environment $\mathcal{E}$ does not interfere with the action system $\mathcal{A}$, and it establishes the data invariant.

The superposition refinement with layers is expressed formally in the following theorem:

Theorem 1 (Superposition refinement with layers). *Let $\mathcal{A}$ and $\mathcal{M}$ be as above. Furthermore, let $g\mathcal{A}$ be the disjunction of the guards of the actions A_i in $\mathcal{A}$, and $g\mathcal{A}^+$ as well as $g\mathcal{B}$ the disjunctions of the guards of the actions A_i and B_j in $\mathcal{M}$. Then $\mathcal{A} \sqsubseteq_R \mathcal{A} + \mathcal{M}$, using $R(x, y, z, f)$, where f denotes the formal parameters of the exported global procedures P_i, if*

(1) $R(x_0, y_0, z_0, f)$,
(2) $R \Rightarrow \mathrm{wp}(P_i + P_i^+, R)$, *for $i = 1, \ldots, k$,*
(3) $R \wedge gP_i \Rightarrow$
$\qquad ((gP_i \wedge gP_i^+) \vee \mathrm{wp}(\textbf{WHILE } \neg(gP_i \wedge gP_i^+) \textbf{ DO}$
$\qquad\qquad\qquad (\textbf{CHOICE } A_1 + A_1^+ \textbf{ OR } \ldots \textbf{ OR } A_m + A_m^+$
$\qquad\qquad\qquad\qquad\qquad \textbf{OR } B_1 \textbf{ OR } \ldots \textbf{ OR } B_n \textbf{ END})$
$\qquad\qquad \textbf{END}, TRUE)),$
$\qquad$ *for $i = 1, \ldots, k$,*

(4) $R \Rightarrow \mathrm{wp}(A_i + A_i^+, R)$, *for* $i = 1, \ldots, m$,
(5) $SKIP \sqsubseteq_R B_i$, *for* $i = 1, \ldots, n$,
(6) $R \Rightarrow \mathrm{wp}(\mathbf{WHILE}\ gB\ \mathbf{DO}\ (\mathbf{CHOICE}\ B_1\ \mathbf{OR}\ \ldots\ \mathbf{OR}\ B_n\ \mathbf{END})\ \mathbf{END}, TRUE)$,
(7) $R \wedge \neg(gA^+ \vee gB) \Rightarrow \neg gA$.

Furthermore,

(8) $R \wedge \mathrm{wp}(E_i, TRUE) \Rightarrow \mathrm{wp}(E_i, R)$, *for* $i = 1, \ldots, h$.

when the environment $\mathcal{E}$ of $\mathcal{A}$ contains the actions $E_1, \ldots, E_h$.

We note that the superposition refinement with layers is a special case of the superposition refinement presented by Back and Sere [5]. The conditions (1), (2), (4) and (5) originate from the data-refinement conditions. Since the guards of the refined actions/global procedures in $\mathcal{A} + \mathcal{M}$ of the form $gA_i \wedge gA_i^+$ trivially imply the guards of the corresponding old actions/global procedures in $\mathcal{A}$ of the form gA_i, and the computation of $\mathcal{A}$ is obviously not changed in $\mathcal{A} + \mathcal{M}$, we only have to show that the refined procedures and actions preserve the data invariant R in the conditions (2) and (4) in order to prove that the global procedures and the actions of $\mathcal{A} + \mathcal{M}$ are correct refinements of the corresponding procedures and actions in $\mathcal{A}$. Condition (6) can be referred to as a non-divergence condition for the auxiliary actions, while conditions (3) and (7) are progress conditions for the global procedures and the actions, respectively.

Proof Obligations for the Layers Within the B-Method. Previously, Waldén et. al. have shown [8, 17, 18] how to prove that an action system is a refinement of another action system, $\mathcal{A} \sqsubseteq_R \mathcal{A} + \mathcal{M}$, within the B-Method. In particular they showed that the proof obligations generated within the B-Method imply the conditions within the superposition refinement method. However, they used the machine specification $\mathcal{A}$ and the refinement machine $\mathcal{A} + \mathcal{M}$ in order to prove the superposition refinement $\mathcal{A} \sqsubseteq_R \mathcal{A} + \mathcal{M}$.

Since a purpose of using layers in the derivation is to decrease the amount of redundant information of the algorithm within the derivation, we will now discuss how to extend the B-method in order to generate proof obligations that correspond to the conditions of the superposition refinement with layers in Theorem 1 directly from the machine specification $\mathcal{A}$ and the layer machine $\mathcal{M}$.

The proof obligations for the conditions (1), (2), (4) and (5) can easily be generated considering the statements in the *initialisation*-clause and the procedures and actions in the *global_procedures*-, the *actions*- and the *auxiliary_actions*-clauses. These proof obligations would even be part of the proof obligations created for the corresponding constructs in the original B-Method. We note that the procedures and the actions given as $P_i + P_i^+$ in the theorem all are of the form $\mathbf{SELECT}\ gP_i \wedge gP_i^+\ \mathbf{THEN}\ sP_i; sP_i^+\ \mathbf{END}$ and their preconditions are considered to have the value $TRUE$. The progress condition (7) can also directly be generated from the guards of the actions and the auxiliary actions in the layer $\mathcal{M}$ and the guards of the actions in the machine $\mathcal{A}$.

The proof obligations for the conditions (3) and (6) involves calculating the weakest precondition of a WHILE-loop and are not as trivial to generate as the proof obligations for the other conditions. In order to generate the proof obligations for a WHILE-loop, an invariant and a variant are needed. Since in order to prove the loop:

WHILE G **DO** S **END**

with **INVARIANT** R and **VARIANT** E the following conditions need to be proven:

(i) $R \Rightarrow E \in \mathbf{N}$,
(ii) $(\forall l. \ (R \wedge G) \Rightarrow [n := E]([S](E < n)))$,

where l denotes the variables modified within the loop. Thus, (i) the variant E should be an expression yielding a natural number, and (ii) when the guard G of the loop holds, the body S should decrease the variant E. The invariant given in the layer machine can serve as the loop invariant for the conditions (3) and (6). The variant for the loop of the condition (3) should be an expression that is decreased each time an action of $A + M$ is executed. This variant could be given in a *variant*-clause in the layer machine M. Condition (6) contains a loop of the auxiliary actions and, thus, we also need a variant that is decreased each time an auxiliary action in M is executed. This variant could also be introduced within the layer machine M in a separate clause called *auxvariant* to distinguish it from the other variant. Using these clauses containing the variants as well as the global procedures, actions and auxiliary actions from their respective clauses, the proof obligations for the conditions (3) and (6) can be generated.

Hence, proof obligations corresponding to all the conditions in Theorem 1 can easily be generated within the B-Method considering the machine specification A and the layer machine M.

Derivation by Superposing Layers. Successive superposition refinements with layers are modelled as follows: If $A \sqsubseteq_{R_1} A + M_1$ and $A + M_1 \sqsubseteq_{R_2} A + M_1 + M_2$, then $A \sqsubseteq_{R_1 \wedge R_2} A + M_1 + M_2$. Thus, during a derivation a number of layers might be superposed on the original action system A. In order to get the resulting distributed algorithm all these layers need to be added to A following the description in this section. In Figure 2, n layers are superposed to the action system A during the derivation. We might also have to introduce procedures during a derivation to attain a distributed action system, as explained in Section 2. Such a step is only rewriting of the algorithm and does not involve refinement. In Figure 2 the rewritten parts of the algorithm are given in the middle column.

4 Conclusions

In this paper we have investigated an important and powerful special case of the original superposition method [5], namely, that of considering each new mech-

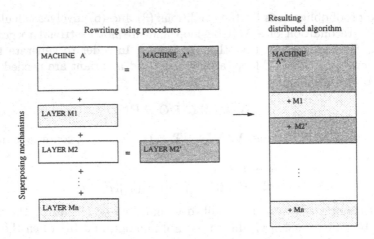

Fig. 2. Composing the derivation

anism as a layer that only reads the variables of the previous layers. The superposition refinement with layers structures the presentation of the derivation. Within this method also the correctness proofs are easier than in the original superposition rule in the sense that part of the conditions in the original rule becomes trivially true. An example of this refinement method is given in [15].

Layers were introduced by Elrad and Francez [10] for decomposing distributed algorithms into communication closed layers. Later Janssen [12] introduced a layer composition operator and developed an algebraic law for deriving algorithms using these kind of layers. Their layers, however, differ from ours. Namely, during the derivation Janssen first decompose the algorithm into layers and then refine these layers, while we add a new layer to the algorithm at each derivation step. Thus, a layer of theirs does not contain a single mechanism as ours does.

Since the superposition method with layers yields large refinement steps with many complicated proof obligations, the tool support is important for getting confidence in these proofs. The B-Method [1] is well suited for representing action systems and superposition refinement [17, 18]. We have, however, proposed an extension to the B-Method, in order to make it more suitable for representing the layers. Thereby, we provide a good basis for generating the proof obligations as well as assisting in proving the superposition refinement with layers correct and will have a tool support for our method.

Acknowledgement

The author would like to thank Kaisa Sere for fruitful discussions on the topics treated here, as well as the referees of the paper for their useful comments. The work reported here has been carried out within the Irene-project and the Cocos-project supported by the Academy of Finland.

References

1. J.-R. Abrial. *The B-Book*. Cambridge University Press, Cambridge, Great Britain, 1996.

2. J.-R. Abrial. Extending B without changing it (for developing distributed systems). In *Proc. of the First Conference on the B-Method*, pp. 169 – 190, IRIN, Nantes, France, November 1996.

3. R. J. R. Back and M. Butler. Exploring summation and product operators in the refinement calculus. In B. Möller, editor, *Proc. of the Third International Conference on Mathematics of Program Construction*, LNCS 947, pp. 128 – 158, Kloster Irsee, Germany, July 1995. Springer–Verlag.

4. R. J. R. Back and R. Kurki-Suonio. Decentralization of process nets with centralized control. In *Proc. of the 2nd ACM SIGACT-SIGOPS Symposium on Principles of Distributed Computing*, pages 131–142, 1983.

5. R. J. R. Back and K. Sere. Superposition refinement of reactive systems. *Formal Aspects of Computing*, 8(3):324 – 346, 1996.

6. R. J. R. Back and K. Sere. From action systems to modular systems. In *Proc. of FME'94: Industrial Benefit of Formal Methods*, LNCS 873, pp. 1 – 25, 1994. Springer–Verlag.

7. M. J. Butler. An approach to the design of distributed systems with B AMN. In *Proc. of the 10th International Conference of Z Users (ZUM'97)*, University of Reading, UK, April 1997. Also, University of Southampton, Declarative Systems & Software Engineering Technical Reports, DSSE-TR-96-6, September 1996.

8. M. J. Butler and M. Waldén. Distributed system development in B. In *Proc. of the First Conference on the B-Method*, pages 155 – 168, IRIN, Nantes, France, November 1996.

9. E. W. Dijkstra. *A Discipline of Programming*. Prentice–Hall International, 1976.

10. T. Elrad and N. Francez. Decomposition of distributed programs into communication-closed layers. *Science of Computer Programming*, 2:155 – 173, North-Holland, 1982.

11. N. Francez and I. R. Forman. Superimposition for interacting processes. In *Proc. of CONCUR '90 Theories of Concurrency: Unification and extension*, LNCS 458, pages 230–245, Amsterdam, the Netherlands, August 1990. Springer–Verlag.

12. W. Janssen. *Layered Design of Parallel Systems*. Ph.D. thesis, Department of computer science, University of Twente, The Netherlands, 1994.

13. S. M. Katz. A superimposition control construct for distributed systems. *ACM Transactions on Programming Languages and Systems*, 15(2):337–356, April 1993.

14. K. Sere and M. Waldén. Data refinement of remote procedures. In *Proc. of the International Symposium on Theoretical Aspects of Computer Software (TACS97)*, LNCS 1281, pages 267 – 294, Sendai, Japan, September 1997. Springer–Verlag.

15. M. Waldén. Layering distributed algorithms. TUCS Technical Reports, No 121, Turku Centre for Computer Science, Finland, August 1997.
http://www.tucs.abo.fi/publications/techreports/TR121.html

16. M. Waldén. Derivation of a distributed load balancing algorithm. In E. Sekerinski and K. Sere, editors, *Refinement Case Studies with B*. Manuscript 1998. Forthcoming book.

17. M. Waldén and K. Sere. Refining action systems within B-Tool. In *Proceedings of Formal Methods Europe (FME'96): Symposium on Industrial Benefit and Advances in Formal Methods*, LNCS 1051, pages 84 – 103, Oxford, England, March 1996. Springer–Verlag.

18. M. Waldén and K. Sere. Reasoning about action systems using the B-Method. In *Formal Methods in System Design*. Kluwer Academic Publishers. To appear.

Two Strategies to Data-Refine an Equivalence to a Forest

Philipp Heuberger*

Turku Centre for Computer Science (TUCS) and Åbo Akademi
DataCity, Lemminkäisenkatu 14 A, FIN-20520 Turku, Finland
e-mail: pheuberg@abo.fi

Abstract. Well-known strategies give incentive to the algorithmic refinement of programs and we ask in this paper whether general patterns
also exist for data refinement. In order to answer this question, we study
the equivalence relation problem and identify the motivations to replace
the equivalence relation by a data structure suitable for efficient computation.

1 Introduction

The equivalence relation problem consists of the specification and implementation of a manager that maintains an equivalence relation over a given set. The
manager allows for the dynamic addition of related (equivalent) elements together with an equivalence test of two elements.

Abrial distinguishes between three orthogonal aspects of refinement [1], i.e. the
decreasing of non-determinism, the *weakening of the precondition* and the *changing of the variable space*. The third aspect is illustrated by our treatment of
the equivalence relation problem, where a relation in an initial specification is
replaced by a function. The motivation for using two different mathematical
objects to present the problem is that a relation is well suited for the abstract
description and the pointer structure is close to the concrete representation in
the implementation.

Algorithmic refinement has singled out reoccuring patterns for the introduction
of a loop construct. Dijkstra [6] motivates formally each development step with
great care and Gries [8] and Cohen [4] formulate strategies like "deleting a conjunct" or "replacing constants by fresh variables". In the examples treated by
them variables are not changed and consequently no strategy for doing so is
formulated.

There are many ways to specify an equivalence relation manager. We present a
variety of them in the B specification method and propose general strategies that
guide the changing of the equivalence to the data structure known as "Union-
Find" or "Fischer/Galler-Trees".

---

* This work has been financed by the Swiss-TMR-Fellowship of the Federal Office for
  Education and Science and is supported by The Swiss National Science Foundation.

The equivalence relation problem is well known and described in many algorithmic textbooks, e.g. [6, 3, 5]. It has been formally treated thoroughly before in VDM [12], based on the mathematical object of a set partition. Fraer has carried out a development in B on a larger example that includes the treatment of the equivalence relation problem [7]. His major strategy is "design for provability". Our approach is different: we look for heuristical guidance to find a suitable data refinement in order to calculate the refined program by proof and in this paper we present two strategies to data-refine an equivalence to a forest. The goal is to identify general strategies for data refinement. In an initial attempt documented in [10], we have refined a specification corresponding to the VDM treatment on which we have partly reported in [11]. We have used the B-Toolkit [2, 13] in the initial development and have generated the machines in this document with AtelierB.

2   The Equivalence Relation Problem

An equivalence relation (or equivalence for short) θ on a set A is a subset of $A \times A$ such that the following three properties hold for $a, b, c \in A$, where $a\,\theta\,b$ stands for $(a, b) \in \theta$:

$$
\begin{array}{ll}
a\,\theta\,a & \text{(Reflexivity)} \\
a\,\theta\,b \Rightarrow b\,\theta\,a & \text{(Symmetry)} \\
a\,\theta\,b \wedge b\,\theta\,c \Rightarrow a\,\theta\,c & \text{(Transitivity)}
\end{array}
$$

For a better understanding of the algebraic definition, let us consider the representation by graphs. In general, every relation corresponds to a graph. The domain set A of a relation corresponds to the set of nodes in a graph and the relation θ corresponds to the set of edges in the graph. Equivalences belong to a particular type of graph, i.e. graphs which consist of fully connected subcomponents only. The equivalence relation problem basically is the construction of the smallest equivalence containing an arbitrary user-given relation. In mathematics, the construction is called the *reflexive, symmetric and transitive closure* or *equivalence closure* for short. In figure 1, the relation represented as a graph to the right is the equivalence closure of the one to the left. Observe that the single-edged cycles at each node are due to the reflexivity and the bi-directed edges to the symmetry. Moreover, symmetry and transitivity together demand an edge between b and c.

The equivalence closure gives a very static and functional view of the problem, i.e. there is one input, i.e. the user-given relation, and one output, i.e. the equivalence. For an equivalence manager though, the problem is more involved. The relation is not passed as a whole, but every pair of connected elements is submitted separately. The user may update the relation and inquire the equivalence dynamically many times in arbitrary order. Translated into the functional view, the transitive closure is applied to a dynamically changing input.

An equivalence manager basically has two operations: an update operation and a query operation. For simplicity, pairs of related elements are only added by

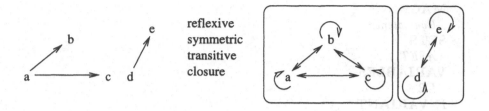

Fig. 1. The reflexive, symmetric and transitive closure of a relation

the update operation. The query operation allows to inquire the equivalence. Initially, the equivalence relation is the identity relation, i.e. the equivalence closure of the empty relation. We name the two operations *equate* and *test* (, as in the VDM example). In terms of our first specification in the next section, the manager maintains an equivalence. The operation *equate* relates two elements to each other and any transitively reachable element. A call to the operation *test* returns the equivalence relationship of two elements.

3 A Variety of Specifications

The B notation allows us to express the equivalence properties of a relation by built-in relational constructs. By that, the reflexivity, symmetry and transitivity of a relation is expressed in an elegant way without referring to the individual elements. (The relation is denoted with RR because variables need to contain at least two letters in B.)

$$\text{id}\,(ASET) \subseteq RR \quad \text{(Reflexivity)}$$
$$RR^{-1} \subseteq RR \qquad \text{(Symmetry)}$$
$$RR;\, RR \subseteq RR \quad \text{(Transitivity)}$$

This formulation of the equivalence properties corresponds to the previous definition. We can convince ourselves for example that symmetry is still symmetry. Reflexivity and transitivity can be shown to correspond as well.

$$RR^{-1} = RR$$
$=$ { relational equality }
   $(\forall\, x, y \cdot x\, RR^{-1} y \equiv x\, RR\, y)$
$=$ { definition of an inverse relation }
   $(\forall\, x, y \cdot y\, RR\, x \equiv x\, RR\, y)$
$=$ { ping-pong argument }
   $(\forall\, x, y \cdot (y\, RR\, x \Rightarrow x\, RR\, y) \wedge (x\, RR\, y \Rightarrow y\, RR\, x))$
$=$ { universal quantification distributes over conjunction }
   $(\forall\, x, y \cdot x\, RR\, y \Rightarrow y\, RR\, x)$

It is customary to omit the universal quantification in algebraic definitions. Hence, the last line coincides with the algebraic symmetry. The machine with the reformulated invariant is given next.

MACHINE
  Equivalence
SETS
  ASET
VARIABLES
  ER
INVARIANT
  $ER \in ASET \leftrightarrow ASET \land$
  $\text{id}(ASET) \subseteq ER \land$
  $ER^{-1} \subseteq ER \land$
  $(ER;ER) \subseteq ER$
INITIALISATION
  $ER := \text{id}(ASET)$
OPERATIONS
  equate$(aa,bb) = $ **PRE**
    $aa \in ASET \land$
    $bb \in ASET$
  THEN
    $ER := \text{closure}(ER \cup \{aa \mapsto bb, bb \mapsto aa\})$
  END;
  $equivalent \leftarrow$ **test**$(aa,bb) = $ **PRE**
    $aa \in ASET \land$
    $bb \in ASET$
  THEN
    $equivalent := \text{bool}(aa \mapsto bb \in ER)$
  END
END

The function **closure** is the reflexive transitive closure of a relation, which is denoted hereafter as in algebra by a postfix asterix *. There is even a simpler way to express that RR is an equivalence relation. Consider the function rst that returns the symmetric reflexive transitive closure of a relation. The function rst is constructed by applying the reflexive transitive closure to the unification of the relation with its inverse. Note that the transitive reflexive closure maintains the symmetry of a relation.

$$rst \,\hat{=}\, \lambda\,x.(x \cup x^{-1})^*$$

The function rst is the equivalence closure. Applied to an equivalence, the equivalence remains unchanged. Hence, a relation is an equivalence relation, if it is a fixpoint of the function rst, i.e. $RR = rst(RR)$ or explicitly

$$RR = (RR \cup RR^{-1})^*$$

Hence, for the specification, we have a choice of writing the invariant in two different ways, either as a conjunct of reflexivity, symmetry and transitivity or simply by the fixpoint equality. This is a purely notational difference, which nevertheless affects the proofs.

MACHINE
  EquivalenceClo
SETS
  ASET
CONSTANTS
  rst
PROPERTIES
  $rst \in ASET \leftrightarrow ASET \rightarrow (ASET \leftrightarrow ASET) \wedge$
  $rst = \lambda\, rr.(rr \in ASET \leftrightarrow ASET \mid \mathbf{closure}(rr \cup rr^{-1}))$
VARIABLES
  ER
INVARIANT
  $ER \in ASET \leftrightarrow ASET \wedge$
  $ER = rst(ER)$
INITIALISATION
  $ER := \mathbf{id}(ASET)$
OPERATIONS
  same as in the machine Equivalence
END

An important semantic difference is obtained from observing that the machine Equivalence is very eager to compute the function *rst*. It is not necessary to compute *rst* as soon as the update information is available. Consider to compute the function at another instant. Indeed, the computation can be delayed for until the equivalence is inquired. Hence, *rst* can be computed right away (eager) when the update operation is performed or later (lazy) when the test operation is performed. In the latter case, the state space invariant does not denote an equivalence in order to satisfy the specifications of the two operations. In fact, it suffices to store the user-given relation. Consequently, the machine UserRelation specified below simply stores the user input.

MACHINE
  UserRelation
SETS
  ASET
CONSTANTS
  rst
PROPERTIES
  $rst \in ASET \leftrightarrow ASET \rightarrow (ASET \leftrightarrow ASET) \wedge$
  $rst = \lambda\, rr.(rr \in ASET \leftrightarrow ASET \mid \mathbf{closure}(rr \cup rr^{-1}))$
VARIABLES
  UR
INVARIANT
  $UR \in ASET \leftrightarrow ASET$
INITIALISATION
  $UR := \emptyset$

```
OPERATIONS
  equate(aa,bb) = PRE
    aa ∈ ASET ∧
    bb ∈ ASET
  THEN
    UR:= UR ∪ {aa ↦ bb}
  END;
  equivalent ← test(aa,bb) = PRE
    aa ∈ ASET ∧
    bb ∈ ASET
  THEN
    equivalent:=bool(aa ↦ bb ∈ rst(UR))
  END
END
```

The eager machine Equivalence (or EquivalenceClo) and the lazy machine User-Relation are extreme in the distribution of the computational effort among their operations. Consider an implementation where the relation in question is stored as a Boolean bit matrix. In the eager specification, where the equivalence closure is stored, the test operation is cheap and requires only a lookup in the matrix, but the equate operation needs to perform the expensive closure operation. In the lazy specification, where the user-given relation is stored, the equate operation is cheap: it flips a bit in the matrix. The test operation, however, requires an expensive search through the reachable elements. Hence, in both extreme cases, the computationally cheap implementation of the one operation goes to the expenses of an overly costly implementation of the other operation.

Both specifications are also extreme in a further aspect. First, observe that an invariant in the B-method (in contrast to the Z specification method) is completely redundant. The invariant could be left out and the specification would retain its meaning. In both specifications, the invariant is the strongest possible, i.e. all non-reachable states are excluded by the invariant. However the invariant of the machine Equivalence enjoys an additional property. Its invariant is *tight*, i.e. within the mathematical object of a relation and for a given sequence of updates, the state of the machine Equivalence is uniquely determined by its invariant to exhibit the future behavior whereas the state of the machine UserRelation is loose and depends on the input sequence. There are other states which produce the same future behavior. Such a unnecessary dependency of state and input is not compelling for a specification.

The tightness of the specification invariant appears to be an objective criteria to discriminate among equivalent specifications. For example, think of a specification variant of the machine UserRelation that includes the last inquired present relationship into the relation. Such a specification already includes an optimization that is comparable with a cache. Indeed, there are many possible ways to select a relation, such that its equivalence closure corresponds to the equivalence closure of the relation given by the user. All the possible relations can be characterized formally by

$$\{\theta \mid rst(\theta) = rst(u)\}$$

where u is the user-given relation. This variety of states is the starting point for applying our strategies. The goal is to exploit the given freedom in order to minimize the cumulated effort of the update and test operations.

4 Two Strategies to Data-Refine an Equivalence to a Forest

From the previous section, we know that any relation whose equivalence closure is the same as the equivalence closure of the user-given relation may constitute the state space. So, we have many more relations than the two extreme ones to select from. Let us search for a restriction of the selection that gives a good compromise between the computational effort of the two operations.

Our first choice is guided by a general heuristic.

Heuristic 1: *Replace relations by functions*

The restriction of a relation to a function may be used as a heuristic because finite functions have immediate computational counterparts, i.e. arrays or pointer fields in a record structure. In general a relation must be replaced by several functions. Fortunately, one function suffices for the particular case of an equivalence. Moreover, we restrict a relation to a total and finite function. A total function is preferable because no test is needed to guard against undefined function applications.

The dereferencing of pointers or the calculation of array elements from indices repeatedly occur in reachability operations and there is a risk that pointers or indices are followed ad infinitum, if the function is cyclic. We could impose the function to be acyclic. But, "acyclicity" is a very restrictive requirement that inhibits elegant solutions in general. Nevertheless, a second general heuristic lays the base for the termination argument of loops in the operations.

Heuristic 2: *Eliminate non-detectable cycles.*

Since the function is desirably total, we can not be absolutely strict in eliminating all cycles. But, there is an elegant way to state the desired property such that only trivial cycles, which are easy to detect, remain.

The desired property is expressed by the antisymmetry of a transitive relation. Algebraically, antisymmetry is defined as follows:

$$a \, \theta \, b \wedge b \, \theta \, a \Rightarrow a = b \text{ (Antisymmetry)}$$

and has a relational counterpart

$$RR \cap RR^{-1} \subseteq \text{id} \, (ASET) \text{ (Antisymmetry)}$$

The remaining cycles are reflexive and can be detected without the explicit introduction of additional state.

In the particular example of an equivalence manager, we introduce a function $f\!f$. The function is not transitive and we need to substitute RR by the transitive closure of ff, i.e. ff^+. Because the mere transitive closure is not available in the B-Toolkit and AtelierB, we use the reflexive transitive closure, i.e. ff^* and obtain a property which we call *transitive antisymmetry*.

$$ff^* \cap (ff^*)^{-1} \subseteq \text{id}\,(ASET) \text{ (Transitive Antisymmetry)}$$

Intuitively, "acyclicity" may be observed as follows. Consider the directed edges of the graph as an indication of the direction of a current. The graph is acyclic, if there is no possibility to cover a distance going once exclusively in one direction and then exclusively in the opposite direction of the current.

What we have found by the two heuristics is the characteristics of a forest. Moreover, we found it by two generally applicable strategies. A forest is a set of trees, such that every root of a tree has a reflexive cycle (see figure 2) [1]. The trees in a forest are also called "Fischer/Galler-Trees".

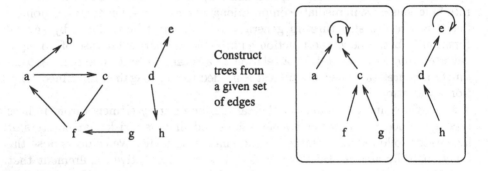

Fig. 2. A forest which represents an equivalence

The taken choices yield a trade-off between the computational effort of the operations. On the one hand, the operation equate is implemented by joining two trees to one. We do so by replacing the reflexive cycle of the one root by an edge to the other root. The operation involves the search for the root for the two given elements. On the other hand, the operation test reduces to the search for a common root in the forest representation and the operation involves the root search for two elements. Hence, we have drastically reduced the cumulated computation cost of the equate and test operation by introducing the forest representation. The root search is specified by the function root which is built from the sequential composition of the transitive reflexive closure of the forest function and the reflexive root cycles.

---

[1] Note that the reflexive transitive closure of the function is a partial order and that the figure 2 can be regarded as a Hasse diagram.

REFINEMENT
 Forest
REFINES
 EquivalenceClo
VARIABLES
 ff
DEFINITIONS
 root == (**closure**(*ff*);**id**(*ASET*) ∩ *ff*)
INVARIANT
 ff ∈ *ASET* → *ASET* ∧
 closure(*ff*) ∩ **closure**(*ff*) $^{-1}$ ⊆ **id**(*ASET*) ∧
 rst(*ff*) = *ER*
INITIALISATION
 ff:=**id**(*ASET*)
OPERATIONS
 equate(*aa,bb*) = **PRE**
  aa ∈ *ASET* ∧
  bb ∈ *ASET*
 THEN
  ff:=*ff* <+ {*root*(*aa*) ↦ *root*(*bb*)}
 END;
 equivalent ← **test**(*aa,bb*) = **PRE**
  aa ∈ *ASET* ∧
  bb ∈ *ASET*
 THEN
  equivalent:=**bool**(*root*(*aa*) = *root*(*bb*))
 END
END

4.1 An Alternative Strategy to eliminate non-detectable cycles

There is an alternative way to apply the second heuristic. After using the same first heuristic - restrict the relation to be a total function - we choose a simpler property to eliminate non-detectable cycles: we require the function to be idempotent, i.e.

$$(\theta\,;\,\theta) = \theta \quad \text{(Idempotency)}$$

This is a stronger restriction than the previous transitive antisymmetry because the forest consists now of trees not higher than a single edge. For convenience, we call them *flat forest*. The representation of an equivalence by an idempotent function results in a straight-forward specification of the operations. The operation equate needs to redirect all edges from the members of one tree to the root of the other tree. Compared with the redirection of a single edge before, it seems to be more work even though no search for a root is necessary. The test operation, obviously, is cheaper, since no iterative search for the root is necessary. The following specification uses the identification function to state the idempotence for typing reasons.

REFINEMENT
FlatForest
REFINES
EquivalenceClo
VARIABLES
fs
INVARIANT
$fs \in ASET \rightarrow ASET \wedge$
$(fs;fs) = (fs;\text{id}(ASET)) \wedge$
$rst(fs) = ER$
INITIALISATION
$fs := \text{id}(ASET)$
OPERATIONS
equate(aa,bb) = **PRE**
$aa \in ASET \wedge$
$bb \in ASET$
THEN
$fs := fs \Lleftarrow fs^{-1} [\{fs(aa), fs(bb)\}] \times \{fs(aa)\}$
END;
$equivalent \leftarrow$ test(aa,bb) = **PRE**
$aa \in ASET \wedge$
$bb \in ASET$
THEN
$equivalent := \textbf{bool}(fs(aa) = fs(bb))$
END
END

The restriction of the data representation to flat forests is stronger than to arbitrary forests. Figure 3 gives an overview of the different restrictions. The variety of all relations that have the same (unique) equivalence closure e as the user-given relation u is indicated as well. We need to distinguish between the behavioral non-determinism observable from the outside and the representational freedom of the data structure. Nothing prevents us from relaxing the single edged trees to arbitrary forests in a second data refinement. The refinement relation is the root function from before.

REFINEMENT
DeepForest
REFINES
FlatForest
VARIABLES
ff
DEFINITIONS
$root == (\textbf{closure}(ff);\text{id}(ASET) \cap ff)$
INVARIANT
$ff \in ASET \rightarrow ASET \wedge$

$fs = root$

INITIALISATION

$ff{:}={\bf id}(ASET)$

OPERATIONS

equate$(aa,bb) = {\bf PRE}$

$aa \in ASET \wedge$

$bb \in ASET$

THEN

$ff{:}=ff \mathbin{\Leftarrow} \{root(aa) \mapsto root(bb)\}$

END;

$equivalent \leftarrow {\bf test}(aa,bb) = {\bf PRE}$

$aa \in ASET \wedge$

$bb \in ASET$

THEN

$equivalent{:}={\bf bool}(root(aa) = root(bb))$

END

END

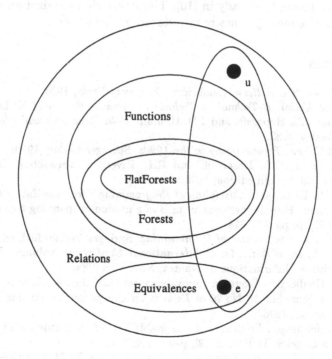

Fig. 3. Restrictions of Relations

5 Concluding Remarks

The B method offers powerful operators on relations, which are well suited to specify the equivalence relation problem. We have presented several machines, which are all equivalent with respect to refinement (refinement-equivalent). The refinement order gives no hint of how to order the specifications even though the state space of the machines varies considerably between the two extremes of an eager and lazy specification. To discriminate among various specifications, the tightness of the invariant appears to be a criteria for the quality of a specification in a model-based approach.

Exploiting the variety of specifications, we have identified two heuristics: *replace relations by functions* and *eliminate non-detectable cycles*. Functions can be mapped directly to computational equivalent structures and *detectable cycles* guarantee the possibility to establish termination conditions for repeated function applications.

The heuristics have been combined to two strategies by avoiding non-detectable cycles in two ways: by *transitive asymmetry* and by *idempotence*. Both elegant formalizations lead to different restrictions of the initial variety: *transitive asymmetry* and *idempotence* characterize *forests* and *flat forests*, respectively, where idempotence implies asymmetry for functions. We have documented the idempotence property already in [10]. The direct characterization of forests by *transitive antisymmetry* is newly introduced in this paper.

References

1. J-R. Abrial. *The B-Book*. Cambridge University Press, 1996.
2. J-R. et al Abrial. *B-Technology Technical Overview*. B-Core (UK) Ltd., 1993.
3. A.V. Aho, J.E. Hopcraft, and J.D. Ullman. *Data Structures and Algorithms*. Addison Wesley, 1983.
4. Edward Cohen. *Programming in the 1990s*. Springer Verlag, 1990.
5. T.H. Cormen, C.E. Leiserson, and R.L. Rivest. *Introduction to Algorithms*. McGraw-Hill, second edition, 1990.
6. Edsger W. Dijkstra. *A Discipline of Programming*. Prentice Hall, 1976.
7. Ranan Fraer. Formal development in B of a minimum spanning tree algorithm. In Habrias [9], pages 305–328.
8. David Gries. *The Science of Programming*. Springer Verlag, fifth edition, 1989.
9. Henri Habrias, editor. *1st B International Conference*, volume 86. Institut de Recherches en Informatique de Nantes, November 1996.
10. Philipp Heuberger. Exercise: Equivalence relation. In *Specification Case Studies with B*, volume Ser. B, No 26 of *Reports on Computer Science and Mathematics*. Åbo Akademi, 1996.
11. Philipp Heuberger. Proving on a reasonable level of abstraction with programmer-designed theories. In Habrias [9], pages 297–302.
12. C.B. Jones. *Systematic Software Development using VDM*. Prentice-Hall International, second edition, 1989.
13. D.S. Neilson and I.H. Soerensen. The B-technologies: A system for computer aided programming. In *6th Nordic Workshop on Programming Theory*, Aarhus, 1994.

Specification of an Integrated Circuit Card Protocol Application Using the B Method and Linear Temporal Logic*

Jacques Julliand[1], Bruno Legeard[1], Thierry Machicoane[2], Benoit Parreaux[1], and Bruno Tatibouët[1]

[1] Laboratoire d'Informatique, 16 route de Gray, 25030 Besançon cedex, France,
Tel +33 (0)3 81 66 64 55, Fax +33 (0)3 81 66 64 50,
{julliand, legeard, parreaux, tati}@lib.univ-fcomte.fr
http://lib.univ-fcomte.fr
[2] Schlumberger Industries, Terminaux Urbains et Systemes,
Parc Lafayette, 6 Rue Isaac Newton, 25000 Besançon, France
machicoa@besancon.ts.slb.com

Abstract. In this paper we propose a construction method of multi-formalism specifications based on B and linear temporal logic. We examined this method with a case study of a communication protocol between an integrated circuit card and a device such a terminal. This study has been carried out in collaboration with the Schlumberger company. We show the current advantages and limits in combining many specifications formalisms and the associated toolkits : Atelier B and SPIN. Finally, we draw conclusions about future directions of research on the proof of heterogeneous specifications, incremental verification and ontool cooperation to assist in the verification step (e.g. a prover, a model-checker and an animator).

1 Why and how heterogeneous cooperation formal methods should be used?

The need to use formal methods is growing in industry, especially for critical reactive applications such as transport, and the nuclear industry where security is an imposed goal. In the scientific community, examples such as [9] are chosen to compare various approachs such as VDM, Z, B, Lustre, Esterel, Lotos, SPIN, etc. Each method is efficient for some aspect (functionalities, state, concurrency, etc) but, it is very rare that real applications are reduced to a single aspect.

In this paper, we present an approach using several parallel formal techniques for the specification of the half duplex protocol which manages the communication between the Integrated Circuit Card (ICC) and an interface device such as a terminal.

The cooperation between heteregeneous formal techniques[5] is today an active line of research[2][22] designed to provide complementary advantages to

---

* Specification is available on http://lib.univ-fcomte.fr/RECHERCHE/P5/ICC.html

formal methods. In this way, our approach is centred on a joint use of the *B method*[1] and *Linear Temporal Logic*[18][19] (LTL), as well as on the associated checking tools : Atelier B[20] and SPIN[15].

Our project, originating from a pragmatic approach to the specification of a problem demonstrates the necessity to combine many formalisms. From this point of view, our work is comparable to the elements of construction method proposed in [22] and [17] to extend B or other formal descriptions such as Z++ and VDM++[16]. In contrast our work is different because it is based on model checking to verify temporal properties.

The half duplex protocol of the communication between a card and a device is a complex application whose requirements analysis is presented in European standard EN 27816[8]. This standard describes, through rules and scenarios, the expected properties of ICC-device communication. These properties correspond on one hand to the invariant in the relationship between variables and, on the other hand, dynamic properties such as the evolution of the system with time. In this standard, the description remains informal, and all the properties are expressed in natural language but perfectly structured.

The Schlumberger division, Urban Terminals and Systems at Besançon, is developing different vehicle parking control systems. This suggests the use of ICC for electronic credits or traditional bank cards. In this context, the company is developing device applications which must respect the EN 27816 standard. The use of a formal approach in this framework is designed at the same time to be able to certify the device software and also to be able to detect cards which do not meet the standard. The company also wishes to understand better the EN 27816 standard so that it may detect certain inconsistencies within it.

In this article, we demonstrate how this multi-formal approach allows one to take specifications into account more precisely and completely, and how the joint implementation of the checking tools (Atelier B and SPIN) helps the definition of formal specifications. This approach using heteregeneous specifications presents numerous unresolved problems, as much at the theoretical level in the proof of the specification as at the level of the refinement strategy. But this experiment carried out in an industrial context and on a large scale application demonstrates the value of coupling the B method and LTL and also the complementarity between the proof approach, and verification by model checking.

In the rest of this article, we present first of all the ICC application in section 2 and we then describe our formal approach in section 3. Then, in section 4 we present the formal specification before describing the results of the verification process in section 5. Our conclusions are presented in section 6.

2 Informal Presentation of an Integrated Circuit Card application

This example belongs to the domain of communication protocols, more precisely between an integrated circuit card (referred to below as Card) and an interface device such as a terminal (called here after Device) shown in figure 1. This system is used in many applications such as the electronic purse. The requirement analysis is described in depth in the European Standard EN 27816[8] written in April 1992 by a committee of The ISO. This draft covers many aspects such as voltage levels, current values, parity conventions, operating procedure, transmission mechanism and communication with the integrated circuit card.

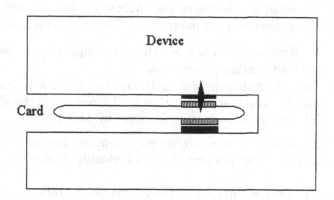

Fig. 1. Terminal to read integrated circuit cards

The principle of the operating procedure has five steps :

1. activation of the contacts by the Device,
2. reset of the Card by the device,
3. the Card's reply to the resetting,
4. information exchange in the case of an asynchronous Cards,
5. deactivation of the contacts by the Device.

Because of the complexity of this system, we have limited our work to one possibility of asynchronous protocol in step four. We suppose that reset is performed correctly and that the device and the card execute the selection of exchange protocol. In Section 2.1, we define intuitively the chosen protocol called protocol T=1 in [8] and our intent in section 2.2 is to include an explanation of the standard in no more detail than is necessary.

2.1 Protocol T=1, asynchronous half duplex block transmission

This protocol defines the exchange of messages transmission in an asynchronous half duplex block transmission protocol between a Device and a Card. A *message* can be divided into one or many *slices*. The transmission of the smallest data unit (a slice) which is performed by a *block* exchange, called an *information block* (denoted by *I-block*), which is made up of a data slice and some pieces of control information such as an identification of the block. The acknowledgment of an I-block is an I-block for the last slice of the messages and a *response block* (denoted by *R-block*) for each slice of data except for the last. The Device and the Card can exchange control blocks, called also *supervisory blocks* (denoted by *S-block*) allowing then to modify the exchange parameters to require for example an adjustment of the length of slices or of response delay, the abortion of a message transmission, etc. In summary, the card and the device transmit three types of blocks :

- I-blocks - denoted by *I(identification, chaining)* - their primary purpose are to transmit application layer information. They are composed of :
  - an identification which is a bit which is comparable to the alternating bit in the alternating bit protocol,
  - chaining information indicating if the slice of data is the end of the message; if this is true, we say that the I-block is non chaining (denoted by *NoLink*), else it is chaining (denoted by *Link*),
- R-blocks - denoted by *R(identification)* - contains positive or negative acknowledgments. They contains the block identification of the expected I-block,
- S-blocks - denoted by *S(type of request)* - the block which contains transmission control information; 4 pairs of request and response are possible : *WtxReq* and *WtxRep* adjust the response delay to continue exchanges, *IfsReq* and *IfsRep* to change the length of slice of data, *ResynchReq* and *ResynchRep* to resynchronise transmission, *AbortReq* and *AbortRep* to abort chaining exchanges.

Three kinds of error are possible: transmission error, a loss of synchronisation and a total loss of message detected by a watch dog. To simplify the level of modelling explained in what follows, few details are specified for the error cases. The dialogue for error recovery is hidden at this refinement. However we specify the failure of recovery which leads to the sudden rejection of the card by the device without explaining the reasons more precisely.

The processing principles for computing the identifications are as follow. An I-block carries its send sequence number denoted $N(S)$ which consists of one bit and is counted modulo 2. Its value starts with 0 either after the start of the block transmision protocol or after resynchronisation and is incremented after sending each I-block. The numbers of I-blocks sent by the device and blocks sent by the card are counted independently with respect to each other. Acknowledgment of an I-block is indicated when the number $N(S)$ of the next received I-block is different from the $N(S)$ of the previously received I-block.

An R-block carries $N(R)$, which is the value of $N(S)$ in the next expected I-block. Acknowledgment of an I-block is indicated when the $N(R)$ of the received R-block is different from the $N(S)$ of the sent I-block (see rule 2.2 section 4.2.4).

If a response does not come before the end of a delay fixed by the protocol, the device sends a request initiated by a watch dog. This situation handles the cases of loss of a slice of a message.

2.2 The European standard EN 27816

The standard described in [8] explains in a very structured manner the results of the requirement analysis step. We have used three parts in particular:

1. the main principles of processing procedures outlined above,
2. the description of the 22 rules for transmission operations,
3. 35 examples of scenario fragments of behaviour of system.

To illustrate the last two parts, the reader can find a few examples of rules in section 4.2.4. and can see scenario number 5 in table 1 and scenario number 3 in table 2. Scenario 5 shows exchange of message between card and device. Deleting the events 1, 2, 3 and 4 in table 1, we obtain scenario number 1 which shows an exchange of messages in a single slice. Scenario 3 in table 2 shows a request for an adjustment of length of slice. Deleting the events 2 and 3 in table 2, we obtain also scenario number 1 which shows an exchange of messages in a single slice.

3 Presentation of the formal construction method

The formal approach illustrated in figure 2 is based on a stage of verifying consistency formed of two elements: a descriptive specification and an operational specification.

The descriptive specification is a B Abstract System[2][4][6], that to say a data model essentially describing system variables which must satisfy the invariant properties. This is completed by a group of LTL formulae describing the behavioural properties of the system such as rule 2.1 (section 4.2.4) in the example.

Event	Device→	← Card	Observations	Rule
1	I(0,Link)		Sending of the first slice of message	1
2		R(1)	Acknowledgment of reception of the second slice	2.2,5
3	I(1,Link)		Sending of the second slice of message	5
4		R(0)	Acknowledgment of reception of the third slice	2.2,5
5	I(0,NoLink)		Sending of the third and last slice of message	5
6		I(0,NoLink)	Acknowledgment with sending of a new message in one slice	2.1
7	I(1,NoLink)		Acknowledgment with sending of a new message in one slice	2.1
8		I(1,NoLink)	Acknowledgment with sending of a new message in one slice	2.1
	etc.			

Table 1. Exchange of messages composed of one or more slices

The operational specification is the final outcome of the stage of formal design by a transition system described by the B events. An event is an action which modifies a guarded state. From a formal point of view, the transition system is totally "flat" in such a way that its dynamic behaviour is the sum of the possible interleavings of events which act at the atomic level. But the choice of events involves the physical structure of the system such that the model approaches reality and real life operation. We approach the operational specification by breaking up the system, by identify the localization or generalizing state variables and designing events on the basis of physical reality.

These two parts of the specification are based upon the standard document[8]. They constitute two different views of the system which must be checked for consistency. This stage is approached in different ways:
- first we check the invariant properties by using the prover of Atelier B [20],
- second we check behavioural properties by model checking techniques using the SPIN environment[12][15].

We chose this solution for practical reasons such as the inmaturity of LTL proof techniques and the technological power of the SPIN environment. In effect, SPIN allows one to consider all the properties which can be expressed in LTL as well also integrating better techniques of reducing the complexity of model checking such as partial order[21], optimisation of the memory representation of states[13][14] and heuristics. Despite all these advantages, there remain two problems, firstly the combinatorics explosion[10][11] continues and secondly we must represent the abstract B model in PROMELA with all the risks involved. We noted however that the simplicity of the model based on the data given by the example allows systematic approach to the task, so limiting the risk.

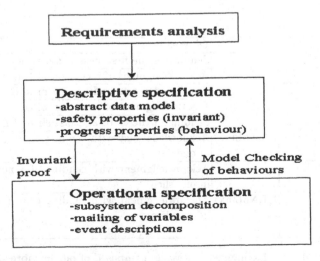

Fig. 2. Method of formal construction

The approach presented above can be coupled with an approach by successive refinement[3] [4]. Although it is not the object of our presentation, we note that the approach we have applied permits us to present a simplified model. Finally we note that this has at least three advantages: it facilitates the transfer from expression of requirements to full specification, it leads to implementation and it allows one to do incremental model checking which is a response to the problem of complexity identified above. In this example, we have proceeded by successive refinements in four stages taking more and more details into account:

- Level 1 : exchange of message in an atomic event,
- Level 2 : taking into account the exchange of messages with several slices,
- Level 3 : taking into account the modifications of conditions of the dialogue by exchange of S-blocks,
- Level 4 : taking recovery of errors into account.

In section 4 we present level 3.

4 Formal specification of Integrated Circuit Cards

We present the specification in three parts :

- the intuitive description of the main goal,
- a *descriptive specification* divided in two parts, the data model of the system, and its safety and progress properties,
- an *operational specification* composed of two parts, the decomposition of the system towards many subsystems, and the formal description of operations called events in the case of reactive systems.

4.1 Goal

The level of specification chosen allows the exchange of messages composed of one or many slices. It also specifies the possibility of aborting the transmission of a chain of slices and of adjusting many parameters of the exchange such as the response time (Wtx), the length of slice (Ifs), the synchronisation parameters (Resynch), sending a control request (Req) and acknowledging (Rep) by transmission of a control block called S-block (see section 2.1). For example, the scenario number 3 in figure 4 shows a dialogue changing the length of slice. Note that we are not concerned with the value of length.

4.2 Descriptive specification

The descriptive specification is divided into three parts:

- the *Data Model* defining the sets and the state variables,
- the *Invariant* defining the safety properties,
- the *Behavioural Properties* defining the progress properties of the system.

Event	Device	Card	Observations	Rule
1	I(0,Link) →		Sending a message composed of one slice	1
2		←S(IfsReq)	Request modifying the length of slice	3
3	S(IfsRep) →		Acknowledgment of the request	3
4		←I(0,NoLink)	Acknowledgment of message and sending of an other messsage	2.1
	etc.			

Table 2. Scenario 3, request and acknowledgment of a change in the length of slice

4.2.1 Data Model The exchange of messages between the Card and the Device requires knowledge of the sending of the last block sent by the card and by the device. These are implemented by the variables TC and TD. The variables TC_tr and TD_tr indicate if the last block is either acknowledged or not. The variable *Dialogue* indicates the state of transmission which is either active or interrupt.

To change the exchange conditions during a message transmission, we must memorise the last I-block sent during the exchange of S-block. The variables ATD and ATC in the data model memorise the last I-block which is waiting for an acknowledgment. After an interruption of a transmission of an information message by an S-block exchange, the message transmission restarts normally using these variables. In order to ensure that the values contained in the variables are correct, we will use the acknowledgment variables ATC_tr and ATD_tr.

The set of blocks called BLOCK is the cartesian product of four fields, the type of block (I, R or S), identification for I-blocks and R-blocks, binding information for I-blocks (indicating if the block carries the last slice of message or not) and a sort of control message for S-blocks.

The B abstract machine is composed of the set descriptions, the definition of applications *Negation* and *Next* allowing respectively inversion of the acknowledgment and computation modulo 2 the state variables. The values *Indef* are interpreted as undefined values for each field of the cartesian product; for example it allows us to indicate that the chaining information is not defined for R-blocks and S-blocks.

SETS
    ACK={Yes, No};
      – "Yes" indicates that the block is acknowledged
    LINKING={Link, NoLink, Indef};
      – "NoLink" indicates that the transmitted slice of message is the last
    DIALOGUE={Active, Interrupt};
      – "Active" indicates that the transmission continues
    IDENT={Zero, One, IndefI};
      – half duplex identification : 0=Zero and 1=One
    TYPEBLOCK={I, R, S};
      – type of blocks : Information, Response, Control

CONTROL={ResynchReq, ResynchRep, IfsReq, IfsRep,
AbortReq, AbortRep, WtxReq, WtxRep, IndefS}
– type of S-blocks

ABSTRACT_CONSTANTS

BLOCK, Next, Negation

PROPERTIES

Negation $\in$ ACK$>\!\!\!-\!\!\gg$ACK$\wedge$ Negation(Yes) = No $\wedge$ Negation(No) = Yes $\wedge$
Next $\in$ {Zero, One}$>\!\!\!-\!\!\gg${Zero, One}$\wedge$ Next = {(Zero$\mapsto$One), (One$\mapsto$Zero)}$\wedge$
BLOCK = TYPEBLOCK$\times$ IDENT $\times$ LINKING $\times$ CONTROL
– type of block

VARIABLES

TC, TD, ATC, ATD, TC_tr, TD_tr, ATC_tr, ATD_tr, Dialogue

4.2.2 Invariant

Notations of variables:
- w, w' : Identification of blocks ($\in$ IDENT or $\in$ ID=IDENT-{IndefI}),
- x, x' : binding ($\in$ LINKING or $\in$ LI=LINKING-{Indef}),
- y, y' : Type of control block ($\in$ CONTROL or $\in$ CONTROL-{IndefS}).

The invariant is described in many parts:
- the type of variables :

TC $\in$ BLOCK $\wedge$ TD $\in$ BLOCK $\wedge$ ATC $\in$ BLOCK $\wedge$ ATD $\in$ BLOCK $\wedge$
TC_tr $\in$ ACK $\wedge$ TD_tr $\in$ ACK $\wedge$ ATC_tr $\in$ ACK $\wedge$ ATD_tr $\in$ ACK $\wedge$
Dialogue $\in$ DIALOGUE $\wedge$

- restrictions of type relative to the type BLOCK for TD (the same properties are require for TC):

$\forall$(w, x, y).((w $\in$ IDENT $\wedge$ x $\in$ LINKING $\wedge$ y $\in$ CONTROL $\wedge$ TC=(((I$\mapsto$w)$\mapsto$x)$\mapsto$y))
$\Rightarrow$(w $\neq$ IndefI $\wedge$ x $\neq$Indef $\wedge$ y=IndefS)) $\wedge$
$\forall$(w, x, y).((w $\in$ IDENT $\wedge$ x $\in$ LINKING $\wedge$ y $\in$ CONTROL $\wedge$ TC=(((S$\mapsto$w)$\mapsto$x)$\mapsto$y))
$\Rightarrow$(w = IndefI $\wedge$ x = Indef $\wedge$ y $\neq$IndefS)) $\wedge$
$\forall$(w, x, y).((w $\in$ IDENT $\wedge$ x $\in$ LINKING $\wedge$ y $\in$ CONTROL $\wedge$ TC=(((R$\mapsto$w)$\mapsto$x)$\mapsto$y))
$\Rightarrow$(w $\neq$ IndefI $\wedge$ x = Indef $\wedge$ y = IndefS)) $\wedge$

- the waiting blocks are always I-blocks containing a message slice:

$\exists$(w, x).(w $\in$ ID $\wedge$ x $\in$ LI $\wedge$ ATD=(((I$\mapsto$w)$\mapsto$x)$\mapsto$IndefS)) $\wedge$
$\exists$(w, x).(w $\in$ ID $\wedge$ x $\in$ LI $\wedge$ ATC=(((I$\mapsto$w)$\mapsto$x)$\mapsto$IndefS)) $\wedge$

- *rule 6* which indicates that the request of a new synchronisation cannot be sent by the card, and also that the response cannot be transmitted by the device:

TC $\neq$ (((S$\mapsto$IndefI)$\mapsto$Indef)$\mapsto$ResynchReq) $\wedge$
TD $\neq$ (((S$\mapsto$IndefI)$\mapsto$Indef)$\mapsto$ResynchRep) $\wedge$

- *rule 3* which indicates that the request of the response time modification cannot be transmitted by the device, and also that the response cannot be transmitted by the card :

TD $\neq$ (((S$\mapsto$IndefI)$\mapsto$Indef)$\mapsto$WtxReq) $\wedge$

TC $\neq$ $(((S \mapsto IndefI) \mapsto Indef) \mapsto WtxRep)$ $\wedge$
- the acknowledged block is the same as the last block sent if this is a message slice:
$\forall(w, x).((w \in ID \wedge x \in LI) \Rightarrow$
    $(TC=(((I \mapsto w) \mapsto x) \mapsto IndefS) \Rightarrow ATC=TC)$
    $\wedge$ $(TD=(((I \mapsto w) \mapsto x) \mapsto IndefS) \Rightarrow ATD=TD))$ $\wedge$
- the half duplex behaviour: $TC\_tr = Negation(TD\_tr)$ $\wedge$
    - there is at most one I-block waiting an acknowledgment, either in the Device or in the Card:
$(ATC\_tr=No \Rightarrow ATD\_tr = Yes) \wedge (ATD\_tr=No \Rightarrow ATC\_tr = Yes)$

4.2.3 Behaviour Properties The progress properties are expressed by the 9 rules, concerned at this level, described in the standard of ISO/IEC[8]. The set of rules mainly describes response properties in the classification of Manna and Pnueli in [18][19]. They are described using the three main operators of linear temporal logic[18][19] denoted $\Box$, O and $\Diamond$ which are respectively interpreted by *Always*, *Next* and *Eventually*.

We introduce a few significant examples of different kinds of formula :

- *rule 1* defines the initial state of any execution,
- *rules 2.1, 2.2* and *5* are typical examples of response (type of progress) properties,
- *rule 3* is an example of immediate response using the Next operator.

- **Rule 1** : The device sends the first block, either an S-block or an I-block (with identification zero and with or without a link).
  $\exists y \in \{ResynchReq, IfsReq\}. \exists x \in LI.$
  $(((TD=(((I \mapsto Zero) \mapsto x) \mapsto IndefS) \wedge ATD=TD \wedge ATD\_tr=No)$
  $\vee (TD=(((S \mapsto IndefI) \mapsto Indef) \mapsto y) \wedge ATD=(((I \mapsto One) \mapsto NoLink) \mapsto IndefS) \wedge$
  $ATD\_tr=Yes))) \wedge ATC\_tr=Yes \wedge ATC=(((I \mapsto One) \mapsto NoLink) \mapsto IndefS) \wedge$
  $TD\_tr=No \wedge Dialogue=Active)$
  Note : "$ATC\_tr=Yes \wedge ATC=(((I \mapsto One) \mapsto NoLink) \mapsto IndefS)$" determine the first identification of card to Zero alternating with One in the next transmission.

- **Rule 2.1** : $I(N_A(S), NoLink)$ sent by A, is acknowledged by $I(N_B(S), x)$ sent by B to transmit application data and to indicate readiness to receive the next I-block from A.
  – case where B is the card
  $\forall w, w' \in ID. \forall x' \in LI. \exists x \in LI.$
  $\Box(ATD= (((I \mapsto w) \mapsto NoLink) \mapsto IndefS) \wedge ATD\_tr=No \wedge$
      $Dialogue=Active \wedge ATC=(((I \mapsto w') \mapsto x') \mapsto IndefS))$
      $\Rightarrow \Diamond ((TC= (((I \mapsto Negation(w')) \mapsto x) \mapsto IndefS) \wedge TC\_tr=No \wedge$
      $\vee ATD\_tr=Yes) \; Dialogue=Interrupt)$

- **Rule 2.2** : $I(N_A(S), Link)$ sent by A is acknowledged by $R(N_B(S))$ sent by B (where $N_A(S)\neq N_B(S)$) to indicate that the received block was correct and the readiness to receive the next I-block from A. (or by an S(AbortReq), cf. rule 9).
  - case where B is the card
  $\forall$ w $\in$ ID. $\Box$(ATD= $(((I \mapsto w)\mapsto Link)\mapsto IndefS) \wedge ATD\_tr=No) \Rightarrow$
  $\Diamond$ $(((TC=(((R\mapsto Negation(w))\mapsto Indef)\mapsto IndefS) \vee$
  $TC=(((S\mapsto IndefI)\mapsto Indef)\mapsto AbortReq)$
  $\vee TC=(((S\mapsto IndefI)\mapsto Indef)\mapsto AbortRep))$
  $\wedge TC\_tr=No \wedge ATD\_tr=Yes) \vee Dialogue =Interrupt))$

- **Rule 3** : If the card requires more time to handle the previously received I-block, it sends S(WtxReq). The device acknowledges by S(WtxRep).
  $\Box$ $((TC=(((S\mapsto IndefI)\mapsto Indef)\mapsto WtxReq) \wedge TC\_tr=No \wedge Dialogue=Active) \Rightarrow$
  O $((TD=(S\mapsto IndefI)\mapsto Indef)\mapsto WtxRep) \wedge TD\_tr=No) \vee Dialogue =Interrupt))$
  Note : A part of rule 3 is described in the invariant.

- **Rule 4** : $I(N(S), NoLink)$ is a non chained I-block or the last block of a chain. $I(N(S), Link)$ is a part of a chain and will be followed by at least one chained block.
  - chained transmission of card
  $\forall$ w $\in$ ID. $\exists$ w' $\in$ ID. $\Box((ATC=(((I\mapsto w)\mapsto Link)\mapsto IndefS) \wedge$
  $ATC\_tr=No \wedge Dialogue=Active)$
  $\Rightarrow \Diamond$ $((ATC = (((I\mapsto w')\mapsto NoLink)\mapsto IndefS) \wedge ATC\_tr=No)$
  $\vee (TD = (((S\mapsto IndefI)\mapsto Indef)\mapsto AbortRep) \wedge TD\_tr=No)$
  $\vee (TD=(((S\mapsto IndefI)\mapsto Indef)\mapsto AbortReq) \wedge TD\_tr=No)$
  $\vee Dialogue=Interrupt))$

4.2.4 Operational specification

The operational specification is divided into two parts :

- the system decomposition which is the result of an informal design step; this step divides the system into processes, maps the variables and defines the guarded events of each subsystems.
- the transition system made up of a formal description of each guarded event.

1. *System decomposition*
   We divide the system in two processes as shown in figure 3, the card and the device which can transmit messages using events *EmC* and *EmD* and can abort an exchange of messages using events *CardChainedTransStop* and *DevChainedTransStop*. The device can interrupt transmission rejecting the card using event *RejectC*. The set of variables is global at this abstraction level. In contrast, the variables will be located in processes in the next refinement step which will be a more realistic model.

2. *Transition System*
   The transition system consists of describing the initial state and each event. The specification of events for the Card and the Device being symmetric, we only present the initialisation, the card events and the reject operation of the Device.

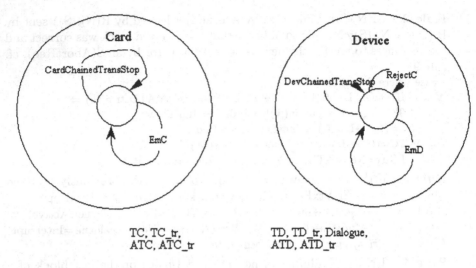

Fig. 3. System Decomposition

(a) *Initialisation* (implements rule 1)

TC_tr := Yes || TD_tr := No || Dialogue := Active|| ATC_tr := Yes ||
TC := (((I↦One)↦NoLink)↦IndefS) ||
ATC := (((I↦One)↦NoLink)↦IndefS) ||
CHOICE
   TD := (((I↦Zero)↦NoLink)↦IndefS) ||
   ATD := (((I↦Zero)↦NoLink)↦IndefS) || ATD_tr := No
OR TD := (((I↦Zero)↦Link)↦IndefS) ||
   ATD := (((I↦Zero)↦Link)↦IndefS) || ATD_tr := No
OR TD := (((S↦IndefI)↦Indef)↦IfsReq) ||
   ATD := (((I↦One)↦NoLink)↦IndefS) || ATD_tr := Yes
OR TD := (((S↦IndefI)↦Indef)↦ResynchReq) ||
   ATD := (((I↦One)↦NoLink)↦IndefS) || ATD_tr := Yes
END

(b) *Event Transmission by the card*
Many cases are possible according to the response that the card and the
device wait and the block that the device sent. An exhaustive analysis
of cases limits the nomber of cases to three :
   i. if either the card sent a message and the device answered the last
      received block either by an I-block or by an R-block or the card
      transmitted a request and the device accepted it, then the card an-
      swers:
      – either by an I-block, chained or not,
      – or by an S-block transmitting a Wtx, Ifs or Abort response.
   ii. the device sent an information message or it accepted a request and
      waits for an acknowledgment for the last transmitted block, the card

answers either by an R-block whose identification is inverse, or by an S-block transmitting a Wtx, Ifs or Abort request,

    iii. the device sent a request, the card answers by an acknowledgement.

(c) *Event Rejection of Card*

At this level of abstraction we can give very little detail because we have not yet specified the handling of the error. We verify simply that the dialogue is interrupted without knowing the reasons.

RejectC = SELECT Dialogue=Active THEN Dialogue := Interrupt END

(d) *Event Stop chained exchange by the card*

The end of chained exchange occurs when the card receives an abort request which it then accepts :

CardChainedTransStop = SELECT

    (Dialogue=Active $\wedge$ TD_tr=No $\wedge$ TD=((($S\mapsto$IndefI)$\mapsto$Indef)$\mapsto$AbortReq))

THEN – the card accepts the abort request

    TC := ((($S\mapsto$IndefI)$\mapsto$Indef)$\mapsto$AbortRep)

END– ChainedTransStop

5 Formal Proof and Verification

The verification was performed with the "atelier B" to prove the invariant and with SPIN to model-check the progress properties. Below, we report our experiment with these tools and sum up the results of using both B and SPIN.

5.1 Using "atelier B"

Our basic specification was written using the B syntax and does not have any progress properties. We used version 3.2 of the tool to type-check it and to verify the invariant with the prover. The "atelier B" automatically proved the 450 proof obligations, which demonstrates that the prover was mature.

Operations	obvious Proof	Proof Obligations	Interactive proof	Automatical proof	%
Initialization	21	52	0	52	100
EmC	205	194	0	194	100
EmD	185	184	0	184	100
DeviceChainedTransStop	22	10	0	10	100
CardChainedTransStop	22	10	0	10	100
Total	481	450	0	450	100

Table 3. Status of B Machine

We obtained this result by studying the proof obligations that were not proved after the first step. This study leads to the correction of our specification. These proof obligations originated from mistakes in our specification or limitations of the prover.

We pointed out some errors out at the descriptive level as well as at the operational level. For example, our first operational specification allowed us to resume a message exchange after a control dialogue even if this dialogue did not stop any exchange. At most one device should be waiting for the acknowledgment of a message block: this property was violated by our specification. We have also corrected a faulty expression of the type restriction at the descriptive level.

Another difficulty in realising the proof obligations originates from limitations of the prover. For example, the following test, defining the function *Next* in the PROPERTIES clause, makes the prover fail, although it was equivalent to the section 4.2.1. clause.

$$\text{Next} \in \{\text{Zero, One}\} \rightarrowtail\!\!\!\twoheadrightarrow \{\text{Zero, One}\}$$
$$\wedge \text{ Next(Zero)=One} \wedge \text{Next(One)=Zero}$$

Proofs were performed on a SS4 SUN Station with 32 MB. This did not induce any major problems of performance or memory size with the most recent version of the specification. Previous versions was more space-consuming.

5.2 Using SPIN

We used the PROMELA language with the SPIN tool to verify linear temporal logical properties. The first step consisted of translating the B specification into PROMELA, the second consisted of putting verifications with the model checker into action. Finally we recapitulate using SPIN working on our specification. Translating B specifications into PROMELA presents the following two questions:

- How can one represent the abstract data model and the B actions using the PROMELA concrete types?
- How can one carry out the atomic events?

These two questions did not cause difficulty in the example given because the data was simple and the atomicity notion already existed in PROMELA. The PROMELA text is close to the original specification. It consists of three processes, the first, called init, cames out some initialisations and launches the two processes Card and Device. These processes consist of a loop with a non-deterministic choice among the different events, realised in the form of a guarded action. The reject event caused an exit from the loop. The verification consists of a liveness property such as the absence of deadlock and the unreachable code, the invariant and the LTL properties described into section 4.2.4. to perform these verifications. The user has to solve three kinds of problems:

- the *next* operator encoding which is not provided by SPIN,
- realisation of the fairness conditions,
- a strategy between combinatory explosion and the memory used by exhaustive verification.

SPIN uses an LTL next-free[12]. To cope with the unavailability of the following operator, we transform rules of the form $\Box(p \Rightarrow \bigcirc q)$. Such rules mean that if p holds, q holds for the next state. This rule becomes $\Box(p \Rightarrow (p \, \mathcal{U} q))$, that is, if a state verifying p is reached, p holds until a state verifying q is reached. This latter property is not as strong as the former, but seems to us to be sufficient in the sense that the following operator is often replaced with a "eventually" operator after refinement.

Some property verifications require fairness conditions amongst events and different cases about events. For example, a weak fairness is necessary in order that some control dialogues do not stop a message exchange. However SPIN allows us to define weak fairness condition among processes but not among transitions. There are three solutions to this problem, first, encoding fairness with counters to bound the number of message blocks, second, encoding it within Linear Temporal Logical properties, third, putting subsets of fair transitions as processes. We chose the first solution because it was the simplest to implement whereas the LTL encoding increases the complexity of verification. In addition, the first solution makes the rule easy to read. This technique limits the complexity graph exploration, but bounds the range of our verification to a maximum number of blocks. However, this limit is in an acceptable range for this example: if the exchange is correct for a message of 0 to 5 blocks, it is probably right for n blocks.

The verification storage without fairness requirement did not cause any problems with memory, because the accessibility graph was reasonably sized. With the fairness counter, the naive verification was not possible. We used two new compression modes in SPIN Version 3.0.0 : Collapse compression mode and BDD based compression. These improvements were efficient, because verifications were successful, although for some properties, it took approximately ten hours of computation with a R10000 processor and 512 MB of memory. Without compression the memory needed was near to 3 GB. SPIN was very efficient within a memory reduction but it was desirable to express the weak and strong fairness among transition efficiently with PROMELA.

5.3 Mistakes detected by the joint use of B and SPIN

With SPIN, the verification was made in three steps: unreachable code and deadlock detection, invariant verification and lastly, verification of progress properties.

In the first model, we detected some unreachable code and no deadlock. The unreachable code was eliminated by SPIN, which indicates the unreachable line in the specification text. B does not detect this problem because the invariant was fulfilled. At the second step, the whole of the invariant of the second specification was verified successfully.

Another mistake was pointed out during the verification of property 3. In the first version it was possible to put an I-block instead of an R-block. This mistake had not already been detected because neither the invariant nor the other rules were violated. The trace provided by SPIN helped us understand why this property was not fulfilled. As soon as the mistake, which was located in a conditional expression, was fixed, this property was verified easily in the operational specification.

The verification of the response properties, expressed with next operators, did not cause any difficulty. On the other hand, the properties including the eventually operator were very time-consuming and required much memory (ten hours operation on an Ultrasparc).

Using both the "atelier B" and SPIN allowed us to detect a mistake in the specification. This mistake was due to a bad translation of the property: "there is at the most one I-block waiting for the acknowledgment sent by the device or by the card". This was originally expressed initially with the formula: "ATC_tr=Yes $\Rightarrow$ ATD_tr=No $\wedge$ ATD_tr=Yes $\Rightarrow$ ATC_tr=No" related to the use of pseudo B. In fact, ATD_tr was originally for "device block waiting for acknowledgment". Because this variable name was considered ambiguous, one of the people involved in the specification changed the interpretation of ATD_tr to "there is a waiting block". Three different people participated; one did the specification, another the verification using B, and the last the verification using SPIN.

As a first step, the people who performed the verification using B modified events in order to achieve the proof. This way the mistake in the property above mentioned was carried foward to the operational specification. It is likely that the impossibility of performing the verification of some liveness properties with SPIN caused us to go back to the original specification and correct this property. We successfully verified this new property with B and SPIN.

This mistake may seem to be minor but such a mistake in interpretation is common in the case of cooperative work on a large problem involving many changes.

5.4 Summary of the verification

Using the prover resulted in a very pedagogic approach since inconsistencies between our logical formulae and event descriptions were emphasized and such corrections were guided. However, we reasoned about the interpretation of formulae by steps involving the checking of formulae, events, and operations pointed out by proof obligations that are not yet validated, this latter checking being systematic but manual. It could be thought that the tool guides the user. In the version used, it only signals that the formula has not been proved, and that we have to analyse all of the proof obligations ourselves.

Take for example the checking of a part of the 184 invariant induced proof obligations where 10 were not automatically proved. Each of these 10 proof obligations was described using two or three pages. The normalisation done by the prover produces an overcrowded presentation with much irrelevant information. As end-users, we would like to get more synthetic information identifying the nonproved part of the invariant, more precisely the list of events that made the prover fail.

We could consider the prover as a guide to the actions. But this is not possible since the prover cannot know if this results from its own failure or if the property itself is false. On the contrary, a model-checker could answer such a question, provided that the generated graph is not too complex.

Practically, using the SPIN model-checker for an invariant helped us finalise the specification: firstly, it tells if the invariant is not fulfilled, secondly, the SPIN simulator allows us to replay the scenario violating this property, that is, we can debug the operational specification. Given this observation we suggest two ways to couple these two kinds of tool. Having a model-checker at the level of abstract data model, could:

- make information from the user complete when a proof obligation failed: he would know if the property is not validated or if the prover is not able to verify it automatically,
- provide a scenario violating a property in order that an "animator" can rerun this scenario again.

6 Conclusions and Prospects

This full scale experiment in implementing a formal approach based on multi-formalism B/BTL allows us to draw several conclusions:

- on the cost of such an approach
- on the real benefits of the application
- on the difficulties associated with such an approach and the technical changes necessary.

6.1 The work involved in the specification

The specification of the protocol ICC is a significant application which involves several hundred lines of B/LTL formalisation and more than 50 man-days of work (cf. table 4) on the specification by refinement.

TASKS	TIME IN MAN-DAYS
Analysis and understanding the problem	5
B/LTL Formalisation	15
Checking and proof with Atelier B	15
Representation and model-checking with SPIN	15
Total	50

Table 4. Time of work partition

This phase of specification and checking took place over a period of approximately 6 months. It involved on one hand the project manager in SCHLUM-BERGER, Urban Terminals and Systems division, in charge of the ICC application and on the other hand 4 researchers from the LIB who have a good knowledge of the techniques of formal B or LTL specification.

6.2 Benefits of the formal approach

This use of the formal specification in SCHLUMBERGER gives perfect control of the EN 27816 standard describing the Half Duplex ICC/Device protocol. Different aspects of the protocol, which are difficult and complex to understand by means of a normative document, have thus been specified, refined and better understood. For example Rule 6.1 leaves one with the impression that the 2 mechanisms play symmetrical roles in the detection of loss of synchronisation whereas Rules 6.2 and 6.3 imply that only the device can produce a resynchronisation.

Work based on this formalisation is continuing in three principal directions :

1. Using the formal specification to check the conformity between cards from various sources. The idea is to record the sequences of the ICC/Device communication over several transactions and to replay these scenarios through the animator of formal specifications. This encourages the detection of instances where the card does not respect the protocol.
2. Checking the respect of the standard by an existing application. Schlumberger's Urban Terminals and Systems Division has an application that has already been written in the Device group and which they would like to check is truly appropriate to the specification. This is in effect a process of "reverse engineering" in which they will abstract the source code of the application.
3. This specification must finally act as the basis for the full development of an ICC/Device specification.

6.3 Heterogeneous Specifications : Opportunities and limitations demonstrated by the experiments

These experiments on the application show the benefits of a multi-formalism B/LTL approach on two levels : the power of expression and the synergy of the checking tools. Several rules expressed in the standard define both the static invariant properties and the dynamic properties of progress. Thus Rule 3 of the standard defines that:

1. only the card may ask for a change in the response time (invariant),
2. a request for modification must immediately be acknowledged by the device.

The joint B/LTL specification allows an accuracy of expression which strengthens the specification. Thus Rule 3 can be formalised in the following manner:

1. (TD $\neq$ (((S$\mapsto$IndefI)$\mapsto$Indef)$\mapsto$WtxReq) $\wedge$
   TC $\neq$ (((S$\mapsto$IndefI)$\mapsto$Indef)$\mapsto$WtxRep)) $\wedge$
2. $\Box$ ((TC=(((S$\mapsto$IndefI)$\mapsto$Indef)$\mapsto$WtxReq) $\wedge$ TC_tr=No $\wedge$ Dialogue=Active) $\Rightarrow$
   O ((TD=(S$\mapsto$IndefI)$\mapsto$Indef)$\mapsto$WtxRep) $\wedge$ TD_tr=No) $\vee$ Dialogue =Interrupt))

The authors' experiment is that the joint expression of the invariant and the progress properties facilitate the expression of the specification. All properties can be taken directly into account without having recourse to tricks of representation, as for example one is sometimes driven to do in order to express progress properties in B. In addition the parallel use of the checking tools Atelier B and SPIN allowed one to discover specification errors (cf. Section 5), which are difficult to discover with each technique independently. Our experience is that this strengthens the specification and avoids the temptation to adapt the specification to the checking tool. One is obliged to refine the specification in order to detect an error, in a different but complementary manner, with the two different checking tools and then to correct it. The limitations of this multi-formalism approach are related both to the theoretical aspects and to the problem of setting up the tools. In the approach presented here, given the limited development of proof techniques in LTL, we used a verification approach based on model checking. The dimensions of the problem and the machine used, (a Multi-Processor Power Challenge machine SGI R10000) allowed us to run exhaustively through the state spaces using SPIN. Nevertheless this does not represent proof, particularly taking account of the technique used to encode fairness. The other difficulty is related to the lack of a link between the checking tool B and the verification of properties in LTL. The checking process remains in parallel, which is still a valid process since it involves checking each property individually, but this poses practical problems. In particular the use of SPIN has the inconvenience that one must not use the abstract data model in PROMELA, i.e. without using abstract structures (sets, applications....) but rather classical computing data structures. For our application this did not create any great difficulties because of the simple data model used. But it represents a difficulty in the approach.

6.4 Future prospects

This experiment allows one to identify future research opportunities in three fields :

- in the theoretical aspects linked to the cooperation of various formalisms,
- in the methodological aspects relating to the structuring of specifications,
- and also in the toolkits designed to help checking.

At the theoretical level the joint use of the B/LTL statements poses the question of proof and the sense to be given to the notion of refining temporal properties. By analogy with the incremental proofs based on refinement, we study the means of carrying out incremental model checking based on temporal refinement.

At the methodological level, it is necessary to integrate a design approach which will produce a structured specification, for example from the physical structure of the system, and which would justify breaking it up into sub-systems and into events.

As far as the toolkits are concerned, we study a model checker acting with an abstract data model in order to make the three functions, proof, model checking and animation operate together.

References

1. J. R. Abrial - The B Book - Cambridge University Press, 1996 - ISBN 0521-496195.
2. J-R. Abrial - Extending B without Changing it (for Developping Distributed Systems) - 1st Conference on the B method - November 1996. Nantes.
3. J-R. Abrial, Mussat L - Specification and Design of a transmission protocol by successive refinements using B - to appear in LNCS. 1997.
4. J. R. Abrial - Constructions d'Automatismes Industriels avec B - Congrés AFADL - ONERA-CERT Toulouse - Mai 1997.
5. G. Bernot, S. Coudret, P. Le Gall - Heterogeneous formal specifications - Proc. of the 5th Int. Conf. on Algebraic Methodology and Software Technology - AMAST'96 - pp 548-472 - LNCS 1101.
6. M. Butler, M. Walden - Distributed System Development in B - 1st Conference on the B method - November 1996 - Nantes.
7. C. Courcoubetis, M. Vardi, P. Wolper, M. Yannakakis - Memory efficient algorithms for the vérification of temporal properties - Formal Methods in System Design I - pp 275-288.
8. European Standard - Identification Cards - Integrated circuit(s) cards with contacts - Electronic Signal and transmission protocols - ISO/CEI 7816-3 - 1992.
9. Formal Methods for Industrial Applications : Specifying and Programming the Steam Boiler Control - ISBN 3-540-61929-1 - Springer Verlag - 1996.
10. R. Gerth, D. Peled, M. Vardi, P. Wolper - Simple on-the-fly automatic verification of linear temporal logic - Proc. PSTV95 Conference - Warsaw - Poland - 1995.
11. P. Godefroid and G. Holzmann - On the verification of temporal properties - Proc. IFIP/WG6.1 Symp. On Protocols Specification, Testing and Verification - PSTV93 - Liege - Belgium - June 1993.
12. G. Holzmann - Design and validation of protocols - Prentice hall software series - 1991.
13. G. Holzmann, D. Peled and Y. Yannakakis - On the nested depth-first search. Proc. 2nd Spin Workshop - American Mathematical Society - DIMACS/32 - 1996.
14. G. Holzmann - State compression in SPIN. Proc. 3rd Spin Workshop - Twente University - April 1997.
15. G. Holzmann - The model checker SPIN. IEEE Trans. On Software Engineering - Vol. 23, No 5.
16. K. Lano - Formal Object-Oriented Development - Springer-Verlag - 1995.
17. K. Lano, J. Bicarregui, A. Sanchez - Using B to Design and Verify Controllers for Chemical Processing - 1st Conference on the B method - November 1996 - Nantes.
18. Z. Manna, A. Pnueli - The Temporal Logic of Reactive and Cocurrent Systems : Specification. ISBN 0-387-97664-7 - Springer-Verlag - 1992.
19. Z. Manna, A. Pnueli - Temporal Verification of Reactive Systems : Safety. ISBN 0-387-94459-1 - Springer-Verlag - 1995.
20. Manuel de référence du langage B - Steria Méditerranée - Décembre 1996.
21. D. A. Peled - Combining partial order reduction with on-the-fly model checking - Proc. 6th Int. Conf. On Computer Aided Verification - CAV94 - Stanford - 1994.
22. D. Mery - Machines abstraites temporelles - Analyse comparative de B et de TLA+ - 1st Conference on the B method - November 1996 - Nantes.

Test Case Preparation Using a Prototype

H. Treharne[1], J. Draper[2] and S. Schneider[1]

[1] Department of Computer Science, Royal Holloway,
University of London, Egham, Surrey, TW20 0EX, UK.

[2] Mission Avionics Division, GEC-Marconi Avionics Ltd,
Airport Works, Rochester, ME1 2XX, UK.

E-mail: helent@dcs.rhbnc.ac.uk

Fax: +44 (0)1784 439786

Abstract. This paper reports on the preparation of test cases using a prototype within the context of a formal development. It describes an approach to building a prototype using an example. It discusses how a prototype contributes to the testing activity as part of a lifecycle based on the use of formal methods. The results of applying the approach to an embedded avionics case study are also presented.

Keywords: Prototype, B-Method, Formal Software Lifecycle.

1 Introduction

This paper describes a formal development lifecycle and the practical application of the B-Method [1] within that lifecycle to the production of an executable prototype. The prototype is derived from an abstract specification for use in test case preparation. Knowledge of the B-Method is assumed when reading this paper.

The prototyping approach described in this paper forms part of a software development process which addresses the requirements of the UK Defence Standard 00-55 [13]. It addresses the requirement that tests generated from the executable prototype of a software specification are repeated on the final code.

This work was mainly carried out as part of the Measurable Improvement in Specification Techniques (MIST) [5] project and extended during the SPECTRUM project within GEC Marconi Avionics Limited (GMAv). The MIST project was an ESSI Application Experiment which investigated the development of safety-critical software using an integrated approach which combined formal and conventional software engineering techniques for software development. SPECTRUM was an ESPRIT RTD project looking at the feasibility of integrating the formal methods B and VDM and the industrial benefits of such an integration.

The rest of this paper is laid out as follows. Section 2 describes a software development lifecycle which uses the B-Method. Section 3 details the typical testing activity carried out in a software development lifecycle. Section 4 describes the testing process in a formal development lifecycle. Section 5 shows how test cases are built based on the use of a prototype. The final sections contain results of building a prototype for an embedded avionics case study, a discussion, and conclusions.

2 Overview of Formal Development Lifecycle

A formal development lifecycle (shown in figure 1), which would be used to develop critical functions of embedded avionics systems within GMAv, starts with a set of requirements written in an informal but structured notation. The B-Method is used to re-specify these requirements and produce a formal abstract specification written in Abstract Machine Notation (AMN) to provide an operational description of the software. This includes a description of all the inputs and outputs of the system and all the critical functions that will be provided by the formally developed software. Some of the lower level implementation details are not included at this abstract level.

The abstract specification is animated, formally proved consistent and, typically, reviewed by an independent verification and validation team. The abstract specification contains enough detail to continue development along two independent parallel paths. The abstract specification may contain some limited non-determinism. The issues arising from prototyping non-deterministic specifications are discussed in section 7.

Both parallel development paths produce executable code. The main development is the formal refinement process which leads to an AMN implementation that is currently hand translated into Ada code. Ada is the preferred programming language for safety-critical software.

In the refinement there are a number of intermediate levels where algorithms and data types are expanded by adding more detail. This design process is discussed in [7] and [8]. The Ada code is verified by review and tested using test cases that are generated using the prototype, as described in section 4.

The secondary development path involves the production of a prototype and the automatic generation of C code which can be executed to produce test cases which are applied to the Ada code. The efficiency of the C code of the executable prototype is not a concern because it is not used in the final system.

3 Testing in a Conventional Software Development Lifecycle

In a software development lifecycle the testing process can be broken into 4 stages; Test Planning, Test Case Preparation, Test Performance and Test Output Review.

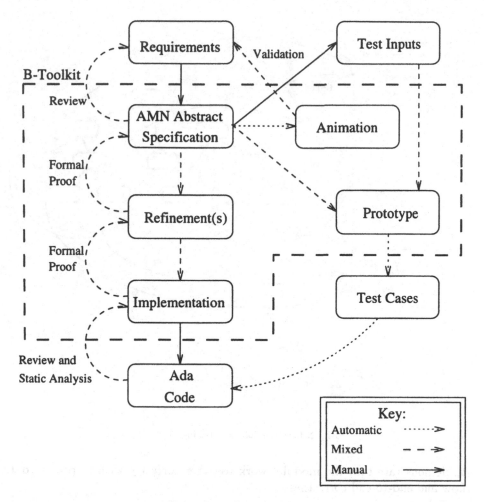

Fig. 1. Formal Development Lifecycle

Test planning is the process of identifying and documenting the required tests for a software system. In software testing there are three levels; Software Unit Testing, Software Integration Testing and Hardware/Software Integration Testing.

The levels of testing are illustrated in figure 2, which shows the scope of each level in terms of the code objects being tested and their relationship with the design or requirement target.

Software Unit Testing (SUT) tests each individual software module against the low level requirements for that module specified in the software detailed design.

Software Integration Testing (SIT) test groups of integrated modules which implement a specific function described in the top level design. The main aim is

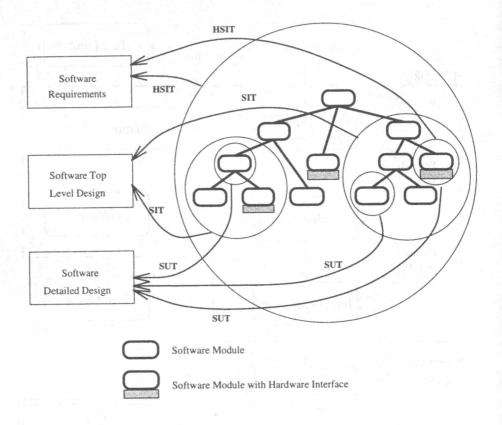

Fig. 2. Levels of Software Testing

to demonstrate that the modules work together correctly with respect to data flow and end-to-end correctness.

Hardware/Software Integration testing (HSIT) tests the fully integrated software within the target environment. It tests the software against the external interfaces and functionality described in the software requirements. It may also test individual interface modules as a addition to the basic unit tests.

The test environment for each level of testing (host or target) is also documented during test planning. In addition to deciding what functionality will be tested, test coverage measurements are defined that must be achieved during testing of each level. This will provide some assurance of the quality of the software in certification and provide evidence that the software has been exercised thoroughly.

These measurements fall into two groups based on functional (black box) and structural (white box) testing [12]. For example, during Software Unit Testing the minimum functional measurement would be that each function or procedure is tested at least once. More stringent requirements would be that each parameter of a procedure or function is is tested with a range of values. For numeric values there would need to be a test case for the minimum, maximum, intermediate and out of bound values. Measurements based on structural testing would consider which statements have been exercised and which branches have been traversed. In addition to traversing each branch of a conditional statement it may also be necessary to achieve a decision coverage measurement which ensures that every boolean value is combined in all the different combinations at least once.

During Software Integration Testing it is expected that the functional test coverage measurement will ensure that combined functions and procedures are being called rather than individual functions and procedures. Furthermore the structural measurement will ensure that all the lower level procedures and functions have been called.

Test case preparation is the next stage in the testing process. In this stage, test case inputs are selected and expected outputs (or a range of acceptable outputs)are identified. The test cases are validated to ensure that the functional coverage metrics have been met.

The test performance stage is the process of applying the test inputs to the software and recording the generated outputs. Tools support the test performance process by automatically applying the test and recording the results, usually by generating a test harness. Tools can also generate stubs for lower level modules to allow higher level modules to be tested before they are integrated.

The final stage in the testing process is the test output review. This checks that the generated outputs are equivalent to the expected outputs and that the structural coverage metrics have been satisfied. Tools can help the output review process by automatically comparing the actual and expected output and by calculating the coverage metrics.

4 Testing in a Formal Development Lifecycle

If the software has been developed using the B-Method then it is possible to use the formality of the top level specification and the automatic features of the B-Toolkit to assist in the test case preparation of the testing process. A prototype is built, as shown in section 5, and is used in the following three phases [14].

Firstly, the abstract specification is analysed in order to identify all the behaviours to be tested. At present it is done manually but tools are being developed which will automate the process for B and Z [9]. Once the behaviours have been identified, input values are chosen which will exercise these behaviours. Boundary value analysis and equivalence partitioning are used to choose these inputs. The inputs for the different behaviours are combined using a cross product to give a large set of test inputs. In order for the executable prototype to run with the test inputs they are translated into a suitable format. The prototype has a simple menu driven interface, offering the system operations. The inputs are extracted from the input list and written into a text file with the appropriate operation calls inserted where required. This formatting is currently performed with ML [16] but could be done with any suitable tool.

The executable prototype is run with the test inputs and the resulting outputs are stored in a file. The combination of test inputs and expected outputs gives a large suite of test cases.

The second phase is the refinement of the test cases into a format that is suitable for use on the Ada code. All the values used in the test cases are abstract representations which must be converted into concrete form to match the interface to the final Ada code using ML. Most of the conversions are simple mappings but some will require complex calculations. For example, an input might be modelled as an enumerated set at the abstract level and refined into a sequence of booleans representing hardware registers at the Ada code level. The result of test case refinement is a test description file which describes the concrete test cases in a format that is suitable for use by the test case application tools.

The last phase is the execution of the Ada code with the test cases. This phase is supported by test application tools, such as AdaTest and TestMate. These tools generate test harnesses and test stubs, as well as applying the test, recording and comparing the actual and expected results. Any test failures are reviewed to see whether they were caused by an error in the main development path or an error in the test case generation. Coverage analysis is also carried out to confirm that all the functionality of the Ada code has been exercised.

The test cases generated using the prototype contribute to the functional testing of all the levels of testing described in section 3. Test cases which exercise the abstract inputs and outputs of the top level functions of the specification will form part of Hardware/Software Integration Testing. The tests of the top level functions which call lower level functions contribute to Software Integration Testing. Testing of the lower level functions will be used in Software Unit Testing.

The test cases are derived from examining the structure of the formal specification, therefore the functional coverage measurement of the unit tests and the structural coverage of the software integration tests are expected to be high. It is also anticipated that, since there are a large number of tests produced, the structural coverage of unit testing will also be high. However, not all the requirements of the system are necessarily embodied in the executable prototype because it is derived from an abstract specification. The abstract specification contains only what is required to describe the safety functions and properties of the software in the system. This obviously affects the coverage metrics that can be achieved during testing. It may be necessary to consider an incremental development of the prototype to cover the new functionality introduced during the refinement process. Alternatively, additional tests can be added manually.

5 Example Prototype

This section uses a small example to illustrate the process of building a prototype using Version 4 Beta Release of the BToolkit [2]. The input to the process is an AMN abstract specification which is a formal description of the functionality of the system. A prototype **MACHINE** and **IMPLEMENTATION** are manually written based on the abstract specification, as shown in figure 3.

This effectively provides a test harness for the specification. The automatic coding features of the Base Generator are used to generate all the **MACHINE**s which support the prototype **IMPLEMENTATION** [3]. The **IMPLEMEN-TATION** together with its **IMPORT**ed **MACHINES** form one development layer and capture all the functionality of the system. Once the **IMPLEMEN-TATION** is written, the Interface generator is used to provide a menu-driven interface which allows testing of the **OPERATIONS** in the prototype. This example only discusses those parts of the process which requires human intervention.

The example used is a simple, embedded system. The software receives input commands from one hardware interface, validates them and stores the input commands which are used by the main functions of the software. This is typical functionality of embedded safety-critical systems where inputs are received from the system and used by the embedded software.

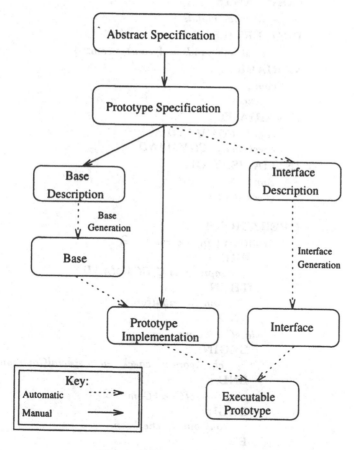

Fig. 3. Prototyping Lifecycle

5.1 Abstract Specification

In the abstract specification the states of a system are represented as **VARI-ABLES** in **MACHINE**s. These variables have a type and an initial state. For example, in figure 4 the variables *com* and *checkcom* which represent part of the state of the system have the type subset of *COMMAND* and are initialised to the empty set.

Operations which manipulate and query the state are also defined in a **MA-CHINE**. In the example there are three operations; the load operation which takes commands as inputs (via the parameter *inputcoms*) and assigns them to the state variable *com*, the get operation which provides a query to retrieve the

> **MACHINE**
>   *Abstract*
> **SETS**
> $COMMAND = \{\ com1\ ,\ com2\ ,\ com3\ \}$
> **CONSTANTS**
>   *specialCommands*
> **PROPERTIES**
> $specialCommands = \{\ com1\ ,\ com2\ \}$
> **VARIABLES**
>   *com* ,
>   *checkcom*
> **INVARIANT**
> $com \subseteq COMMAND \land$
> $checkcom \subseteq COMMAND$
> **INITIALISATION**
> $com := \emptyset\ \|$
> $checkcom := \emptyset$
>
> **OPERATIONS**
> $LoadCom\ (\ inputcoms\ )\quad \widehat{=}$
>   **PRE**
> $inputcoms \subseteq COMMAND$
>   **THEN**
> $com := inputcoms$
>   **END** ;
> $UpdateCheckCom\quad \widehat{=}$
>   **BEGIN**
> $checkcom := checkcom \cap specialCommands \cup com$
>   **END** ;
> $outcom \longleftarrow GetCheckCom\quad \widehat{=}$
>   **BEGIN**
> $outcom := checkcom$
>   **END**
> **END**

Fig. 4. Example Abstract Machine

validated state *checkcom* and the update operation which provides a validation function which updates the validated state.

The validation function makes use of the constant *specialCommands*. The constant is defined in the **CONSTANTS** clause and the explicit property of this constant is included in a **PROPERTIES** clause. In some instances properties of the declared constants may still be abstract. However, all constants must have explicit properties in order to write a prototype **IMPLEMENTATION**. The structuring mechanisms provided by the B-Toolkit support the adding of these explicit properties during the prototyping process. This separation of concerns provides a way of clearly identifying the extra detail added during prototyping.

5.2 Prototype Specification

The purpose of the prototype **MACHINE** is to capture the functionality of the system so that it can be exercised using a menu-driven interface and to remove non-determinism in the abstract specification. This example is deterministic and therefore concentrates on providing a suitable reference basis for test case generation.

The prototype **MACHINE** is built on top of the abstract specification using the **INCLUDES** clause. This means that the prototype **MACHINE** inherits all the state (*com* and *checkcom*) and can use all the **OPERATIONS** of the abstract specification.

OPERATIONS which do not have any input or output arguments can simply be promoted into this new specification **MACHINE** as shown by *UpdateCheckCom* in figure 5. However, **OPERATIONS** with abstract inputs and outputs need to be handled differently. These **OPERATIONS** are replaced by new **OPERATIONS**. The new **OPERATIONS** simply define a new interface but the information content will be the same. This is necessary so that inputting and outputting of parameter values can be implemented in the body of these new **OPERATIONS** using the support of the automatic coding features of the BToolkit.

For example, in the abstract specification there is an **OPERATION** which loads commands, *LoadCom*, and assigns the input argument *inputcoms* to the state variable *com*. In the prototype specification, *Proto*, the operation is replaced with *PLoadCom*. The body of the specification indicates how the state of the system changes; a set of the correct type is assigned to the state *com* via a call to *LoadCom*. This clearly shows that the effect on the system is the same whether *LoadCom* or *PLoadCom* is called. However, the interface to the *PLoadCom* **OPERATION** makes it possible to write an implementation which allows the user to input each element of the set interactively using the menu-driven interface.

Another **OPERATION** which illustrates this interface refinement is the query **OPERATION** *PGetCheckCom*. The purpose of this **OPERATION** is to output the value of the state *checkcom*. Notice that the specification for this new output **OPERATION** is different to *PLoadCom*. *PGetCheckCom* does not

```
        MACHINE
            Proto
        INCLUDES
            Abstract
        PROMOTES
            UpdateCheckCom

        OPERATIONS
            PLoadCom  ≙
                ANY    comset   WHERE
                    comset ⊆ COMMAND    THEN
                    LoadCom ( comset )
                END ;
            PGetCheckCom  ≙
                BEGIN
                    skip
                END ;
            PGetCom  ≙
                BEGIN
                    skip
                END
        END
```

Fig. 5. Example Prototype Specification Machine

change the state *checkcom* and so the function skip was used in the body of the specification to indicate that the value of the variable does not change.

The prototype specification also provides new **OPERATIONS** so that all the state variables in the system can be set and retrieved. This is important during test case generation because the system must be put into a specific state before running the test scenario. Thus in this example the prototype specifies an additional access **OPERATIONS** for the state variable *com*, *PGetCom*.

5.3 Base Generation

The state of the prototype system defined in the specification must be completely encapsulated in the prototype **IMPLEMENTATION** to allow a direct translation into C source code. The example needs to encapsulate the state variables, *com* and *checkcom*. The state is not of simple types such as naturals, strings or booleans and so the Base Generator is used to build appropriate encapsulating structures for these sets.

The Base Generator takes as its input a description of the structure of the state it captures. Figure 6 shows declarative statements for *cmd* and *checkcmd*. The identifiers are of the same set type, *COM*, with a maximum size of three elements. The identifiers must be different from the state variables but a link between the commands will be established in an **INVARIANT** when the prototype **IMPLEMENTATION** is written in section 5.4.

The Base Generator uses this description to build a system **MACHINE** containing a collection of **OPERATIONS** which form a basic instruction set that can be used to manipulate the *cmd* and *checkcmd* data structures. For example, an **OPERATION** *add_cmd* with one input argument will add a command to the set *cmd*. The **OPERATION** returns a boolean value indicating whether the command element has been added to the set *cmd* successfully. These instruction sets are used to implement **OPERATIONS** in the prototype **IMPLEMENTATION**.

Sets and sequences which are **CONSTANTS** also need to be encapsulated using base generation. Thus the declarative statement for the identifier *specialcmd*, in figure 6, is used to encapsulate the structure of the constant set *specialCommands* in the example. Again a link will be provided between the identifier and the constant in the **INVARIANT** of the prototype **IMPLEMENTATION**.

> **SYSTEM**
> *ProtoBase*
> **SUPPORTS**
> *Proto_1*
> **IS**
> **GLOBAL**
> $cmd \in$ SET (*COM*) [*3*] ;
> $checkcmd \in$ SET (*COM*) [*3*] ;
> $specialcmd \in$ SET (*COM*) [*3*]
> **END**
> **END**

Fig. 6. Example Prototype Base Description

5.4 Prototype Implementation

The final manual stage in producing the prototype is to make use of the **MACHINE**s generated from the system building block in the prototype **IMPLEMENTATION**.

The **IMPLEMENTATION** is written in a restricted subset of AMN. It contains constructs which are familiar to programmers, such as **IF THEN ELSE** and **CASE** statements.

In order to produce code, all the state of the system must be encapsulated in instantiations of library **MACHINE**s or **MACHINE**s produced during base generation using the **IMPORTS** clause, as shown in figure 7. When importing the system **MACHINE** (*ProtoBase*) the abstract enumerated set *COMMAND* is passed as a parameter. This is matched with the formal parameter *COM* in the generated system **MACHINE** which is derived from the set name used in the system declarative statements in figure 6. A *basic_io* **MACHINE** is also **IM-PORT**ed so that input and output facility provided by the system **MACHINE** can be used.

The **INVARIANT** clause in the **IMPLEMENTATION** allows the definition of relationships between the abstract and concrete state. For example, in figure 7 the set variable *cmd* in the system **MACHINE** is connected with the variable *com* in the abstract specification.

In a **MACHINE**, sets are declared in the **SETS** clause, constants are declared in a **CONSTANTS** clause and their properties are defined in the **PROPERTIES** clause. In an **IMPLEMENTATION**, constants and sets are captured in a Base description. When the generated system **MACHINE** is **IMPORT**ed these constants and sets are not initialised. The **INITIALISA-TION** clause contains **OPERATIONS** to fill the sets with their enumerated elements and provide constants with the appropriate values. For example, *cmd* is initialised to the empty set using the operation *clear_cmd*. Any temporary storage declared in the system **MACHINE** is not initialised until it is used.

The style adopted in a prototype **IMPLEMENTATION** is important. The structure of the clauses should remain as close to the original specification as possible to aid manual verification by review. For example, in a parallel composition of two **OPERATIONS** their sequential implementation should have the same order as that of the specification. This is illustrated by the **INITIALISATION** clauses of figure 4 and figure 7.

Prototype **OPERATIONS** which are specified using a parallel composition of **OPERATIONS** are implemented as one **OPERATION** containing the combined functionality. This tends to lead to a very large flat implementation. However, provided the code is commented clearly it is easy to identify the **OPERATION** boundaries and provide traceability back to the abstract specification. This aids the process of manually verifying the low level AMN against the specification.

The **OPERATIONS** used to load and retrieve the state make use of the *read_cmd*, *write_cmd* and *write_checkcmd* from the system **MACHINE** to handle the inputting and outputting of sets automatically. Notice *outbool* is simply a report boolean indicating success or failure of the operation which is called.

5.5 Interface Generation and Code

Once all the supporting constructs have been generated and the prototype **MA-CHINE** and **IMPLEMENTATION** have been analysed, code generation is an entirely automatic and straightforward process. An Interface description is introduced which contains all the **OPERATIONS** from the prototype. This list of **OPERATIONS** is reviewed and any that are not needed can be removed.

```
IMPLEMENTATION    ProtoI
REFINES
    Proto
SEES
    Bool_TYPE , Scalar_TYPE , String_TYPE
IMPORTS
    ProtoBase ( COMMAND ) , basic_io
INVARIANT
    com = cmd ∧ checkcom = checkcmd ∧ specialCommands = specialcmd
INITIALISATION
    VAR    outbool  IN
        clear_cmd ; clear_checkcmd ; clear_specialcmd ;
        outbool ⟵ add_specialcmd ( com1 ) ;
        outbool ⟵ add_specialcmd ( com2 )
    END

OPERATIONS
    PLoadCom    ≙
        VAR    outbool  IN
            clear_cmd ;
            outbool ⟵ read_cmd
        END ;
    PGetCheckCom   ≙
        write_checkcmd ;
    PGetCom    ≙
        write_cmd ;
    UpdateCheckCom    ≙
        VAR    spec , cc , outbool   IN
            spec ⟵ val_specialcmd ;
            inter_checkcmd ( spec ) ;
            cc ⟵ val_cmd ;
            outbool ⟵ union_checkcmd ( cc )
        END
END
```

Fig. 7. Example Prototype Implementation Machine

The Interface Generator is used to build the interface **MACHINE**s and automatically carry out all the code translation and linking to provide an executable prototype in C code.

6 Results

The main aim of the MIST project was to apply the B-Method to a Case Study and to compare this with a parallel development of the same system using a conventional software development process [6]. This allowed the B-Method to be evaluated and procedures to be developed which can be used on future avionics projects within GEC Marconi Avionics Limited.

The Case Study used for the MIST project addressed part of the software controlling a Station Unit on a military aircraft. The Station Unit holds one store (e.g. a fuel tank or missile). The Station Unit receives commands from a central armament control unit. These commands can order a store to be armed or released, or the Station Unit to perform tests on itself. Before reacting to any commands, the Station Unit checks that the message containing the command is valid by performing a number of data encoding checks. The Case Study was restricted to the main control and function of the Station Unit. It did not include the tests performed continuously, on power-up or on demand, nor any of the minor functions performed by the software. The Case Study covers 36% of the total software for a Station Unit.

This section summarises a testing comparison for the main control of the Station Unit (about 9% of the total software). The effort required to code, unit and integration test these functions using the formal approach was 78% of the effort taken using the standard approach. This reduced effort later in the development lifecycle compensates for the greater effort needed in the requirements and specification phases early in a formal lifecycle.

The effort taken to write tests for these critical functions using the formal approach was 12 man weeks. This included 3 man weeks for writing the prototype which could be considered as part of the validation effort for the abstract specification. The effort expended on writing the tests using the conventional approach was only 9 man weeks. However the number of tests that were produced using the formal approach was significantly more than the number developed manually, in the order of 40 times more tests. It has already been stated that 100% coverage of statement, branch and LCSAJ (Linear Code Sequence and Jump) may not be achieved for all operations using tests based on the prototype due to the level of abstraction in the abstract specification. However, the conventional approach achieved lower coverage than the formal approach. It would not be impossible to write the tests needed to achieve the same level of coverage but it would increase the effort required. The highly automated nature of the formal test case generation means that no more effort is needed to produce large combinations of tests. It is also felt that the formally produced tests would be more robust in terms of coverage against minor changes to the Ada code.

The formal development lifecycle is based on an integrated verification approach [10] where each step in the specification and refinement process is verified. Given the high degree of verification it was expected that errors introduced during specification and refinement would also be found early in the lifecycle. This means that any errors found during testing would mostly be due to errors in coding. For example, figure 8 shows where the errors were introduced and detected during the formal development of the critical functions of the case study. As was expected most of the errors were detected by the verification and validation processes. The two errors detected during testing were introduced when translating the AMN design into Ada code.

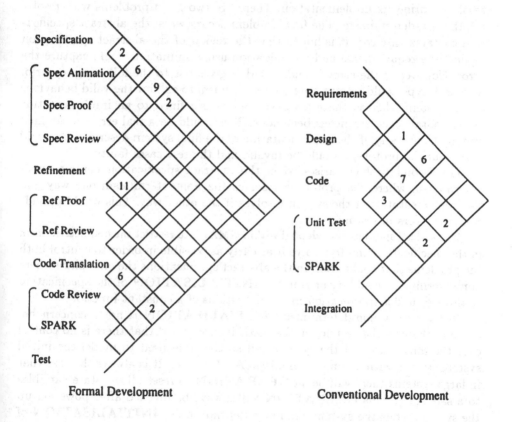

Fig. 8. Errors in Developments

A fault grid [4] was also produced for the same critical functions which were developed using conventional development methods, shown in figure 8. It shows that most of the errors were found during testing. For example, seven errors were found during unit test which were introduced during the design phase. It is clear that the conventional development lifecycle detects many more errors later in the lifecycle which means that the cost of re-work is relatively high.

7 Discussion

The example in section 5 showed that prototyping deterministic specifications is not difficult. However, there are further issues involved in prototyping non-deterministic specifications.

A prototype **IMPLEMENTATION** cannot contain any non-determinism which means that non-determinism present in an abstract specification must be resolved during its implementation. There are two main problems with resolving the non-determinism. The first problem occurs when the abstract specification contains an error. It is hoped that the review of the abstract specification against the requirements and its validation using animation would capture the error. However, if the error is undetected it gives rise to the following scenario. The prototype could resolve the non-determinism to exhibit the valid behaviour of the system whereas the main development is refined to an implementation which contains the erroneous behaviour. This would be a real error in the final system. Conversely, if the implementation of the final system described the valid behaviour the prototype would be invalid and the test cases faulty.

The second problem arises when the abstract specification contains non-determinism where the prototype resolves the non-determinism one way and the implementation of the system resolves it the other way. This would provide spurious errors in testing.

The style of specification adopted within GMAv is to restrict the non-determinism in the specification and to resolve it as early as possible in order to control both the problems that could arise. In the abstract specifications the only place where non-determinism could occur is in the **INITIALISATION** of the specification or through under-specification in the definitions of a constant function.

In practice, a non-deterministic **INITIALISATION** is not a concern because of the way the system will be used. It is assumed that there is no control over the initial state of the system and so the style used to model the initial system state is with a non-deterministic **ANY** clause. It is always the case that in large systems there will be an **OPERATION** to reset all the state variables to a safe state. This **OPERATION** will always be invoked after powering up the system. Thus the system will never depend on the **INITIALISATION** of the **MACHINE**.

The following **CONSTANT** function, *checkfun*, illustrates how non-determinism is resolved for under-specified functions.

$$checkfun \in \mathbb{P} \, (\, COMMAND \,) \times CHECKDATA \to BOOL$$

Checkfun takes two inputs of a power set of type COMMAND and CHECK-DATA. In the abstract specification the set COMMAND is enumerated but CHECKDATA is under-specified and remains abstract. This is because it will be refined to several different inputs but the details are unimportant in the abstract specification.

Before the prototyping process can begin the non-determinism must be resolved. Thus the prototyping specification would include an enumeration for CHECKDATA by introducing another enumerated set of *good* and *bad* elements and stating in the **PROPERTIES** clause that this set is equivalent to CHECK-DATA. It would also include a property resolving the non-deterministic function. For example,

$$\forall \, ss \, . \, (\, ss \in \mathbb{P} \, (\, COMMAND \,) \Rightarrow checkfun \, (\, ss \, , \, good \,) = TRUE \,) \wedge$$
$$\forall \, ss \, . \, (\, ss \in \mathbb{P} \, (\, COMMAND \,) \Rightarrow checkfun \, (\, ss \, , \, bad \,) = FALSE \,)$$

It would have been possible to include this detail in the abstract specification but this would have introduced too much unnecessary detail. It would also have involved writing a more complex refinement relation in the main development which would increase the proof effort. However, by excluding it there is a danger of resolving the non-determinism in a different way in the prototype and in the main development. Thus the test cases produced from the prototype would not be appropriate for application to final Ada code.

Nevertheless, the way the non-determinism was resolved still retained the shape of the function. The barest minimum of detail was introduced to make it deterministic and implementable so that when the test cases are refined from abstract to concrete values they could still be refined to be compatible with the final code. There is no explicit refinement relation between the prototype and the refinement specification in the main development, the relationships are embedded into the ML which performs the conversion from abstract to concrete test cases.

One alternative solution would be to produce a set of possible outputs for each case of non-determinism in the specification. Even in this situation the prototype would still have to define all the abstract sets in order to be able to build the prototype. Producing sets of outputs would add an extra level of complexity when building the prototype and is a topic for further research.

The prototyping aims to be a fast process as shown by the results of the Case Study. This was made possible by building the prototype as one development layer and using B-toolkit library **MACHINE**s. A layered design approach was not adopted. However, in very large systems the prototype **IMPLEMEN-TATION** would simply be too large to control as one entity. In such cases a layered development approach would be necessary but the principles of resolving the non-determinism early would still apply.

In this paper an executable prototype has been used in the testing process. It could also be used to provide preliminary validation of the formal specification which is another requirement of the Defence Standard 00-55. In the lifecycle described in section 2 preliminary validation of the specification, to identify errors in expected behaviour against the informal requirements, was carried out using the animation facility of the B-Toolkit.

The Ada code produced from a formal development may not be the code for the whole system. Other functions may have been developed using a conventional development lifecycle. Thus all the Ada code would be integrated together to provide the source code for the complete system. The test cases produced for the formally developed code would still be valid and would form almost all the test cases needed to test these formally developed software functions. The only additional tests, developed using conventional testing methods, would be ones needed to achieve the required structural coverage metrics.

8 Conclusions

This paper described an integrated approach to formal software development and focused on a testing process based on the use of a prototype. The approach to prototyping using the automatic code generation features of the B-Toolkit enabled a prototype to be produced rapidly from a formal specification. Tests were generated using this prototype taking no significantly greater effort than the equivalent tests produced using the conventional approach but provided a much higher number of tests and a higher test coverage.

The formal development lifecycle has been tested on a large Case Study which captured all the safety critical functions of a typical avionics system. When a formal approach is used within the development of systems less effort will be required during testing.

Acknowledgements

The authors would like to thank GEC Marconi Avionics Limited for permission to publish this paper. The views expressed in this paper are those of the authors and do not necessarily represent the views of GEC Marconi Avionics Limited.

References

1. Abrial J. R.: *The B Book: Assigning Programs to Meaning*, Cambridge University Press (1996).
2. B-Core(UK): *B-Toolkit Version 4 Beta Release*, Magdalen Centre, The Oxford Science Park, UK (1997).
3. B-Core(UK): *Case Study: Design Using Generated Base Objects*, Magdalen Centre, The Oxford Science Park, UK (1994).
4. Dick J. and Maisey D.: *Fault grids: Another Way of Presenting Fault Counts*, Proceedings of Software Quality Management 1996, Cambridge, UK (April 1996).
5. Draper J.: *Applying the B-Method to Avionics Software: an Initial Report on the MIST Project*, Encress 1995 Conference Proceedings.
6. Draper J., Treharne H. *et al.*: *Evaluating the B-Method on an Avionics Example*, Proceedings of DASIA, Rome (1996).
7. Draper J. and Treharne H.: *The Refinement of Embedded Software with the B-Method*, Proceedings of Northern Formal Methods Workshop, Bradford, UK (September 1996).
8. Hoare J. P.: *Application of the B-Method to CICS*. Chapter 6 in H. Bowen, editor, Application of Formal Methods, pp. 97-123, Prentice-Hall International (1995).

9. Hörcher H-M. and Peleska J.: *Using formal specifications to support software testing*, Software Quality Journal 4, pp. 309-327 (1995).

10. Kemmerer R. A.: *Integrating Formal Methods into the Development Process*, IEEE Software (September 1990), pp. 37-50.

11. Lichter H., Schneider-Hufschmidt M. and Züllighoven: *Prototyping in Industrial Software Projects - Bridging the Gap Between Theory and Practice*, IEEE Transactions on Software Engineering, **20**(11) (1994), pp. 825-832.

12. Myers G. J.: *The Art of Software Testing*, Wiley (1979).

13. UK Ministry of Defence: *The Procurement of Safety Critical Software in Defence Equipment*, Defence Standard 00-55 (1997).

14. Ormsby B.: *An Approach to Testing during Formal Development with the B-Method*, Industrial Report, Proceedings of 22nd EUROMICRO conference, Prague (September 1996).

15. Waeselynck H. and Boulanger J-L.: *The Role of Testing in the B Formal Development Process*, Proceedings of 6th International Symposium on Software Reliability (ISSRE '95), Toulouse, France (October 1995), pp. 58-67.

16. Wikström A.: *Functional Programming using Standard ML*, Prentice Hall, International Series in Computer Science (1987).

Author Index

Abrial J.-R.   1, 83

Banach R.   129
Behm P.   26, 29
Bicarregui J.   148
Burdy L.   29

Chartier P.   66

Desforges P.   26
Draper J.   293
Dunne S.   226

Galloway A.   226

Heuberger P.   261

Julliand J.   273

Lamboley P.   198
Legeard B.   273

Machicoane T.   273
Malioukov A.   162
Matthews B.   148
Méry D.   198

Meynadier J.-M.   26, 29
Morel G.   198
Morgan C.   9
Mussat L.   83

Parreaux B.   273
Pétin J.-F.   198
Pilarski F.   27
Poppleton M.   129
Potet M.-L.   46

Ritchie B.   148
Rouzaud Y.   46

Schneider S.   293
Sekerinski E.   182
Shore R.   226
Stoddart B.   226

Taouil-Traverson S.   210
Tatibouët B.   273
Treharne H.   293

Vignes S.   210

Waldén M.   243

Lecture Notes in Computer Science

For information about Vols. 1–1315

please contact your bookseller or Springer-Verlag

Vol. 1316: M. Li, A. Maruoka (Eds.), Algorithmic Learning Theory. Proceedings, 1997. XI, 461 pages. 1997. (Subseries LNAI).

Vol. 1317: M. Leman (Ed.), Music, Gestalt, and Computing. IX, 524 pages. 1997. (Subseries LNAI).

Vol. 1318: R. Hirschfeld (Ed.), Financial Cryptography. Proceedings, 1997. XI, 409 pages. 1997.

Vol. 1319: E. Plaza, R. Benjamins (Eds.), Knowledge Acquisition, Modeling and Management. Proceedings, 1997. XI, 389 pages. 1997. (Subseries LNAI).

Vol. 1320: M. Mavronicolas, P. Tsigas (Eds.), Distributed Algorithms. Proceedings, 1997. X, 333 pages. 1997.

Vol. 1321: M. Lenzerini (Ed.), AI*IA 97: Advances in Artificial Intelligence. Proceedings, 1997. XII, 459 pages. 1997. (Subseries LNAI).

Vol. 1322: H. Hußmann, Formal Foundations for Software Engineering Methods. X, 286 pages. 1997.

Vol. 1323: E. Costa, A. Cardoso (Eds.), Progress in Artificial Intelligence. Proceedings, 1997. XIV, 393 pages. 1997. (Subseries LNAI).

Vol. 1324: C. Peters, C. Thanos (Eds.), Research and Advanced Technology for Digital Libraries. Proceedings, 1997. X, 423 pages. 1997.

Vol. 1325: Z.W. Raś, A. Skowron (Eds.), Foundations of Intelligent Systems. Proceedings, 1997. XI, 630 pages. 1997. (Subseries LNAI).

Vol. 1326: C. Nicholas, J. Mayfield (Eds.), Intelligent Hypertext. XIV, 182 pages. 1997.

Vol. 1327: W. Gerstner, A. Germond, M. Hasler, J.-D. Nicoud (Eds.), Artificial Neural Networks – ICANN '97. Proceedings, 1997. XIX, 1274 pages. 1997.

Vol. 1328: C. Retoré (Ed.), Logical Aspects of Computational Linguistics. Proceedings, 1996. VIII, 435 pages. 1997. (Subseries LNAI).

Vol. 1329: S.C. Hirtle, A.U. Frank (Eds.), Spatial Information Theory. Proceedings, 1997. XIV, 511 pages. 1997.

Vol. 1330: G. Smolka (Ed.), Principles and Practice of Constraint Programming – CP 97. Proceedings, 1997. XII, 563 pages. 1997.

Vol. 1331: D. W. Embley, R. C. Goldstein (Eds.), Conceptual Modeling – ER '97. Proceedings, 1997. XV, 479 pages. 1997.

Vol. 1332: M. Bubak, J. Dongarra, J. Waśniewski (Eds.), Recent Advances in Parallel Virtual Machine and Message Passing Interface. Proceedings, 1997. XV, 518 pages. 1997.

Vol. 1333: F. Pichler. R.Moreno-Díaz (Eds.), Computer Aided Systems Theory – EUROCAST'97. Proceedings, 1997. XII, 626 pages. 1997.

Vol. 1334: Y. Han, T. Okamoto, S. Qing (Eds.), Information and Communications Security. Proceedings, 1997. X, 484 pages. 1997.

Vol. 1335: R.H. Möhring (Ed.), Graph-Theoretic Concepts in Computer Science. Proceedings, 1997. X, 376 pages. 1997.

Vol. 1336: C. Polychronopoulos, K. Joe, K. Araki, M. Amamiya (Eds.), High Performance Computing. Proceedings, 1997. XII, 416 pages. 1997.

Vol. 1337: C. Freksa, M. Jantzen, R. Valk (Eds.), Foundations of Computer Science. XII, 515 pages. 1997.

Vol. 1338: F. Plášil, K.G. Jeffery (Eds.), SOFSEM'97: Theory and Practice of Informatics. Proceedings, 1997. XIV, 571 pages. 1997.

Vol. 1339: N.A. Murshed, F. Bortolozzi (Eds.), Advances in Document Image Analysis. Proceedings, 1997. IX, 345 pages. 1997.

Vol. 1340: M. van Kreveld, J. Nievergelt, T. Roos, P. Widmayer (Eds.), Algorithmic Foundations of Geographic Information Systems. XIV, 287 pages. 1997.

Vol. 1341: F. Bry, R. Ramakrishnan, K. Ramamohanarao (Eds.), Deductive and Object-Oriented Databases. Proceedings, 1997. XIV, 430 pages. 1997.

Vol. 1342: A. Sattar (Ed.), Advanced Topics in Artificial Intelligence. Proceedings, 1997. XVII, 516 pages. 1997. (Subseries LNAI).

Vol. 1343: Y. Ishikawa, R.R. Oldehoeft, J.V.W. Reynders, M. Tholburn (Eds.), Scientific Computing in Object-Oriented Parallel Environments. Proceedings, 1997. XI, 295 pages. 1997.

Vol. 1344: C. Ausnit-Hood, K.A. Johnson, R.G. Pettit, IV, S.B. Opdahl (Eds.), Ada 95 – Quality and Style. XV, 292 pages. 1997.

Vol. 1345: R.K. Shyamasundar, K. Ueda (Eds.), Advances in Computing Science - ASIAN'97. Proceedings, 1997. XIII, 387 pages. 1997.

Vol. 1346: S. Ramesh, G. Sivakumar (Eds.), Foundations of Software Technology and Theoretical Computer Science. Proceedings, 1997. XI, 343 pages. 1997.

Vol. 1347: E. Ahronovitz, C. Fiorio (Eds.), Discrete Geometry for Computer Imagery. Proceedings, 1997. X, 255 pages. 1997.

Vol. 1348: S. Steel, R. Alami (Eds.), Recent Advances in AI Planning. Proceedings, 1997. IX, 454 pages. 1997. (Subseries LNAI).

Vol. 1349: M. Johnson (Ed.), Algebraic Methodology and Software Technology. Proceedings, 1997. X, 594 pages. 1997.

Vol. 1350: H.W. Leong, H. Imai, S. Jain (Eds.), Algorithms and Computation. Proceedings, 1997. XV, 426 pages. 1997.

Vol. 1351: R. Chin, T.-C. Pong (Eds.), Computer Vision – ACCV'98. Proceedings Vol. I, 1998. XXIV, 761 pages. 1997.

Vol. 1352: R. Chin, T.-C. Pong (Eds.), Computer Vision – ACCV'98. Proceedings Vol. II, 1998. XXIV, 757 pages. 1997.

Vol. 1353: G. BiBattista (Ed.), Graph Drawing. Proceedings, 1997. XII, 448 pages. 1997.

Vol. 1354: O. Burkart, Automatic Verification of Sequential Infinite-State Processes. X, 163 pages. 1997.

Vol. 1355: M. Darnell (Ed.), Cryptography and Coding. Proceedings, 1997. IX, 335 pages. 1997.

Vol. 1356: A. Danthine, Ch. Diot (Eds.), From Multimedia Services to Network Services. Proceedings, 1997. XII, 180 pages. 1997.

Vol. 1357: J. Bosch, S. Mitchell (Eds.), Object-Oriented Technology. Proceedings, 1997. XIV, 555 pages. 1998.

Vol. 1358: B. Thalheim, L. Libkin (Eds.), Semantics in Databases. XI, 265 pages. 1998.

Vol. 1359: G. Antoniou, A. Ghose, M. Truszczynski (Eds.), Learning and Reasoning with Complex Representations. Proceedings, 1996. X, 283 pages. 1998. (Subseries LNAI).

Vol. 1360: D. Wang (Ed.), Automated Deduction in Geometry. Proceedings, 1996. VII, 235 pages. 1998. (Subseries LNAI).

Vol. 1361: B. Christianson, B. Crispo, M. Lomas, M. Roe (Eds.), Security Protocols. Proceedings, 1997. VIII, 217 pages. 1998.

Vol. 1362: D.K. Panda, C.B. Stunkel (Eds.), Network-Based Parallel Computing. Proceedings, 1998. X, 247 pages. 1998.

Vol. 1363: J.-K. Hao, E. Lutton, E. Ronald, M. Schoenauer, D. Snyers (Eds.), Artificial Evolution. XI, 349 pages. 1998.

Vol. 1364: W. Conen, G. Neumann (Eds.), Coordination Technology for Collaborative Applications. VIII, 282 pages. 1998.

Vol. 1365: M.P. Singh, A. Rao, M.J. Wooldridge (Eds.), Intelligent Agents IV. Proceedings, 1997. XII, 351 pages. 1998. (Subseries LNAI).

Vol. 1367: E.W. Mayr, H.J. Prömel, A. Steger (Eds.), Lectures on Proof Verification and Approximation Algorithms. XII, 344 pages. 1998.

Vol. 1368: Y. Masunaga, T. Katayama, M. Tsukamoto (Eds.), Worldwide Computing and Its Applications — WWCA'98. Proceedings, 1998. XIV, 473 pages. 1998.

Vol. 1370: N.A. Streitz, S. Konomi, H.-J. Burkhardt (Eds.), Cooperative Buildings. Proceedings, 1998. XI, 267 pages. 1998.

Vol. 1371: I. Wachsmuth, M. Fröhlich (Eds.), Gesture and Sign-Language in Human-Computer Interaction. Proceedings, 1997. XI, 309 pages. 1998. (Subseries LNAI).

Vol. 1372: S. Vaudenay (Ed.), Fast Software Encryption. Proceedings, 1998. VIII, 297 pages. 1998.

Vol. 1373: M. Morvan, C. Meinel, D. Krob (Eds.), STACS 98. Proceedings, 1998. XV, 630 pages. 1998.

Vol. 1374: H. Bunt, R.-J. Beun, T. Borghuis (Eds.), Multimodal Human-Computer Communication. VIII, 345 pages. 1998. (Subseries LNAI).

Vol. 1375: R. D. Hersch, J. André, H. Brown (Eds.), Electronic Publishing, Artistic Imaging, and Digital Typography. Proceedings, 1998. XIII, 575 pages. 1998.

Vol. 1376: F. Parisi Presicce (Ed.), Recent Trends in Algebraic Development Techniques. Proceedings, 1997. VIII, 435 pages. 1998.

Vol. 1377: H.-J. Schek, F. Saltor, I. Ramos, G. Alonso (Eds.), Advances in Database Technology – EDBT'98. Proceedings, 1998. XII, 515 pages. 1998.

Vol. 1378: M. Nivat (Ed.), Foundations of Software Science and Computation Structures. Proceedings, 1998. X, 289 pages. 1998.

Vol. 1379: T. Nipkow (Ed.), Rewriting Techniques and Applications. Proceedings, 1998. X, 343 pages. 1998.

Vol. 1380: C.L. Lucchesi, A.V. Moura (Eds.), LATIN'98: Theoretical Informatics. Proceedings, 1998. XI, 391 pages. 1998.

Vol. 1381: C. Hankin (Ed.), Programming Languages and Systems. Proceedings, 1998. X, 283 pages. 1998.

Vol. 1382: E. Astesiano (Ed.), Fundamental Approaches to Software Engineering. Proceedings, 1998. XII, 331 pages. 1998.

Vol. 1383: K. Koskimies (Ed.), Compiler Construction. Proceedings, 1998. X, 309 pages. 1998.

Vol. 1384: B. Steffen (Ed.), Tools and Algorithms for the Construction and Analysis of Systems. Proceedings, 1998. XIII, 457 pages. 1998.

Vol. 1385: T. Margaria, B. Steffen, R. Rückert, J. Posegga (Eds.), Services and Visualization. Proceedings, 1997/ 1998. XII, 323 pages. 1998.

Vol. 1386: T.A. Henzinger, S. Sastry (Eds.), Hybrid Systems: Computation and Control. Proceedings, 1998. VIII, 417 pages. 1998.

Vol. 1387: C. Lee Giles, M. Gori (Eds.), Adaptive Processing of Sequences and Data Structures. Proceedings, 1997. XII, 434 pages. 1998. (Subseries LNAI).

Vol. 1388: J. Rolim (Ed.), Parallel and Distributed Processing. Proceedings, 1998. XVII, 1168 pages. 1998.

Vol. 1389: K. Tombre, A.K. Chhabra (Eds.), Graphics Recognition. Proceedings, 1997. XII, 421 pages. 1998.

Vol. 1391: W. Banzhaf, R. Poli, M. Schoenauer, T.C. Fogarty (Eds.), Genetic Programming. Proceedings, 1998. X, 232 pages. 1998.

Vol. 1393: D. Bert (Ed.), B'98: Recent Advances in the Development and Use of the B Method. Proceedings, 1998. VIII, 313 pages. 1998.

Vol. 1394: X. Wu. R. Kotagiri, K.B. Korb (Eds.), Research and Development in Knowledge Discovery and Data Mining. Proceedings, 1998. XVI, 424 pages. 1998. (Subseries LNAI).

Vol. 1396: G. Davida, M. Mambo, E. Okamoto (Eds.), Information Security. Proceedings, 1997. XII, 357 pages. 1998.

Vol. 1397: H. de Swart (Ed.), Automated Reasoning with Analytic Tableaux and Related Methods. Proceedings, 1998. X, 325 pages. 1998. (Subseries LNAI).

Vol. 1398: C. Nédellec, C. Rouveirol (Eds.), Machine Learning: ECML-98. Proceedings, 1998. XII, 420 pages. 1998. (Subseries LNAI).